Praise for *The Case For Pragmatic* ...

"Daniel Fishman cuts through rhetoric with clear writing and a razor-sharp wit. The chapter on education is like the welcome beam of a lighthouse in a fog. As schools follow the case-study approach this book recommends, they can put themselves on a sure path toward meeting their goals. Fishman extends lifelines that can help the field reinvent and reinvigorate itself for the benefit of society."

—Maurice J. Elias, coauthor of *Social Problem Solving: Interventions in the Schools*

"At a time when psychology is wracked with debate and self-doubt, Daniel Fishman finds a way for the field to re-assert its social relevance and value while acknowledging its limits. Steering between the shoals of positivism and postmodernism, Fishman makes the case for a pragmatic psychology in unusually lucid and forceful prose. This book should be read not only by professional psychologists but by all interested in the future of mind-related science."

—John Horgan, author of *The End of Science*

"This book could not be more timely. There is a pressing need for the development of new methods of scientific inquiry and data analysis. Fishman provides elegantly reasoned, scholarly arguments that provide a basis for such a new pragmatic science of psychology. A must read for all psychologists."

—Kenneth I. Howard, coauthor of *The Measurement & Management of Clinical Outcomes in Mental Health*

"Fishman's pragmatic psychology paradigm holds out for me the promise of unification of the clinical and research enterprises to produce the wealth of information on psychotherapy outcomes for which we have been searching. It's a pleasure to endorse an enterprise as exciting as this book, for which many of us have waited for so long."

—Peter E. Nathan, coeditor of *A Guide to Treatments That Work*

"The breadth of this work is astonishing: it is a vast and complex historical, theoretical, epistemological, methodological, and philosophical argument. At the same time, it is a work which speaks directly to the most passionate commitments of both the spirit and the discipline."

—Yvonna S. Lincoln, coeditor of *Handbook of Qualitative Research*

The Case for Pragmatic Psychology

Daniel B. Fishman

Foreword by Donald R. Peterson

NEW YORK UNIVERSITY PRESS
New York and London

NEW YORK UNIVERSITY PRESS
New York and London

Library of Congress Cataloging-in Publication Data
Fishman, Daniel B.
The case for pragmatic psychology / Daniel B. Fishman ;
foreword by Donald R. Peterson.
p. cm.
Includes bibliographical references and index.
ISBN 0–8147–2674–7 (hardcover : alk. paper)
ISBN 0–8147–2675–5 (pbk. : alk. paper)
1. Psychology—Philosophy. 2. Psychology—History. I. Title.
BF38.F57   1999
150.19'8—dc21   98–40189
                   CIP

Grateful acknowledgment is made to Guilford Publications for
permission to reprint excerpts from Calhoun, K. S., & Resick, P. A.
(1993). Post-traumatic stress disorder. In D. H. Barlow, ed.,
Clinical handbook of psychological disorder: A step-by-step treatment manual, 48–98. 2d ed. New York: Guilford Press.

New York University Press books are printed on acid-free paper,
and their binding materials are chosen for strength and durability.

Manufactured in the United States of America

10 9 8 7 6 5 4 3 2 1

To Claire, Debbie, and Amie—
the ultimate support system

Most nonpsychologists have very foggy ideas about the nature of our discipline. . . . Listen to us. "We're a profession, but we aren't really a profession, we're a science. We do research, but most of us don't actually do any research. We aren't really scientists, we aren't really professionals, we're scientist-professionals. We aren't exactly scientist-professionals, we're scholar-professionals. We're sort of like scientists, but we aren't general scientists, we're local scientists. What we do isn't exactly research, it's disciplined inquiry." We sound like Jackie Mason.

—Donald R. Peterson, *Educating Professional Psychologists:*
History and Guiding Conception
(1997, 190)

The tradition in Western culture which centers around the notion of the search for Truth, a tradition which runs from the Greek philosophers through the Enlightenment, is the clearest example of the attempt to find a sense in one's existence by turning away from solidarity to objectivity. . . . By contrast, those who wish to reduce objectivity to solidarity—call them "pragmatists"—do not require either a metaphysics or an epistemology. They view truth as, in William James' phrase, what is good for *us* to believe. . . . They see the gap between truth and justification . . . simply as the gap between the actual good and the possible better.

—Richard Rorty, "Solidarity or Objectivity?"
Objectivity, Relativism, and the Truth
(1991, 21–23)

If we have any lesson to learn from the experience of the 1960s and '70s, this (I have come to believe) is our need to reappropriate the wisdom of the 16th-century humanists, and develop a point of view that combines the abstract rigor and exactitude of the 17th-century "new philosophy" with a practical concern for human life in its concrete detail. Only so can we counter the current widespread disillusion with the agenda of Modernity, and salvage what is still humanly important in its projects.

—Stephen Toulmin, *Cosmopolis:*
The Hidden Agenda of Modernity
(1990, x–xi)

Contents

List of Figures and Tables   *xiii*

Foreword by Donald R. Peterson   *xv*

Preface   *xix*

Acknowledgments   *xxv*

Introduction: A Better Way to Help by
Reinventing Psychology   1

   Turning Mainstream Psychology Upside Down   1

   The Emergence of the Pragmatic Paradigm
   from Postmodernism   5

   Supporting the Beleaguered Practitioner   9

   Two Faces of Psychology: "Nature" versus "Culture"   21

   A Reader's Guide   24

I History   29

1   1600 to the Early 1960s: Psychology and Positivism—
A Marriage Made in Enlightenment Heaven   31

   Origins: 1600 to 1879   32

   Pendulum Swings in History   36

   Psychology Comes of Age: 1879 to the Early 1960s   38

2   The 1960s and Beyond: The Postmodern Invasion   44

   Psychologists Proliferate   45

   Psychological Topics Proliferate   46

   Psychological Methods Proliferate   57

II Philosophy   73

3   "Postpositivism": Revolution within the Family   75

Targeted Hits 75

Expanding the Critique 80

The End of Science? 88

4 The Dialectic: Putting It All Together 93

The Players 94

Not So Fast 97

Boiling It Down to Three Paradigms 98

5 Transcending the Dialectic: The Emergence of
Postmodern Pragmatism 102

The Family Tree 103

Pragmatists Weigh In 109

A Balinese Cockfight and Schizophrenia 124

On to the Case Study Method 130

III Method 133

6 The Pragmatic Case Study: Psychology's Tool for
Enhancing Human Services 135

Addressing Psychosocial Problems 135

Measuring the Bottom Line: Program Evaluation 137

Collaborating with Clients: Community Psychology 146

"What Works and Why We Have So Little of It" 149

7 Nuts and Bolts: The Pragmatic Case Study Method 153

Let the Games Begin 154

Quality Control 180

Linking Frameworks 188

From Single Case to Database 190

IV Application 197

8 Psychology and Psychotherapy: From "House of
Cards" to "House of Cases" 199

An End to Our "Era of Good Feeling" 200

The Battle 204

A Pragmatic Proposal 217

A Case in Point 237

9 Educational Reform: From "Culture Wars" and
"Silver Bullets" to the Real Classroom 245

 The Factory Model 246

 The Combatants Square Off 249

 Many Promising Reform Ideas 255

 Ideas Are Cheap, Successful Cases Are Not 261

V Implications 281

10 Manifesto for a Pragmatic Psychology 283

 Prologue: A Call for Pluralism 283

 Pragmatists Unite! An Action Plan for
Making Case-based Psychology a Reality 285

 Vision: Staying in Touch with Our Roots 289

 The Challenge Ahead 292

 Notes 295
 References 339
 Index 361
 About the Author 387

Figures and Tables

Figure 1.1. Professional Activity as Applied Science   10

Figure 1.2. Professional Activity as
           Disciplined Inquiry   11

Table 4.1.   Illustrative Differences among
           Epistemological Paradigms   99

Table 7.1.   Typical Organization and Content of a
           Research Report in the Three Paradigms   156

Table 7.2.   Quality-of-Knowledge Procedures in the
           Three Paradigms   160

Table 7.3.   Major Points of Correspondence
           between Figure 1.2 and Table 7.1   189

Foreword

Daniel B. Fishman's book, *The Case for Pragmatic Psychol-ogy*, is revolutionary, both in substance and in portent. I mean that lit-erally. Instead of assuming, as prevailing ideology would have us do, that practically useful, socially beneficial psychology must begin with a science that is passed on through a closely sifted technology to more or less routine application by practitioners, Fishman proposes that we turn psychology upside down. As practitioners, we begin with our clients, be they people in distress, dysfunctional families, failing corporations, or violent, culturally deteriorating communities. We take them as they come, in all their natural complexity; bring our best knowledge, experi-ence, skill, and creative ingenuity to bear in understanding and improv-ing the condition of each client; and in organized cooperation with other practitioners accumulate a database of successful and unsuccessful cases. On this base, we inform future generations of professionals and progressively extend the mass of useful knowledge that any true profes-sion must embody and that the people who purchase our services de-serve and demand.

If faithfully enacted, the program Fishman proposes will revolution-ize the psychological professions. The intuitions and lore on which many professional actions are currently based will gradually be replaced by systematic records of comparable cases, though there will always be room for creative innovation in the ever-expanding range and ever-changing flow of problems that professional psychologists encounter. Results of pertinent research can be readily incorporated in the knowl-edge base that practitioners bring to each new case. Useful theoretical developments, whenever they appear, can be integrated with prior con-ceptions in guiding each inquiry. The emerging result will be, of all things, a science-based profession, in the pragmatic sense intended by William James, John Dewey, and contemporary pragmatists like Richard Rorty, Richard Bernstein, and Stephen Toulmin, whose thinking Fishman skillfully integrates in forming the epistemological foundations of his argument.

I shall not try to summarize the contents nor elaborate the merits of Fishman's book in this brief appraisal. Better for you, my reading partner in the search for a better way to do the psychologist's job, to get on with the author's clear, deeply thoughtful, richly informed, inspiring message. All I shall attempt are a few summary opinions about the main contributions Fishman has offered to our profession, and exposure of some nonsequiturs that I have repeatedly had to disqualify in countering critical objections to my own arguments along lines that are comparable, if not exactly parallel, with those pursued in this book.

To my mind, the pragmatic epistemology that Fishman articulates is the strongest statement yet to be seen of a useful, philosophically defensible guide for inquiry in the practice of psychology. Comparison and contrast of the pragmatic paradigm with neopositivist and hermeneutic approaches to the stupefying complexities of the human condition lay out a path for sensible investigation that successfully avoids the rigidities and needless restrictions of the former alternative and the vague, "anything goes" license that endangers those who wander into the hermeneutic field. The specificity with which Fishman elaborates the pragmatic approach, the details of the program, and the rich examples he provides bring new clarity to useful, systematic practice. All these carry the live authenticity that will allow practitioners not only to learn about disciplined inquiry, but actually do it and teach it to others. The major contribution of the work, in my opinion, is the detailed plan for moving "from single case to database," as Fishman puts it. It is a splendidly fortunate historical coincidence that the rationale for making this leap and the technology that will allow us to accomplish it have come along at just the same time.

In the matter of nonsequiturs that Fishman is likely to encounter in critical objections to his proposal, I must wearily note that the pragmatic arguments are not antiscientific. No one—not Fishman, nor I, nor any sane person—can dispute the value of scientific method nor its success in advancing knowledge about human behavior. Anyone who has the slightest doubt about that needs only to compare William James's *Principles of Psychology*, published in 1890, with any current textbook in the field to see how far we have come. Philosophically brilliant, linguistically charming, and rich in the insights of a wise and observant man, James's volumes are nearly devoid of scientifically established facts, except for the results of early German experiments that James himself often dismissed as demonstrations of the obvious. Any introductory textbook will show dramatically that a century of research in psychology has taught us a great deal about the way human beings sense, perceive, think, feel, learn, and act. Fishman says we do not have to *start* with traditional scientific research before we can proceed with useful practice, but he does not say that scientific research should not be done.

More wearily still, I remind readers familiar with my work that encouragement of pragmatically guided, systematic case study does not detract from the value of quantitative, group-based research as a way to examine the important issues that quantitative, group-based research is designed to examine. In determining which diagnostic method is better, on average, for answering which diagnostic question, or which form of treatment works better, on average, for which form of ailment, the carefully planned, properly instrumented, quantitatively analyzed group-comparative studies that constitute a large share of Ph.D. dissertations and much of the faculty research in contemporary clinical and counseling psychology are clearly required. Moreover, the current fact and future likelihood that systematic case studies will be more readily accepted and more actively promoted in professional schools than in academic departments of psychology does not detract from the value of the scientist-practitioner programs that flourish in many academic departments. Fishman does not argue that we stop doing the kind of research that goes on in those programs. His only plea is that we start doing the kinds of disciplined inquiry that his book so clearly describes, that systematic case study be given a place on the legitimate epistemic stage.

If that is done, we will take a long step toward resolving the dilemma between rigor and relevance that has bedeviled psychology from the beginning. We will study conditions that matter, but do so in a disciplined way, and over the long range accumulate a body of case material to accompany other forms of research in creating and progressively improving a scientifically credible, practically useful profession of psychology.

It has been my pleasure to know Dan Fishman as a friend, and my privilege to work with him as a colleague, for more than twenty years. It is now my pleasure and privilege to commend his book, heartily and without reservation, to all those who seek in psychology a science and profession that works in the public good.

Donald R. Peterson

First Dean, Graduate School of Applied and Professional Psychology (GSAPP), Rutgers University

Former President, National Council of Schools and Programs of Professional Psychology (NCSPP)

Author, *Educating Professional Psychologists: History and Guiding Conception* (1997)

Preface

On December 1, 1995, a memo came across my desk that threatened my professional role and identity as well as my job. The Chair of the department of psychology at my university was calling for the abolition of our graduate school of professional psychology, the institution where I had been employed for almost twenty years. His reason:

> It is not clear to me why the University should be involved at all with a psychotherapy-related professional school. The value of advanced training for talk therapy has been seriously questioned by recent data which show quite conclusively that such advanced training is totally unnecessary (see Robyn Dawes' [1994] *House of Cards: Psychology and Psychotherapy Built on Myth*). . . . There is the legitimate question of why taxpayers should subsidize an unnecessary route to licensing for private practice and third-party payments.

Robyn Dawes is a well-established psychologist who places great faith in the findings of a "natural science" psychology, that is, a psychology grounded in the laboratory-based, theory-testing paradigm modeled after such natural sciences as physics and chemistry. The "data" mentioned in the memo related to Dawes's contentions (a) that there was no evidence that doctorally trained professional psychologists were more effective as psychotherapists than less trained professionals or even than "paraprofessionals"; and (b) that statistical formulas were superior to doctoral professionals in making such clinical predictions as final psychiatric diagnosis on the basis of intake data for inpatients, and the likelihood of a mentally ill individual committing a violent crime sometime in the future.

I had heard about the hornet's nest of uproar that Dawes's book had stimulated at the time of its publication a year earlier, but this memo made it all hit home. A series of rebutting thoughts and questions raced through my mind. How "conclusive" were Dawes's data? I knew of methodological questions about the data, and I had heard that Dawes had only reviewed a select sample of relevant studies. Also, most studies of psychotherapy and clinical versus statistical prediction were based upon the positivist assumptions of experimental psychology, and this paradigm seemed to me an inappropriate one to apply in evaluating the effectiveness of any type of human services. In fact, I had just read a study of psychotherapy outcome in the November 1995 issue of *Consumer Reports* concluding that psychologists were more effective than marriage counselors and family doctors. This study had been directed by Martin Seligman,[1] a respected research psychologist, but it had used a nonexperimental research design, and this work itself subsequently raised tremendous controversy.[2]

Also, the labeling of our professional school's mission as teaching "talk therapy"—suggesting that this was an activity in which the professional simply talked to the patient—was both a travesty against the variety and complexity of the psychotherapeutic interventions taught at our school and against the spectrum of other knowledge and skill areas in which a number of my colleagues and I were involved, such as program evaluation, community psychology, and applied organizational psychology.

The 1995 memo was the immediate catalyst for this book. But the project has much deeper and wider roots—in fact, forty years' worth. This book contrasts two visions of psychology: one "scientific," in the natural science sense, and one "pragmatic." I write with a good deal of passion about these two visions, because over the forty years I have been living with them intellectually in serial monogamy.

I first fell in love with the natural science vision in 1958 when I majored in psychology as an undergraduate at Princeton. This vision fit perfectly with the times, since the 1950s were in many ways the height of the worldview of "modernism."[3] Modernist thinking, and the "positivist" philosophy that underlies it, places a particularly high value on reason and its flowering in natural science. Natural science is viewed as a specially privileged, objective, "value-free" means for uncovering the true, underlying nature of the physical and human world, independent of our minds and culture. As our natural scientific knowledge increases, both in the physical and social worlds, it is translated into cumulative technological advancement and related moral progress in our culture and way of life as a whole.

While I received my doctoral degree in clinical psychology and social relations from Harvard and continued my love affair with the natural scientific vision of social science, the stability, optimism, self-discipline, and conformity of the 1950s was broken by the "counterculture" revolution and political upheavals of the 1960s. The changes in the '60s were associated with the emergence of an interrelated family of alternative visions called by such names as "postmodernism," "neopragmatism," "social constructionism," "deconstructionism," "cultural criticism," "hermeneutics," "interpretive theory," and "antifoundationalism." While there are very important differences among these frameworks, they all contrast themselves to modernism, assuming that reality is, to a large extent, "constructed" or "invented" by individuals and groups as a function of particular personal beliefs and historical, cultural, and social contexts. Thus, "postmodernism" (the term I use to refer to these alternative views as a group) conceives of the nature of reality as relative, depending upon an observer's point of view.[4] The postmodernist argues against the modernist's claim to achieve fundamental and objective knowledge about the world through the natural science method. Postmodernism takes the position of perspectivism, that is, the view that knowledge is always limited by the subjective and cultural context of the knower, and the "eternal" truths promised by natural science are limited to particular cultural and historical perspectives.[5]

Postmodernism's rise has been stimulated by the enormous growth of the media, which has made public more and more details of everyday life.[6] In spite of popular nostalgia for the 1950s, contemporary media has also exposed their dark side. After all, racism, homophobia, sexism, poverty, crime, alcoholism, social injustice, and environmental pollution were present in the '50s, they were just more hidden from view and more accepted. Hodding Carter writes that in 1954, when he was at Princeton and I was just about to enter it, there was only one black student out of three thousand undergraduates. Also at this time, Princeton was all male, there was no public acknowledgment of homosexuality as an alternative lifestyle, and anti-Semitism was quite open and explicit. Today's picture is dramatically different. Princeton's admitted class of 1998 is 48 percent female, 7 percent African American, 6 percent Hispanic, and 12 percent Asian American;[7] it has an active gay and lesbian community; and it has a Jewish president. These changes are reflected in the eating clubs, perhaps the most conservative and historically the most discriminatory institution at the university. Today one of these clubs is kosher and another publicly promotes its gay-oriented activities.[8]

Postmodernism has had a growing impact on psychology and the other social sciences. For me, disenchantment with the natural science vision of psychology started slowly, as I realized more and more that the thousands of laboratory-like studies being generated by the field were having frustratingly little impact upon major social and psychological problems. In my particular field of clinical psychology, I had to admit that the waxing and waning of areas like psychoanalysis, encounter groups, community mental health, family therapy, and behavior therapy—while of great interest and appeal to me—were much more dependent on fad and fashion than on the "data" and "results" of natural science studies. In fact, since the data from these studies were not consistent, and since the studies were not replicated, it was difficult to derive any policy conclusions from them.

My discontent with the natural science vision crystallized in an article I wrote with William Neigher in 1982, entitled "American Psychology in the 1980s: Who Will Buy?"[9] Written at the beginning of President Ronald Reagan's "cut, slash, and chop" approach to the federal social program budget, we reviewed the very disappointing substantive results of natural science-based psychology in developing solutions to individual and social problems. As a more effective alternative to this scientific model, we proposed a "technological" model of applied psychology and discussed a number of contrasts between the two.[10] While natural science emphasizes academic freedom of the individual researcher, technology is guided by goals and objectives that are established by the society. While natural science ideally takes place in the laboratory, technology is conducted "in the field," within the actual situation in which a problem presents itself. While basic research focuses on testing hypotheses derived from academic theories, technology focuses on directly altering conditions in the real world. While natural science focuses upon the parameters in its laboratory experiments, technology develops systematic pictures of psychological and social phenomena in the outside world, using standardized measures and large-scale norms like the U.S. Census, national economic indicators such as the inflation rate, school achievement scores, and crime statistics. Finally, while the goal of natural science is theory development and "truth," the goal of technology is to guide practical action by suggesting effective solutions to presenting problems within the constraints of a particular body of knowledge, a given set of skills, and available resources.

In 1985 I teamed up with a senior colleague at Rutgers, Donald Peterson, to design a conference that would further develop the idea of the technological model. We brought together leading applied psychologists to talk about the potentials of the technological model for psychological assessment methods that spanned across "systems" levels and different organizational settings. Included was work at the biopsychological level on the role of the home-based computer in brain function therapy, and uses and misuses of psychophysiological measures such as heart rate in lie detector tests. At the individual-behavior level we looked at the assessment of patients in mental hospitals and inmates in prisons. In the area of group functioning, we reviewed the measurement of family patterns in which certain parental behaviors perpetuate the aggressive and violent behavior of adolescent children, and the evaluation of determinants of safety-related performance problems within airline crews. Finally, our consideration of organizational functioning included the topics of assessing decision making in community mental health centers, and measuring management performance in corporations.

The conference led to a book, *Assessment for Decision*,[11] whose title reflected the theme of the project: how assessment that is focused on practical problem solving is always conducted with the goal of providing clients with concretely useful information for specific decisions. Some of decision-relevant information we explored included whether a particular prison inmate should be released on parole, whether a particular airline crew is showing signs of dysfunction that could lead to a crash, and whether management role descriptions in corporations could be improved so as to increase organizational productivity and morale.

In the book we documented the very disappointing results of natural-science-based psychology.[12] One project was singularly striking and telling in this regard. In a survey conducted by *Psychology Today* for its fifteenth-anniversary issue,[13] eleven distinguished psychologists, "the best minds in the field," were asked to describe what each considered to be "the most significant work in psychology over the past decade and a half." Their "astonishing" answers to this question were summarized in a *New York Times* editorial:

> "Significant work" implies work generally agreed to be important, but the 11 Best Minds in psychology agree on hardly anything. Stanley Milgrim of the City University of New York hails the teaching of sign language to apes as an enduring recent achievement. But another contributor, Ulric Neisser of Cornell, cites as important the evident failure to teach sign language to apes.
>
> B. F. Skinner, alleging himself not well informed of recent progress in

other fields of psychology, recounts the advances in behavioral psychology, which he pioneered. But two other sages, Jerome Bruner of the New School for Social Research and Richard Lazarus of Berkeley, laud the escape from Skinnerian psychology as the most significant accomplishment. . . .

The failure of the 11 psychologists to agree on almost anything evinces a serious problem in their academic discipline. . . . Can psychology be taken seriously as science if even its leading practitioners cannot agree on its recent advances?[14]

As my thinking progressed to become more explicitly postmodern, the "technological" paradigm became the "pragmatic paradigm." It is true that in contrast to theory-testing natural science, technology does focus on real-world problem solving. However, "technology" is in many ways a modernistic concept, connoting an emphasis upon a simplifying, mechanistic view of the world at the expense of the complexities of the psychological, social, and cultural systems in which human beings function. On the other hand, "pragmatism," the philosophy developed by William James and John Dewey at the turn of the century, has been embraced and incorporated into postmodernism by such writers as the philosopher Richard Rorty and the psychologist Donald Polkinghorne, who refers to his postmodernly updated version as "neopragmatism."[15]

At some point soon thereafter I clearly switched my allegiance to this pragmatic vision, and the more I became attached to it, the more alienated I felt from the natural science vision.[16] This is one of my motivations for writing this book: to review the history of psychology so as to understand how the natural science vision became and remains dominant in the field, in spite of its glaring shortcomings for many of our concerns. My other motivation is a passionate belief that the natural science vision is fatally flawed and severely limited in its capacity to address our social crises, and that it is the pragmatic vision that has that capacity. This book will contend that yes, there is a better way. Given an equal chance to compete with the natural science paradigm, the pragmatic model will demonstrate its superior practical payoff in the development, operation, and refinement of effective social programs that grapple with our crippling social crises.

Acknowledgments

This book has emerged from forty years of active professional engagement in the diverse worlds of applied psychology: research, scholarship, direct practice, administration, program planning, and program evaluation. Along the way, I have been most fortunate to experience wonderful mentors and their supporting institutions who have expertly and persuasively modeled a variety of paradigms in our discipline and guided and encouraged me as I pursued my own path among these: Silvan Tomkins at Princeton University; Justin Weiss and Elliot Mishler at the Massachusetts Mental Health Center; Carl Zimet at the University of Colorado Health Sciences Center; Henry Frey and Youlon Savage at the Adams County (Colorado) Mental Health Center; Henry Foley at the National Institute of Mental Health; and Peter Nathan and Don Peterson at the Graduate School of Applied and Professional Psychology (GSAPP) of Rutgers University.

Since 1976 I have enjoyed a marvelous group of colleagues at Rutgers-GSAPP who are distinguished by a most unusual combination of outstanding professional achievement, collegiality, scholarly engagement, and broad-mindedness. Pragmatism's ultimate value upon continuing dialogue and the related call for pluralism in psychology that I issue in the last chapter are both embodied in our faculty community. This environment has been complemented by a superb group of professional psychology graduate students, whose intellectual talents, emotional skills, and passion for service have inspired me to seek a paradigm that truly matches their potential.

Five close Rutgers colleagues and friends have been particularly absorbed with this project and have provided special expertise and support as I moved more and more to think "outside the box." Cary Cherniss has unfailingly been there from the beginning, providing penetratingly insightful, down-to-earth, and enormously useful feedback at every stage, from all the way back when this book was just a glimmer in my eye. His caring and encouragement have been particularly appreciated during the inevitable rocky times.

From his first moment at Rutgers, Louis Sass has welcomed me into his deep, sophisticated intellectual engagement with the philosophical and cultural dimensions of psychology. His gracious feedback on drafts of this book has been a seminar in contemporary philosophy and in how to throw off the shackles of "social science speak" and connect with the clear, graceful literary voices to be found in the humanities.

Both in conceptualization and in professional practice, Don Peterson, former dean of GSAPP, has pioneered the "disciplined inquiry" paradigm upon which this book builds. His great intellect, pragmatic brilliance, and moral centering have been an inspiration for me to focus on the ultimate social good of applied psychology: working in a systematic fashion toward human betterment with critical self-reflection and public accountability.

An expert in the philosophy of psychology and its ramifications for psychotherapy research and scholarship—and a "closet" pragmatist—Stan Messer has generously shared his wide-ranging knowledge to bring a critically constructive perspective to the psychotherapy chapter. His continuing staunch backing of my project has been an important source of strength.

Finally, Brent Ruben, a senior faculty member of the Rutgers School of Communication, Information, and Library Studies with whom I have collaborated on a number of projects designed within the framework of pragmatic psychology, is a model of the effective applied social scientist. I have greatly appreciated his enthusiasm for my project, his keen insights, and his sage advice.

Four other close professional colleagues—Maurice Elias, John Kalafat, Jonny Morell, and Bill Neigher—have been there since the late 1970s with their informed, perceptive, and sustaining encouragement and with their prototypic modeling of pragmatic psychology.

Three editorial reviewers—M. Brewster Smith, Donald Polkinghorne, and Yvonna Lincoln—had the open-mindedness and broad perspective to see the potential in an unusual manuscript. Their encouragement and profound understanding of the positive possibilities of pragmatism for psychology were enormously encouraging. Their enthusiasm, support, and wonderfully crafted and sensitively offered feedback came at just the right moments.

Two editors were most helpful. Martha Heller of Rutgers University

Press provided early guidance and backing that legitimized a unique approach to applied psychology. Tim Bartlett of NYU Press took on the stodginess of earlier drafts and sensitively but effectively inspired me to "lighten up" without sacrificing substance. Tim also helped me to envision and then to create the book as an integrated whole. In addition, Despina Papazoglou Gimbel was an ideal managing editor; and Martin L. White, an expert indexer.

Close friends from outside the field were a breath of fresh air as they shared their perspectives in reaction to drafts of parts of the book. Three public education teachers—Jerry Shulman, Connie Shulman, and Judy Underberg—brought years of classroom-gained wisdom to their insightful readings of the education chapter; and Bob Dunn brought his special knowledge of the computer world and the concept of "case-based reasoning" to fleshing out the section in chapter 7, "From Single Case to Database." Jerry was also particularly helpful as he shared his expertise in clear, engaging writing and his infectious enthusiasm for the potential contribution of my new ideas. Lastly, I want to thank Susan Katz, a graphic designer and art director, who lent her impressive talent toward the creation of the front cover layout for the paperback edition.

Finally, it has been a joy to have a family that is not only deeply loving, but also "in the business"—my wife, Claire, my fellow traveler since graduate school; my daughter Debbie, the third doctoral clinical psychologist in the family, following in our footsteps and then some with her sharply honed clinical perspectives, sensitivities, and compassion; and my daughter Amie, a de facto community psychologist, social activist, and writer/editor par excellence. They have inspired me to create a paradigm that captures the special devotion and humanity they emanate by engaging human problems and misery: always deeply empathetic and caring, and always informed by theory and self-reflection attuned to the contextual complexities of their case situations. They have been intensely devoted to this project from its inception with unfailing confidence—not always shared by me—in my capacity to do it justice. Claire especially has unwaveringly been my support, literary adviser, and in-house editor, hour by hour and day by day for the seven years this project has taken to reach final fruition—a herculean task if there ever was one!

Introduction
A Better Way to Help by Reinventing Psychology

Turning Mainstream Psychology Upside Down

The human troubles of our times demand the attention of psychology. We seem caught in a web of social crises, powerless to generate effective solutions. Drugs and violence seem to pervade small towns, suburbs, and cities alike; homelessness abounds; the middle-class lives with job insecurity and worry that their health insurance will be discontinued; the public school system seems to be in a state of disarray and ineffectiveness; alienated white males join paramilitary militias devoted to racism, anti-Semitism, and violent resistance to government authority; and "culture wars" proliferate over issues like abortion, prayer in schools, school choice, gay rights, and welfare dependence. Overseas, two disturbing, antidemocratic trends appear to dominate more and more each day: tribalism, with different ethnic, racial, and religious groups murderously pitted against one another; and globalism, with the homogenization of cultures and economies across countries created by international corporations, undermining distinctive ethnic traditions and identities.[1,2]

How can psychology help? For the last one hundred twenty years, since Wilhelm Wundt's establishment of the first scientific psychological laboratory, mainstream psychology has primarily offered one answer, building upon two positivist assumptions from such natural sciences as physics, chemistry, and biology. These state (a) that the search for general theory precedes application, and (b) that general theory proceeds analytically by breaking complex processes into small parts and individual variables; developing broad, abstract laws to correlate these variables; and then experimentally testing these laws in controlled, laboratory settings.

This book argues a radical proposal: to improve psychology's capacity to help address human difficulties and crises, we must turn the mainstream model upside down. Based upon recent philosophical developments in the areas of postmodernism and pragmatism, I will contend that application—the need to solve a particular problem in a local situation—comes first, and that theory and research are then directed by the problem at hand. Moreover, theory and research must deal with problems as they holistically present themselves in actual situations. The pragmatic paradigm thereby argues that actual cases—in all their multisystemic complexity and contextual embeddedness—should be the starting and ending points of psychological research that purports to be effective in contributing to the solution of real-life problems. In short, in this book I will show that there are compelling practical and epistemological reasons for radically deconstructing psychology, and then reinventing the field by getting down to cases—both literally and figuratively.

It is true that a substantial segment of the public and government leaders see psychology, along with mainstream social science in general, as a major resource for studying and addressing social problems. Psychological research annually guides policies for the investment of hundreds of billions of government and foundation dollars. Yet for the layperson, the domain of academic social science frequently seems a realm that is completely alien to the troubles of our times. What appears is a pristine, "scientific" world of general behavioral theories posited in abstruse, mechanistic terms, detached from the nitty-gritty complexity of everyday life; a world of preoccupation with methodological controls to simulate laboratory conditions for studying human action; a world of complex numbers and statistics; and a world of empirical findings which, while described as "suggestive" and "worthy of further study," seem typically to be either inconsistent, obvious, or irrelevant.

It is not surprising that some members of Congress—both Republican and Democratic—have waged a frontal attack on the funding of social science research, describing social scientists as "the foolish fringe folly of researchers who use tax money like the dilettante squanders his inheritance,"[3] as engaging in "an intellectual boondoggle undeserving of the research appropriations given other scientific fields,"[4] as giving the public a "golden fleecing,"[5] as "a very expensive way of confirming what we already know," and using jargon to belabor the obvious by "chopping their way through open doors."

Representative Barbara Mikulski has been particularly dramatic and articulate in her criticism of a particular piece of alcoholism research:

Not one rummy has been taken off of Baltimore streets by this research. Not one drunken husband has been dissuaded from beating his wife or one drunken mother from beating her child. These research projects are like exotic, expensively mounted butterfly collections, hidden away in vaults and only exhumed from time to time to display to other collectors of the rare and unusual in mutual reaffirmation of their elite status.[6]

It is tempting to join these politicians and see a conspiracy among social scientists to defraud the public of billions of dollars in the pursuit of intellectual games for "mutual reaffirmation of their elite status." However, this book contends that the positivist, natural science scientific model predominates today, not as a result of corrupt or fraudulent individual professionals, but rather as a result of academic psychology's continuing, misplaced faith in the philosophy of modernism. This philosophy has gained tremendous intellectual and political favor over the past one hundred years because of its intimate association with movements, such as the Enlightenment and the Industrial Revolution, that underlie contemporary civilized life in developed societies.

Modernism—the natural-science-centered worldview deriving from the Enlightenment—is a seductively attractive belief system in its promise of clear, absolute, "objective" answers in a complex, ambiguous, troubled world. However, modern psychology's delivery on its promise to date has been scant at best, especially in light of the major resources devoted to it, such as the federal government's annual investment of at least $1.8 billion for psychological and related social science research.[7]

Of course, the lack of dramatic results to date and the divergence of psychological conceptualizations of human behavior from lay conceptualizations are not per se damning of the field. The response of mainstream psychology to its meager results is to urge patience. The field reminds us that it is holding a philosophical promissory note with the American public. Based on the discipline's underlying, modernistic philosophy of science and knowledge, psychology has promised that investment in the laboratory-based, theory-testing research model of positivism will eventually pay off with the discovery of general laws that can then be deductively applied to solve specific social problems.[8] Some believe it is still possible that the special language and perspective of psychology will one day spawn a "psychological Newton" or a "psychological Einstein" who will develop laws that gain broad consensus in the discipline concerning their distinct and superior capacity to predict and control individual and social functioning with dramatically increased power over other explanatory models.[9]

However, there are growing reasons to question the "full faith and credit" of the philosophy behind the promissory note, reasons deriving from "postmodern"[10] critiques of mainstream psychology. This book will explore these critiques and use them as a foundation for proposing an alternative, case-based model, philosophically embedded in postmodern pragmatism,[11] for more effectively addressing social problems.

Postmodernism's critiques of mainstream psychology's modernistic thinking are reflective of postmodernism's broad critique of the modernistic philosophy that underlies the contemporary institutions in Western, industrialized society. Since the Enlightenment, modernism has promised increasing social progress with the growth of science and associated technology, social progress based on the rational application of universal laws about human nature that are "discovered" through social science research. Modernists have proclaimed that this process will lead to homogeneous liberal democracies around the world and an end to major ideological differences among national and ethnic groups.[12]

However, at an increasing rate over the past forty years, change and diversity have predominated, with great variation depending on local conditions. Today in this country, radical change is in the air: institutions are being "deconstructed" and then "reinvented." Government is being reinvented by rethinking and reworking the basic nature and structure of government programs that have developed over the past sixty-five years.[13] The "family" is being reinvented by including gay and lesbian couples and their children (adopted and natural) within the rubric of a "normal" family.[14] Business and education are being reinvented to move from a nineteenth-century, hierarchical, "factory" culture to a contemporary, "smart" culture that emphasizes decentralization, teamwork, and the provision of information in a technology-rich format.[15] The "melting pot" concept of American society has changed into one of a "salad bowl" mosaic emphasizing diversity and multiculturalism. And even the basis of modern life is being questioned in a book titled *The End of Science*,[16] by a senior editor of the prestigious journal *Scientific American*.

It is this environment of postmodern change and diversity that sets the stage for a fundamental rethinking of the nature of psychology as a discipline. And it is from this environment that a new, case-based, pragmatic psychology springs. To provide an initial understanding of postmodernism and pragmatic psychology's place in it, a whirlwind tour of postmodernism is in order.

The Emergence of the Pragmatic Paradigm from Postmodernism

What's What in Postmodernism

A core idea in postmodernism is that we are always interpreting our experienced reality through a pair of conceptual glasses—glasses based on such factors as our present personal goals in this particular situation, our past experiences, our values and attitudes, our body of knowledge, the nature of language, present trends in contemporary culture, and so forth. It is never possible to take the glasses off altogether and view the world as it "really is," with pure objectivity. All we can do is change glasses and realize that different pairs provide different pictures and perspectives of the world. Which glasses we "should" use in an individual situation depends not on which pair purports to correspond best to the "real" external world, but rather on a variety of other criteria, which are an ongoing subject of discussion and dialogue. Because postmodernism posits that there are no clearly superior, that is, "privileged" criteria, it is not surprising that there several variants of postmodernism that differ according to which criteria should predominate. All these variants, however, can be understood in terms of six major themes emphasized by postmodern epistemology.[17]

The first of these themes is "foundationlessness," the notion that there is no objectively knowable external reality that forms a foundation to knowledge, but rather that all knowledge is partial and limited to one of many possible perspectives, consisting of constructions based on human organizing capacities. A second theme is "fragmentariness," the idea that the real is not a single, integrated system, but rather a collection of disunited, fragmented, disparate elements and events. Another theme is "constructivism," the notion that human knowledge is not a mirrored reflection of reality, but rather a constructed interpretation of the undifferentiated "flux" of experience.

A fourth theme is "critical theory," the neo-Marxist view that all knowledge-generation is driven by economic, political, and cultural forces, either pitting those in authority against the disadvantaged and disenfranchised, or empowering the latter in their striving toward social dignity, equity, and justice.[18]

A fifth theme is the "ontological hermeneutics" of Heidegger and Gadamer. "Hermeneutics" is the science or art of interpretation. Initially it focused on biblical texts, and later it was extended to all texts, and then to human behavior *as text*. Ontological hermeneutics takes the analytic methods of hermeneutics and transforms them into the basic constituents of human experience. In Sass's words, ontological hermeneutics is "a recognition that processes of understanding and interpretation are not merely tools of the human sciences [the humanities], but constitute the very essence of human existence itself."[19]

Last is the theme of "neopragmatism." Accepting the view that much of our experienced reality is socially constructed in cultural and historical context, neopragmatism focuses on the contextual goals and purposes that specific human groups do in fact have, and it evaluates the "truth" of a body of knowledge in terms of its capacity to help achieve those goals and purposes. In Donald Polkinghorne's words:

> Neopragmatism . . . [does not] accept that a postmodern discipline has to be solipsistic and relativistic. Human beings do make choices, complete projects and accomplish purposes in the world. Their everyday choices of which actions to pursue in order to bring about a desired result are most often informed by previous experiences rather than theoretical predictions.[20]

Neopragmatism allows for scientific effort, although the purpose of science is revised. Instead of being a search for underlying laws and truths of the universe, science serves to collect, organize, and distribute the practices that have produced their intended results.[21]

Within the framework of these six themes, four types of postmodernism can be differentiated in terms of which of the themes they emphasize: "skeptical" postmodernism emphasizes the first three, more deconstructive themes—foundationlessness, fragmentariness, and constructivism;[22] "critical" postmodernism emphasizes critical theory;[23] "ontological" postmodernism emphasizes ontological hermeneutics;[24] and "affirmative," "neopragmatic"—or what I am simply calling "pragmatic"—postmodernism highlights neopragmatism.[25]

The Pragmatic Paradigm as a Response to Psychology's
"Culture Wars"

Within psychology, it is mainly the skeptical and critical visions of
postmodernism that have gained prominence. These visions are in many
dramatic ways an explicit rebellion against the hegemony of modernist,
positivist psychology. The dialectical debate between positivist psychology and these versions of postmodernism—psychology's version of the
"culture wars"—has been strongly polarizing the field and splitting it
apart.[26] Now psychologists frequently battle against one another rather
than against human distress and social conflict. For example, critical
postmoderns are viewed by positivists as blatantly antiscientific in their
ideological politicalization of all psychological issues; while positivists
are viewed by critical postmoderns as strongly and naively aligned with
perpetuating the political status quo of contemporary oppressive, corporate capitalism.

Positivists are angered by skeptical postmoderns. Emphasizing the limitations of knowledge, skeptical postmoderns put their energies into the
provocative deconstruction of accepted realities, ideas, and institutions.
While this can have a salutary effect upon unfreezing ossified and destructive belief systems, and while this process sometimes results in a playful, ca-
cophonous, flamboyant celebration of the diversity of human images and
ideas, ultimately the skeptical postmodern does not explicitly propose more
useful belief systems.[27] In short, the purpose of the skeptical postmodern is
deconstructive, not constructive. While skeptical postmodernism's dramatic, confrontive qualities have helped it to achieve notice in its clash with
positivist psychology, these qualities have exacerbated polarization within
the field. The choice presented by positivism versus skeptical postmodernism seems to many a choice between a "formal," "technical," "objective," "rigorous," and ultimately "socially irrelevant" psychology, on the
one hand, and a "subjective," "personal," "deconstructive," "critical," and
ultimately "nihilistic" psychology, on the other.[28]

Not surprisingly, a related dialectic occurs between skeptical and critical postmoderns. The skeptic condemns the critical theorist for proposing foundational, "essentialist," "totalizing" political values, not acknowledging the contextually limited, constructivist nature of them;
while the critical theorist castigates the skeptic for radical relativism and
associated political nihilism.[29]

Ontological postmodernism is less combative than skeptical and critical postmodernism, and thus has been less caught up in the dialectic with positivism. Ontological postmodernism stresses the philosophical complexity and ambiguity of knowledge, emphasizing an epistemological humility that contrasts with the tendency toward epistemological provocation and rhetorical flamboyance among many skeptical and critical postmodern authors.[30] However, ontological postmodernism's focus on extra-empirical, esthetic, "philosophical" truth results in a deemphasis on practical problem solving for today's pressing social concerns.

The debate among positivism, skeptical postmodernism, and critical postmodernism in psychology over the past forty years has reached a point of diminishing returns. The skeptics have made their point that there are fundamental limitations on the knowledge generated by positivist psychology, and the critical postmoderns have sensitized us to the political and economic agendas running throughout psychological research projects. Yet the positivists have held their ground, still politically and economically dominating the field of organized psychology. Even though the practical value of all these years of positivist psychology are disappointingly meager, the positivists have staked out psychometrically sophisticated and inventive methodologies that set high standards for rigorous, critical, and ingenious thinking about the complexities of measuring psychological phenomena. In addition, positivists have developed a rich supply of psychological theories and ideas that explore a variety of the vast array of possible perspectives that can be taken upon human behavior and action.

The *pragmatic paradigm* in psychology seeks to transcend psychology's dialectical culture wars by developing an integrative alternative. This approach combines the epistemological insights and value awareness of skeptical, critical, and ontological postmodernism—hereafter referred to in group as the *hermeneutic paradigm*—with the methodological and conceptual achievements of the *positivist paradigm*. Thus the natural science methodologies and concepts of positivism are employed, but with a nonpositivist purpose: they are used to achieve the democratically derived program goals of particular, historically and culturally situated social groups, not to uncover purported general laws of human nature. In political terms, pragmatism can be viewed as staking out a middle, centrist position between modernistically traditional, conservative positivism on the right, and radically liberal, skeptical and critical postmodernism on the left.[31] An important purpose of this book is to enlarge the number of psychologists who are attracted to join this centrist position, and to encourage the establishment of disciplinary structures—journals, funding for research projects, and training programs—to help institutionalize pragmatism within organized psychology.[32]

The call for a pragmatic centrist position between the dialectical polarities of "leftist" skeptical and critical postmodernism versus "rightist" positivism resonates with the academic "culture wars" on college campuses and on the broader political scene. The intellectual historian Russell Jacoby and the political scientist Benjamin Barber write about how the culture wars, as reflected in the ideological battles on today's campuses, have misled America, diverting public attention from the real problems corroding education and society:

> Conservatives, liberals, and radicals argue over which books should be taught in schools; meanwhile few books are read. . . . Faculty and students dispute which words violate the rights of which groups; while society turns increasingly violent. . . . Citizens wrangle over multiculturalism . . . ; meanwhile the irresistible power of advertising and television converts multiculturalism into a monoculture of clothes, music, and cars.[33]
>
> Conservatives want to teach the canon, critics want to teach multiculturalism: Who wants to teach democracy? Private agendas abound: Who will teach the public agenda?[34]

On a more philosophical level, in the words of the anthropologist Nancy Scheper-Hughes, it is time to resist the present forces of political polarization, when "the cultural right is demanding moral and epistemological certainties and the cultural left is calling for a capitulation to the ultimate nihilism of postmodernism."[35]

Supporting the Beleaguered Practitioner

The practical value of psychology as a discipline results from the activities of applied and professional psychologist practitioners. Broadly speaking, one can distinguish at least two models of professional practice, paralleling the epistemologies of positivism and pragmatism.

The Modern, Positivist Model

In the modern, positivist model, practitioners are appliers of "basic" knowledge. Donald Peterson[36] terms this model "professional activity as

Figure 1.1. Professional Activity as Applied Science (from Peterson 1991). Reprinted by permission of the publisher.

applied science," and his outline of it is presented in figure 1.1. As shown, basic research begins by discovering the underlying laws of human nature, which leads to applied research, which in turn generates technologies (such as "manualized" cognitive-behavior therapy for panic attacks or whole language techniques for teaching reading), which are then applied by professional practitioners working directly with clients. This is a linear model, in which the most challenging and valued work is done by the basic researcher on the left of the figure, and the applied psychologist on the right is viewed as a technician applying highly operationalized procedures.

From a postmodern perspective, the problems with the positivist view of applied psychology are twofold: the "basic" science" upon which the practitioner is to act is epistemologically flawed—it is not possible to "discover" "basic laws of human nature"; and the results of the enterprise are substantively irrelevant to the nonlaboratory world—because of the contextual embeddedness of psychological knowledge.

The Postmodern, Pragmatic Model

The alternative view of applied psychology, the postmodern, pragmatic model, provides an epistemological conception of what many claim psychological practitioners actually do.[37] Peterson calls this model "professional activity as disciplined inquiry," and an outline of it is presented in figure 1.2. As shown, the model has three major parts: a *client* (component A), who presents with a desire for change, receives a *program* of services (components B–K), which then goes through an *evaluation* of its effectiveness in helping attain the client's change goals (component L).

More specifically, the model starts with the "client" and the client's problems and goals for change (component A in the figure). The client can be an individual, group, organization, community, or even a society. For example, in the educational domain, the client can be an individual student, a class, a school or school district, the community in which a

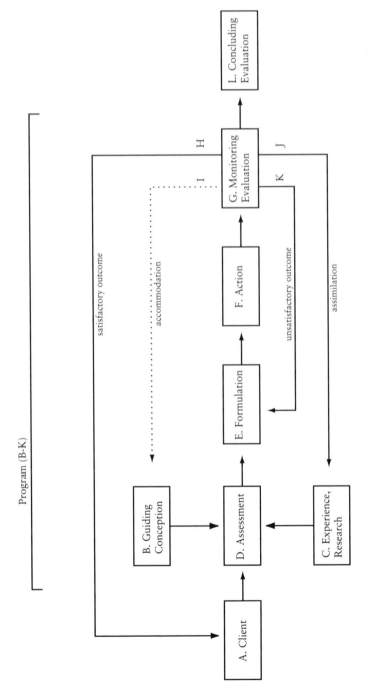

Figure 1.2. Professional Activity as Disciplined Inquiry (adapted from Peterson 1991). Reprinted by permission of the publisher.

school district is located, or the nation's school system as an integrated whole (in the instance of federal programs such as Title 2 funding for children in poverty, special education funding for learning handicapped students, and the school lunch program).

The first step in disciplined inquiry is assessment (D). It is orchestrated by a "guiding conception" (B) of the process under study, which includes the practitioner's assumptions about theory, epistemology, program goals, and ethics.[38] The assessment is also influenced by the examiner's knowledge of relevant empirical research and by the examiner's remembered examples of similar cases (C). The assessment is then employed to create a specific formulation of the client's situation (E). This is the assessor's best understanding of the particular case, and frequently he or she will at this point reframe the issues the client initially presented. This formulation implies some sort of action (F), "either an intervention that offers the best available prospect of benefit to the client or a decision that will be useful to the client."[39] The effectiveness of the action is then evaluated (G).

If the client and practitioner agree that the changes they have accomplished or the decisions they have reached suffice for the client, or that further efforts are not promising, the project is completed and a concluding evaluation can be conducted (L). However, if either client or practitioner consider the outcomes insufficient and both consider that additional efforts promise improvement, "further cycles of reformulation, action, and evaluation may continue until an acceptable outcome is reached [H–K]."[40]

In proper practice, each case is a learning experience for the practitioner:

> Each case the practitioner studies adds to the store of knowledge he or she can bring to the next case. Usually the experience is assimilated within the body of comparable experiences the practitioner has accumulated previously [component J in the figure]. Occasionally, however, the outcomes or other characteristics of a case are so sharply inconsistent with the guiding conception the practitioner has followed until that time that an accommodating change in the conception is required [component I in the figure].[41]

When functioning within the pragmatic model, writers such as Peterson, Polkinghorne, and Schön[42] emphasize the importance of the practitioner's history of personal professional experience, which develops an internal database of accumulated case studies upon which the practi-

tioner draws for guidance in dealing with the problem at hand. Polkinghorne compares the positivist and pragmatic models of applied psychology with Dreyfus and Dreyfus's[43] typology of cognitive processes used by
"novice" and "expert" practitioners, respectively, in a variety of professions. Novice practitioners, as in the positivist model, follow the rules
and procedures they were taught in training in a cookbook type of manner. On the other hand, expert practitioners rework these procedures to
meet the unique nature of a particular applied situation. Expert knowledge is produced by interaction between an expert's repertoire of cognitive understanding and environmental cues in the case situation at hand.

Schön describes the intellectual process of the expert practitioner as
"reflection-in-action":

> When someone reflects-in-action, . . . he is not dependent on the categories
> of established theory and technique, but constructs a new theory of the
> unique case. His inquiry is not limited to a deliberation about means which
> depends on a priori agreement about ends. He does not keep means and
> ends separate, but defines them interactively as he frames a problematic sit-
> uation. . . . Because his experimenting is a kind of action, implementation
> is built into his inquiry.[44]

In contemporary American psychology, psychological practitioners
are beleaguered, caught between two unattractive alternatives. If they attempt to follow the applied science model and base their actions on the
scientific literature, they do not receive relevant and effective substantive
guidance for dealing with the context-specific complexities of the individual case. On the other hand, if practitioners follow the disciplined inquiry, reflection-in-action model, they are accused of not being "science-
based" by politically and academically dominant, positivist researchers.
While there are some published proponents of the disciplined inquiry
model—such as Peterson, Schön, and Polkinghorne—systematic development of this approach is still in a preliminary stage and very few if any
empirical studies have been completed employing the model. This book
will build upon the conceptual work already completed to bolster the argument for an alternative epistemological foundation—pragmatism—
upon which to legitimate the actual work of highly functioning applied
and professional psychologists. Moreover, once this foundation is established and fully articulated, the disciplined inquiry work of applied psychologists can become much more systematic and effective. For there will
then be positive sanctions and incentives for the establishment of a for-

mal knowledge base of case studies, conducted within the disciplined inquiry model, which will have enormous practical value in guiding future practitioners in addressing their new individual cases.

Peterson, Schön, and Polkinghorne all advocate that in the context of the growing postmodernist movement, this is the time to acknowledge, recognize, and promote the pragmatic, postmodern epistemology that actually does underlie psychological practice. In fact, Polkinghorne argues that as postmodern critiques of modernist academic psychology increase, the pragmatic epistemology underlying psychological practice can be seen as an excellent alternative for psychology to transform itself into a postmodern discipline.[45]

In chapter 8, the dilemma of the psychological practitioner and the promise of the pragmatic case study for resolving this dilemma will be explored for a crisis now taking place in professional psychology: threats—both economic and positivist—to the viability of the clinical psychology practice of psychotherapy precipitated by the growth of managed health care.

Two Cases in Point

Education Reform. Chapter 9 will illustrate the potential of pragmatism for addressing the challenges of educational reform. Psychologists are drawn to this area for a variety of reasons. Historically, the first applied psychology—Lightner Witmer's clinic established in 1896—was educational psychology,[46] and thus over the past one hundred years psychologists have been closely linked with the history and evolution of education. Also, over the past fifteen years, difficulties in our national school system have engendered strong public concern and political visibility since these problems were highlighted by a series of nine reports issued by high-profile, national educational organizations in the early and mid-1980s.[47]

In addition, professional psychologists find schools an excellent site for prevention programs addressing many of the social problems that plague us, such as illiteracy, deficits in job skills, violence, drugs, single teenage pregnancy, and intergroup prejudice and discrimination. The schools are the one community and governmental institution through which almost all children pass, and so finding ways to create effective schools and classrooms has tremendous payoffs for the society as a whole.[48]

There are currently over fourteen thousand school districts, with a total of more than eighty thousand schools.[49] Each school is a case study in how to accomplish generally agreed-upon academic, interpersonal, affective, and character goals in the education and socialization of the nation's next generation.

Why not use the resources of psychology to study systematically and document a sample of these "cases" to see which ones are successful, to try to understand why they are successful in their local contexts, and then to see how this knowledge can provide guidelines for other schools to improve themselves?

The traditional, modernist approach to increasing educational effectiveness seeks general "laws" that "explain" educational performance—"laws" that link better educational performance to one or two single factors, such as smaller classes, or longer days, or more parental involvement, or more updated curricula, or "progressive" teaching techniques, or better teacher-administration relations, or one of today's favorites, "vouchers." In search of these laws, groups of schools that are high versus low on each of these variables but otherwise appear similar are compared to see if a systematic connection emerges between the "high-scoring" schools and better educational performance.

By contrast, in the pragmatic approach, systematic case studies are conducted at well-functioning model schools and, for comparison, at poorly functioning schools. "Model" versus "poor" functioning is explicitly defined in measurable, partly quantifiable, and partly qualitative terms, involving, for example, factors like teacher morale, student enthusiasm for learning, student initiative in learning, and academic performance. The criteria for such a definition of excellence have to be established through political dialogue, policy setting, and decision making. Defining goals, then, is viewed as a sociopolitical and *not* a scientific question. To obtain the broadest understanding of how "model" schools attain their success, all the variables that seem relevant in that school setting are included in the case study, not just one or two isolated factors.

From this perspective, it seems clear that it is crucial to look at multiple levels and facets of a school in understanding how it works. This might begin with individual *student demographics*, such as the percentage who are affluent versus poor, who are minority, and who come from single-parent families. Then we might look at individual *student abilities*, including student learning styles, and *student past educational experience*. Next might be a consideration of *student subculture* with regard to whether learning and studying hard are valued, or whether they are viewed as "uncool." Also important are *parent* demographics, attitudes toward the school, and participation in school programs. Then of course there are *teachers*—what are their abilities, training, demographics, openness to new programs, and morale? As important are characteristics of the *central administration*, the superintendent, principal, vice principals, secretaries, and so forth: What are their demographics, competencies, morale, and subculture? What are their capacities to relate to children, teachers, and parents? Of course, don't forget the role of *school board* members, who have their own demographics, competency, and morale, and of *other relevant community, media, and government leaders*. Also, what are the *physical facilities, financial support, curriculum materials*, and *learning technologies*, such as instructional television and computers, that are available to the school? Finally, while each of these levels and facets is important in and of itself, the interactions, relationships, and interdependencies among them are also of major significance. In fact, some, like the psychiatrist-educator James Comer,[50] believe that *collaboration* among and within students, faculty, administration, parents, and community members is absolutely necessary if a school is to be successful.[51]

In sum, the case study adopts a holistic, systems approach rather than the molecular, single-variable, mechanistic framework of modernism. Case study reports of the model and poorly functioning schools are designed to provide practitioners and policymakers with guidelines for working with whole schools to help them attain higher levels of educational performance and organizational effectiveness.

A Tale of Two Studies. Another, more specific educational example will further highlight the fundamental differences in the kind of research generated by the traditional scientific model and that produced by the pragmatic model proposed here.[52]

An African American student at a prestigious Ivy League university chose a topic for an undergraduate psychology honors thesis on the basis of her deep concern about flagrant non-use of condoms by teenagers, and especially by African American teens. She wanted to develop an educational program for promoting teenagers' knowledge about the importance of using condoms and for increasing such usage. After a discussion with her adviser, who taught the traditional scientific model, the student's study became essentially a test of a general theory of behavior—specifically, the "Theory of Planned Behavior," or "TPB" as it is called.[53] The student learned to state the theory in abstract, "scientific" terms:

> [TPB] theory postulates that an individual's intention to perform or not perform a volitional behavior, combined with subjective norms, attitudes, and perceived behavior control, determine whether or not a person will attempt to perform a particular behavior. The TPB further asserts that intentions are a product of an individual's personal nature and social influences. . . . An individual's evaluation of a particular behavior as positive or negative constitutes his attitude toward the behavior. The social influences, or subjective norms, are defined as the person's perceptions of social pressure to perform the particular behavior.

This formal, "technical" vocabulary seems to many lay people to make the direct and obvious into the obscure and inaccessible. It is not surprising that it can turn off activists, not to mention policymakers. Translated into ordinary discourse, the theory simply says that a person's particular behavior in a particular situation—such as condom use before sex, or completing income tax forms on time, or violently counterattacking another person in self-defense—is determined by a variety of factors, including the person's own attitudes toward the behavior, his view of attitudes toward the behavior by people important in his life, his perceived ability to be in control of the behavior, and the strength of his intention to perform the behavior.

In carrying out her research, the student's emphasis, as dictated by the standard scientific approach in which she was being taught was on developing measures of attitudes that flowed from the theory and would test it. For example, she created a questionnaire that asked her research subjects to indicate how much they believed statements such as, "If condoms are used, sex doesn't seem natural" (own attitude), "Saying we have to use a condom would make my sexual partner think I am having sex with other people" (others' attitudes), "Condoms cost too much" (perceived ability to control the behavior), and "I plan to use condoms if I have sex in the next six weeks" (intention).

In her study, the student recruited ninety-eight college sophomores. She administered her questionnaire before and after the research subjects experienced a five-hour, small-group educational experience of games, exercises, and films. There were three different groups. One focused on promoting knowledge about AIDS and condom use by employing Afrocentrically oriented materials, one promoted such knowledge without the

Afrocentric orientation, and a "control" group focused on the promotion of general health.

The student's hypothesis was that her African American student subjects would respond most strongly to the specifically designed Afrocentric program as compared to the other two groups. Would this be surprising? And if, as indeed they did, the students in the Afrocentric group increased their stated pro-condom-use attitudes and beliefs on the questionnaire, how would this relate to actual changes in behavior? Since behavioral outcome was not recognized as a required part of her study, the researcher never learned whether actual condom use changed after the educational experience. All that was needed for her scientific purpose of testing the Planned Theory of Behavior was administering questionnaires right before and after the five-hour educational experience. The research was propelled and constrained by a model that assumes that real-life issues will be impacted upon ultimately by findings in basic research.

In graduate school, this student had an opportunity to redesign her project within the pragmatic paradigm. This allowed her to be inspired by a wish first and foremost to solve a real-life problem. This is what is meant by "problem-driven" research as opposed to the student's "theory-driven" thesis project.

In line with the problem-driven way of thinking, the ultimate goal in the student's pragmatic research design was an increase in condom use over time. A parallel increase in pro-condom-use attitudes, emphasized in the undergraduate thesis, is desirable only if it translates into behavior. Therefore, in redesigning her study, it was essential that the student build in ways to assess her subjects' actual condom use after the educational experience in ongoing follow-up.

The student began the pragmatic research design with a question similar to her original one: With what educational curriculum would individuals most likely alter their condom-use behavior? The difference in the proposed research from that point on was dramatic. The pressing questions raised were as follows: How do these young people view AIDS, condom use, sexuality, peer pressure, mortality, and so forth, and how are their views related to their behaviors? The need was to engage these young people in interviews, dialogue, and focus groups, using the emerging information to tailor an educational experience that was best suited to their needs and subculture.[54]

Next was the creation of an advisory committee of like individuals, with whom the researcher would work collaboratively throughout the research. Such a committee was intended to engage the young people more fully in developing and participating in the project by engendering a sense of "ownership" in the research and to provide crucial input about developing the program from their own point of view as participants.

In designing the program, the goal was to put together as rich an educational experience as feasible so as to maximize impact. If the student's program for AIDS education could be shown to have a major impact, and if her results were sufficiently replicated, then this level of impact could become a "standard." In other words, this program could become a model case study. Later attempts to isolate the "effective ingredients" of the program and to eliminate other components that were not effective—in order to make the program more cost-effective—could then be judged against the programs's original standard of effectiveness.

The design of the study began with two considerations. The study had limited resources, and prior knowledge of the subculture of the participants argued that there was a high probability that the Afrocentric AIDS education group would be more effective than either of the control groups in the original study. On the basis of these factors, the student decided to focus all the available resources on (a) enriching the Afrocentric group intervention, so as to increase condom use as much as possible over base rate at the beginning of the study, (b) creating a "no intervention" control group, that is, a group of demographically comparable subjects who received no intervention, but who would be monitored in the same way as the intervention group to assess whether the latter increased their condom use relative to the control group, and (c) following up the impact of the study over an extended period of time.

An important aspect of the program's impact certainly has to be follow-up. One isolated, five-hour educational experience surely doesn't seem sufficient if we are trying to change teenagers' practices regarding sex and condom use.

Magnify this one undergraduate thesis thousands of times, and add to this number tens of thousands of masters' theses, doctoral dissertations, and academic research projects conducted in psychology each year. The studies, and commentaries on them, have accumulated in huge numbers over psychology's last one hundred years. (As of June, 1998, "PsycINFO," the American Psychological Association's electronic database of formal publications in disciplinary psychology, was listing 1,065,577 records of published material since 1887!) These are the resources going primarily into standard, scientific, theory-driven research.

And like the project of our illustrative student research, a substantial number of these studies could be redesigned into pragmatic, problem-driven projects with a much greater chance, I am arguing, of making a difference in the world of everyday reality.

In a reinvented, pragmatic psychology, then, psychologists "get real." They work not in laboratories and college classrooms but in those places in which pressing psychological problems present themselves. They work directly and collaboratively with the individuals who experience these problems. Their focus, then, is not on deriving universal laws but rather on achieving the particular social goals in specific social programs that the public most cares about.

Psychology's Journals: A New Vision

Consistent with its down-to-earth focus, implementation of a case-based, pragmatic paradigm would have dramatic practical impact on the focus and content of psychological research. Instead of today's journals filled with "theory-driven" group studies, the field would have journals filled with systematic, comprehensive case studies. These case studies could then be organized into a computerized database by various categories. Practitioners working with the problems and goals and contexts of a particular case situation could then access those case studies in the database that best matched the target situation and employ those studies for suggestions and guidelines for addressing the target case. Researchers and theorists would conduct comparative analyses across specific types of cases to yield pragmatically focused generalizations about what interventions work to accomplish certain types of goals in specific kinds of case situations.

Thus, a new elementary school principal taking over a city school that is in ethnic, racial, and linguistic conflict could address the database and learn about the La Escuela Fratney or, in English, the Fratney School in Milwaukee: a multicultural, two-way bilingual elementary school that has created a most promising model. Drawing on the diversity of its neighborhood, the school developed a series of six themes, each lasting six weeks, which constituted the first school year: Our Roots in the School and Community, The Native American Experience, The African-American Experience, The Hispanic Experience, The Asian-American/Pacific American Experience, and We Are a Multicultural Nation. Traditional school subjects, such as math, science, social studies, and art, were interwoven into each theme. Moreover, within each of them, teachers taught one entire segment almost entirely in Spanish. An example was "Insect Life on the River," which was that portion of the fourth-grade science curriculum that was linked to the first theme on the local community.[55]

Adopting the pragmatic perspective means, then, that psychology's knowledge base would in some ways look like that of court law. The basic knowledge unit in court law is the completed individual case. These cases are then used to develop guidelines and precedents for new cases. In addition, legal scholars and researchers analyze the collection of cases to derive general judicial guidelines for practical policymaking.

Two Faces of Psychology: "Nature" versus "Culture"

A theme that organizes this book is differentiation between the natural sciences and the humanities, that is, between the sources of modernist and postmodernist psychology, respectively. To understand this concept, it is useful to employ Baumeister's[56] division of reality into two broad categories, corresponding roughly to nature and culture. The natural sciences primarily study the former, and the humanities the latter. The first category involves physical things, such as trees, rocks, tables, water, windows, dogs, and electricity. Modern science tells us that these objects are made up of atoms and molecules and follow certain natural laws.

The second category is meaning and intention.

> Meaning is real [because] people act on the basis of meanings, and these actions produce physical consequences. Buildings, for example, do not come into being by the mere confluence of natural forces. Buildings exist as meanings (such as ideas in the architect's mind) before they exist as physical things. Blueprints, contracts, zoning restrictions, building codes, and other meanings play a vital role in the creation of a building. . . .
> [While] meaning is real, . . . [it] is not the same thing as physical reality. . . . Language is not made up of atoms and molecules. It is possible to describe a book in terms of its physical properties, such as the chemical composition of the paper and the number of small ink squiggles on the pages, but such a description would completely miss the point of what a book is.[57]

The study of white mice running through laboratory mazes, of human beings as "information-processing systems," or of personality as a collection of behavioral traits exemplifies a psychology based in nature, a discipline that attempts to explain all human behavior in observable, physical terms. A psychology grounded in culture brings in such nonmaterial concepts as beliefs, attitudes, intentions, social process, and cultural roles to understand behavior. Thus, nature involves "the causal interactions of objects," while culture encompasses "the rational conduct of agents."[58]

Such a perspective presents human behavior in terms of consciousness and intentionality, focusing on people as agents of their own actions. From this perspective, human life is inescapably enmeshed in a web of meanings, intentions, plans, goals, and purposes. Removing these meanings from our actions irretrievably loses the essence of these phenomena.[59]

Applying a pragmatic perspective to the culture perspective yields such studies as how to develop effective management for a public housing complex, how to increase safe sex, how to reduce conflict in married couples, how to increase the efficiency of drug rehabilitation programs, and how to reduce the violence and popularity of teenage gangs.

In contrast, modernism frequently views humans in mechanistic terms as entities and forces that do not have free will and are not therefore agents of their own actions.[60] This allows explanations of human behavior to be directly parallel to explanations of the behavior of nonhuman systems, both living and nonliving. For example, as gravity attracts planets and DNA directs the physiological development of the growing organism, food rewards guide white mice through mazes, personality traits direct an individual's independence behavior, peer pressure pushes adolescents, positive incentives on an assembly line increase the occurrence of workers' carefulness, tax incentives for companies stimulate investment in new equipment, and negative political advertising, properly timed, increases positive attitudes toward the candidate who sponsors it.

The history of psychology was dominated by modern, "nature-based" explanations from the late nineteenth century until the early 1960s, when postmodern, "culture-based" concepts began to compete for attention. In the 1950s, this meant that the major research in psychology involved the study of animal learning within the psychological theory of "behaviorism," which focuses on predicting and controlling overt actions that involve muscle movements (as opposed to "mentalistic" phenomena like thoughts and feelings). Typical animal learning experiments explored how food rewards affect the learning of mice in running mazes or pressing bars in their cages.

From a layperson's perspective, this work seems so distant from complex, everyday human experience. However, in line with modernistic natural science, this research was predicated on the assumption that underlying all the complexities and variation in animal behavior (and humans were viewed biologically as one type of animal), there are a few fundamental laws relating experience of the environment to behavioral learning and change, similar to the basic laws in physics put forth by Newton and Einstein, or Mendeleyev's periodic table of elements in chemistry.

Laboratory mice are attractive in this model because they can be systematically bred to be genetically identical and raised in an identical way, so differences in inheritance and experience are eliminated as determinants of their behavior. Also, a hallmark of the natural sciences is the study of phenomena that can be objectively, directly, and reliably observed. Animal behavior would seem to fit this criterion well, since what was being observed in the mice experiments was "a matter of stimulus and response, of physical environment, and of muscle movement."[61] Not fitting this criterion are subjective human experience and actions that are imbued with the symbolic meanings of language and culture, such as conscious thought, verbal exchanges, and cultural images.

In the 1950s, the dominant focus in psychology on externally observable behavior and the rejection of concepts reflecting mental phenomena was a critical aspect of the discipline's culture. As two historians of the period point out:

> In mid-century American psychology, it would have cost a career to publish on mind, consciousness, volition, or even imagery.[62]
>
> Behaviorists [those advocating an exclusive focus on externally observable behavior] taught two generations of American methodologists to lower their voices when speaking of "purpose," "experience," "knowledge," "thinking," or "imagination." These words were taboo, along with the rest of the common-sense vocabulary that applies to human beings.[63]

Compare this historical picture to a recent postmodernist perspective on the learning studies with laboratory mice: "In retrospect we find it disturbing that the scholarly world could believe [that] the fundamentals of human nature could be laid bare by the antics of a small number of laboratory animals, . . . [that] the mind of man could be revealed by the behavior of the rat at a choice point."[64]

What a change as we turn to the 1990s. Here we find a significant group—although still a minority—of psychologists who turn to the humanities for their models of understanding human behavior. Instead of studying white mice running through laboratory mazes, or human beings as "information-processing systems," or personality as a collection of behavioral traits, postmodern psychologists study human phenomena such as the "self," "lived experience," "consciousness," and "intention."[65] And instead of using scientific methods of experimentation and quantification, postmodern psychologists frequently use historical and literary methods of analysis. A recent paper by the psychologist Philip Cushman, entitled "Why the Self Is Empty: Toward a Historically Situated Psychology," illustrates this approach:

> This article presents a contextualized treatment of the current configuration of self, some of the pathologies that plague it, and the technologies that attempt to heal it. Of particular interest is the historical shift from the Victorian, sexually restricted self to the post-World War II empty self. The empty self is soothed and made cohesive by becoming "filled up" with food, consumer products, and celebrities.[66]

A Reader's Guide

I begin in part 1 with a history of psychology and its broader cultural context. This exploration first reveals the modernistic forces that created the positivist paradigm in the late nineteenth century and provided support for its dominance (chapter 1). It then goes on to document the rise of postmodernism since the 1960s, which is intimately linked with the diversification of psychology in its epistemologies, theories, and methods (chapter 2). This diversification provides a nurturant intellectual climate in which a case-based, pragmatic alternative to positivism can take root.

Part 2 next focuses on one aspect of this intellectual climate: the philosophical foundations of the pragmatic paradigm. These can be found in the postpositivism movement (chapter 3); in an emerging dialectic between "modern positivism" and "postmodern constructionism" (chapter 4); and in the rediscovery of the pragmatism of James and Dewey by such postmodern philosophers as Bernstein, Rorty, and Toulmin (chapter 5).

In Part 3 I translate the philosophy of pragmatism into the pragmatic case study method. A pragmatic case study examines individual human service programs and employs concepts from the established psychological fields of program evaluation and community psychology (chapter 6). The nitty-gritty details of conducting such a study in a rigorous manner become clear when a typical study in this method is systematically compared with typical studies in the other main established paradigms in psychology today: positivism and hermeneutics (chapter 7).

In Part 4 I illustrate the practical advantages of the pragmatic paradigm for two controversial areas: psychotherapy reform (chapter 8) and educational reform (chapter 9). The book concludes in part 5 with an action plan for fully realizing the exciting potential of pragmatic psychology (chapter 10).[67]

The proposal for a new, pragmatic psychology should be important for a variety of audiences. Since this paradigm directly challenges the majority of mainstream psychologists and is a "call to arms" for minority dissenters from that model, the arguments for it must be convincing to readers in the academic psychology and philosophy of psychology communities. At the same time, the arguments have to be addressed to those outside academia who are the funders and consumers of psychology and who thus have a great stake in how their money can be used most effectively in addressing psychosocial problems. These include individuals like government policymakers, managed health care officials, psychotherapy patients, school board members, parents, and reflective citizens. In addition, the ideas in the book should be of considerable interest to undergraduate and graduate students of applied psychology. I have striven to keep these various audiences in mind when writing this book by trying to avoid jargon and otherwise make the writing understandable and engaging, while at the same time presenting the arguments in a rigorous, scholarly manner with ample endnotes.[68]

To accommodate the nonprofessional reader, I have written the book to be as "freestanding" as possible, without assuming more than a general understanding of applied psychology. In parts 1 and 2—History and Philosophy—I provide a selective and critical summary of others' ideas to demonstrate that the historical and philosophical arguments for the pragmatic paradigm have already been established by respected scholars, although their pieces and links require assembling and integration. Overall, I believe that the original contributions of the book are fourfold: (a) this distinctive selection and weaving together of historical and philosophical themes into an argument for the pragmatic paradigm; (b) writing about the relevant ideas in a way that is particularly accessible to a lay audience, including undergraduate and beginning graduate students; (c) the concrete development of a distinctive and rigorous methodology for conducting and documenting pragmatic case studies and organizing them into practitioner-friendly databases; and d) illustrations of the practical value of the pragmatic case study method in addressing social needs, such as improving cost-effectiveness and accountability in psychotherapy and public education.

To bolster my argument that the epistemology underlying mainstream psychological research is flawed, I draw upon a number of philosophical works. In doing so, my main goal is to summarize the relevant philosophical arguments and positions in a generally nontechnical way, so as to keep the flow of the argument accessible. For authority I cite well-known professional philosophers and classic philosophical statements about the relevant issues. Readers with a developed philosophical interest are encouraged to consult these primary sources for the technical details of the philosophical points being summarized.[69]

Of course the philosophical authorities I cite are not without their critics. Throughout its history and perhaps for its unlimited future, philosophy has been dialectic: any idea and position that has been set forth has been criticized and opposed by an alternative position. While there have been particular times and places when consensus forms (for example, the reign of logical positivism in Britain and America during the late 1920s and early 1930s), this has later evaporated. Moreover, as discussed in chapters 1 and 2, these periods of consensus generally occur in "unifying" historical periods that emphasize stability in the culture; and as these periods naturally swing, pendulum-style, into "diversifying" periods of change and pluralism, the disappearance of consensus is accelerated. Beginning around 1960 and with accelerating force, we have been in a diversifying period. Thus, the lack of consensus upon a single philosophical position at this time is not only not surprising, some would say it is entirely predictable.

However, the crucial point of my thesis of the need to reinvent psychology is that we need to incorporate diversity more systematically in our epistemological and resulting methodological models. I will not claim philosophic consensus upon the need to adopt totally the pragmatic paradigm and the associated case study method for the discipline. Rather, my claim will be that there is sufficient disagreement upon positivist epistemology—the epistemology that justifies the dominant modern, "scientific" paradigm—and there is sufficient agreement upon an alternative pragmatic epistemology to support the here-proposed, case-based paradigm. Thus, I will focus on summarizing the supportive ideas of established philosophic thinkers whose ideas command respect and legitimacy—respect and legitimacy that are reflected frequently in the degree to which they are debated and critiqued. Because the thrust of my argument is toward a plea for diversity, I consider a full attempt to settle these debates and critiques beyond the scope of the present project.

Because of my background as a psychologist, the book will focus on references and examples from this discipline in pursuing my argument. However, because psychology is a social science, it shares much in common with the larger discipline, and thus I make references frequently to this larger context and literature. In fact, there are numerous other books on the history and contemporary nature of the social sciences, with emphases in the nonpsychology disciplines, which make clear that the themes explored in this book cross the various social sciences, even though they frequently manifest themselves somewhat differently within the particular historical and cultural contexts of each discipline.[70] These other books do share a thematic overlap with the present one in terms of documenting the impact of postmodernism on the various social science disciplines and the dilemma now faced in the field between philosophically problematic positivism and seemingly nihilistic, skeptical postmodernism. However, the present book is distinctive in presenting a way out of the positivism versus skeptical postmodernism dilemma by developing an alternative, pragmatic paradigm in psychology, which in many ways retains positive elements from both approaches while discarding their negative ones. Because of commonalities among the social sciences, I believe this distinctive aspect of my book has many important ramifications and applications beyond psychology for the other social sciences.[71]

Coming Down from the Ivory Tower

I argue in this book that the urgent nature of today's psychological and social crises and pathologies demand that we look for alternative, more effective paradigms. The book sets forth one such model based on the philosophy of pragmatism and centered around the method of the systematic case study. The goal of the book is to further the widespread adoption of this pragmatic paradigm so that its conceptual promise can be empirically implemented and evaluated.

Kurt Lewin, the famous social psychologist who developed the concept of action research,[72] is frequently cited for his statement in defense of theory: "There's nothing so practical as a good theory." My proposal to reinvent psychology in the image of pragmatism is an attempt to prove a variant of Lewin's dictum: "There's nothing so practical as a good epistemology." In fact, because within pragmatism only contextually based practical knowledge is possible, within this paradigm a more extreme version of Lewin's dictum emerges: "The only meaningful psychology is applied psychology."

Morris Parloff has playfully captured the need for psychology to be more responsive to today's social crises:

> The basic question, then, is what must we as researchers do in order to respond more usefully to the pragmatic questions which now face the field. . . . We cannot remain in the aloof stance caricatured in the familiar picture of the basic scientist who prefers to seek after truth untrammeled by the noisy yammerings of the secular world. The fact is that in the practice world in which we must find support for our research we can only hope to settle for half-aloof.[73]

I contend that as the pragmatic paradigm begins to show its power, more and more psychological scientists will come down from the ivory tower, will "set up shop" within the very places they wish to influence, will collaborate on equal terms with a target situation's stakeholders, will finally pay attention to the contextual embeddedness of human behavior, and will focus not on "discovering" general "truths" but rather on achieving particular public goals in particular social programs.

PART I

History

To contextualize my argument for the pragmatic paradigm in psychology, I begin with the history of psychology. Chapter 1 brings the reader back to the Enlightenment and its links to the establishment and entrenchment of positivism and the natural science method as the foundation of modern psychology, which "officially" began with the creation of Wilhelm Wundt's laboratory in 1879. I draw upon Irwin Altman's concept of pendulum swings for understanding shifts between different historical periods, with his arguments as to why the era from 1879 to the early 1960s can be viewed as a modern period of unification, and the era since as a postmodern one of diversification.

In chapter 2, I explore this diversification within psychology since the early 1960s and its connections to the growth of postmodernism in the larger culture. The movement toward a variety of coexisting and competing approaches is reflected in the development of such contrasting theories as humanistic psychology, cognitive psychology, and general systems theory, and of such different methods as hermeneutics, qualitative research, and feminist research approaches. This recent, postmodern age of diversity and associated pluralism creates the intellectual and sociopolitical environment for challenging the dominance of positivism and for developing an alternative, case-based, pragmatic psychology.

1

1600 to the Early 1960s

Psychology and Positivism—A Marriage
Made in Enlightenment Heaven

The closest we can ultimately come to "objective reality" is history—the specific events that have actually happened to particular people and their contexts and meanings. Psychological experiments in artificially controlled environments can suggest general principles for predicting human action in concrete situations, but the final "test" of whether an action has occurred is history. Thus, the events of history are a vital empirical database for understanding our human identity, experience, and behavior.[1]

Postmodernists point out that while history might be a crucial database of human action, there is no way to be fully objective in our perception of it. Any view of history, just as any view of behaviors in a laboratory experiment, is one of a variety of possible interpretations of the events themselves. On the other hand, there are accepted criteria for judging the value and usefulness of any particular view of history, such as the quality of the evidence martialed, the clarity of the analysis, the self-reflectiveness of the historian, and the degree of consensus associated with the particular historical interpretation. Reasoned, informed, scholarly, self-aware history, then, is a crucial place to begin if we are to understand the contemporary potential of a discipline like psychology, together with the debates, controversies, and battles that today pervade the field.

A perspective on history that appears particularly relevant for understanding contemporary psychology's creation and development focuses on three time periods: a "pre-discipline" time from the origins of the Enlightenment, around 1600, to 1879, the year of the "big bang" in which Wilhelm Wundt is credited with creating the independent discipline of contemporary psychology by establishing a psychological research institute; the years from 1879 to the early 1960s, in which converging forces spawned a prospering and unified, "modern" discipline; and the years from the early 1960s, in which psychology has become increasingly pluralistic and dialectical, that is, increasingly "postmodern." Such a tripartite division is admittedly arbitrary and simplified—as is any attempt to impose a structure on the complex, multidimensional flux of history. The rationale for this particular structure is that it highlights certain critical themes that have organized psychology's historical development and identity over the last four hundred years.

Origins: 1600–1879

Contemporary psychology, along with the other social sciences, evolved as the application of models and methods from the natural sciences—physics, chemistry, and biology—to social and psychological issues and problems. The origins of contemporary social science can be traced to the origins of contemporary natural science, in the Enlightenment, the period associated with the rise of modernism.[2] The Enlightenment (roughly 1600–1800) was characterized by the glorification of empiricism and reason—the two hallmarks of natural science. There was a strong political motive behind the movement, for it provided a basis for questioning the religious and royal authority that dominated at that time. Enlightenment philosophers credited reason for all the achievements made in science and philosophy, and blamed people of authority, particularly the leaders of the Catholic Church, for promulgating reason's antitheses—ignorance and superstition—to maintain their own personal power.[3]

The search for more accurate theories about the natural world was also stimulated as the expanding commercial economies of the Renaissance generated the need for new technology, such as improved methods of navigation and building construction.[4] Copernicus's "heliocentric" theory, proposed in 1543, introduced the radical idea that the earth revolved around the sun, and not vice versa, upsetting the Church's view that humans were the center of the universe. In the early 1600s, Galileo devised the first telescope and made observations that supported the Copernican theory.

Building on the work of Copernicus and Galileo, Isaac Newton's *Principia*, published in 1687, dramatically demonstrated the comprehensive power of mathematics to explain the natural world. Newton argued that four fundamental, mathematical principles—a universal law of gravitation and three laws of motion—were able to explain the movement of any and all physical bodies in the universe; and as time went on, empirical confirmation of these laws accumulated.[5] Suddenly, scientists saw the universe in a new, elegantly and simply ordered way. It could be viewed as a gigantic machine, in which all matter constitutes the parts of the machine, and Newton's laws are the motor that keeps the parts working in a highly predictable manner.

The ability of Newton's elegant theory to predict and control the physical world was a triumph of reason and the reasonableness of nature. Inspired by Newton, Enlightenment philosophers of the eighteenth century, such as Montesquieu, Hume, and Adam Smith, made the assumption that human nature is as mechanistically well ordered as the physical universe. In *The Spirit of the Laws* (1748), Montesquieu wrote: "The material world has its laws, the intelligences superior to man have their laws, the beasts their laws, and man his laws."[6]

Likewise, David Hume urged application of the new "experimental" method to the human world, to observe the "uniformity among the actions of men, in all nations and ages."[7] Throughout the writings of these philosophers, the difference between modern, technologically evolving societies and their feudal forerunners is emphasized. A "social science" was needed to guide modern society into the future.[8]

One of the earliest forerunners of contemporary political science theory was Thomas Hobbes. In the spirit of the new mechanistic physics, Hobbes believed political institutions could be best understood by analyzing their most basic parts:

> Everything is best understood by its constitutive causes. For as in a watch ... the matter, figure, and motion of the wheels cannot be well known, except it be taken asunder and viewed in parts; to make a more curious search into the rights of states and duties of subjects, it is necessary (I say, not to take them asunder, but yet that) they be so considered as if they were dissolved.[9]

Newton's ideas influenced a group of eighteenth-century philosopher-psychologists who were known as the "British Empiricists," typified by David Hume. As Newton had worked out the fundamentals of the science of material "stuff," Hume saw that his task was to develop a parallel "mental mechanics" of consciousness.[10] The mental atoms were "perceptions of the mind," and the forces operating on and between them were associations. The infant's mind is a "blank slate," and all substantive knowledge which that person later possesses derives from his or her sense experience, as processed by the mind according to certain "laws of association." These laws selectively connect certain sensations and ideas, in a computer-like way, according to such criteria as whether the mental units resemble one another in structure or appearance, are contiguous in time, or are related by cause and effect. The cumulative bombardment of the "mind" by sensations creates mental pictures that correspond to "outside reality." This process was seen as a justification for an experimental science founded on sensory observation.

Hume articulated one of the major tenets of modernist social science: the distinction between fact and value. Social science is viewed as only being able to "discover" or "describe" psychological and social patterns as they occur, independent of whether they are judged "good" or "bad." These value judgments take place outside the "science," and fall into the "personal," "political," or "cultural" realms.

Applying Newton's ideas to economics, Adam Smith assumed that just as there are natural physical laws, there are natural economic laws.[11] In addressing the basic problem of how social order and human progress can be possible in a society where individuals follow their own self-interests, Smith's answer is that within a free market, that is, a market in which government does not interfere, the natural economic laws (such as supply and demand) direct the self-interests of the participating individuals to mesh together in a complementary way, guided "as if by an invisible hand," so that the overall effect is a positive one for the society as a whole. Smith's ideas have been characterized as a type of "social Newtonianism," because they reduce economic institutions to habits of thought and action that can be fully explained by a few, rather simple laws of individual behavior, just as Newton was able to explain all physical motion by his four basic laws of gravity and motion.[12]

In his six-volume *The Course of Positive Philosophy* (1830–1842), Auguste Comte framed his "law of the three states." This law proposes that individuals and societies strive to understand the workings of the physical and social worlds by advancing through three sequential, increasing valid stages of conceptualizations. The first encompasses theological explanations; the second, metaphysical explanations including abstract concepts such as "first causes" and "ultimate purposes"; and the third, "positive" explanations using the empirically based methods of science. The third stage is characterized by a systematic collection and correlation of observed facts and abandonment of unverifiable speculation about such notions as "first causes." In the course of human history, each of the sciences—mathematics, astronomy, physics, chemistry, and biology —progressed through the first two stages and had become, in turn, positive. Now "social physics" had become sufficiently positive to become a basis for scientifically derived social reform and rational government.[13]

In his later four-volume work, *System of Positive Polity* (1851–1854), Comte argued for a three-part social science: a "sociology" to study the historical development of human social thought; a physiology to study the functioning of the brain; and a new, integrative science of "morale," to study the individual in relation to the results of sociology and brain physiology.[14] Thus, Comte was one of the first social science thinkers to see the field as an integrated whole consisting of separate subdisciplines.

In 1879, Wilhelm Wundt, the "father of modern psychology," founded a prototypical "psychological institute" around a psychophysical laboratory, studying phenomena such as reaction time and the nature of color perception and optical illusions. The institute was similar to a contemporary university scientific department in the wide variety of activities in which it engaged —conducting programs of research, publishing monographs and textbooks, editing journals, and attracting an international group of students. The institute was strongly identified with the natural sciences, particularly physics, through its laboratory filled with brass instruments that precisely controlled the administration of stimuli and carefully measured sensory reactions. This identity with physics helped to legitimize scientifically the "softer" activities in which the institute engaged: creating introspective methods for systematically studying an individual's "mental contents" (inner experience); studying the processes of word association, judgment, and emotion; and developing psychological interpretations of the data of history and anthropology.

The success of Wundt's institute was crucially instrumental in creating psychology as an organized, scientific, and autonomous discipline. In recognition of this, in 1979 the American Psychological Association (and other groups of psychologists within and outside the United States) celebrated the centenary of the founding of Wundt's laboratory as the "hundredth anniversary" of the establishment of scientific psychology.[15]

Far from being the realization of the Enlightenment thinkers' hopes, the Industrial Revolution revealed great poverty, entrenched class conflict and economic exploitation, political tyranny and corruption, alienation and loss of community, and violent political revolution.[16] A variety of nineteenth-century intellectuals, including Marx, Darwin, and Freud, directly attacked the Enlightenment image of human nature as dominated by reason, cognition, and free will. Marx's economic determinism refuted the idea that individuals are in control of their personal, social, political, and cultural lives. Rather, systemic economic forces are the underlying determinants of all aspects of human interaction and experience. Even knowledge itself—whether in the humanities or the natural sciences—depends on social and economic forces rather than on independent intellectual inquiry.[17]

Darwin attacked the idea that humans, in their capacity for reason, self-reflection, and civilization, were completely separated from animal species. Instead, his theory of evolution by natural selection emphasized linkages between humans and other species in terms of such noncognitive areas as emotions, impulses, "flight or fight" responses to threat, sexual behavior, and predisposition to form families and hierarchical social structures.[18] A recent development in the application of Darwinian thinking to human behavior is "human sociobiology," also called "evolutionary psychology," which combines evolutionary biology and the social sciences to look for the origins of human social behavior in the social behavior of other animals.[19]

Finally, Sigmund Freud's theory of psychoanalysis challenged the idea that our psychological life is equivalent to our conscious experience.[20] Rather, he argued, there is a powerful realm of unconscious life, full of conflict and primitive asocial and antisocial impulses, that underlies our conscious experience and, frequently unbeknownst to us, has the potential for major control over our thoughts and actions.[21]

Pendulum Swings in History

To understand underlying themes in different historical time periods, the psychologist Irwin Altman has introduced the concept of historical cycles that alternate between periods dominated by "centripetal" or "unifying" forces, which have consolidating and unifying qualities, and "centrifugal" or "diversifying" forces, which have diverging and separating qualities.[22] Each of these forces is viewed as having both positive and negative attributes: thus, unifying forces can provide harmony and stability on the positive side, but continuation of the status quo, stagnation, inflexibility, and resistance to change on the negative. On the other hand, diversifying forces can lead to innovative ideas, creative change, enrichment, and new directions on the positive side, but divisiveness, turbulence, and disunity on the negative.

Altman applies his theory of historical alternation between unifying and diverging periods to the development of psychology. In his analysis, he identifies three time periods: the years preceding 1879, 1879 to roughly 1960, and the years since 1960. Consistent with the postmodern point of view, in Altman's approach to the historical development of psychology the different phases the discipline has gone through are inseparable from their social, political, and cultural context. For example, he argues that the unifying development of psychology during the 1879 to 1960 period reflected unifying forces in American society at large.

Altman does not attempt to explain in theoretical or historical detail why unifying and diversifying periods alternate across time, except to propose that reality is intrinsically dialectic, with both of these forces always present but with one usually dominating. As the dominant force in a society plays itself out over time, its excesses and negative attributes emerge and motivate the society to focus upon the other force, in a "the grass is always greener," pendulum-like manner. This cyclical theory could, of course, be one explanation for the change that gained major momentum around 1960 from a unifying, stable period of Western modernism to a diversifying, fragmenting, and turbulent period of Western postmodernism. Altman's concept would be consistent with Toulmin's[23] thesis that the unifying period of the Enlightenment, which emphasized consensus upon a universal view of scientific, rational, and objective reality, was a pendulum swing away from the premodern period of the Renaissance, with its diversifying values of skepticism, pluralism, and practical truth in context.[24] In any event, from the perspective of this book's theme, it is not necessary to view Altman's ideas as more than a description of alternating sociocultural, historical eras and their manifestations in different areas of life such as politics and such intellectual disciplines as psychology and the other social sciences. The important point in the present argument is that there have been two separate periods since the founding of psychology in 1879: a unifying, modern era, followed, around 1960, by a diverging, postmodern era; and that the present, postmodern era provides the intellectual, philosophical, and sociopolitical context and rationale for the pragmatic reinvention of psychology.

The Enlightenment, the source of modernism, was a unifying time because of the converging social agreement upon the intellectual primacy of natural science, objectively discoverable truth, logic, and technology as unifying elements in Europe's and then America's political and moral worldviews. Consensus upon the "privileged" epistemological status of natural science, in America generally and in the social sciences specifically, continued until around 1960, at which point this consensus started to break down. Accompanying this breakdown has been a strong rise in belief by significant segments of the population in the epistemological paradigms of perspectivism, social constructionism, and relativism which are associated with postmodernism. In other words, at the epistemological level, the converging consensus upon the primacy of natural science that began in the Enlightenment reflects the unifying nature of modernism, and the breakdown of this consensus starting around 1960 reflects the diversifying nature of postmodernism.

Having said this, I shall examine some of the forces, both within psychology and in the larger culture, that led to the postmodernism movement and how they particularly manifested themselves in psychology. In this chapter, I shall describe the history of modernistic psychology; and in the next two, postmodern psychology and related developments in philosophy. Then, in chapter 4, I summarize the contrasting elements of modern and postmodern psychology.

Psychology Comes of Age: 1879 to the Early 1960s

Before 1879, writers of psychology were typically identified with other disciplines, such as philosophy, biology, or medicine. There was little sense of a defined field of psychology with common values, methods, and approaches.[25] Altman labels this period, with its lack of unifying forces, as diversifying.

The founding of Wundt's laboratory ushered in a unifying period. Psychologists began to study human behavior and experience in its own right and by distinctive methods, not just as an extension of other disciplines. In America, this process led to the formation of the American Psychological Association in 1892 and the subsequent establishment of formal psychology departments and programs in universities. Until the early 1920s, the unifying forces led to the formation of a limited number of grand theories—called "systems" or "schools"—of psychology around which individual psychologists, books, journals, and academic departments clustered. For example, "structuralism" emphasized the introspective study of the thoughts and feelings of inner mental life; "instinct theory," the role of evolution-linked, animal instincts in the motivation of human activities; "functionalism," the practical purposes and consequences of those activities; and "behaviorism," the learning of overt, muscle-based behaviors (as opposed to "mentalistic" phenomena like thoughts and feelings).[26]

The unifying forces during this time stimulated further consolidating. By the 1930s behaviorism had risen to dominance and provided the unifying anchor for American psychology through the 1950s, until its loss of dominance around 1960.[27]

Altman points out that during this 1879 to 1960 period, a similar unifying pattern took place concerning research methodology. Psychology closely allied itself with the natural sciences, emphasizing quantitative, experimental, laboratory-oriented research, and it rejected or downplayed earlier methods that were linked with the humanities, such as case studies, field research, introspection, and self-report.[28] In fields where experimentation was not possible, such as the assessment of personality and intelligence, researchers emphasized rigorous quantification and measurement, called "psychometrics." The convergence upon these methodological values became a strong consolidating force in the field and helped psychology to achieve a unified and distinctive identity.[29]

The values derived from behaviorism and natural science methodology—quantification, experimentation, a focus on behavior that can be directly and objectively observed, and the search for general laws (as opposed to context-based knowledge like history)—were supported during the first half of the twentieth century by the predominance in Anglo-American philosophy of the view known as "logical positivism." This view is associated with a group of philosophers who gathered around Moritz Schlick and Rudolf Carnap in the 1920s and who were known, by the place they met, as the "Vienna Circle." Logical positivists argued that all the old philosophical questions, such as the nature of reality ("metaphysics"), truth ("epistemology"), and morality, were answered by the assumptions and methods of modern natural science. Stated simply, the logical positivists proposed that there are only two kinds of knowledge: the truths of logic and the "positive" facts of sense experience (empiricism), which are determined by good experimental science in the tradition of the physical sciences.[30]

Applying this position to traditional metaphysical and moral topics, the logical positivists stated that questions about such issues as the "first causes" of reality and the characteristics of "natural moral law" are not even meaningful questions, because they cannot be answered on the grounds of logic or sense experience. In his classic 1936 statement of the logical positivist position, *Language, Truth, and Logic*, A. J. Ayer summarizes the view as follows:

> To test whether a sentence expresses a genuine empirical hypothesis, . . . I require . . . that some sense-experience should be relevant to the determination of its truth or falsehood. If a putative proposition fails to satisfy this principle, and is not a tautology, then I hold that it is metaphysical, and that, being metaphysical, it is neither true nor false but literally senseless. . . . [Thus] it can not be significantly asserted that there is a non-empirical world of values, or that men have immortal souls, or that there is a transcendent God.[31]

From this view Ayer developed his "yea-boo" theory of ethics. Ethical statements expressing, for example, that one should honor one's parents or that killing is wrong are simply expressing the speaker's emotions about these topics, giving a "yea" to express approval for honoring one's parents, and a "boo" to express disapproval of killing.[32]

In effect, then, the logical positivists were reducing philosophy to the philosophy of science. This position helped to raise natural science to a preeminent position in the intellectual world during the 1879 to the early 1960s period. It bolstered the dominance of the modernist perspective, which is built upon an absolute belief in the special status of scientific knowledge and the capacity of science to bring about social, political, and economic progress. Psychology and the other social sciences found enormous advantages in allying themselves with behaviorism, natural science method, and logical positivism—that is, in presenting themselves as "real" scientists with what Dorothy Ross calls a commitment to "scientism."[33] The enhanced public image and prestige of social science resulted in a crucial payoff: increasing financial support from government, business, and foundations.

During the period from 1879 to the early 1960s, psychology was expanding not only in research and academic theory development, but also in a wide variety of practice areas, such as intelligence testing, vocational assessment, personnel selection, psychotherapy, and consultation with businesses and government organizations. During World War II, for example, psychology was called upon to deal with these types of tasks and with new issues such as military team composition and organization, training of military personnel, human engineering (designing machines to be in tune with the cognitive and behavioral capacities and limitations of human functioning), mass communications and propaganda, leadership selection and training, and vision and perception in night combat.[34] However, the research coming out of academic psychology laboratories, which was dominated by animal learning experiments, was too abstract and disconnected to be of use for the down-to-earth problems the practitioner faced. On the other hand, the activities of the practitioner were not controlled and rigorously scientific enough for researchers to take seriously.

These differences in interest and values between researchers and practitioners propelled periodic splits in the national organization, the American Psychological Association, and subsequent unifying efforts within the Association to change its structure and expand its scope so that all psychologists could be at home under a single umbrella.[35]

Perhaps the capstone unifying action in response to the conflicts between psychological researchers and practitioners during this period was a model of clinical psychology training that was agreed upon at a national conference in Boulder, Colorado, in 1949.[36] This "Boulder model" includes a unifying definition of the clinical psychologist as a "scientist-practitioner," that is, as *both* a scientist and a practitioner, who would continue to receive the generic psychology research degree, the Ph.D. (doctor of philosophy), but who would also be trained for clinical practice.

In her definitive work, *The Origins of American Social Science*, Dorothy Ross describes the embrace of scientism by other social sciences, such as sociology, economics, and political science, in the 1920s. The defining feature of natural science was now its method. The guiding principles involved laboratory control, behavioristic theorizing, replicable and exact measurements, and statistics.[37]

Ross points out that identification with scientism had the important effect of distancing the social sciences from taking (or at least appearing to take) ideological positions on societal issues. Up until that time, these social sciences had been intimately involved with "political" issues such as liberalism, Marxism, socialism, the proper role of democratic institutions, and the best policies for regulating business. The stance of scientism helped social scientists to present themselves as being "apolitical," as simply collecting "facts" and developing "true theories" about the structure and functioning of society and not taking political sides.[38]

The Larger Social and Political Context

Altman reveals how the unifying development of psychology during the 1879 to 1960 period reflected unifying forces in American society at large. He begins his analysis by acknowledging that there were massive disruptive events during this period, including World Wars I and II, the Korean War, the Russian and Chinese communist revolutions, the rise of Nazism and imperial Japan, worldwide depression in the 1930s, the Holocaust, racism and race-related conflicts, and the vast European migration into the United States between 1890 and 1930. However, Altman argues that strong unifying factors prevailed in America over these diversifying factors. For example, during this time,

> the average person had a fundamental faith in the democratic system; in spite of occasional scandal and calls for a new political system, the American presidency and governing structure were accepted and rarely questioned by citizens at large. The epitome of stability was reflected in the unprecedented four-term presidency of Franklin D. Roosevelt through the depression and World War II. Moreover, although the world wars of these decades created stress and enormous difficulties, they also unified American society. To some extent in World War I, and especially in World War II, American society was unified in purpose, and the citizenry readily accepted sacrifices. These wars, particularly World War II, were the "wars to end all wars," to "save democracy," and they were accepted as the responsibility of all Americans.[39]

In addition, Altman points out that the disruption and tensions introduced by the waves of immigrants in the early 1900s were moderated by the idea of America as the "melting pot," which was a powerful unifying force. Also, despite the suffering and economic disruption during the 1930s' depression, the strong role of government in developing new social welfare programs reflected the concern of the government for its citizens. These unifying trends continued after World War II and throughout the 1950s, with the benefits of higher education and material prosperity being extended to more and more of the population.

The unifying nature of these times was reflected by themes of societal conformity in a number of the major popular social science books written during this period. For example, David Riesman's *The Lonely Crowd*[40] talked about pressures to be "other-directed" so one could be ultrasensitive to what was socially acceptable; William Whyte's *The Organization Man*[41] focused on how the individual worker was expected to be highly loyal to his corporation; and C. Wright Mills's *White Collar: The American Middle Classes*[42] argued that middle-class managers had lost their individuality and initiative and had become technocrats, subservient to the wishes of corporate America.

The next two chapters turn to the period since the early 1960s, reviewing the move toward diversity in the general culture and society at large and, reflecting this broad sociopolitical and cultural context, in psychology (chapter 2) and in the philosophy of science (chapter 3), particularly.

2

The 1960s and Beyond
The Postmodern Invasion

Those of us who lived through the 1950s vividly experienced the stark contrast between the seeming stability and sense of unity during those times and the creative turmoil, innovation, and fragmentation of the 1960s and 1970s. Accepted roles, identities, and authority relationships were overturned by forces like the anti-Vietnam War protests, the civil rights movement, the women's movement, the sexual revolution, "hippie" counterculture, and the growth of multiculturalism, the concept of America as a "salad bowl" rather than a "melting pot" of different racial and ethnic groups.

The universities led the way in the turmoil. In 1964, at the University of California's Berkeley campus, there evolved a Free Speech Movement that questioned the bureaucratic, business mentality of the university and advocated, sometimes with civil disobedience,"student power." This movement, fueled by civil rights and anti-Vietnam War protests, inspired and spawned the New Left movement, associated with the Students for a Democratic Society (SDS). The attacks on established ways of thinking turned on traditional disciplines and subjects such as the "great books." The traditional approach to education was accused of being either exploitive and chauvinistic, or irrelevant.

One of the disunifying factors in the larger culture occurring during this time, with particular importance to psychology, was the release of many mentally ill and mentally retarded individuals from institutions back into the community (a process called "deinstitutionalization"). Traditional neighborhoods have been strained. Large numbers of highly visible homeless people are now a fixture in our cities. Also, the popularization of "mind-expanding" drugs in the 1960s has led to a drug problem of enormous proportions, cutting the ties of victims to their families and communities and to general social norms.[1]

Postmodernist psychologists, positively identified with the vast intellectual and social changes that started in the 1960s, have successfully launched an invasionary force on the shores of modernism and positivism. While the modernists have generally withstood the postmodern barrages and still dominate mainstream psychology, the postmodernists have created an established encampment and stronghold. What has emerged for psychology, then, is a discipline in intense dialectical tension, conflict, and diversification. The all-pervasive "culture wars" from the broader society have found fertile ground for creating our own "psychology wars." The present chapter reviews some of the forces and ideas within psychology that, over the last 35–40 years, have increasingly challenged the field's dominant, positivist, behavioral modern paradigm.

Psychologists Proliferate

After World War II, higher education in the United States entered a boom period that reached its height in the 1960s and '70s. These years were energized by such developments as growth in enrollment coming from the baby boom children born after World War II; infusions of money by state and federal government for program development, construction, faculty, and student aid; and a strong commitment in American culture to mass education.[2] During this time, the modern, scientistic image of psychology and the other social sciences made the discipline very attractive to the country at large as a vehicle to address social problems, and this helped the social sciences to function as an active participant in the higher-education boom. This not only led to an increased need for social scientists to staff academic departments in colleges and universities, but these growing departments had increased capacity to train graduate students and in turn started producing a higher rate of new social scientists each year.

With the proliferation of psychologists came a proliferation of geometrically increasing specialties. This resulted in part from the growing numbers of academics and the "publish or perish" career imperative in which psychologists participated along with other academics. Publication became the "coin of the realm" for a psychology faculty member to become promoted, tenured, and respected by his or her colleagues, and two major criteria determined publication. The first was methodological rigor, the degree to which the methods of the research were consistent with the scientistic standards of the physical sciences. Such rigor was generally held to be more important than the substance of the research per se. One critical commentator in psychology described the results of this criterion: "We now have journals that are full of research that is methodologically impeccable and intellectually vapid."[3] The second criterion was innovation, writing about something new, which was held to be more important than replicating and consolidating previous work.[4]

The mix of a large number of psychologists pressing for publication, and publication criteria that emphasized methodological rigor and innovation, fueled a tremendous outpouring of divergent, disparate information. The process was described by one reviewer in 1985 as follows:

> In recent years it has become increasingly characteristic for investigators to stake out a small and relatively isolated terrain to homestead as one's own. With a single assumption about human motivation, several variables, and a half dozen relevant experiments, one can establish an identifiable arena of study. If one does not, at least at the outset, threaten one's neighbor's assumptions, and one's experiments meet the commonly shared standards of rigor, the professional rewards can be considerable. . . . [This leads many areas of research to be] marked by a plethora of small, relatively isolated, and independent principalities.[5]

The growth and diversification of psychology is reflected in the membership statistics of the American Psychological Association (APA). In 1960, the APA had eighteen thousand members, while today it has grown to more than seventy thousand members, a growth rate almost three times greater than that of the general population.[6] Moreover, the APA has grown from nineteen major "divisions" in 1948 to fifty today, covering such diverse specialties as military psychology, population and the environment, women's psychology, psychology and the law, lesbian and gay issues, ethnic minority issues, media psychology, exercise and sports, and peace psychology. This diversifying specialization is reflected even further by a recent edition of the APA Membership Directory in which a taxonomy of over 350 "psychological specialties" was listed for describing the activity of individual Association members.[7]

Psychological Topics Proliferate

Paralleling expansion in the structure of psychology in the period after 1960, the content of psychology was diversifying. From the 1950s' focus

on overt behavior, particularly in laboratory animals, psychological research branched out into views of the person from the humanities, into
the domain of cognition and consciousness, and into views of the person,
family, organization, and community as reflecting different variants of
general systems.

Humanistic Psychology

In the 1960s the "countercultural revolution" against the modernist
culture of the 1950s found a unifying voice in 1971, when Charles Reich,
a law professor at Yale University, wrote *The Greening of America*,[8] a
passionate, scathing, detailed, and articulate manifesto of this "revolution." The book was in essence an early critical postmodernist critique of
1950s American culture. Coming at the right moment, it became a num-
ber-one best-seller and drew enthusiastic reviews. Reich argued that
America at that time was in crisis, with at least seven focal elements:

1. "Disorder, corruption, hypocrisy, war," resulting in "a breakdown
   of the social fabric."
2. "Drastic poverty among affluence" because the nation's economy
   was dominated by special, wealthy, private interests.
3. Uncontrolled physical technology leading to the destruction of the
   natural environment, and the excessive power of bureaucracy,
   "which is the application of technology to social institutions" and
   which causes the logic of the organization to take precedence over
   more human values.
4. The "decline of democracy and liberty; powerlessness." "Democracy has rapidly lost ground as power is increasingly captured by
   the giant managerial institutions and corporations, and decisions
   are made by experts [and] specialists."
5. The artificiality of work and culture," with our working days used
   for "making useless or harmful products, or serving the bureaucratic structures."
6. "Absence of community: . . . modern living has obliterated place,
   locality, and neighborhood, and . . . the family, the most basic social system, has been ruthlessly stripped to its functional essentials.
   . . . Protocol, competition, hostility, and fear have replaced the
   warmth of affection which might sustain man [sic] against a hostile universe."

7. "Loss of self: . . . Beginning with school, if not before, an individual is systematically stripped of his imagination, his creativity, his heritage, his dreams, and his personal uniqueness, in order to style him into a productive unit for a mass, technological society. Instinct, feeling, and spontaneity are repressed by overwhelming forces."[9]

Just as the experience of the 1960s created a ripe climate for Reich's popularization of neo-Marxian critiques of modernist capitalism, these times created a ripe climate for a group of psychologists who declared war upon scientistic psychology. Launching their "movement" at a 1964 conference at Old Saybrook, Connecticut, this group included theorists and spokespeople such as Abraham Maslow, Carl Rogers, Rollo May, and Fritz Perls. These psychologists argued that American psychology's love affair with science had shut the field away from important ideas, methods, and experiences in the humanities. To emphasize their embrace of human experience and the humanities, they called their approach "humanistic psychology." This viewpoint was presented as a "third force" in psychology, as a third alternative to the scientistic, deterministic psychological theories then present, behaviorism and psychoanalysis.[10]

Humanistic psychology brought together three major streams in Western European thought. The first was humanism, which emphasizes the elements of human conscious experience, such as the imposition of "meaning" upon the contents of experience, transcendence above immediate experience, intentionality, the organizing and integrating functions of the self, and the importance of free will and choice.[11] In addition, humanism emphasizes the perfectibility of individual human beings, a notion that is reflected in Maslow's notion of "self- actualization."[12]

The second stream of thought was "phenomenology," an approach developed by the philosophers Edmund Husserl and Martin Heidegger. This view emphasizes the study of "pure experience," whether it refers to the experience of concretely existing objects, of fictions, or of itself. All we can know definitively are the phenomena of experience; the existence of a reality independent of human observers is not presumed. We construct reality, then, out of our own sense experience and that of others. In short, phenomenology turned behaviorism on its head: while behaviorism rejected the study of inner experience and emphasized the importance of external observation of overt behavior, phenomenology rejected the study of overt behaviors and limited its purview to investigating the nature of an individual's inner experience of the world. In humanistic psychology, these ideas led to Carl Rogers's client-centered psychotherapy, with the therapist showing "empathetic understanding" and "unconditional positive regard" in order to help the client in a process of "self-exploration" to find his or her "true, inner self" and become self-actualized.[13]

The third stream of thought in humanistic psychology was existentialism, associated with such thinkers as Søren Kierkegaard, Friedrich Nietzsche, Albert Camus, and Jean-Paul Sartre.

> [Existentialism is] an attitude or a way of perceiving man [sic] and the world. . . . To be consciously aware of happenings, to be anguished by perplexities, to glory in possibilities, to savor sensations and prize experiences, is to operate in an existential mode. More importantly, though, to recognize that the individual cannot borrow value, truth, and meaning from without, but must create them from within . . . is to be truly existential. . . . Life is a burden pressed upon each of us as a result of his inevitable confrontation with the "ultimate concerns" of individual existence—isolation, meaninglessness, responsibility, death; freedom to experience; freedom to choose; . . . and along with it must come an acceptance of responsibility for the form that his existence comes to assume.[14]

M. Brewster Smith describes some of the "resonances" between humanistic psychology and the 1960s counterculture:

> "Individualism," with personal satisfaction and self-fulfilment as primary values; the belief in "human perfectability," with a de-emphasis upon the need for political or ethical institutions; the stress on "self-disclosure" and intimacy, sexual and otherwise; an emphasis on the "here and now"; and "irrationalism," manifested in a downplaying of science and rational problem solving, in a reliance on intuition over other evidence, and in the celebration of "expanded consciousness" and experiential "highs" induced by drugs, music, and other stimulants.[15]

The "Cognitive Revolution"

In parallel with the development of humanistic psychology in the 1960s, a radical change occurred in the theoretical concepts of laboratory-based, experimental psychology. Before this time, from the 1930s through the 1950s, the dominant theory in psychology was "behaviorism," as bolstered by the philosophy of science of logical positivism. The epitome of this paradigm was the work of Clark Hull at Yale. Hull was sometimes seen as the Newton of twentieth-century psychology, and the success of behaviorism as a whole seemed to be identified by many psychologists with the success of Hull's program. Following Newton's model, Hull developed a general mathematical formula to predict whether an animal or human being will engage in a particular behavior.[16] While from today's perspective this formula seems both simplistically grandiose and quaint as a way of explaining all animal and human behavior, within the context of the 1940s and early 1950s it was taken very seriously. From the formula Hull was able to derive seventeen postulates that could be combined into 133 specific theorems and numerous corollaries.

Great initial excitement accompanied the work of Hull and his associates. However, as the theory was tested repeatedly, the testable predictions consistently failed, and each new failure led to new ad hoc stopgaps. At the time Hull's magnus opus appeared, shortly before his death, his students and collaborators knew that the entire project was deeply flawed. The intense excitement surrounding Hullian theory turned to disillusionment, and even despair.[17]

In the late 1950s Sigmund Koch, a former follower of Hull who had become an early critic, edited a massive, comprehensive, scholarly and at that time definitive evaluation of all psychological theory, including Hull's theory and all other learning theories. Published in seven volumes and entitled *Psychology: A Study of a Science*, Koch's conclusions included the following:

> Consider the hundreds of theoretical formulations, rational equations and mathematical models of the learning process that we have accrued; the thousands of research studies. And *now* consider that there is still no wide agreement, even at the crassest descriptive level, on the empirical conditions under which learning takes place.[18]

The failure of Hullian learning theory and the broader disappointment with all learning theory stimulated a general discrediting of behavioristic, scientific psychology and a search in experimental psychology for alternative theories. During the late 1950s the "cognitive revolution" presented itself as the sought-after alternative.

The "cognitive revolution" can be traced to the year 1956, which saw ground-breaking publications in cognitive psychology involving two individuals who were to become major leaders in the field, George Miller and Jerome Bruner, and two major conferences (at MIT and Dartmouth

College) on the emerging connections among cognitive psychology research, "information theory" from engineering, and the "artificial intelligence" of computers.

The thesis of Miller's compelling paper is contained in its title, "The Magical Number Seven, Plus or Minus Two: Some Limits on Our Capacity for Processing Information."[19] Miller assembled considerable evidence to support his conclusion that an individual's ability to make absolute distinctions among stimuli such as numbers or phonemes (different language-related sounds), and to remember a variety of discrete items, all seemed to undergo a crucial change at about the level of seven items. Up to this level, the ability to discriminate was fine, but above this level, it fell off sharply. Miller concluded: "There seems to be some limitation built into us either by learning or by the design of our nervous systems, a limit that keeps our channel capacities in this general range."[20]

In his scholarly and engaging history of the cognitive revolution, *The Mind's New Science*,[21] psychologist Howard Gardner summarizes a number of reasons why Miller's paper was a rallying cry to psychologists with interests in cognition. First, the paper synthesizes a wide variety of research studies that had previously been disconnected. Secondly, Miller's "discovery" of a striking limitation in human information processing capacities redirected research attention toward exploring the nature and structure of such central nervous system limitations *within* the person, and away from behavioristically looking at human action from the *outside*. Finally, Miller's explanation of the "seven plus or minus two" limitation employed "information theory," which had been developed by Claude Shannon, an electrical engineer at MIT, in the late 1930s.

Information theory viewed information apart from any particular transmission device, whether the "on-off" flow of electrons in computers or the firing versus nonfiring of neurons in the brain. This idea made it possible to draw the close connection between human "cognition" (thinking) and computers: both can be conceptualized as "information-processing devices." In the analogy between human and computer functioning, the brain's neurological "wetware" is seen as parallel to a computer's physical "hardware," and the mind as parallel to a computer's logical, "software" operations.

Norbert Wiener, an MIT mathematician, dramatically extended information theory with his new feedback science of "cybernetics." Working during World War II on "servomechanisms"—devices that kept anti-aircraft artillery, guided missiles, and airplanes on course—Wiener focused on the nature of feedback information and how it is a vital part of self-correcting and self-regulating systems, be they human or mechanical.[22] For example, feedback provides the information for a thermostat to regulate a house heater so as to maintain a constant room temperature; and ongoing feedback in computerized learning programs provides information to reinforce correct knowledge acquisition in the student.

Nineteen fifty-six also saw the publication of *A Study of Thinking*, by Jerome Bruner, Jacqueline Goodnow, and George Austin,[23] in which the authors studied concept formation, a well-established area of experimental psychology that looked at the process by which an individual classifies heterogeneous-appearing elements into categories. The researcher would focus on a particular concept, such as the class of all cards with one red figure, or the class of all cards containing red squares. The subject was not told the concept, but simply presented the cards one at a time and asked whether the card fell into the pre-determined concept. After the subject answered, she was told whether her response was right or wrong. The subject's task was to try and figure out what the concept was. Bruner's work was innovative and influential because rather than treating subjects like deaf and mute animals, he simply told the subjects what to do and relied heavily on their comments as an aid in analyzing the results. In contrast to behavioristic principles, the subjects were treated as active, strategic problem solvers, and their introspections were taken seriously. In short, Bruner and his colleagues discarded behavioristic theories and methods for studying concept formation and substituted in their place an information-processing model.[24]

The cognitive revolution's metaphorical comparison of computer and mind endowed upon this movement the scientistic credentials needed to maintain an identity with experimental psychology. Thus, to meet the objections of behaviorism against "mentalistic" concepts requiring introspection to measure, the cognitive scientists could point to the computer as a means for studying human information processing that did not involve introspection and that had the scientistic credentials of electrical engineering behind it. However, once the cat was out of the bag and cognitive psychologists were given "permission" to look inside the human mind, all sorts of spinoffs emerged. As time went on, while one group of researchers continued to adhere to the assumption that the mind should be studied as a very complex computer, other researchers branched out to study traditional "mental" topics, such as consciousness, the self, intention, and meaning. The distinction between these two groups of researchers follows the physical world of nature and the natural sciences, on the one hand, and the symbolic world of culture and the humanities, on the other. As an example of the humanities-based approach, Jerome Bruner argues for the importance of studying "meaning" rather than "information."

> Information is indifferent with respect to meaning. . . Information processing inscribes messages . . . and then manipulates them in prescribed ways: it lists, orders, combines, compares precoded information. The system that does all these things [for example, a computer] is blind with respect to whether what is stored is words from Shakespeare's sonnets or [random] numbers. . . . Information processing needs advance planning and precise rules. It precludes such ill-formed questions as "How is the world organized in the mind of a Muslim fundamentalist?" or "How does the concept of Self differ in Homeric Greece and in the postindustrial world?" and it favors questions like "What is the optimum strategy for providing control information to an operator to ensure that a vehicle will be kept in a predetermined orbit?"[25]

The wide-ranging nature of the cognitive revolution, including its bridging of natural science-oriented and humanities-oriented investigators, predictably led to its evolution into an interdisciplinary field, frequently labeled "cognitive science." Some of the major disciplines involved include psychology (both from its experimental and humanistic traditions), artificial intelligence (from the computer analogy to cognition), neuroscience (in the study of the brain's "wetware"), anthropology (in the study of meaning and culture), linguistics (also in the study of meaning), and philosophy (in terms of fundamental analyses of such questions as the mind-body problem or the nature of knowledge).[26]

General Systems Theory

In 1942, the philosopher Stephen Pepper published *World Hypotheses: A Study in Evidence*,[27] which proposed that scientific and philosophical theories or "hypotheses" about the world—either the physical world or the psychological and social ("psychosocial") world—fall into four basic categories, each associated with a particular "root metaphor," that is, an analogy with something we know from everyday experience. Pepper's framework made clear that modernism is built upon only two of the categories ("mechanism" and "formism"), leaving two additional categories ("organicism" and "contextualism") for the development of theoretical alternatives to modernism. These alternatives form psychology's home in postmodernism; and many of the dialectical differences between modern and postmodern psychologists can be traced to different choices they make in their Pepperian world hypotheses.

"Formism," with its root metaphor of similarities and differences in the intrinsic qualities of entities, views behavior as emerging from traits within the individual.[28] Thus, individuals act as they do primarily because of their inherent natures, without much attention given to the temporal aspects of behavior or to the contexts within which the behaviors are embedded. When an individual's behavior is explained in terms of his or her "attention deficit disorder" or "intelligence," a formistic model is being employed.

"Mechanism," with its root metaphor of the machine, treats the person and the environment as separate, underlying entities that interact in a linear, causal, predictable manner, as do the parts of a spring-driven watch or a water pump, or the sequential actions of billiard balls initiated by a billiard shot. Using mechanism, one analyzes psychosocial phenomena in terms of the antecedent environmental conditions that lead to certain behaviors, which then lead to various consequent conditions, which in turn become antecedent conditions for certain subsequent events. For example, in the classroom, seeing other children pay attention (antecedent) can be perceived by a particular child as encouragement to pay attention also (behavior), which can then lead to the teacher's approval (consequent), which in turn, as a reward, can increase the chance of the child's paying attention the next day. Within mechanism, the goal of theory development is to enhance the ability to predict and control behavior.

"Organicism," with its root metaphor of the living organism, conceives of both person and environment as a system with complex, reciprocal, and dynamic relationships and influences among the individual parts. For example, in the individual human being, the different organs (or "subsystems"), such as the brain, heart, and lungs, work together in a give and take manner to maintain each other and to sustain the overall organism. The lungs provide oxygen needed to create energy for the heart and brain and the lungs themselves; the heart circulates the oxygen to itself and to the lungs and brain; and the brain monitors the availability of oxygen in the environment and ensures that the person does not work so hard as to exhaust all the oxygen that is internally available. Change usually occurs in accord with underlying regulatory mechanisms that both maintain a system's short-term status quo ("homeostasis") and direct long-range, directional change. Examples at different systems levels are an individual person's development from birth to adulthood, a good group therapist's ability to keep the members of the group constructively engaged with one another and with group tasks; and the process of a nation's economic development from a Third World to a First World country. A system is seen as having an ideal end point toward which it optimally develops.

Finally comes "contextualism," with its root metaphor of the historical event, such as D-Day in World War II, or the purposive act, such as an individual runner winning the Boston Marathon. This view is basically limited to the psychosocial area. In contextualism,

> The world is seen as an unlimited complex of change and novelty, order and disorder. Out of this total flux we select certain contexts; these contexts serve as organizing gestalts or patterns that give meaning and scope to the vast array of details that, without the organizing pattern, would be meaningless or invisible.[29]

Because the world outside our minds is "an unlimited complex of change and novelty, order and disorder," it is not possible to attain a "true," "objective" picture of this world. Rather, the "truth" of a concept is a function of its practical usefulness in particular contexts.[30] The contextualist worldview forms the basis of the "pragmatic paradigm," the central subject of this book.

Pepper's notion of philosophically contrasting assumptions in the theories of the physical, biological, and social sciences was stimulated by dramatic changes in physics associated with the Newtonian (interactional) versus the Einsteinian (contextual) perspectives; and Pepper's ideas were an early forerunner to the postmodern critique of the mechanistically dominated, scientific ideas of the Enlightenment and positivism. Writing just after Pepper, John Dewey and Arthur Bentley[31] proposed a similar distinction among "self-action," "interaction," and "transaction," which correspond to Pepper's world hypotheses of formism, mechanism, and contextualism, respectively. Recently, psychologists Irwin Altman and Barbara Rogoff have built upon and elaborated these distinctions, focusing specifically upon the foundational assumptions, or what they call the "world views" in psychological theory.[32] Altman and Rogoff's parallel terms for Pepper's four-world hypotheses are the "trait," "interactional," "organismic," and "transactional" world views, respectively.

As discussed in chapter 1, from the 1920s until around 1960, there was a general consensus within psychology that Newton's model of science was the view to follow. And his model was a quintessentially mechanistic one, with his image of the universe as a gigantic clock. The developments described above in the late 1950s and early '60s—critical theory, humanistic psychology, and the humanities-oriented branch of the cognitive revolution—all rejected this wholly mechanistic model and introduced contextualist elements into social science theories.

At this same time in the 1950s, a movement was developing in the social sciences to challenge the mechanistic world hypothesis in another way by promoting the worldview of organicism. Called "general living systems theory," or simply, "general systems theory," the origins of this movement trace back to the ideas of the biochemist and sociologist L. J. Henderson and the philosopher Alfred North Whitehead in the 1920s.[33] Other influences were Einstein's relativistic "field" theory, which emphasized two-way causal relationships among elements, as opposed to one-way, linear relationships; "gestalt" psychology, which highlighted how humans tend to perceive organized wholes, not individual parts that are merely added together; Norbert Wiener's newly created science, described above, of "cybernetics"; and the writings of Ludwig von Bertalanffy, a philosophically oriented biologist, particularly his 1950 essay in *Science*, "The Theory of Open Systems in Physics and Biology."

Two of Bertalanffy's basic tenets were (a) to formulate general principles and laws of systems independent of their special type, whether they be biological, psychological, or social; and (b) to build upon the similarities across different types of systems to create a unified science. A major figure in carrying out these ideas was the psychologist James G. Miller, who convened an interdisciplinary group at the University of Chicago, called the Committee on Behavioral Sciences, which began regular meetings in 1952. Included were "senior professors in history, anthropology, economics, political science, sociology, social psychology, psychology, psychiatry, medicine, neurophysiology, and mathematical biology."[34] Between 1953 and 1955 Miller wrote articles that outlined a specific way to carry out Bertalanffy's tenets.[35] Over the years he worked on expanding this outline, and in 1978 he published a brilliant, grand compendium of his work, covering over one thousand pages.[36]

Miller differentiates seven types of living systems: the cell, the organ, the individual, the group, the organization, the society, and the supranational system. He demonstrates how each can be conceptualized in terms of the same structures, functions, and terms.[37] The major part of Miller's book consists in organizing scientific information in the fields associated with these different system levels—biology, individual psychology, social psychology, organizational science, sociology, and political science—and framing this information in terms of common systems terms, like "boundary" and "memory." Miller shows how the interactions of matter, energy, and information among the systems at one level can be conceptualized as creating the next higher level, a process he calls "shred out."

Many of the ideas from general systems theory were later transported into the area of psychotherapy with families, resulting in a field known as "family systems therapy." In this way of thinking, an individual with emotional problems is reflecting a family system that is in some way dysfunctional, and the family as a whole is treated to address this dysfunction. Sometimes this is accomplished by changing roles and communication patterns within the family as a whole to stimulate more healthy functioning by individual members.[38] In Miller's terms, this approach believes it is most effective to treat emotional disorder at the level of the group (the family), rather than the level of the individual person.

Psychological Methods Proliferate

The Separation of "Human Science" from "Natural Science"

As discussed in the Introduction, reality can be usefully divided into two broad categories, corresponding roughly to the world of physical objects (such as trees, rocks, water, dogs, and tables), and the world of cultural meanings (such as a person's intention or the English language). This differentiation can be historically traced back to late nineteenth-century Germany and the heated debate over the character of the "natural sciences" (*Naturwissenschaften*), as opposed to the "human sciences" (*Geisteswissenschaften*). Philosophers such as Dilthey and Rickert argued that the study of human action was centrally concerned not with the prediction and control, that is, the "explanation" of the physical aspects of behavior per se, but rather with "understanding" the meaning of the behavior as experienced and interpreted by other human beings.[39]

For example, if a person walking in the street is struck from behind, her reaction will depend less on the physical properties of the blow itself and more on the action's meaning to its originator. If the individual who administered the blow now seems to be laughing at the walker's plight, the walker might conclude that the act was designed to harm her in some way and she might plan to retaliate. However, if the blow appeared to be unintentional and the seeming assailant is now apologetic, the stroller might conclude that the blow was an accident and that no harm was intended.[40]

In natural science, the object of study—such as human behavior—is viewed "from the outside" as something outside of and separate from ourselves. In contrast, in human science human behavior is viewed "from the inside," so that we understand it by sympathetically responding to the behavior in terms of our own conscious inner life, with its mixture of thoughts, feelings, sensations, images, and intuitions.[41]

In the rush toward scientism and behaviorism during the 1900 to 1960 period, the notion of "human science" as distinct from "natural science" disappeared from mainstream psychology and the other social sciences, which took the fields of physics and chemistry as their model. However, the distinction was rediscovered in Peter Winch's influential 1958 book, *The Idea of a Social Science and Its Relationship to Philosophy*.[42] Winch maintained that while the objects that natural science studies have an existence independent of the concepts used to understand them, this is not true of human action. He illustrates the distinction by comparing an act of obedience with a clap of thunder:

> In the case of . . . [the thunder], although human beings can think of the occurrences in question only in terms of the concepts they do in fact have of them, yet the events themselves have an existence independent of those concepts. There existed electrical storms and thunder long before there were human beings to form concepts of them or to establish that there was any connection between them. But it does not make sense to suppose that human beings might have been issuing commands and obeying them before they came to form the concept of command and obedience.[43]

Winch's ideas found a fertile ground because of the other challenges in the 1960s to the natural science model of the social sciences, discussed above. A particularly influential and dramatic extension of Winch's ideas was presented by Kenneth Gergen in his 1973 paper, "Social Psychology as History."[44] His theme was that unlike the general laws discovered in physics, psychological theories are always limited to particular times and cultures, and thus these theories are "primarily reflections of contemporary history" that change as historical conditions change.

Gergen's argument is twofold. First, unlike with nonhuman objects of scientific study, humans' behavior can be altered by providing feedback to them. Human behavior is self-reflexive. Not only are we acting in response to our environment, but we are also aware that we are acting, and this awareness can itself affect how we behave. Thus, if the public becomes aware of the "universal laws of human behavior" that psychologists "discover," then the public's awareness of these laws can alter their behavior and thereby invalidate the purported general laws. In this vein, Gergen notes that our value of individual freedom provides a strong incentive to invalidate psychological "laws" of behavior, so as not to fall victim to manipulation by others.

Gergen's second argument against transhistorical laws in psychology is based on findings that observed regularities in relationships among psychological and social variables change over time, that is, they are historically dependent. Studies of political activism in the 1960s and early '70s found that variables that successfully predicted political behavior during the early stages of the Vietnam War were different from those that successfully predicted activism during later periods.

As another example, Gergen cites the theory of "cognitive dissonance," which states that individuals will rationally act to reduce inconsistencies between their beliefs and their behaviors. For example, if we stand in line for three hours to buy tickets to a play, the theory says that we will be likely to justify this effort by judging the production favorably.[45] However, there are many historical counterexamples to this tendency. Early existentialist writers celebrated the inconsistent act, and paradox and irony have been a staple of revered literature and drama during certain historical eras.

Gergen concludes by pointing out that the self-awareness of human beings and the dominating importance of cultural meanings in human behavior preclude psychology from adopting the model of the natural sciences. While the velocity of falling bodies or the compounding of chemical elements are highly stable and quantitatively measurable events across time and situations leading to the derivation of general, mathematical laws, psychology is primarily a historical inquiry, dealing with facts that are largely unrepeatable and fluctuate markedly across time.[46]

Hermeneutics

Gergen's arguments, published in 1973 in a prestigious, mainstream psychological research journal, *The Journal of Personality and Social*

Psychology, signaled a growing movement to view the domain of psychology as narrative interpretation, similar to qualitative history, literature, and journalism, rather than as a laboratory-based search for universal, quantitative laws. This "turn to interpretation" created new links between a significant number of psychologists and the intellectual movement called "hermeneutics."

"Hermeneutics" is the science or art of interpretation. The term refers to Hermes, Greek messenger of the gods and god of eloquence. Initially, hermeneutics was developed for the examination of biblical texts in order to uncover and decipher the message of God that was hidden within them. Later, hermeneutics became generalized as a method of textual interpretation that was not restricted to religious works.[47] In the eighteenth and nineteenth centuries, with the stimulation of writings by Schleiermacher and Dilthey, it was generalized still further to apply also to human action.[48] In contrast to the natural science model, "when we adopt a hermeneutic approach to human action, we essentially treat the action as though it has a semantic and 'textual' structure."[49]

Over the last twenty-five years, hermeneutics has evolved into a broad array of approaches, which are represented in both the social sciences and the humanities, particularly in philosophy and literary criticism. The different forms of hermeneutics are united in their opposition to the natural science approach to understanding and explaining human behavior. In effect, the social sciences are "caught" in the middle of the scholarly disciplines, being tugged in one direction to be like the natural sciences (viewing human action as "nature," to be explained in terms of the "behavior of organisms"), and being tugged in the other direction by the humanities (viewing human action as "culture," to be understood in terms of literary narrative and qualitative history). A recent book exploring the application of hermeneutics to psychology articulated three types of hermeneutics: "methodological," "ontological," and "critical."[50]

Methodological hermeneutics focuses on applying hermeneutic principles to the interpretation of human behavior. Unlike objectivist social science, this view

> does not strive for decontextualized facts, but emphasizes meanings as experienced by individuals whose activities are rooted in given sociohistorical settings. The hermeneutic approach insists upon the inseparability of fact and value, detail and context, and observation and theory. Methodological hermeneutics utilizes qualitative description, analogical under-

standing, and narrative modes of exposition. It deemphasizes quantification and controlled experimentation, and does not seek a neutral, objective vocabulary with which to characterize social phenomena.[51]

An important concept in methodological hermeneutics is the problem of the double hermeneutic in psychology.[52] For in this discipline we have an observer trying to understand and interpret the experience and behavior of another person, who is in turn trying to understand and interpret his or her own world. Added to this situation is the notion that the humans are self-reflexive: a person involved in a study is reactive to the fact of being involved in the study. Following the idea of the double hermeneutic, we can additionally say that the psychological study is doubly self-reflexive, for both the observer and the study subject are influenced by the knowledge of being part of the study and by the behaviors of the other. Thus, four interactive factors have to be addressed in the psychological study: the interpretive process of the observer, the interpretive process of the research subject, and how the study process interacts upon both the observer and the research subject. This complexity raises major questions about the limits of psychological knowledge generally, and the validity of mainstream studies in empirical psychology specifically, since they typically do not acknowledge or address these interactive processes.

Because to understand something new inevitably involves reference to something that is already known, the process of understanding operates in a circular, dialectical fashion. This is referred to within methodological hermeneutics as the "hermeneutic circle."[53] An example of this phenomenon: while the meaning of a sentence derives from the individual words it contains, our interpretations of word meanings are also dependent on the relationships among the words and the meaning of the sentence as a whole. Thus, when we attempt to interpret a strange culture, practice, theory, language, and so on, our interpretation occurs within a circle in which the parts are always interpreted within some understanding of the whole, which in turn is understood by coming to understand the constituent parts.[54]

Ontological hermeneutics focuses on the role of interpretation in the nature of human existence itself. It is based on the work of thinkers like Heidegger and Gadamer, who posit that our fundamental mode of "being-in-the-world" is that of creatures who understand and interpret. Heidegger argued that the fundamental mode of human existence is engaged, practical activity, as exemplified in the carpenter hammering a nail.

For Heidegger, the paradigmatic object in the human world is something like a carpenter's hammer—that is, not a mere physical thing or a sensation or an idea contemplated from a position of scientific or philosophical detachment (as the empirical [natural scientists] would have it), but a tool that is used. . . . Thus, a hammer is not a "hammer" by virtue of some objective characteristics that it has "in itself," apart from its place in the human world. . . . The hammer's "hammerness" is experienced as out there in the world, inseparable from the substance it imbues, and the external world is "always already" imbued with human purpose and meaning.[55]

Finally, *critical hermeneutics* was developed by Habermas as an outgrowth of work on neo-Marxist "critical theory." In the Marxist tradition, critical hermeneutics employs interpretive techniques to criticize the moral and ideological underpinnings of contemporary social practice and institutions, in order to foster emancipation from arbitrary, unjust forms of cultural and political domination. For example, critical hermeneutics looks at the political functions and implications served by the natural and social sciences, and it concludes that these functions frequently are in the service of maintaining and rationalizing existent institutions of political oppression.

Social Constructionism

The themes of the two related movements described above—the separation of "human science" from "natural science" and hermeneutics—were crafted by a group of social scientists into a position that has come to be called "social constructionism."[56] Social constructionist inquiry is principally concerned with explaining the processes by which people come to describe and account for the world, including themselves. Social constructionism assumes that objective observation is not possible. To have an understanding of what they sense, people must bring preconceptions to the observation process. Thus, instead of being "discovered," the social reality of any group or "language community" is constructed through the communal interchange of the group's members.

Social constructionism began as a marginal view in the early 1970s and steadily grew in authority and prestige. By the mid-1980s, it was appearing in mainstream and high-profile psychological journals. For example, here are three representative quotes expressing social constructionism that appeared in the mid-1980s in the *American Psychologist*, among the most prestigious journals in psychology:

It is neither physically nor philosophically possible to obtain knowledge without first choosing some assumptive framework. This framework is un-determined by observations; rather it constitutes the [interpretive or] hermeneutic context for generating "facts" and giving meaning to obser-vations.[57]

How can theoretical categories be induced or derived from observation . . . if the process of identifying observational attributes itself relies on one's possessing categories? How can theoretical categories map or reflect the world if each definition used to link category and observation itself re-quires a definition?[58]

All the world's a stage, but the script is not *As You Like It*, it is *Rashomon*. Each of us has our own reality of which we try to persuade others. Facts do not have an independent existence. Rather, facts guide the selection of observations and the invention of reality. . . .

[In short], we do not discover scientific facts; we invent them. Their use-fulness to us depends both on shared perceptions of the "facts" (consen-sual validation) and on whether they work for various purposes, some practical and some theoretical.[59]

Once we accept that the categories for describing and understanding human behavior action are constructed, we are subject to "radical doubt" about the "taken-for-granted world."[60] This has led social con-structionists to challenge our basic psychological and social categories, such as the gender dichotomy of man and woman, emotional attributes like anger and fear, and the notions of altruism, domestic violence, and suicide. For example, is suicide "unnatural" and "wrong," as was cul-turally unquestioned until just recently, or can suicide be a rational re-sponse to an existence of unending pain and severe disability? One way of challenging the "naturalness" of our social concepts is to compare the present with earlier historical periods. Social constructionists' his-torical investigations have revealed substantial variation over time in the concept of the child, of romantic love, of mother's love, and of self. In certain periods, childhood was not considered a specialized phase of development, romantic and maternal love were not components of human nature, and the self was not viewed as isolated and au-tonomous.[61]

A recent illustration of social constructionist thinking in the media ap-peared in the *New York Times Magazine* in an article entitled "Date Rape's Other Victim: In Their Claims of a Date-Rape Epidemic on Cam-pus, Feminists Subvert Their Own Cause."[62] The author focuses on a typ-ical questionnaire item used to define rape: "Have you had sexual intercourse when you didn't want to because a man gave you alcohol or drugs?" The constructionist analysis proceeds:

> The phrasing [of the question] raises the issue of agency. Why aren't college women responsible for their own intake of alcohol or drugs? A man may give her drugs, but she herself decides to take them. If we assume that women are not all helpless and naive, then they should be held responsible for their choice to drink or take drugs. If a woman's "judgement is impaired" and she has sex, it isn't necessarily always the man's fault; it isn't necessarily always rape.[63]

Further analysis reveals that the traditional concept of rape is embedded in a cultural concept of women as passive and nonsexual property, as chaste objects, as "virtuous vessels to be 'dishonored,' 'ruined,' 'defiled.'"[64] Their value to the men to whom they belong has been measured by their degree of purity. The author concludes that paradoxically, the feminist goal of empowering women to view themselves and to be viewed by men as active, forceful, responsible, sexual, and independent persons who are not "property" is being undermined by many of the ideas embedded in the present feminist construction of the date-rape crisis.

Qualitative Research

Positivist social scientists identify their discipline with the physical world of nature and the natural sciences, where the essential units of analysis are numbers. Hermeneutically oriented social scientists identify their discipline with understanding of an individual's lived experience and the symbolic world of culture and the humanities, where the essential units of analysis are qualitative data—speech, the written word, music, and images. Quantitative psychologists study social class or psychological dependency by rating them on numerical scales. Qualitative psychologists replace these ratings with a narrative description of the various concrete details concerning an individual's class status or dependency, using methods such as "open-ended, creative interviewing; . . . life history; life-story; [and] personal experience and self-story construction."[65]

One of the attractions of qualitative research is its accessibility to the nonsocial scientist. Words provide context, chronological flow, and local causality as they create narrative stories. "The findings from qualitative studies have a quality of 'undeniability.' . . . Words, especially when they are organized into incidents or stories, have a concrete, vivid, meaning-ful flavor that often proves far more convincing to a reader—another re-searcher, a policy-maker, a practitioner—than pages of numbers."[66]

Early advocates for qualitative research methods were the sociologists Barney Glaser and Anselm Strauss, who introduced them in conjunction with their concept of "grounded theory."[67] In contrast to positivist social science, which develops theory first and then deductively derives quanti-tative hypotheses from the theory to test on observed phenomena,[68] grounded theory is inductively derived from first descriptively studying the phenomena. Thus, in grounded theory, data collection, analysis, and theory stand in reciprocal relationship with one another.[69] Since theory is stated in verbal, qualitative terms, it is necessary for a grounded theory to be derived from data that are themselves qualitative in form.

An important concept in qualitative research is that of "thick" versus "thin" description, which is associated with the description of "nature" versus "culture," respectively.[70] Thick description captures the meanings, intentions, and experiences that have occurred in a complex human situ-ation in a rich, dense, highly contextualized manner; while thin descrip-tion summarizes "objective facts" in a general, abstract, summary man-ner.[71] Anthropologist Clifford Geertz is known for having popularized this concept in the social sciences. He illustrates by analyzing a blink of the eye among boys. The blink can indicate an "involuntary twitch" from a neurological disorder, "a conspiratorial signal to a friend," a par-ody of the second person's wink as "amatuerish" and "obvious," or the practicing of the parodying wink.

> [Thus is the difference between] the "thin description" of what the re-hearser (parodist, winker, twitcher . . .) is doing ("rapidly contracting his right eyelids") and the "thick description" of what he is doing ("practicing a burlesque of a friend faking a wink to deceive an innocent into thinking a conspiracy is in motion").[72]

Narrative versus Propositional Modes of Thought

A number of the above described movements—humanistic psychol-ogy, hermeneutics, social constructionism, and qualitative research—have attacked the possibility of objective, verifiable, "scientific" truth in human behavior. Adherents of these views have turned away from the usual mode of thinking in the natural sciences—called by Bruner[73] *propo-sitional* thought. Instead, they have turned to *narrative* storytelling—a staple of history, literature, and journalism, for example—as a more appropriate medium for understanding social phenomena.[74]

The literary critic Kenneth Burke points out that fully formed stories include five elements: an Actor, an Action, a Goal, a Scene, and an Instrument—plus Trouble, which consists of an imbalance between any two or more of the five elements.[75] Thus stories describe intentioned heroes and villains in their conflicts and struggles over time—both against themselves, others, and external barriers—to reach goals. The success of heroes creates comedies, and failure, tragedies. The narrative mode stresses the particulars of personal experience as they take place over time, emphasizing personal agency and language that can be uncertain, subjective, and symbolically suggestive. The author of a story frequently has an emotional relationship to the actors and actions within it.[76]

Propositional thinking, on the other hand, consists of abstract principles and logically constructed theories, and formal, clear, rigorous methods for measuring them and testing them against experience. Familiar examples are statements such as Newton's laws of motion and the theorems of geometry. The propositional mode stresses general laws and concepts that are universal over time, focusing on mechanistic forces that determine human behavior, and using language that is as clear, explicit, and "value-free" as possible. The author-researcher in propositional thinking is emotionally independent of the "subjects" being investigated.[77]

Bruner[78] contends that the cognitive revolution has been hijacked by a model that views the person as a mechanistic "information processor," thus assuming that propositional thought is "natural." He argues instead that humans exist within the shaping hand of culture, which operates through processes of narrative meaning-making. He discusses the central importance of "folk psychology"—how the lay public thinks about behavior in narrative terms—in understanding social behavior.

With its emphasis upon statements that are abstract, formal, quantitative, precise, "value-free," and mechanistic, propositional thinking seems clearly linked with thinking that views the world as nature. Just as clearly, the characteristics of narrative thinking associate it with viewing the world as culture. These characteristics include the identification with the particulars of personal experience in historical context; the focus on personal agency and language which can be uncertain, subjective, and symbolically suggestive; and the appeal to imagination, empathy, caring, and commitment.

Feminist Research Methods

The feminist movement of the 1960s and '70s attacked the role and traditional image of women in modernist culture, as exemplified by the 1950s. In the eyes of the movement, this image involved notions of women as subservient to men, as needing to be protected by men, as overly dominated by feeling rather than reason, and as suited to be housewives and mothers in the home and not as employees and professionals in the workplace.

Feminist theorists embrace postmodern and social constructionist positions in offering a critique of modernist representations of women, viewing the modernist image as a cultural creation to be deconstructed and reformed so as to provide women a more equal role and status in society. Since historically psychology has been monopolized by men, feminist psychologists argue that traditional scientific psychology is dominated by traditional male values, with its great emotional separation between the "detached" researcher and the "object" being studied; and its experimental laboratory involving control and manipulation of the object of study.[79]

Some feminist psychologists have emphasized the importance of gender differences.[80] For example, in her well-known studies of moral decision making, Carol Gilligan[81] found that while men tend to arrive at conclusions based on individual reflection and abstract principles, women typically reach solutions through relating to others—considering the feelings of their friends, families, and relevant others. Women see themselves as existing in a web of relationships held together by bonds of caring. Also, women tend to identify more with "communion" (orientation to others, seeing the self as part of a social whole), while men tend to identify more with "agency" (individual orientation, focus on the self and self-expansion).[82]

Some women in the social sciences have adapted these ideas to create distinctively "feminist" research methods. Applying the value they place on social relationships, they work in cooperative, egalitarian teams rather than in hierarchical groups with an individual senior researcher at the top. Also, they don't strive for emotional detachment from and "above" their research subjects; rather they "collaborate" with their subjects and are open to personal elements in relationships with their subjects. Applying the value they place upon intuition and feeling in addition to reason, these feminist researchers are open about their personal values and feelings as they relate to the research process. In addition, they use the context of real relationships in their studies. They work naturalistically, "in the field," rather than in the artificiality of the laboratory; and in their work they use the language of real relationships, qualitative description, and interpretation of life stories and personal experiences.[83]

Other women in the social sciences are critical of an emphasis on gender differences and "feminist" research methods.[84] They accuse advocates of such ideas as guilty of modernistic "essentialism." Certainly there are instances of male social scientists who reject emotional separation between research subject and researcher, instead emphasizing collaboration in the research relationship.[85] In any event, whether distinctively "feminist" or just distinctively "postmodern," there are ardent advocates for a radical alternative to the traditional, modern experimenter-subject relationship in social science research.

Postmodernism

To summarize and expand upon earlier discussions, "postmodernism" can be characterized as a broad cultural movement that blossomed in the 1960s and still pervades contemporary intellectual life.[86] Postmodernism represents a direct reaction against modernism, so a good place to begin in understanding postmodernism is with modernism.

The term "modernism" has been applied to the thinking of the Enlightenment and its technological, political, and cultural consequences in creating highly industrialized, urbanized, contemporary cultures in "first world," "Western" societies.[87] The Enlightenment was characterized by valuing empirical observation and reason as the most authoritative source for achieving fundamental truth about the natural and social worlds.[88]

Four interrelated values distinguish modernism.[89]

1. *Technicism*, a focus on developing formalized, systematic, and objectified techniques for achieving the predictable control of events.
2. *Rationality*, which emphasizes the use of the intellect and excludes "all that is purely traditional, charismatic, or ritualistic."[90] Rationality is associated with the values of "balance, restraint, order,

reason, and sobriety," and thus it rejects the values of "extremism, intensity of experience, spontaneity, emotionality, and passion."[91]

3. *Amorality*, "the modern separation of fact and value and the removal of 'the good' from the objective order of things."[92] This separation is related to the cultural rise of secularism, science, and technology, which are explicitly designed to be "value-free."

4. *Classical humanism*, which opposes all irrational authority and arbitrary privilege and dedicates itself to the active enhancement of human liberty.[93]

The history of postmodernism is traced by some to radical ideas that came out of the political left in the 1960s, both in this country and in France—ideas that directly attacked the values and assumptions of modernism.[94] This attack was led in part by postmodern thinkers identifying with those groups who were socially marginal and oppressed in modern society, and who in the 1970s and 1980s formed new civil rights or "identity politics" movements—groups such as women, gays and lesbians, blacks and other peoples of color, the mentally ill, the physically disabled, and prisoners.[95]

A persuasive argument has been made[96] that the development of postmodernism has been, paradoxically, hastened and powered by the modernistic forces of science and technology. These forces have led to the development of new travel and communication technologies (jet planes, affordable and available individual automobiles, telephones, television, the Internet, and so forth), so that today the typical individual is exposed—via real and media travel—to a vast variety of new, exotic, and contrasting places, cultures, lifestyles, values, and political and social conflicts. This exposure attacks the assumption of a single, "true" picture of the world and of a single, "correct" way of living. Rather, we are all put in the position of anthropologists, whose exposure to cultural differences has led to a culturally relativistic view of the world that emphasizes temporal, geographic, and social context as determinants of meaning and truth.

Several types of postmodernism were reviewed in the Introduction. The two most controversial and provocative are "critical" and "skeptical" postmodernism. "Critical" postmodernism is identified with the goals of classical humanism, as is modernism, but argues that modernism has subverted these goals through its fostering of the development of industrialized societies characterized by corporate capitalism.[97]

"Skeptical" postmodernism emerged from a group of 1960s Paris philosophers. Pessimistic about the possibility of ever reaching the goals of classical humanism,[98] they asserted that individuals are not free to make their own decisions, and that the world isn't what it appears to be. Instead, we and the world are permeated by giant, hidden, impersonal structures.[99]

Skeptical postmodernism questions all-encompassing world views, like Christianity, traditional Marxism, fascism, capitalism, liberal democracy, feminism, and modern science. A major method used in this questioning is "deconstruction," a process of analysis whose goal is to reveal the arbitrariness, contradiction, or injustice of the constructions and assumptions of any particular conventionally held concept or view.[100]

Because skeptical and critical postmodernism provocatively and scathingly attack the political and philosophical foundations of modern society, they are highly controversial. This controversy has flourished in academia, where many of the 1960s campus political radicals have become tenured faculty in the humanities and social sciences and have continued to pursue the philosophical and political themes of postmodernism. Following in the footsteps of the 1960s critical and skeptical postmodernists, these scholars use the methods of deconstructive criticism to attack the assumptions and values of the present political and cultural establishment, which are viewed as reflecting "the oppression, inequality, and exploitation that exists, not only in the United States, but globally."[101] Identifying with "identity politics," these "tenured radicals"[102] advocate a heightened sensitivity to the rights and needs of disadvantaged groups within universities. Because of their postmodern sensitivity to language, they pay particular attention to the words used to talk about these groups, such as "differently abled" instead of "physically disabled."

The postmodernist deconstruction of the superiority of any particular culture has led academic radicals and liberals to develop and advocate the idea of appreciating and respecting multiple cultures and backgrounds, frequently referred to as the value of "ethnic and racial diversity" and "multiculturalism," and labeled by those opposed to this point of view as "political correctness," or simply, "P.C." This has led, for example, to the introduction of feminist, black, and Asian writers in introductory civilization courses, the idea being that the traditional "great books" in these courses only represented the ideas of white European men.

There has been an intense, highly public conservative backlash against the ideas and actions of the "tenured radicals," who are viewed as destroying the very foundations of our free society.[103] This has generated intense, polarizing, ideological debates between the liberal advocates of postmodernism and the conservative defenders of modernism. We will revisit the resulting attack, counterattack, and polarization—termed the "culture wars"—in some detail in chapter 9, when we review their embodiment in policy and program issues in the arena of educational reform.

In Berman's *Debating P.C.: The Controversy over Political Correctness on College Campuses*,[104] the dust cover captures the emotionality of the conflict between postmodernists and modernists:

> White male Eurocentrism . . . or an essential cultural heritage? The supporters of what has become known as "P(olitical) C(orrectness)" call the traditional courses at America's top universities racist, sexist, and homophobic. They seek diversity and multiculturalism. Their opponents fear a tyranny of "P.C." do-gooders. They treasure the old-fashioned courses on Western culture as bastions of civilization. Open-minded . . . or "politically correct"? Educational reformers want to fight prejudice and discrimination by insisting on *freshperson* v. *freshman*, *Native American* v. *Indian*, *differently abled* v. *disabled*. Opponents see a "P.C." threat to free speech . . . [and] the profound value of the literary canon.

Here one can see clearly the interaction of politics and epistemology. The modernist believes in the knowability of an objective physical reality that yields truths about the physical and social worlds. Gergen[105] points out that modernists in the humanities have extended this belief to include the knowability of objective esthetic and moral values and truths.[106] This draws modernists to a conservative political position, believing in the discovery of universal truths from the Enlightenment to the early 1960s, and desiring to retain the institutions and policies built upon these truths. Modernists decry changes in these values and institutions.

In contrast, postmodernists believe that all views of the physical, social, esthetic, and moral world are constructed based on historical and cultural context, with no objective, universal standards. Thus, diversity and multiculturalism are valued, and the elevation of past standards and practices as universal is attacked and deconstructed: both because assertion of their universality is false, and more specifically because these standards are used to perpetuate the political subjugation of historically disempowered groups.

PART II

Philosophy

It is now time to delve more deeply into the philosophies of knowledge associated with postmodernism. Chapter 3 examines the one that most directly challenges positivism, the writings of such authors as Kuhn, Quine, and Wittgenstein that go under the rubric of "postpositivism."

To better understand the location of the pragmatic paradigm in "epistemological space," in chapter 4 I draw together the diverse historical and philosophical trends reviewed in previous chapters, viewing them as various strands of two competing visions. One is modernism, with its scientific, positivist epistemology that assumes the possibility of discovering objective truth. The other is postmodernism, with its social-constructionistic epistemology that rejects this possibility. I label these visions "modern positivism" and "postmodern constructionism," respectively. The pragmatic paradigm's home is within the latter. I conclude the chapter by systematically comparing the conceptual foundations of three psychology paradigms: positivism, pragmatism, and hermeneutics, the other distinct paradigm emerging from postmodernism that offers its own alternative to positivism.

Chapter 5 next homes in on the philosophy of pragmatism, the most direct epistemological foundation for pragmatic psychology. It reviews how the postpositivist attacks on positivism were joined by complementary critiques from Continental philosophy to justify epistemological alternatives. One of these alternatives is pragmatism, first developed by the philosopher-psychologists William James and John Dewey at the turn of the century and updated in a postmodern context by such philosophers as Richard Bernstein, Richard Rorty, and Stephen Toulmin. I explore in some detail the ideas of these thinkers and demonstrate how their arguments can be employed to provide epistemological justification for the systematic case study method that is at the heart of the "pragmatic psychology" which I am advocating.

3

"Postpositivism"

Revolution within the Family

Psychology's diversification since the 1960s has been supported by intellectual challenges to logical positivism by philosophers who were originally identified with it. These "postpositivistic" attacks from within on the philosophical foundation of modernistic psychology have shaken up the pre-1960s complacency and self-confidence of the field and have stimulated a search for a revised foundation in mainstream academic psychology.[1] Postpositivist challenges to traditional positivism inform my argument for a radical, pragmatic reinvention of psychology.

Targeted Hits

Karl Popper's "Falsifiability"

Perhaps the first successful criticism of the classic logical positivist position was articulated by the philosopher Karl Popper in his 1935 book, *The Logic of Scientific Discovery*.[2] Popper attacked the positivist view of science, arguing that it isn't possible to verify conclusively scientific propositions, because no matter how many observed instances there are of experiments that are consistent with the proposition, it is always possible for an additional instance to be inconsistent. Theories engender confidence to the extent that they are repeatedly tested without yielding either falsification or arbitrary modification to sidestep disconfirming data.

The problem Popper identified arises from the nature of induction. If statement A, "All swans are white," is true, then it logically follows that statement B, "All observed swans have been white," will be true. However, it does *not* follow that if B is true, then A must be true—that is, "If all observed swans have been white, then all swans are white"—because it is never possible to observe all possible swans, now, everywhere, and in the future; and there is always the possibility of observing a nonwhite swan somewhere in the future. This is the logical fallacy of "affirming the consequent." If the hypothesis "If A, then B" is posited and B turns out to be true, it does not logically follow that A is true.

Popper's analysis challenged the long-held view that science was inductive, characterized by the use of observation and experiment and not by logical argument per se in reaching its results.

> The great difficulty was that no run of favourable data, however long and unbroken, is logically sufficient to establish the truth of an unrestricted generalization. This led immediately to the disquieting conclusion that science (or at least the important part of it that deals in such generalizations) simply had to live by faith in some kind of uniformity of nature, hard to define satisfactorily, and seemingly impossible to prove without circularity.[3]

In short, Popper's arguments lead to the conclusion that science's assumptions about the world have to be taken on faith, suggesting that the foundation of science is not that different from religion.

In his analysis, Popper goes on to point out that while universal generalizations cannot be verified, they can be falsified. For example, while no amount of observations of white swans verifies the statement, "All swans are white," observation of one black swan falsifies it. Of course, as a scientific theory is shown to be consistent with more and more empirical observations together with the absence of inconsistent observations, the empirical justification for characterizing the theory as true increases. However, the theory always remains falsifiable, and thus can never be viewed as resting on indubitable foundations.

Thomas Kuhn's Scientific Paradigms

While Popper's work gently raised doubts about the rational certainty of science, in 1962 the dominance of logical positivism was shaken at its very roots by Thomas Kuhn's radical book, *The Structure of Scientific Revolutions*.[4] Both a philosopher and historian of science, Kuhn studied historical growth and change in the natural sciences. From this historical analysis, Kuhn contended that scientific progress often did not take place in a continuous, linear, logical sequence. Progress had often been sudden, with abrupt changes that swept away the foundation of existing theory. He gave as examples the "scientific revolutions" of Copernican astronomy, Darwinian evolution, Freudian psychoanalysis, Watsonian behaviorism, and Einsteinian physics. Kuhn chose the term "revolution" explicitly to emphasize the connection between a radical scientific shift in an assumptive framework and a political revolution, in which the "old order" is drastically overturned.

To understand these "revolutions," Kuhn introduced the concept of a scientific "paradigm." By this he means the underlying, fundamental assumptions or premises a scientific field makes in order to develop new knowledge. Most of these premises have never been "scientifically proven"; in fact, they are not in a form to be scientifically proven even in principle. One example is the assumption in Darwinian evolutionary biology that there is a single overarching organization connecting all types of animals and that this organization has a natural explanation. An example from psychology is the assumption in behaviorism that a person's activities can be properly explained without recourse to her inner thoughts and feelings. In line with Popper's analysis, in neither of these instances is it logically possible to collect enough empirical data to "prove" these assumptions right or wrong. Rather, these are the types of assumptions that must be taken for granted if more detailed scientific hypotheses are to be deductively generated and empirically tested.

Kuhn points out that when representatives of two paradigms enter into debate about paradigm choice, "their role is necessarily circular. Each group uses its own paradigm to argue in that paradigm's defense. . . . [And yet] the status of the circular argument is only that of persuasion. It cannot be made logically or even probabilistically compelling for those who refuse to step in to the circle."[5]

Kuhn views a paradigm as having at least three different facets. On one hand, it refers to the basic worldview of a scientific discipline, which Kuhn describes in such terms as "a new way of seeing," "an organizing principle governing perception itself," and a cognitive "map" of reality. In addition, a discipline's paradigm refers to its concrete, basic tools, such as its instruments, procedures, and methods for collecting data; its mathematical and other methods for analyzing data; and the codification of its basic knowledge, in textbooks and other exemplary writings. Finally, Kuhn states that a paradigm cannot be separated from the people who use it. So while the concept has an abstract sense, it also has a sociopolitical sense that reflects a discipline's need for communication, organization, perpetuation through teaching students, and recognition and support by the public at large. Kuhn described this facet of paradigm as involving a group of "universally recognized scientific achievements" and "a set of political institutions."

Kuhn conceives the sudden changes that constitute scientific revolution as taking place within a cyclical process in which knowledge develops in terms of four sequential stages. The first stage is called the "prenormal" or "preparadigmatic" stage, which exists when individuals or small groups of researchers pursue knowledge of the same phenomenon in an independent manner, without communicating among themselves; and this leads to each using different terms, measures, and theories.

The second stage, called "normal science" or "paradigmatic science," takes place when a group of researchers decide to work cooperatively with one another, using a single underlying framework or "paradigm" with common terms, methods, theories, and criteria for deciding what are the "relevant problems" to be studied. This mutuality of interests and practices defines a discipline. Kuhn called scientific activity in this stage "puzzlesolving"—the solving of delimited problems within the parameters of the established paradigm.

The normal stage gives way to a third, "crisis" stage, when new observational methods and research designs yield "anomalous" data, that is, data that cannot be explained by the paradigm of the second stage. During this third stage, the discipline searches for a new paradigm that will better encompass existing data. When the crisis of the third stage is resolved by the adoption of a new paradigm, the fourth, "revolution" stage has begun. Thus, the movement to the fourth stage involves a "paradigm shift" from the second stage. This shift leads to a new stage of normal science, and the cycle begins again.

A striking example of a paradigm revolution took place in physics in the early 1960s. Paradoxically, this was happening at a time when classical physics appeared to be closing in on consensus for a Grand Unified Theory or "theory of everything" that appeared to explain the behavior of all matter and all types of energy—from the tiniest particles of an atom to the origin of the universe in a "big bang."[6] However, classical physics had problems in explaining the physical behavior of certain types of everyday phenomena, like water eddies in a stream, the course of rising smoke, the changing patterns of clouds, fluctuations of wildlife populations, or the oscillations of the heart or the brain. Another example with tremendous economic implications is classical physics' inability to make long-range weather predictions. Traditionally, these phenomena were considered so "unstable" as to be basically without form or structure, so discontinuous and erratic as to be essentially in "chaos."

In an attempt to understand better the problems of weather forecasting, the MIT meteorologist Edward Lorenz created a mathematical, computer model of the weather in the early 1960s. By chance he discovered that tiny errors in measuring the initial conditions of a particular weather system can lead to enormous divergence between the actual and predicted weather over time. As he explored this phenomenon, he discovered that there were predictable patterns that conformed to mathematical equations—albeit patterns that did not conform to classical physics—in the apparent disorder of long-range weather data, and his work helped to create a whole new paradigm in physics called "chaos" theory. Generally, Lorenz's finding meant that tiny differences in input could soon lead to vast differences in output—a phenomenon that was named "sensitive dependence on initial conditions." In weather this is illustrated in what has only half tongue-in-cheek been termed the "butterfly effect"— the idea that a butterfly stirring the air today in Beijing can transform storm systems next month in New York.[7]

James Gleick illustrates the concept of "sensitive dependence on initial conditions" through the applications of Lorenz's equations to the behavior of a water wheel. The wheel contains buckets with holes at the bottom. Water pours in at a steady rate from the top, above the wheel. If the flow of the water in the wheel is slow, the water drips out of the buckets at the same rate it comes in, and the top bucket never fills up enough to overcome friction, with the result that the wheel never starts turning. If the flow is faster and the bucket fills up before the water drips out, the weight of the top bucket sets the wheel in motion, and it can settle into a rotation that continues at a steady rate.

However, if the flow of the water is faster still, the spin can become chaotic, because of nonlinear effects built into the system. As buckets pass under the flowing water, how much they fill depends on the speed of spin. If the wheel is spinning rapidly, the buckets have little time to fill up. Also, if the wheel is spinning rapidly, buckets can start up the other side before they have time to empty. As a result, heavy buckets on the side moving upward can cause the spin to slow down and then reverse.[8]

In fact, as Lorenz discovered, over long periods the spin can reverse itself many times, never settling down to a steady rate and never repeating itself in any predictable pattern.[9]

Gleick describes the political and sociological aspects of the "revolution" as physicists made a "paradigm shift" to chaos theory. While eventually chaos theory became an accepted part of physics, at first there was political resistance to this "upstart" way of thinking:

> Every scientist who turned to chaos early had a story to tell of discouragement or open hostility. . . .
>
> Those who recognized chaos in the early days agonized over how to shape their thoughts and findings into publishable forms. . . . To some the difficulty of communicating the new ideas and the ferocious resistance from traditional quarters showed how revolutionary the new science was.
>
> Stylistically, early chaos papers . . . went back to first principles. As Kuhn notes, established sciences take for granted a body of knowledge that serves as a communal starting point for investigation. . . . By contrast, articles on chaos from the late 1970s onward sounded evangelical. . . . they declared new credos, and they often ended with pleas for action.[10]

In short, Kuhn saw the dramatic changes that occur in scientific theories over time as more like political revolutions than the uncovering of new mathematical proofs or the disinterested discovery of newly observed phenomena. Rhetoric, persuasion, ideology, and values become important factors in accounting for changes in scientific theory. Since these ideas directly challenge the highly appealing view of science as being objective, value free, and purely rational—as being "above politics"—the first reactions to Kuhn's book were strongly negative: Kuhn's ideas were characterized as "absurd, contradictory, and wrong," and even as "immoral and irrational."[11] However, Kuhn's ideas were reflecting a major change in the philosophy of science that had begun with Popper and would grow strikingly over the next sixty years: postpositivism. So an attack on Kuhn himself could not stem the momentum created by his powerful ideas.

Expanding the Critique

Willard Quine's "Webs of Belief"

Positivists claim that there are only two kinds of knowledge: the truths of logic (such as the proofs of geometry), which they call "analytic" statements and which are true by virtue of the meanings of the words involved; and empirical facts, which they call "synthetic" statements and which are true by virtue of matching some confirming sense experience of the world. Any other kinds of statements—about religion, ethics, esthetics, and so forth—are considered expressions of emotions and thus not true knowledge.

Beginning in 1951, Willard Quine argued cogently that both of these claims are false.[12] He asserted that there is no clear distinction between analytic and synthetic statements. Moreover, the reason underlying this lack of distinction makes it impossible to speak of synthetic statements "matching" a particular part of the world in a determinate way.

Quine argued that the statements we are prepared to assert should be viewed as forming a smoothly interconnected whole, as a seamless "web of belief." Particular observational claims ("there goes a streak of light") lie on the outside of the web; general explanatory principles ("All matter is composed of subatomic particles") are entrenched in the center.

In scientific experiments, we logically derive an observable prediction from a target hypothesis in a theory and assume auxiliary hypotheses. Suppose the prediction turns out to be false. We could reject the rule of inference by which the prediction was derived, the way in which relevant variables were operationalized in the testing process, our perception that the result was correct, the auxiliary hypotheses, the target hypothesis, or some combination of these. In other words, a scientific experiment involves a web or network of assumptions and observations, and any anomaly in this network can be due to a problem in any part of it. Thus, drawing conclusions from the experiment becomes a matter of interpreting patterns among the various elements of the network—much like traditional historical or literary scholarship—rather than like performing a logical, mathematical proof, as implied in traditional, positivist accounts of science.

If data in an empirical study do not match the explanatory principles, something in this web has to be revised.[13] But what? Quine contended that there was nothing in the web that was immune from revision per se. Pragmatically, it makes sense to try to revise as far from the center of the web as possible, since that way less of the more abstract and general parts of the scientific theory in the web will be disturbed. On the other hand, revolutions in science typically involve revisions of this sort: terms like "energy," "mass," and even "space" have been redefined and understood to mean different things. What seemed at first to be unquestionable definitions from the domain of logic that were "analytically" true ("This is just what the concept 'space' means") turned out to be subject to revision after all. *No* statement is necessarily true—unless we decide to treat it that way.

The other end of the web, the observational end, is also subject to revision. Theory is embedded in the language we use, and so this theory seeps into our accounts of what we observe. Quine argued that the same stimuli could with equal coherence be captured by logically incompatible conceptions—where you with your theory speak of seeing "rabbit," I with mine might see "undetached rabbit parts," "rabbit time slices," or "rabbit stages." It seems clear that this is not an empirical dispute, but a conceptual dispute about the language we use to frame our observations. Quine has formalized this idea in his famous thesis of the "indeterminacy of radical translation": the view that a sentence (or word in a sentence like "rabbit") can always properly be regarded as meaning a multitude of different things, with no empirical way of determining what its single, "real" meaning is.[14]

In sum, Quine contended that scientific language is not a mirror of the world. Rather, it is a way of expressing a particular perspective, which reflects certain interests that scientists bring to the world. Thus, when empirical data don't appear to be consistent with theoretical expectations, which part of the "web of belief" is altered is not determined by the outside world, but rather by pragmatic considerations concerning which parts of the web seem most useful to alter. "What is true" becomes "What is true relative to some theory."

Even though Quine identifies rational justification with present scientific standards, he attaches no transcendent significance to them. The standards are valuable insofar as they allow us to anticipate what will happen next, that is, to help us in "predicting . . . episodes of sensory bombardment on the strength of . . . past episodes."[15] Should some system unlike science as we know it (say, astrology) prove a better predictor, we would replace science and likewise our idea of rational justification to incorporate the more successful standards:

> Experience might still take a turn [such that] . . . our success in predicting observations might fall off sharply, and concomitantly with this we might begin to be somewhat successful in basing predictions upon dreams or reveries. At that point we might reasonably doubt our theory of nature in even fairly broad outline.[16]
>
> The utility of science, from a practice point of view, lies in fulfilled expectation: true prediction.[17]

Paul Feyerabend's "Anarchism" in Scientific Method

Paul Feyerabend dramatically expanded upon Quine's epistemological openness to alternatives to traditional science. Like Quine, Feyerabend's starting point was science's ability to help us in the goal of coping with the world. He argued in a variety of iconoclastic, rhetorical ways that this goal is most successfully reached using a pluralistic methodology. In any field, he claims, knowledge has been best obtained "from a proliferation of views rather than from the determined application of a preferred ideology.[18] The freedom of artistic creation can be "not just as a road of escape but as a necessary means for discovering and perhaps even changing the features of the world we live in."[19]

While not claiming that proliferation guarantees progress, Feyerabend does argue that proliferation has worked in the past and that reason or science *cannot exclude* such a possibility. He suggests that experimentation in modes of reasoning should be tolerated just as experimentation in modes of living, so as to have different types of outcomes from which to choose what seems to work best for particular purposes:

> My *thesis is that anarchism helps to achieve progress in any one of the senses one cares to choose.* Even a law-and-order science will succeed only if anarchistic moves are occasionally allowed to take place.[20]
>
> For nobody can say in abstract terms, without paying attention to idiosyncrasies of person and circumstances, what precisely it was that led to progress in the past, and nobody can say what moves will succeed in the future.[21]

In the end, Feyerabend's goal is not to destroy, but rather to deprivilege the rules of traditional science and to encourage alternative modes of knowledge inquiry.

Quine and Feyerabend argue that, at any moment, we view the world through a particular pair of glasses, that is, with some specific perspective involving a particular "web of belief." It is never possible to take off the glasses altogether and view the world as it "really is." All we can do is change glasses and realize that different pairs provide different views or perspectives of the world. Quine contends that the specific pair of glasses we should use in an individual situation depends not on which pair appears to correspond best to the "real" external world, but rather on which is best pragmatically, that is, which pair is most useful in meeting our particular, practical goals in that situation. It follows that if two different groups have different interests in a certain situation, each might be justifiably led to choose different glasses with which to view the situation. Feyerabend goes further and sees a positive value—based both upon our past experiential track record and the creative aspects of human nature—in using a variety of different glasses per se. The variety of paradigms in approaching the world will be more likely, he proposes, to help us in finding the particular pair of glasses that best meets our needs in a specific situation.[22]

Ludwig Wittgenstein's "Language Games"

As a young man Wittgenstein had written his *Tractatus*,[23] one of the classic works providing a philosophical rationale for positivism. In *Tractatus* Wittgenstein conceives of an objective world composed of "things" that are organized into primitive, knowable "atomic" facts. Corresponding to this world is a language of atomic statements. Each of these atomic statements is a kind of picture of a fact. The basic conditions of being a picture in this sense are a one-to-one correspondence of elements between picture and thing pictured, within a common structure or "logical form." The atomic statements might be compared to dabs of color in a naturalistic painting of a landscape, with the dabs corresponding to the elements distinguished in the landscape, arranged in a way that reflects the pattern of those elements.

In his later years (from the 1930s to his death in 1951), Wittgenstein passionately rejected his earlier position and developed the "linguistic analysis" approach summarized in his famous, posthumous *Philosophical Investigations*.[24] In fact, the latter book is explicitly designed as an attack upon the atomic-facts and language-as-naming model of language that he had set forth in the *Tractatus*. Wittgenstein adopted a view of language as a structure in which we are completely embedded, similar to the way in which we are completely embedded in a Quinian web of belief. What is meant by a concept, Wittgenstein contended, is a function of its use in the context of the interests and purposes of those who invoke the concept. Consider how a child learns the meaning of the statement, "That was a joke!" To learn this is to understand the context—the "form of life"—in which the statement has a point, since the meaning of words in jokes is different from their meaning in more straightforward, serious uses (for example, in satire, words frequently mean the opposite of dictionary definition). In addition, the child must be able to have the type of interests that saying "That was a joke!" expresses.[25]

For the later Wittgenstein, the analogy is not language as a "picture," but rather language as a "tool" and "game." Language is compared to a bag of carpenter's tools—a hammer, pliers, saw, screwdriver, and so forth—each with its own particular function and technique of use. Wittgenstein views the functions of words as diverse as the function of these carpenter's tools.[26] Language is also compared to a range of games, each with its own equipment, rules, and criteria of success and failure. Thus to understand and assess any use of language, we need to know what game is being played, and what its rules and objectives are. A linguistic move can only be judged permissible or impermissible within the context of a particular game. Just as confusion results when a player in a game makes up new rules as he goes along, or misapplies the rules, so it causes confusion and perplexity when a user of language creates new rules, violates old ones, or misconceives language. It is misleading and confusing, then, to think of language as consisting of words that stand for objects. There are many other functions of language: giving orders, making up stories, translating, codifying the rules of language itself, interpreting descriptive reports, and so forth.

Thus, unlike the framework of the *Tractatus*, in the framework of *Philosophical Investigations* there are no universal criteria of understanding and truth. However, there is clearly an interrelatedness among different language games, for we experience them as being of the same cloth. Wittgenstein characterizes this interrelatedness as a "family resemblance." Any member of a family resembles some other member. But there is usually no single pervading feature that defines them as all members of the same family. Rather, there are borderline cases of similarity, and cases in which a characteristic of one family member imperceptibly merges with a characteristic of another. Thus, in comparing games or family members, the result is a complicated network of similarities that overlap and crisscross; sometimes there are overall similarities, and sometimes similarities of detail.[27]

Since language games are related by family resemblances, there is no way to identify the essence of language. Rather, one must examine how language is used in a variety of ways, what its purpose is. Thus, a word's "meaning" can be defined by its use in the language.[28]

Viewing language as a game means that language is intrinsically public. For example, to understand the meaning of John's statement that he feels "pain" does not involve speculating about John's hidden, private experience. Rather, such understanding involves acquiring the technique for using the word "pain." To say that "pain is private" involves the mistake of confusing the grammatical use of the word "sensation" with the nonlinguistic state of my experience. Thus, while it makes sense to say that *other people* doubt whether I am in pain, it does *not* make sense for me to say that *I doubt* I am in pain.[29]

An analogous mistake occurs when it is assumed that to mean something is to think it:

> "When I teach someone the formation of the series . . . I surely mean him to write ... at the hundredth place." —Quite right: you mean it. And evidently without necessarily even thinking of it. This shows you how different the grammar of the verb "to mean" is from that of "to think." And nothing is more wrong-headed than calling meaning a mental activity![30]

Likewise, intending, understanding, feeling, and seeing (in the visual or understanding sense) are techniques, "forms of life," "modes of action" about which we can be clear if we are not confused by misleading parallelisms of grammar.[31]

The family character that belongs to the concept of language is also true of other concepts, such as "name," "meaning," "number", "proof," and "consciousness," in whose nature or essence philosophy has been traditionally interested. The moral taught by the study of language games is that the philosopher's quest for essences is based on a misunderstanding of language. Wittgenstein saw one of the philosopher's roles as a "therapeutic" one. In this role, the philosopher does not offer new solutions to traditional problems, such as "mind-body relations" or "other minds," as traditionally posed. Rather, the role is patiently to assemble reminders of how a term like "mind" actually functions in the language game that is its original home. The goal, then, is to reveal the misunderstandings that give rise to the philosophical problem in the first place.

Anticipating the development of social constructionism, Wittgenstein thus contends that there is no knowable reality outside of language. When learning a language, we assume the conventions that make up social understandings. These conventions are humanity's and philosophy's bedrock; when they have been dissected and displayed, philosophy has reached its endpoint and there is nothing left to say. What is meant by reality, rationality, or rightness is, in the final analysis, simply adhering to a certain set of language rules. Since the nature of rationality is thus found in our deepest habits, we cannot ask if our deepest habits are themselves really rational.

Wittgenstein's work attacked one of the foundational justifications for the dominance of behaviorism from the 1930s through the late 1950s. Behaviorism's preeminence was based in part on the positivist argument that to be like the natural sciences, psychology should only deal with publicly observable behaviors, and that mentalistic terms like "pain," "belief," and "intention" named private, nonpublicly observable states. Wittgenstein's analysis of such mentalistic terms as tools in *public* language games rather than as names or descriptions of private mental states undermined this argument.

It is true that the meaning of many mentalistic terms does entail particular patterns of behavior; for example, John's writhing and yelling are frequently cues to support the legitimacy of the statement, "John is in pain." And in fact B. F. Skinner, the quintessential behaviorist, wrote a carefully reasoned book, *Verbal Behavior,*[32] providing a pure behavioral explanation of the learning and maintenance of language. However, unlike Skinner's other work involving the experimental analysis of the behavior of nonverbal animals, *Verbal Behavior* only involves conceptual analysis and no scientific data per se. Moreover, Wittgenstein's analysis argued directly against the position that Skinner takes in his book: that language functions as names and cues for stimuli in the nonlinguistic world. Wittgenstein's view is that words only have meaning within the context of a language game. The relationships between a language game and the nonlinguistic world—both for "private terms" like "intention" and "feeling," and for "public terms" such as "dancing," "wincing," and "shouting"—are complex and changeable across context, and frequently blurry and even indeterminate.

For Wittgenstein, we can't communicate outside of a language game, and once we enter a language game, we can't talk in a "pure" way about the nonlinguistic world. The characteristics of language itself shape how we perceive and communicate with each other. The linguistic and non-linguistic world thus become unalterably bound together and intertwined with each other.

Linking to the Hermeneutic Circle

Popper, Kuhn, Quine, Feyerabend, and Wittgenstein all sound a similar theme, emphasizing the limitations if not the impossibility of objective, scientific knowledge because of our embeddedness in the logical, cultural, cognitive, and linguistic preconditions of that knowledge—preconditions that change according to historical and cultural context. For Popper, these preconditions include the deductive theoretical principles that we simply have to assume without being able to prove them; for

Kuhn, these preconditions are scientific paradigms; for Quine and Feyerabend, they are webs of belief; and for Wittgenstein, they are language games.

We can never step out of these preconditions and see the world objectively; for our ability to "see" is contingent upon these preconditions being in place. This notion—that the seeking of knowledge is limited by the need to assume preconditions to that knowledge which can't be proven—is very similar to the linguistic concept of the hermeneutic circle, discussed in chapter 2. According to the hermeneutic circle, to understand a strange culture, practice, theory, language, and so forth, interpretation occurs within a circle in which the parts are always interpreted within some understanding of the whole, which in turn is understood by coming to understand the constituent parts. Thus, to understand something new requires reference to something that is already known and has to be taken for granted in order to understand the new; and then in turn we must assume the former, the new learning, to analyze and understand critically the latter, what we originally knew and assumed.

The End of Science?

Newton's law of gravitation and three laws of motion created a simple, elegant, rational picture of the universe as a gigantic machine, in which all matter constitutes the parts of the machine, and the four laws are the motor that keeps the parts working in a highly predictable manner. This deterministic model dealt in concepts of solid, visible objects moving in the types of time we can understand in terms of our direct experience of the everyday world. The accessibility of this model added a sense of reality to it; this seemed a most reasonable picture of how things are. In fact, followers in the spirit of Newton applied his mechanistic, linear-cause-and-effect ideas to politics (Hobbes), psychology (Hume), economics (Smith), sociology (Comte), and biology (Darwin).

This whole way of thinking supported the modernist notion that scientific theories describe real states and structures of nature, and that they replace each other as successive approximations to the full truth—a position characterized as scientific realism.[33] This point of view is reflected in such statements as: "Even though the Milky Way has a romantic name, it is *really* only a very large collection of expanding, mindless bodies of matter"; "the flaws in Jimmy Carter's presidency were *really* due to weakness in his personality"; "schizophrenia is *really* a neuronal disorder of the brain"; and "the problems of the typical alcoholic are *really* perpetuated by the support of co-dependent persons in their lives." In each of these instances, the realist uses the word "really" to imply, first, that it is possible to discover single, objective truths about external reality; and second, that the relevant statement reflects a part of those truths.[34]

Developments in contemporary physics (and other branches of science) over the past 150 years have yielded ideas that are both much less accessible and much more abstract and fanciful than Newton's laws. For example, Maxwell's equations integrating magnetism and electricity speak of electromagnetic fields and electromagnetic radiation such as X rays and microwaves, phenomena that are not directly visible to the naked eye, that do not follow linear, billiard-ball cause-and-effect models, that are conceptually complex in terms of particle-wave duality,[35] and that involve challenging mathematics for their full understanding.

This abstractness, complexity, and at times profoundly counterintuitive quality increases as one considers more recent developments in physics. Examples from particle physics are Heisenberg's Uncertainty Principle (the position and velocity of an electron can't both be precisely measured but can only be determined probabilistically) and the fanciful world of the particle "zoo": gluons, gravitons, neutrinos, hadrons, leptons, and quarks, which in turn come in six different "flavors."[36] Then consider Einstein's theory of relativity, with its notions of time dilation (moving clocks run more slowly, with slowly aging space travelers returning from a voyage to outer space younger than their earthbound children!); of moving yardsticks being shorter than stationary ones; of moving objects being more massive; and mass and energy being convertible into each other $(E = mc^2)$.[37] On top of all this complexity and strangeness is the paradigm revolution of chaos theory, discussed above, which claims that many phenomena, like the weather and the course of rising smoke, cannot be explained by other theories in physics, but require completely new, "nonlinear" theories.

These developments in contemporary physics—which present an image of the physical world that is much less understandable, much less directly related to sense experience, much less intuitive, and much less deterministic than the Newtonian image—raise major doubts about the validity of scientific realism. In Flew's words:

Realism is probably under most pressure when the scientific theory makes it impossible to "understand what is going on," that is, to regard the structures revealed in terms of antecedently intelligible modes and mechanisms. Action at a distance, electromagnetic radiation, subatomic particles, and many other theoretical constructs have all provoked this complaint.[38]

These doubts about scientific realism are compounded by the above-described paradigm clash of atomistic particle physics with the holistic theories of chaos and complexity—which of these radically different theories truly represents reality? All the doubts about scientific realism in turn raise questions about the foundations of modernism, which is built upon a belief in scientific convergence over time upon a single, certain set of objective truths about the natural, psychological, and social worlds. Also, realism is not a necessary assumption for justifying or explaining science. A reasonable alternative is to assume that scientific theories and models are human constructions, "hypothetical constructs,"[39] which function as tools for prediction and technology development, with their validity based upon the accuracy of their predictions and their generativity in creating workable technologies.

In this regard, logical positivism also takes an agnostic position on the issue of scientific realism. On the one hand, logical positivism supports modern faith in cumulative scientific knowledge, which would seem to be getting closer and closer to the way the natural world actually is. On the other hand, many logical positivists depend on sensory data as their ultimate test of truth, adding an element of subjectivity to their position. Moreover, the whole issue of whether the objects of science are "real" seems like one of the metaphysical questions that the logical positivists reject as not meaningful, since there are no sensory experiences that can differentiate whether realism is a true or incorrect doctrine.[40]

John Horgan's book, *The End of Science: Facing the Limits of Knowledge in the Twilight of the Scientific Age*,[41] constitutes the most recent chapter in the attack on scientific realism. A senior science journalist for the venerable *Scientific American*, Horgan describes a process that might be called the "postmodernization" of science. Based on sophisticated and probing interviews with leading scientists in a variety of fields, including physics and evolutionary biology, one of the strong themes that emerges from Horgan's work is a paradox. The history of science is characterized by both a belief that science is getting closer to the underlying laws of nature, while at the same time dramatic new theories keep emerging, suggesting that over time any theory always becomes outdated and is never that close. Moreover, disciplinary, political, and journalistic excitement and recognition in science are associated with innovation and striking "breakthroughs." The possibility that our present theories of, for example, particle physics and evolutionary biology are close to the "truth" is thus a major problem. For how then can radically new theories be posited in order to keep up the excitement and the notoriety of the innovators?

To understand this dilemma of the contemporary scientist, Horgan turned to ideas from the literary scholar Harold Bloom.[42] Just as Bloom argued that no contemporary poet can surpass Milton or Shakespeare, so no contemporary scientist can surpass Newton's laws of motion, Darwin's theory of natural selection, and Einstein's theory of general relativity. Moreover, these theories are empirically supported by data in a way that no work of art can be. Most scientists simply concede that they cannot compete with what Bloom called "the embarrassments of a tradition grown too wealthy to need anything more,"[43] and they work at puzzle solving within the established paradigm—for example, measuring the mass of quarks more precisely or helping to decipher the genome.

But there are also "strong scientists" who seek to be truly innovative. They seek to provide new interpretations—not new data—concerning established theories like quantum mechanics or the big bang or Darwinian evolution, and by doing so, to transcend them. In Horgan's words, these scientists are pursuing science in a "speculative, postempirical mode" that he calls "ironic science." It resembles literary criticism—perhaps the paradigm of postmodernism—in that it offers interpretations that are interesting and provocative, but that do not empirically force the overturn of the established paradigm. These theories are "ironic" because, like literary texts, they can have multiple meanings, none of them definitive.[44]

One of the many examples of postempirical, postmodern, ironic science Horgan describes is the British physicist Roger Penrose's book *The Emperor's New Mind*,[45] which became a best-seller. Penrose asserted that modern science, with all its accomplishments, could still not account for the mystery of human consciousness. The key to consciousness, Penrose speculated, lay in "the fissure" between the two major theories of modern physics: quantum mechanics and general relativity, which physicists have been unsuccessfully attempting to integrate into a single "unified" theory.

> In his book, Penrose sketched out what a unified theory might look like and how it might give rise to thought. His scheme, which involved exotic quantum and gravitational effects percolating through the brain, was

vague, utterly convoluted, utterly unsupported by evidence from physics or neuroscience. But if it turned out to be right in any sense, it would represent a monumental achievement, a theory that in one stroke would unify physics and solve one of philosophy's most vexing problems, the link between mind and matter.[46]

Mainstream psychologists continue to base the privileged nature of their knowledge on its close correspondence to the experimental scientific method used in the "natural" or "hard" sciences like physics and biology. However, as Horgan argues, the boundaries are blurring between the "hard" sciences, traditionally associated with "nature," and such humanities as literary criticism and metaphysical philosophy, traditionally associated with "culture." As these hard sciences are invaded by counterintuitive, fanciful, abstruse, interpretive, ironic, postmodern forces, and "science"—at least as modern positivists know it—comes to an end, one wonders how long mainstream psychology will hold out. Will psychology soon find itself celebrating a "philosophy of science" paradigm from physics, its role model discipline, that is in fact just a historical relic in that discipline?[47]

4

The Dialectic
Putting It All Together

Two competing visions overarch and energize the historical and philosophical details we have been reviewing. Modernism emerged from the Enlightenment not only to promote rationality and science, but also as a way of organizing the world and defining societal values and individual ethics. Postmodernism developed as a rebellion against the perceived faults, deficiencies, and oppressive forces of modernism. In the recent words of one postmodern critic: "Science has failed to deliver utopia: its materialist underpinnings have destroyed the basis of morality and esthetics, and have reduced the status of human beings to a collection of replicating molecules without meaning, sense or purpose in the grand scheme of things."[1]

As modernism is a total worldview, so is postmodernism's planful rebellion against it. Likewise, as modernism is a tightly interrelated system of assumptions, so is its virtual polar opposite, postmodernism. For a full understanding of the implications of the modern-postmodern dialectic, we must pull together the strands of the polarized dichotomies on the disparate issues we have been considering in past chapters and approach these worldviews more holistically. At the same time, such an act of integration must be accompanied by a disclaimer. For "modernism" and "postmodernism" are constructs that necessarily simplify the complexities of the real world. On the one hand, it is important to clarify the underlying dialectic between the modern and postmodern visions for the purpose of justifying and developing a new conceptual and methodological space for a pragmatic, case-based psychology—the task of the remainder of the book. On the other hand, it is important to remember the simplification necessary to accomplish this practical task, and not to shut ourselves off from these complexities in other discussion contexts.

The various polarities we have examined individually are woven into two contrasting descriptions below, with key concepts from the discussion in earlier chapters in italics. I have labeled them "modern positivism" and "postmodern constructionism" to highlight the contrasting epistemologies that underlie each worldview.

The Players

Modern Positivism

Modern positivism is a worldview based on the assumption that physical and social reality are governed by *general laws* that can be stated in *propositional* and *quantitative terms*, that these laws are objectively knowable, and that the *natural science method* is the best means for *discovering* them. The natural sciences conceptualize the world in terms of *nature*, that is, in terms of physical matter such as trees, rocks, tables, dogs, and electricity. Applying this view to human behavior means, in part, that humans are seen as similar to other animals whose behavior is goal-directed toward individual and group survival, as described in *evolutionary biology and sociobiology*. Like other biological phenomena, human behavior is *explained* (that is, predicted and controlled) in terms of a collection of impersonal, mechanistic, *machinelike processes*, which are governed by deterministic, general "laws of nature." Traditional *behaviorism* is a good example of the natural science approach to social action.

The philosophical basis for the natural sciences is *positivism*, which holds that in order to be meaningful or objective, a statement has to be open to verification, or at least falsification, by particular *sense-experiences*, such as seeing a dial reading on a meter. In positivism, statements of cultural or individual *values are subjective* and can and should be separated from the process of acquiring knowledge with the scientific method. Positivism explicates how scientific theories are *deductively* used to generate predictions of events that can be tested through empirical observation. The result of theory testing is the creation of discrete, *atomic statements of fact*. These are phrased in terms of *thin description*, that is, in a general summary manner with a deemphasis on the particularities of context and actors' intentions and experience. Ultimately, the search for truth is guided by data, that is, upon what sense-experience and empirical observation reveal.

The identification of psychology with positivism is sometimes called *scientism*. This term emphasizes that psychology is presented as "apolitical," simply using experimental, quantitative methods to discover empirical "facts" and to develop "true theories" about the structure and functioning of society and not taking political sides. Scientism is sometimes referred to as *masculine science* in that it involves such values as emotional separation between researcher and research subject, quantification, and experimental manipulation of the subject.

Derived from the Enlightenment, modernism emphasizes the value of *rationality* and its embodiment in the scientific method in learning about and coping with the human condition. Because modernism holds that objective truth is possible, that the scientific method is a superior technique for ascertaining this truth, and that this truth is cumulatively progressing toward completeness, periods in which modernism has predominated are characterized as being *unifying* (*centripetal*), that is, as emphasizing forces toward unity and stability, at times to the point of stagnation and inflexibility. Such a period of unity was the 1950s in the United States, with a dominant mainstream culture, *clearly differentiated roles for men and women*, and a *melting pot* goal of assimilating different racial and ethnic subgroups into a single national culture.

Postmodern Constructionism

Postmodern constructionism is a worldview based on the assumption that reality is not objectively knowable. Rather, reality is *constructed* by individuals and groups as a result of particular beliefs and historical, cultural, and social contexts. The nature of reality is relative, depending on the observer's point of view. The *incompleteness*, limitations, and relativity in knowledge are illustrated in the concepts of the *hermeneutic circle*, the *web of belief*, *scientific knowledge as paradigm-driven*, and *language as intrinsic to experienced reality*. While continued application of the scientific method will most probably result in cumulative technological progress, social progress is historically contingent upon the particular conditions, values, and decisions of our time.

Two of the philosophic underpinnings of postmodernism are *hermeneutics* and *social constructionism*. Hermeneutics holds that what is knowable is an individual's holistic experience of engaged, intentional, practical activity, while social constructionism holds that what is knowable is a particular group's experienced social reality, which is created through the communal interchange of the group's members. Both hermeneutics and social constructionism hold that "language" and "experience" cannot be separated; in fact, both take the position that human behavior should be viewed and understood in a way that is similar to how we interpret *written texts*. Thus, understanding the meaning of language describing human behavior is intimately tied to *the interests and purposes of the language users* and the particular *Wittgensteinian language game* in which they are engaged, not just to the relation between the statement and the listener's sense-experience, as claimed by positivists.

Because reality is "constructed," its nature is intrinsically bound up with *culture,* that is, the human, social, and cultural meanings of the objects and events of the individually and socially experienced world. Since the postmodern approach focuses on culture, within postmodernism psychology becomes a *human science*, similar to other humanities disciplines such as historical scholarship and literary criticism. The goal of a human science is *understanding*, that is, making sense of human behavior "from the inside," in terms of the researchers' and research subjects' conscious inner life, with its mixture of thoughts, feelings, sensations, images, intuitions, and *intentions*. The way to capture this understanding is through *qualitative research*, by analyzing words, not numbers. The way to communicate this understanding is through *thick description*, which captures the complex meanings of human experience using language in a rich, dense, highly contextualized, detailed manner, and through *narrative*, storytelling modes of thought. The emphasis on words and feelings, and the use of collaborative relationships between researcher and subject have led feminists to be attracted to postmodern science as distinctively *feminine science*. The lack of clear separation among ideas, emotions, and intuitions has led postmodernists to stress *nonrational forces* in human behavior much more than modernists do. *Humanistic psychology* and the *cognitive revolution* in psychology are examples of postmodern concerns with consciousness, intention, and mental life.

Because reality is constructed from holistic experience, combining perceptions, beliefs, feelings, intentions, and values, it is not possible to separate "facts" from values. Thus, postmodern psychologists are not averse to combining their research with *ideological activism*. Also, the emphasis on personal, holistic experience leads postmodern psychologists to develop their conceptual theories from experience inductively, creating *grounded theory*.

Postmodernism can be viewed as a 1960s reaction against modernism. Since postmodernism emphasizes the limitations and relativity of knowledge, it encourages the development of *diversity* in ideas and in ethnic and racial subcultures. Thus, postmodernism is a *diversifying, (centrifu-*

gal) cultural force, emphasizing new ideas, creative change, and enrichment, at times to the point of turbulence and fragmentation. Postmodernism's diversity is reflected in the *counterculture* of the 1960s and the *feminist* attack on rigid gender roles and stereotypes.

Not So Fast

Of course, reducing the intricacies of modernism and postmodernism to a series of dichotomies between clearly differentiated alternatives downplays the important complexities within the modern and postmodern movements in psychology. For example, the cognitive revolution had two contrasting inspirations—one which viewed the mind as nature, and one which viewed it as culture. Mind-as-nature researchers such as George Miller attempted to preserve positivism in reaction to the failures of behaviorism. Thus, they could go "inside" a person's conscious experience and retain deterministic, mechanistic rigor by treating the mind as a computer, an information-processing machine that could be studied "objectively" as an overtly observable "outside" entity. In contrast, mind-as-culture researchers such as Jerome Bruner advocated the importance of studying "meaning" rather than "information"; and thus they linked themselves to hermeneutics and the humanities disciplines such as history and literature.

As another example, while general systems theorists like James Miller provide an alternative to the mechanistic thinking of the Newtonian physics paradigm, they are still committed to positivistic, natural science models and goals. In Pepper's terms, the root metaphor of psychological theory shifted from the machine to the living organism, but psychology still remained within the purview of the natural sciences, shifting from the domain of physics to that of biology. On the other hand, systems concepts emphasize a holistic rather than an elementistic approach to phenomena, with notions such as reciprocally causal interactions among elements, systems within systems, a system as a whole "seeking" equilibrium, and emergent phenomena. Notions such as these have encouraged some systems theorists to "push the envelope" of positivism, and at times to push through that envelope to, in Pepper's terms, contextualistic theories that emphasize and appreciate the particularity of psychological events, rather than searching for general laws that purportedly underlie them.

As a third example, while the idea of qualitative research challenges the quantitative emphasis that is such a hallmark of positivism, some modernistic researchers have adapted qualitative research to positivist purposes. An example is the methodology of "content analysis," in which small "meaning units" in documents are quantitatively coded as to their presence and strength, and the resulting quantitative data are then treated in traditional positivist ways. On the other hand, many qualitative researchers have been drawn to a hermeneutic position, rejecting content analysis because of its inability to capture the context within which a written text has meaning, for example, such features of a text as its ongoing narrative, its literary tropes, and its connection to experience and knowledge.[2]

As illustrated in these examples, positivist psychologists have frequently attempted to adapt and appropriate new, diversifying ideas to positivist projects and concepts. In this way, they have been able to claim that they are au courant with contemporary thinking. On the other hand, their "adaptation" profoundly alters the idea itself. In effect, a number of these new ideas can be viewed from either the perspective of nature or culture, and which level of discourse is chosen determines whether the resultant idea falls in the modern, positivist or postmodern, constructionist category. My focus on dichotomizing assumptions and perspectives into modern and postmodern categories is intended to highlight the fundamental, epistemological difference in level of discourse. It is this difference which underlies the topographical complexities of the diversifying psychological concepts and movements I have been reviewing.

Boiling It Down to Three Paradigms

The worldview of postmodern constructionism can be divided into the four positions described in the Introduction: skeptical, critical, ontological, and neopragmatic (or what I am simply calling "pragmatic") postmodernism. For purposes of clarifying my main thesis, which argues that pragmatism be given "equal time" in forming a philosophical foundation for psychological research, I shall be comparing and contrasting three paradigmatic alternatives for psychological research: a positivist paradigm, a pragmatic paradigm, and a hermeneutic paradigm. This last groups together the methodological, critical, and ontological branches of hermeneutics, which are parallel to the skeptical, critical, and ontological positions within postmodernism.

Based on previous discussion, table 4.1 lists thirteen major contrasts

TABLE 4.1
Illustrative Differences among Epistemological Paradigms

Paradigm Characteristic	Positivist Paradigm	Pragmatic Paradigm	Hermeneutic Paradigm
1. Underlying epistemology	Logical positivism	Social constructionism	Social constructionism
2. Primary mode of research[a]	Nomothetic	Idiographic	Idiographic
3. Primary site of research[a]	Specially created settings: laboratories, college classrooms	Natural settings	Natural settings
4. Primary source of knowledge[a]	Observation	Observation	Intuition
5. View of how predictable and determined behavior is[a]	Emphasis on behavior as determined and predictable	Emphasis on behavior as determined and predictable	A balance between behavior as predictable versus unpredictable, determined versus indeterminate
6. Primary goal of research	Derivation of theory-based, general psychological laws through laboratory experiments	Solution of context-specific, practical psychological problems	Qualitative understanding of context-specific psychological events and processes
7. Primary type of data employed	Quantitative	Quantitative and qualitative	Qualitative
8. Primary level of analysis[a]	Elemental	Elemental and holistic	Holistic
9. Primary use of empirical or experimental information generated: scientific/scholarly understanding vs. improving the human condition[a]	Scientific theory development	Improving social programs by assistance to decision makers in those programs	Scholarly addition to a cumulative body of commentary about human experience and behavior
10. Primary modes of communication	Publication in academic, highly technical journals	Publication in both academic journals and written reports to lay decision makers concerning their programs and policies	Publication in both academic journals and "intellectual" media like the *New York Times Magazine*
11. Need for complex, quantitative management information systems	Low need: experiments generate relatively small amounts of quantitative data	High need: performance indicators about complex, real-world settings generate large amounts of quantitative data	Very low need: quantitative data are generally a low priority within the paradigm

TABLE 4.1 *(continued)*
Illustrative Differences among Epistemological Paradigms

Paradigm Characteristic	Positivist Paradigm	Pragmatic Paradigm	Hermeneutic Paradigm
12. Exemplars in psychology	Animal experiments to test Hullian learning theory; correlational studies to test personality trait theory	Market research; standardized educational tests, such as the SATs; token economies in behavior therapy	Qualitative interpretation of the Rorschach; interpretation in psychoanalytic therapy; psychohistory
13. Exemplars outside of psychology	Natural sciences (physics, chemistry, and biology)	National economics indicators; U.S. Census; financial accounting data; sports statistics	Investigative reporting; interpretive history; literary criticism

SOURCE: Adapted from Fishman 1988. Reprinted by permission of the publisher.

[a] Kimble (1984) found these six items to define the "scientific" versus the "humanistic" cultures in psychology on his "Epistemic Differential" scale. With the exception of item 9, the positivist paradigm embodies all the characteristics of the scientific culture, and the hermeneutic paradigm all those of the humanistic culture.

among the three paradigms.[3] Included in these comparisons are six items that Kimble found to differentiate empirically between the "scientific" and "humanistic" cultures in psychology.[4] With one exception, these cultures are perfectly aligned with the positivist and hermeneutic paradigms, respectively. (The exception is item 9, in which the humanistic pole involves an emphasis on "improving the human condition" rather than on the "scholarly understanding" of the hermeneutic paradigm.)

In distinguishing among the three paradigms as outlined in table 4.1, it is important to emphasize that this is a representation of three "pure" types, and in actual practice, many combinations of these pure types occur. Thus, while the table might be interpreted as implying that there are only two categorically distinct epistemological paradigms in quantitative psychology, in practice the positivist and pragmatic paradigms outlined in the table form the endpoints of a continuum. This continuum includes a large variety of "mixed" epistemologies that contain varying blends of the elements from the "pure" types at each end, and any particular epistemology can be profiled in terms of where it is located on each of these. However, it is still quite meaningful to speak in terms of *relative* differences among epistemologies with respect to the degree they are located closer to or farther from the "pure" positivist and "pure" pragmatic endpoints of the continuum.

This analysis also applies to differences between the hermeneutic paradigm and the other two paradigms. What I have described as three "pure" paradigms are the endpoints of continua, and in reality most psychologists employ various blends of these in their epistemological models. However, the *relative* differences in the degree to which a particular epistemology is positivist, pragmatic, or hermeneutic is still a crucial consideration in the field.

From table 4.1, we can see that the pragmatic model is a type of hybrid of the other two: items 1–3 are shared with the hermeneutic paradigm; items 4 and 5 are shared with the positivist paradigm; and items 6–11 are unique to the pragmatic paradigm (items 12 and 13 are not classifiable in this manner). This hybrid quality of the pragmatic paradigm will be an important theme in chapter 7, which compares in detail the ways in which the three paradigms conceptualize, design, conduct, and document research in psychology.

5

Transcending the Dialectic

The Emergence of Postmodern Pragmatism

I am calling for a radical restructuring of the way in which psychological research is conducted—from the experimental group investigation to the holistic case study. Since such a far-reaching proposal challenges the underlying philosophy of mainstream psychology, the legitimacy of the proposal requires an alternative foundational grounding. This is located in the philosophy of pragmatism, to which we now directly turn.

This chapter explores the arguments for pragmatism, beginning with attacks on logical positivism. A historical review reveals that such attacks by nineteenth and twentieth century Continental philosophy had little effect until postpositivist critiques from within converged with and legitimized the Continental attacks.[1] Once the conceptual foundation had been prepared, it became a fertile ground for the reinvigoration of the uniquely American philosophy of pragmatism—developed particularly by philosopher-psychologists William James and John Dewey at the turn of the century. In the hands of recent philosophers like Richard Bernstein, Richard Rorty, and Stephen Toulmin, pragmatism has been reworked within the context of postmodernism. The chapter illustrates the distinctiveness of the pragmatic perspective by contrasting it with hermeneutic analyses of two domains of human behavior: a Balinese cockfight and schizophrenia. The chapter closes with an analysis of the logical transition from pragmatic philosophy to the case study method, the topic of the following two chapters.

The Family Tree

Continental and Anglo-American Philosophers Speak the Same Language

Rising to ascendance in the 1930s, logical positivism dominated Anglo-American thinking in philosophy, as it did in the natural sciences and the social sciences. Following the philosophical tradition of British empiricism, and building on the tremendous technological success of the natural sciences in helping to create industrialized Western societies, logical positivism grounded all knowledge in basic sensory experience. It contended that objective knowledge about the external world could be discovered by linking that sensory experience with recent advances in symbolic logic and with the methods of natural science. Applying this position to traditional metaphysical and moral topics, logical positivists like A. J. Ayer stated that questions about such issues are not even meaningful questions.

In effect, then, the logical positivists reduced philosophy—the intellectual foundation of all knowledge—to the philosophy of science, making an absolute separation between empirical "facts," which are based on sense experience and have legitimate claims to knowledge, and values, which are simply the expression of the speaker's emotions and not true knowledge.

Logical positivism bolstered the dominance of the modernist perspective, which is built upon an absolute belief in the special status of scientific knowledge and the capacity of science to bring about social, political, and economic progress. For psychology and the other social sciences, an alliance with logical positivism and "real" science thus had enormous political advantages. It enhanced psychology's public image and prestige, leading to increasing financial support from government, business, and foundation sources.

However, logical positivism was not dominant in other parts of the world. During the nineteenth century and continuing through the 1930s, a very different philosophical tradition was flourishing in Continental Europe, especially in France and Germany. This tradition has at least five strands: phenomenology, existentialism, methodological hermeneutics, ontological hermeneutics, and critical hermeneutics. Fundamentally, all five are united in their direct opposition to the premises of logical positivism specifically and modernism generally, and as such they help to form the intellectual foundation of postmodernism. All five were described in chapter 2,[2] so they will only be briefly summarized here:

- *Phenomenology* emphasizes knowledge through an exclusive focus on the subjective, experienced world of consciousness, the fundamental and undeniable existent. All other philosophical questions about the relationship between the mind and the physical world are to be suspended so that experience can be "bracketed," that is, taken on its own terms.
- *Existentialism* is considered more an attitude than a system, focusing on emotion rather than rationality, and on the anxieties of modern life rather than the search for certain knowledge. In the existential perspective, the problem of being, morality, and value takes precedence over the problem of knowing—that is, the question "How shall we live?" takes precedence over the question "How do we know?" Instead of embracing science, the Industrial Revolution, and the rationality of academic philosophy, as did logical positivism, existentialists attacked these components of modernism as dehumanizing.
- *Methodological hermeneutics* focuses on applying interpretive principles to the qualitative understanding of human behavior in particular sociohistorical settings. These principles include the hermeneutic circle and the inseparability of fact and value, detail and context, and observation and theory.
- *Ontological hermeneutics* addresses the role of interpretation in the nature of human existence itself. It views our fundamental mode of "being-in-the-world" as that of creatures who understand and interpret in the context of engaged, practical activity, as exemplified by a carpenter hammering a nail.
- *Critical hermeneutics* employs interpretive techniques to critique the moral and ideological underpinnings of contemporary social practice and institutions, with the goal of fostering emancipation from arbitrary, unjust forms of cultural and political domination.

The five strands of Continental philosophy oppose logical positivism and modernism in different but interconnected ways. Existentialism and critical theory both attack modernism politically and culturally, seeing it as exploitive and dehumanizing, killing individual freedom, creativity, and centeredness. Existentialism makes its criticism from the perspective of the exploited and alienated individual, while critical theory makes it from the perspective of a society's political and economic structure. Also, both are critical of academic philosophy, accusing it of being a reflection and advocacy tool of modernism rather than as a means of providing an objective analysis of modernism and/or as a means of opposing modernism.

Existentialism, phenomenology, and ontological hermeneutics all stress the foundational nature of conscious experience with its ideas, images, sensations, emotions, impulses, and desires considered as an integrated whole. This is contrary to logical positivism's stress upon atomistic sense impressions, which these other philosophies see as an artificial and a misleading abstraction. Existentialism and ontological hermeneutics, although not phenomenology, additionally put emphasis on the engaged, purposive, volitional quality of conscious experience. This contrasts with logical positivism's view of the individual as a passive recipient of stimuli, which govern behavior by mechanistic rather than volitional forces. Finally, in opposition to the behavioristic focus of logical positivism, methodological hermeneutics stresses the importance of sociocultural context, linguistic meaning, and textual interpretation in understanding human experience.

Before the late 1930s, these Continental forays against logical positivism had relatively little effect on the dominance of this view in American and British philosophy. Continental philosophy was considered softheaded and muddled, based on the sort of "metaphysics" that Ayer had demolished. Existentialism was viewed more as literature than philosophy; methodological hermeneutics was ignored because of its rejection of the natural science method in studying human phenomena; phenomenology and ontological hermeneutics were rejected because of their nonscientific focus on internal experience rather than on overt behavior; and neo-Marxist critical theory was viewed more as political ideology than philosophy, especially by two countries that were ideologically opposed to Marxist thinking. In addition, Heidegger, a central figure in Continental philosophy, was ridiculed for his exceedingly dense and awkward style of writing and attacked for his conversion to Hitler's national socialism.[3]

However, the critique of logical positivism from within by postpositivists such as Popper, Kuhn, Quine, Feyerabend, and Wittgenstein was a different story.[4] The postpositivists concluded that objective, scientific knowledge is severely limited, if not impossible, because of our embeddedness in the cultural, cognitive, and linguistic preconditions of that knowledge—preconditions that change according to historical and cultural contexts. These preconditions include the need to assume deductive theoretical principles without being able to prove or verify them (Popper); and the embeddedness in scientific paradigms (Kuhn), webs of belief (Quine and Feyerabend), and language games (Wittgenstein). Objective perception of the world is not possible because our very ability to "see" is contingent upon these preconditions being in place.

This notion—that the seeking of knowledge is limited by the need to assume preconditions to that knowledge which can't be proven—is very similar to the ideas of Continental philosophy. Existentialism's precondition is each individual's embeddedness in existence, with the need to discover anew how to create meaning and to take responsible action in a world that is in itself meaningless, albeit full of manifold possibilities for constructing meaning. Phenomenology's precondition is to limit knowledge only to the phenomenal world of individual consciousness. Ontological hermeneutics' precondition is embeddedness in holistic, individual conscious experience, which is permeated by qualities of engagement and purposiveness. And critical theory's precondition is the foundational nature of political and economic forces in determining all aspects of individual functioning, both in terms of experience and in terms of behavioral products, such as natural science research. This need to assume nondirectly provable preconditions to knowledge is similar to the concept of the hermeneutic circle, which runs through Continental philosophy: to understand something new requires reference to something that is already known and which has to be taken for granted in order to understand the new; and then in turn we must assume the former, the new learning, to analyze and critically understand the latter, what we originally "knew" and assumed.[5]

This convergence of Continental philosophy and Anglo-American, postpositivistic philosophy is striking, given the almost complete lack of communication between them.[6] In Ronald Miller's words:

> The critique [of logical positivism] is certainly strengthened by its emergence out of two radically disparate traditions that many thought only a few decades ago to be totally irreconcilable. That Heidegger's metaphysics and Wittgenstein's antimetaphysical philosophy would converge with a neo-Marxist [critical theory] epistemology was almost inconceivable, yet it is now a well-documented trend in the current philosophical scene.[7]

The American Experience

The emergence of postpositivism and philosophical hermeneutics freed up American philosophy from the dominance of positivism, with its exclusive focus on the justification of the nature and authority of scientific knowledge. American philosophy was now free to rediscover its uniquely American creation, pragmatism. Cornel West has traced the chronological development of pragmatism from its beginnings in Ralph Waldo Emerson, Charles Peirce, William James, and John Dewey; through its articulation in such thinkers as Sidney Hook, C. Wright Mills, W. E. B. Du Bois, Reinhold Niebuhr, and Lionel Trilling; to its present "pragmatic" resurgence in professional philosophy in individuals such as Willard V. Quine and Richard Rorty. In his classic book, *The American Evasion of Philosophy: A Genealogy of Pragmatism,*[8] West describes how pragmatism "evades" the traditional epistemological focus of academic philosophy, with its focus on the quest for certainty and foundation. Rather, pragmatism views philosophical thought as a vehicle to impact upon the pressing sociopolitical and cultural issues of the day. The fact that these issues are filled with uncertainty and historical contingency loses its daunting quality when the quest for incontrovertible foundation is evaded.

> The distinctive appeal of American pragmatism in our postmodern moment is its unashamedly moral emphasis and its unequivocally ameliorative impulse. In this world-weary period of pervasive cynicisms, nihilisms, terrorisms, and possible extermination, there is a longing for norms and values that can make a difference, a yearning for principled resistance and struggle that can change our desperate plight.[9]

The Originators of Pragmatism: Peirce, James, and Dewey. Two central themes run through the work of the originators: contextualism[10] and the pragmatic theory of meaning and truth. In contextualism, "The world is seen as an unlimited complex of change and novelty, order and disorder. Out of this total flux we select certain contexts; these contexts serve as organizing gestalts or patterns that give meaning and scope to the vast array of details that, without the organizing pattern, would be meaningless or invisible."[11]

Within this way of thinking, truth is "the successful working out of an idea" within a specific, always limited context. The contextualist hesitates to extend a theory beyond the limits of specific working situations; all experiences are fragmentary, limited, partial, and occur within the limits of contexts beyond which is only an infinite universe of indeterminacy. Contexts, then, are humanly created structures that integrate and explain experience.[12]

Because the world that exists independently of our minds is "an unlimited complex of variety, change and novelty," it is not possible to attain a "true," "objective" picture of the world. Rather, pragmatism holds that the meaning and truth of a statement or concept are a function of its practical or "pragmatic" usefulness in particular contexts. Peirce uses hardness and weight to illustrate the pragmatic theory of meaning:

> Let us ask what we mean by calling a thing *hard*. Evidently that it will not be scratched by many other substances. The whole conception of this quality, as of every other, lies in its conceived effects. . . . Let us seek next a clear idea of weight. . . . To say that a body is heavy means simply that, in the absence of an opposing force, it will fall.[13]
>
> The whole function of thought is to produce some habits of action [and] . . . every purpose of action is to produce some sensible result. Thus, we come down to what is tangible and conceivably practical, as the root of every real distinction of thought, no matter how subtle it may be; and there is no distinction of meaning so fine as to consist in anything but a possible difference of practice.[14]

James is most identified with the pragmatic theory of truth. In his words: "Any idea that will carry us prosperously from any one part of our experience to any other part, linking things satisfactorily, working securely, saving labor, is true for just so much, . . . true *instrumentally*. The true . . . is only the expedient in the way of thinking."[15]

Traditional, positivistic science is based on a "correspondence" theory of truth, which holds that the truth of a statement or concept is a function of the degree to which it is a correct reflection of "objective," external reality. Moreover, positivists assume that this objective reality is governed by a few, elegant, discoverable general laws, much like Newton's laws of physics, chemistry's periodic table of elements, or the "double helix" structure of the DNA molecule. The "royal road" to discovering such laws is the scientific method of inquiry, in which phenomena are studied under conditions of high experimental control.

In contrast, because pragmatism views the world as "an unlimited complex of variety, change and novelty," with knowledge consisting of contextually limited guidelines and not general laws, pragmatism emphasizes the tentativeness, fallibility, and incompleteness of any substantive knowledge.[16] However, pragmatism does view the method of scientific inquiry as one of the best techniques to derive useful knowledge. In Dewey's words: "The future of our civilization depends upon the widening spread and deepening hold of the scientific habit of mind."[17] In fact, it was because of the inadequacy of existing and yet-to-be-discovered knowledge that James's and Dewey's prescribed "scientific attitude" was defined *in terms of* an openness toward and search for new but only temporarily valid knowledge in a world of continual change.[18]

The recent rediscovery of American pragmatism is epitomized in the work of three American philosophers: Richard Bernstein, Richard Rorty, and Stephen Toulmin.[19] Each in a different way has argued a common theme: the need to go "beyond" the present logical impasse between advocates of objectivism and those of relativism to focus on the practical problems in contemporary life—social, political, and cultural.

Pragmatists Weigh In

Richard Bernstein's "Praxis"

The theme of Bernstein's work is reflected in the title of his 1983 book, *Beyond Objectivism and Relativism: Science, Hermeneutics, and Praxis.* Bernstein begins with the postpositivist arguments against positivism and its associated doctrine of "objectivism," that is, the assumption that objective knowledge about the world is possible. However, he asks, if we then take positions such as postpositivism and hermeneutics that emphasize the limits of knowledge, are we doomed to the ills of relativism? Bernstein's book explores this question in great depth, and he comes out concluding that the answer is no. Rather, we must travel "beyond" the traditional dichotomous choice of objectivism versus relativism and embrace pragmatism, or the term that he uses, "praxis" (practical as opposed to theoretical discourse).

Objectivism and Relativism. Bernstein defines the concepts of objectivism and relativism as follows:

> By "objectivism" I mean the basic conviction that there is or must be some permanent, ahistorical matrix or framework to which we can ultimately appeal in determining the nature of rationality, knowledge, truth, reality, goodness, or rightness. . . . Objectivism is closely related to foundationalism and the search for an Archimedean point. The objectivist maintains that unless we can ground philosophy, knowledge, or language in a rigorous manner we cannot avoid radical skepticism.
>
> The relativist not only denies the positive claims of the objectivist but goes further. In its strongest form, relativism is the basic conviction that

when we turn to the examination of those concepts that philosophers have taken to be the most fundamental—. . . [like] rationality, truth, reality, right, the good, or norms—we are forced to recognize that in the final analysis all such concepts must be understood as relative to a specific conceptual scheme, theoretical framework, paradigm, form of life, society, or culture.[20]

There have been two standard arguments against relativism. The first is the logical argument. Since Plato, objectivists have argued that relativism is self-referentially inconsistent and paradoxical.[21] For the relativist claims first, directly or indirectly, that his or her position is true; and second, that all truth is relative, that is, what seems true may also be false. It follows that relativism itself may be both true *and* false; and that simply stating the thesis of relativism itself undermines it.[22]

The second standard argument against relativism is a cultural one. If all moral, esthetic, political, and other standards are relative, then culturally we have no way of deciding what is true, good, right, and of artistic value. In the colorful words of anthropologist Clifford Geertz, relativism implies "anything goes, to each his own, you pays your money and you takes your choice, I know what I like, not in the south, *tout comprendre, c'est tout pardonner.*"[23] This argument is at the heart of the "culture wars" that modernist thinkers have waged against postmodernists who attempt to deconstruct the superiority of any particular set of values. Cultural relativism is viewed, says Geertz, as an attack upon the traditions, institutions, and values of our society, as giving license to such forces as "subjectivism, nihilism, incoherence, Machiavellianism, ethical idiocy, esthetic blindness, and so on."[24] For example, one traditional literary scholar has concluded that the relativism movement beginning in the late 1960s has led to "the death of literature," that is, to the death of "the great works of literary art that, with their pretensions to permanence and universal truth, had hitherto been the foundation of liberal education."[25]

Cultural relativism is a particularly controversial topic in anthropology, which created many aspects of the concept. Originally, the idea was an attempt to attack Western racism in prejudicially judging other cultures, particularly less technologically developed, "primitive" cultures. Modernist anthropologists, though, view cultural relativism as a destructive tool of cultural criticism used to undermine the values of Western culture and as an example of inverted racism. Thus, Melford Spiro, a modernist anthropologist who wishes to ground the field in universals about human nature and culture, sees cultural relativism as a means to critique ideologically contemporary Western society. For example, compared to some primitive societies that have less aggressive, competitive, materialistic, and individualistic cultures than ours, our society is seen as "perverted" and dysfunctional.[26]

The "Either/Or" Question. Bernstein views the objectivism versus relativism debates as based on a fallacy: that there are only these two alternatives, that it is an Either/Or question. The driving force behind this fallacy is what Bernstein calls the "Cartesian Anxiety." This is the concern set forth by the seventeenth-century philosopher Descartes in his *Meditations* that to combat possible doubt, deception, and error in thinking, and to counteract unfounded opinions, prejudices, tradition, or external authority as justification for beliefs, philosophy must find a certain foundation for all knowledge, "an Archimedean point upon which we can ground our knowledge."[27]

Bernstein points out the importance of understanding the religious context in which Cartesian Anxiety was fueled. In line with Christian thinking at the time, Descartes' viewed human beings as limited, finite creatures who are completely dependent on an all-powerful, infinite God. This can lead to the terrifying experience of not being sure one is not in a self-deceptive dream world, or nothing more than a plaything of an all-powerful demon—the fear of having "all of a sudden fallen into very deep water . . . [where] I can neither make certain of setting my feet on the bottom, nor can I swim and so support myself on the surface."[28] Thus, *either* there is a fixed foundation for our knowledge, *or* we are doomed to the forces of darkness that envelop us with madness and with intellectual and moral chaos.[29]

Bernstein, along with other pragmatists and related thinkers, has set as a major task to critique and move beyond the anxiety engendered by Descartes' Either/Or question. For "if we question, expose, and exorcise Cartesianism [and the associated Cartesian Anxiety], then the very opposition of objectivism and relativism loses its plausibility."[30]

As an example of the movement beyond objectivism and relativism, Geertz proposes that the question of assuming cross-cultural universals (objectivism) versus assuming cultural relativism does not have an Either/Or answer, but rather involves a comparison of trade-offs.[31] Objectivist approaches recognize the commonalities among different societies (such as language, family structure, and social and religious rituals), and these approaches meet our need for stability and centeredness in viewing the world. However, objectivism carries with it provincialism, "the danger that our perceptions will be dulled, our intellects constricted, and our sympathies narrowed by the overlearned and over-valued acceptances of our own society."[32] Relativist approaches counter this provincialism by helping us to remain open to the considerable variation among cultures, and discouraging us from passing inappropriate and counterproductive judgments on other societies to whom we are increasingly tied in the global village. However, relativism can desensitize us to the cultural practices and values that play important roles in giving our own society coherence and positive meaning.

The approach Geertz suggests, of examining the trade-offs between an objectivist versus a relativist perspective, would seem useful in understanding other related issues. For example, consider the question of moral responsibility for action. Modernist critics argue that postmodernism has led to a relativistic culture in which individuals no longer are held accountable for their actions. In the words of one irate critic:

> [With the disappearance of belief in objective standards of moral responsibility, we are besieged by] pushers of political correctness who would like to see grievance elevated into automatic sanctity. . . . Hence the rise of cult therapies teaching that we are all the victims of our parents, that whatever our folly, venality or outright thuggishness, we are not to be blamed for it, since we come from "dysfunctional families."[33]

The author of this passage certainly sensitizes us to the abuses of attributing all deviant, mean, and violent behavior to factors beyond the actor's control; and such a practice can weaken the models, encouragement, and incentives for moral, law-abiding behavior. On the other hand, a society that can recognize and take into account practical differences in the degree to which individuals have freedom to act and which shows compassion for deviant behavior achieves qualities of mercy and understanding that add in their own way to the society's moral character.

Bernstein addresses the more general issue of the logical argument against relativism. He points out the transitions in thinking brought about by the move from logical positivism to postpositivism:

> In the philosophy of science, and more generally in contemporary analytic epistemology, we have witnessed an internal dialectic that has moved from the preoccupation . . . with the isolated individual term [e.g., Hume], to the sentence or proposition [e.g., Wittgenstein's *Tractatus*], to the conceptual

scheme or framework [e.g., Quine and Kuhn], to an ongoing historical tradition constituted by social practices [e.g., Wittgenstein's language games in the *Investigations*]—a movement from logical atomism to historical dynamic continuity.[34]

Reframing the problem of the Either/Or in these terms, we can say that the objectivists looked to logical positivism to identify and justify atomistic indubitables that corresponded to the nonlinguistic world. As this project was being attacked by postpositivism, the Cartesian response of objectivists was that without the indubitables, all that was left was "anything goes" relativism and incoherence. The postpositivists responded that yes, we are always embedded in a conceptual framework (such as a web of belief, a paradigm, or a language game) whose assumptions cannot be proven logically; these assumptions can only be reflected upon via the hermeneutic circle. However, going beyond the Either/Or question, the postpositivists (and hermeneutic philosophers) argue that the assumptions of the conceptual framework are not arbitrary, trivial, or insubstantial. For these frameworks arise from and are embedded in historical traditions and contemporary sociocultural structures and institutions. And even though this does not endow the framework with absolute authority or certainty, it does provide it with significant momentum and weight in determining the present.

For example, in the industrialized countries of Western Europe, the United States, and Canada over the past 125 years, there have been very strong traditions of striving toward democracy and social justice that are a major moral force in the world today—traditions that can be traced at least back in part to situations and events such as Periclean Greece in the fifth-century B.C., the Magna Carta in 1215, and the Declaration of Independence in 1776. On the other hand, these traditions don't carry objective or absolute moral authority outside of the historical and contemporary sociopolitical context of the last 125 years. The counterexamples of Nazi Germany and fascist Italy in the 1930s and '40s certainly illustrate this lack of absolute authority. However, the fact that these two regimes have mainly been the exception over the past 125 years reflects the very substantial force of the democratic and social justice tradition.

Transcending the Either/Or Question to Practical Action. Bernstein argues strongly for a position outside of the Either/Or of "absolute" objectivism versus "anything goes" relativism. To arrive at this position, he analyzes and synthesizes the ideas of four major contemporary philosophers, drawing from them themes of pragmatism. They include three German philosophers representing the Continental philosophy tradition: Hans-Georg Gadamer, associated with ontological hermeneutics; and Jürgen Habermas and Hannah Arendt, associated with critical hermeneutics. The fourth is the American pragmatic philosopher, Richard Rorty.

Bernstein develops a substantive synthesis of the ideas of the four philosophers. He begins with an appreciation of human plurality, which is based on the "depth and pervasiveness of conflict . . . which characterizes our theoretical and practical lives."[35] He cites Pitkin and Shumer's discussion of the role of conflict in democratic politics:

> Democratic politics is an encounter among people with differing interests, perspectives, and opinions—an encounter in which they reconsider and mutually revise opinions and interests, both individual and common. It happens always in a context of conflict, imperfect knowledge, and uncertainty, but where community action is necessary. The resolutions achieved are always more or less temporary, subject to reconsideration, and rarely unanimous. What matters is not unanimity but discourse. The substantive common interest is only discovered or created in democratic political struggle, and it remains contested as much as shared. . . . Conflict . . . is what makes democracy work, what makes for the mutual revision of opinions and interests.[36]

Bernstein points out that implicit in the idea of productive dialogue for dealing with conflict is a community that underlies the dialogue, a community built upon shared understandings and experiences, shared social practices, and an emotional sense of affinity and solidarity.[37] In the context of contemporary times, when there are multiple threats to the stability and viability of these underlying communities, it becomes all the more imperative for us to foster and nurture them. A crucial component of such communities is "practical rationality," which, while not logically justified by an absolute objectivity, is also not without foundation in an "anything goes" relativism. It is therefore incumbent upon us to nurture the autonomy of practical rationality and show its relevance to all domains of culture. One way to do this is to identify and promote concrete exemplars of the types of dialogical communities in which practical rationality flourishes.[38]

Bernstein concludes by emphasizing the importance of *praxis*, of practical action:

It is not sufficient to try to come up with some new variations of arguments that will show, once and for all, what is wrong with objectivism and relativism . . . ; such a movement gains "reality and power" only if we dedicate ourselves to the practical task of furthering the type of solidarity, participation, and mutual recognition that is founded in dialogical communities.[39]

[Thus,] in the final analysis, the movement beyond objectivism and relativism is not just a perplexing theoretical quandary but a practical task that can orient and give direction to our collective *praxis*.[40]

Richard Rorty's "Radical" Pragmatism

Two important themes run through Rorty's work: a "metacritique" of traditional, modernist philosophy from a postmodern, deconstructionist point of view; and a moral argument for a "pragmatic relativism" with pragmatic dialogue, that is, "the willingness to talk, to listen to other people, to weigh the consequences of our actions upon other people."[41] Pragmatic relativism directs our attention away from issues of finding truth to issues of how to cope with the exigencies of human life as it is embedded in particular sociopolitical, cultural, and historical contexts.

"Metacritique" of Philosophy. In 1979 Rorty published a dramatic, provocative book entitled *Philosophy and the Mirror of Nature*.[42] In it, he reviewed the history of modernist Western philosophy since the Enlightenment, which has focused on "epistemology," the study of mind, knowledge, and the process of knowing. The guiding assumption throughout this period has been correspondence theory, which takes the form of likening the mind to a mirror that reflects "external" reality, and viewing knowledge as concerned with the accuracy of these reflections. In this model, philosophy's role is to discover the foundations of knowledge by investigating the precise nature and functioning of the mirror— whether it is material or mental or linguistic in composition, and whether it works by capturing external perceptions from our sense organs or intuitions from our inner experience.

After reviewing the mirror model, Rorty critically questions its underlying assumptions. He begins by pointing out that each different position in modernist philosophy has taken a particular mode of knowledge—be it sense impression, rational ideas, intuition, emotional insight, holistic experience, Heidegger's "engaged practical activity," or language and social dialogue—and identified this mode as more basic and fundamental than the other modes, with the other modes being derived from the fundamental one. Applying hermeneutic, social constructionist, and postpositivist concepts to the history of philosophy, Rorty argues that there is no fundamental mode of understanding and knowledge. Rather, these modes are all different perspectives, which are interdependent and reciprocally interactive in the knowing process. There is no way to know if one mode somehow "matches" or represents external reality or nature. Yes, there is

> such a thing as brute physical resistance—the pressure of light waves on Galileo's eyeball, or of the stone on Dr. Johnson's boot. But . . . [there is] no way of transferring this nonlinguistic brutality to *facts*, to the truth of sentences. . . . As many *facts* are brought into the world as there are languages for describing [events of brute physical resistance].[43]

Rorty concludes from his analysis that philosophical search for the epistemological foundations of knowledge is doomed to failure, and that it distracts us from the important work of using knowledge to meet better human needs and purposes. Thus, knowledge is to be judged ultimately by its capacity to be helpful to individual and social goals, not by its purported accuracy in reflecting an external, "objective" reality.

Implications for the Social Sciences. In an article entitled "Method, Social Science, and Social Hope,"[44] Rorty spells out the implications of his postmodern pragmatism for the social sciences. He begins by pointing out that all we can conclude from the success of natural science theories like Newton's laws in making empirical predictions is simply that they are effective in making such predictions—not that these concepts actually mirror the "true" nature of the physical world, "things as they *really are*," "Nature's Own Language," or "an absolute conception of reality."

> Galileo and his followers discovered, and subsequent centuries have amply confirmed, that you get much better predictions by thinking of things as masses of particles blindly bumping against each other than by thinking of them as Aristotle thought of them—animistically, teleologically, and anthropomorphically. They also discovered that you get a better handle on the universe by thinking of it as infinite and cold and comfortless than by thinking of it as finite, homey, planned, and relevant to human concerns. . . .
>
> These [types of] discoveries are the basis of modern technological civilization. But they do not . . . tell us anything about . . . the language which nature itself uses, . . . [about] the Book of Nature.[45]

Thus, Galileo had no special philosophical, transcendental method for seeing nature as it really is. Rather, he "just lucked out," because Galileo's terminology was the *only* "secret" he had.

Nature versus culture have comprised two contrasting ways in which psychology and the other social sciences have been conceptualized.[46] Typically, the debate between mainstream versus hermeneutic social scientists has been construed by both groups as a dispute about what "really" constitutes the "essence" of the human condition—is it nature (e.g., "goal-oriented behavior") or culture (e.g., the "lived experience")?

In response, Rorty continues his pragmatic line of reasoning by showing that "natural science" and "human science" are simply two different vocabularies for dealing with the same human behavior. Neither can be shown to be a better statement of the "true" nature of that behavior. Rather, these different vocabularies have to be judged by how well they act as "instruments for coping with things rather than representations of their intrinsic natures."[47] The first of these vocabularies is particularly suited to prediction and control in human affairs (e.g., for deciding the best tax incentives for encouraging job-producing capital investment), and the second, to enhancing the ability of citizens to sympathize and associate with one another (e.g., for altering the culture by encouraging more openness and tolerance toward others who are different in race, ethnicity, gender, or sexual preference).

In sum, positivist explanation and hermeneutic understanding are simply alternative ways of doing social science, each with their own set of pragmatic strengths and weaknesses, just as microscopic and macroscopic descriptions of organisms are alternative ways of doing biology. While a biochemical perspective on cows is the most helpful in dealing with the diseases they acquire, a macroscopic perspective is the one you choose in getting the cows to move from the field to the barn for milking. Likewise, "If you want to know why a square peg doesn't fit into a round hole you had better *not* describe the peg in terms of the positions of its constituent elementary particles."[48]

Thus Rorty argues that there are only different interpretive perspectives on our experience, and it is not useful to hold on to "traditional notions of rationality, objectivity, method, and truth."[49] Rather, we will be more effective in grappling with the challenges of contemporary social life if we agree that rationality is what history and society make it—that there is no over-arching ahistorical structure (the nature of Man, the laws of human behavior, the Moral Law, the Nature of Society) to be discovered. . . . [We must abandon the notion that] there lies something (God, Science, Knowledge, Rationality, or Truth) which will, if only we perform the correct rituals, step in to save us.[50]

To summarize the arguments of Rorty (and also those of his post-positivist contemporaries Kuhn, Quine, and Wittgenstein, reviewed above,[51] which Rorty builds upon), it is as if we are always viewing the world through some pair of glasses with their own specific characteristics—be they blue, red, green, magnifying, distancing, or elongating—that is, with some specific perspective involving a particular "paradigm" or "web of belief." It is never possible to take off the glasses altogether and view the world as it "really is," that is, to view the world with pure objectivity. All we can do is change glasses and realize that different pairs of glasses provide different pictures of the world. It is true that there are aspects of the outside world—Rorty's "brute physical resistance," or James's "external flux"—which impinge upon us. Yet this unstructured input is not coherent and expressible in language or concepts; in other words, it has no expressible meaning per se. Rather, categories, words, attitudes, frameworks, paradigms, context, and so forth have to be imposed upon it to give it meaning. These are in turn mediated by the nature of any observer's particular set of glasses, which include variables such as the observer's "personal," "private" beliefs; the characteristics of the observer's language; the input the observer receives from social interaction with others; the historical and cultural context in which the observer is embedded; and motivations the observer has with respect to what is being observed (that is, the observer's "emotional bias" to "see what he or she wants to see").[52] Which glasses we should use in an individual situation depends not upon which pair purports to best correspond to the "real" external world, but rather which is best pragmatically, that is, which pair is most useful in meeting our particular, practical goals in that situation. It follows that if two different groups have different interests in a certain situation, each might justifiably be led to choose different glasses with which to view the situation.

This idea, that we are always looking at the world through a particular pair of "glasses" that creates a particular perspective, is the philosophical position of "perspectivism." Rorty[53] also calls this position "anti-foundationalism," highlighting the point that pragmatism sees no single, "underlying" foundational perspective that has a unique claim to the truth in comparison with other, competing perspectives.

"Pragmatic Relativism." Rorty argues that "anything goes" relativism does not necessarily follow from perspectivism. An alternative and more useful conception of relativism is one that can be termed "pragmatic relativism," so-called because it is the belief of philosophical pragmatists. This is the view that

> there is nothing to be said about either truth or rationality apart from description of the familiar procedures of justification which a given society— *ours*—uses in one or another area of inquiry. . . . We should drop the traditional distinction between knowledge and opinion, construed as the distinction between truth as correspondence to reality and truth as a commendatory term for well-justified beliefs. . . . [In other words], there is nothing to be said about the truth save that each of us will commend as true beliefs those which he or she finds good to believe.[54]
>
> To say that what is rational for us now to believe may not be *true*, is simply to say that somebody may come up with a better idea. It is to say that there is always room for improved belief, since new evidence, or new hypotheses, or a whole new vocabulary may come along.[55]

This conception of relativism is called "pragmatic" because it holds that while in an ultimate or foundational sense there is no single objective truth, within the context of a particular society at a particular time certain statements and the justification that backs them are judged as better in the sense that they are more relevant to promoting the solidarity and goals of some particular social group, be that a local community, a region of the country, our whole society, or the total global community. Rorty puts it this way:

> Pragmatists . . . view truth as, in William James' phrase, what it is good for *us* to believe. . . . For pragmatists, the desire for objectivity is not the desire to escape the limitations of one's community [to find a "higher, transcendent" truth], but simply the desire for as much intersubjective agreement as possible, the desire to extend the reference of "us" as far as we can. Insofar as pragmatists make a distinction between knowledge and

opinion, it is simply the distinction between topics on which such agreement is relatively easy to get and topics on which agreement is relatively hard to get.[56]

Thus pragmatism emphasizes that the "truth" of a conception consists in the extent to which it is helpful in meeting human needs and drawing people together in solidarity and community, not in the extent to which it corresponds to a foundational reality. In traditional philosophical terms, then, Rorty points out that the value of cooperative human truth seeking has "only an ethical base, not an epistemological or metaphysical one."[57]

Because pragmatism denies any objective foundation in "human nature" for morality, pragmatists have been accused of unleashing a kind of "ethical relativism," wherein everyone can act in their own selfish interest without any rational way of restraining themselves. In his book *Contingency, Irony, and Solidarity*,[58] Rorty answers this accusation. He begins by asking, "Why is it in one's interest to be just?" He responds by pointing out that implied in this concern is the assumption that at the "deepest" level of the self there is no sense of human solidarity, that this sense is a "mere" artifact of human socialization.[59] Yet this is making the "realist" error of believing that there is an objective basis for seeing "things as they really are," that it can be determined that "fundamental" human nature is to be selfish, not communal. Rorty responds that "socialization, and thus historical circumstance, goes all the way down." There is nothing "beneath" socialization or prior history that defines human nature. The question "What is it to be a human being?" should thus be replaced by questions like "What is it to inhabit a rich twentieth-century democratic society?" and "How can an inhabitant of such a society be more than the enactor of a role in a previously written script?"[60]

Stephen Toulmin's "Back to the Future": The Return to Renaissance Values

In his book *Cosmopolis: The Hidden Agenda of Modernity*,[61] the philosopher Stephen Toulmin identifies two opposing worldviews in classical Greek culture and philosophy. One, represented in the writings of Aristotle, is humanistic pragmatism. It is concerned in dealing with practical concerns in the here and now of particular flesh and blood people, with themes of complexity, ambiguity, pluralism, skepticism, contextualism, and practical problem solving. The other worldview, represented in the writings of Plato, is rational formalism. It is concerned with the search for objective, abstract, foundational, rational knowledge, with themes of certainty, clarity, and universalism.

Toulmin's two worldviews parallel the pendulum swings of which Altman speaks.[62] Toulmin's formalist worldview is associated with convergent, unifying forces (such as the universal laws of objectivist, "basic" science), and his pragmatic view is associated with divergent, pluralistic forces (such as those of case studies and contextually delimited "applied" science). When considering similar time periods, Toulmin and Altman agree on their characterization; for example, both view the 1920–1960 period as particularly resonant to modern formalism, and the period since 1960, to postmodern pragmatism.

In a combined historical and philosophical analysis of the time since classical Greece, Toulmin discusses how the Middle Ages were dominated by rejection of both Aristotle's and Plato's worldviews in favor of a theological worldview based on faith (versus rationality) and a focus on the afterlife (as opposed to the world in which we live). This was then followed by thinkers during the Renaissance (such as Erasmus, Rabelais, Shakespeare, and Montaigne) who developed a humanistic, Aristotelian pragmatism, exploring a wide variety of subjects in the sciences and humanities in a highly interrelated and practically oriented manner.

Toulmin describes the traditional, "received" historical view, dominant in the 1920s and '30s, that the Renaissance was in fact a transitional period between the medieval and modern periods. In this view, the early scientific thinking of the Renaissance "blossomed" into the work of thinkers like Galileo and Newton, who provided both the philosophical underpinnings and powerful theoretical models of how the scientific method could lead to foundational knowledge in both the physical and social worlds. This resulted in a "natural" progression from humanistic pragmatism to the formal rationalism of the modern period, a progression that was facilitated by the increasing material comfort and rationality of everyday life brought by continuing scientific and technological development.

In the major portion of his book, Toulmin argues with extensive and persuasive scholarly support against this "received" view of the Renaissance and modernism. He claims that the Enlightenment went off in the direction of formal rationalism because of intense conflict between European Protestants and Catholics, reflected in the religious wars of the seventeenth century and the resultant exaggerated need for rational "certainty." In line with Bernstein, Toulmin sees this need for certainty as grounded in the very influential writings of Descartes. Toulmin argues that the death and funeral of the tolerant, pluralistic King Henri and the ensuing Thirty Years' War (1618–1648) between the Catholics and Protestants created in Descartes, as a representative of his cultural milieu, a profound emotional need to seek rational certainty as an antidote to the theological, political, and economic turmoil and disaster in the world around him.

In Toulmin's view, Descartes' "Quest for Certainty" reflected and articulated the central preoccupation of intellectuals in the seventeenth century, a time that was the exact opposite of the "received" view of modernism: that is, the exact opposite of being economically prosperous, secularly dominated, constructively organized around political movements toward nation-states, and comfortably committed to rational science.[63] In short, the Quest for Certainty of modernism is not a discovery of the true nature of the world, but rather "a by-product of a special occasion: the political and economic breakdown in the political order of early modern Europe, and a concurrent breakdown in the accepted order of nature."[64]

Toulmin then turns to the origins of the "received" view of the 1920s and 30s, which is so at variance with his own revisionist view. He looks at this question "historiographically," that is, in terms of "how the views of the 17th century are influenced by the historical mirrors we use to view it."[65] His analysis concludes that the "distortions" of 1920s and '30s historians resulted because these times strongly paralleled the crises of belief about society and nature in the early 1600s. For example,

> In the 1930s as in the 1630s, the traditional system of European states was in dispute: the dismemberment of the Habsburg Empire redrew the entire map of Central and Eastern Europe, while the economic ruin of Germany opened it up to the demagoguery of Adolph Hitler. . . . [Also,] the scientific work of Albert Einstein [relativity theory] and Werner Heisenberg [the "uncertainty principle"] undermined all the earlier certainties, even the public intelligibility, of [a previously Newtonian] physics.[66]

In context of the above, Toulmin discusses the development of logical positivism, which was created by the Vienna Circle in the 1920s and elaborated and popularized by Ayer in the 1930s.[67] Toulmin views logical positivism's development as a formalistic reaction to the uncertainty and turbulence of the postwar 1920s and the depression-ridden 1930s. Certainly, the Vienna Circle's chief preoccupation with "reviving 'exactitude' and building a 'unified science' around a core from mathematical logic" is consistent with a "nostalgia for the certainties of the 17th century."[68]

In relation to this main theme, Toulmin analyzes and critiques the formal rationalism of modernism for having lost the humanistic vision of the Renaissance. He ends by arguing that postmodernism offers an opportunity to return to the humanistic pragmatism of the Renaissance. Thus his pragmatism helps to link our present concerns to the time before the modern European human project was diverted into the ultimately unproductive path of formal rationalism.

Toulmin identifies four contrasting themes between knowledge in humanistic pragmatism and formal rationalism, themes that have been present in the dialectic between these two worldviews since Aristotle and Plato. These contrasts continue to be most helpful in differentiating the pragmatic and positivist paradigms of psychology, respectively.

The Oral versus the Written. This distinction contrasts a focus on oral communication, which emphasizes dialogue, rhetoric, and Wittgenstein's "language games," with a focus on written language, which emphasizes the soundness or validity of "arguments" as referring not to public interactions with particular audiences, but to written chains of statements whose validity rests on their internal relations. The contrast is thus between *argumentation* among particular people in specific situations dealing with concrete cases, and general *proofs* that are written and judged as such.[69]

The Particular versus the Universal. This distinction contrasts a focus on case analyses, such as takes place in Anglo-American common case law and in medicine, with a focus on the timeless and universal principles that are purported to underlie such abstract concepts as God, freedom, justice, goodness, and mind. For example, in moral philosophy, the contrast is between the careful examination of "particular practical cases" versus the search for "comprehensive general principles of ethical theory."[70]

The Local versus the General. This distinction contrasts a focus on such disciplines as ethnography, geography, and history, which look at knowledge in the particular local context, with a focus on disciplines like mathematics, the "pure" sciences, and modern epistemology, which seek out abstract, general ideas and principles by which particulars can be connected together. In short, this is a contrast between a focus on "concrete diversity" and universal "abstract axioms."[71]

The Timely versus the Timeless. Finally, this distinction contrasts a focus on practical matters that occur in relation to a particular time, with a focus on abstract principles that hold across all time. For example, all problems in the practice of law and medicine are "timely." In these cases, "time is of the essence," and they are decided "as the occasion requires." A navigator's decision to change course 10 degrees to starboard can be as rational as the steps in mathematical deduction; yet the rationality of this decision rests not only on formal computations, but also on the temporal context in which it is decided. The navigator's calculations may have been performed perfectly, but, if the resulting action is done at the wrong time, the decision will become "irrational."

In contrast, problems in "basic" science and philosophy focus on permanent structures underlying all the changeable phenomena of nature, "on timeless principles that hold good at all times equally."[72]

A Balinese Cockfight and Schizophrenia

Table 4.1 summarized three different epistemological paradigms in psychology that emerge from the historical and philosophical analysis. Chapter 7 will present a detailed, technical elaboration of the methodological differences among these three paradigms when they are applied to conducting psychological research, with a special focus on the characteristics of the pragmatic paradigm. As a bridge between these two sections, two examples of hermeneutically oriented research and ways in which this research contrasts with positivist or pragmatic investigation are presented below.

Clifford Geertz's Excellent Adventure

Deemphasizing formal and systematic quantitative study, hermeneutic research emphasizes qualitative analysis and interpretation of current social and cultural "constructions" and written cultural documents, spelling out ethical and conceptual implications of present constructions or alternatives to them. The typical article describing this research reads more like an interpretive essay on philosophical, esthetic, or moral issues than a "scientific" study.

Hermeneutic research is illustrated by the ethnographic writing of anthropologists, which presents a "thick," narrative description and interpretation of the details of a particular culture. A classic example is Clifford Geertz's essay, "Deep Play: Notes on the Balinese Cockfight."[73] Geertz begins with a description of the entry, by himself and his wife, into the life of a small Balinese village in 1958. In this description, the chronological development of the personal relationship between the Geertzes and the villagers is detailed. At first these Western anthropologists seemed to be ignored completely by the Balinese, but later, after the Geertzes joined the spectators at an illegal cockfight, the villagers became quite friendly and involved collaborators. Geertz writes in the narrative form, resulting in a story that might be titled "The Trials and Tribulations of Contacting Balinese Villagers." The role between the researchers and their "informants" is treated as a personal, interactional one, and not as the traditional detached, unemotional relationship sought for between laboratory researchers and their "subjects."

After describing the development of a personal and social relationship between the villagers and himself and his wife, Geertz turns his attention to the cockfight. In the event, two roosters are fitted with small steel swords and placed in close proximity. What then typically happens is that "the cocks fly almost immediately at one another in a wing-beating, head-thrusting, leg-kicking explosion of animal fury so pure, so absolute, and in its own way so beautiful, as to be almost abstract, a Platonic concept of hate."[74] All this is accompanied by a good deal of ritual in terms of the preparation and handling of the roosters, betting upon the results, and the resulting implications for the relative social status of the handlers and betters. Geertz discusses the symbolic role of the cockfight in Balinese culture: "To anyone who has been in Bali any length of time, the deep psychological identification of Balinese men with their cocks is unmistakable. The double entendre here is deliberate. It works in exactly the same way in Balinese as it does in English, even to producing the same tired jokes, strained puns, and uninventive obscenities."[75]

Balinese men spend an enormous amount of time in grooming and feeding their cocks, in discussing them with one another, and in trying them out against one another.

> In identifying with his cock, the Balinese man is identifying not just with his ideal self, or even his penis, but also, and at the same time, with what he most fears, hates, and ambivalence being what it is, is fascinated by— "The Powers of Darkness." The connection of cocks and cockfighting with such Powers, with the animalistic demons that threaten constantly to invade the small, cleared-off space in which the Balinese have so carefully built their lives and devour its inhabitants, is quite explicit.[76]

Within the hermeneutic tradition, Geertz concludes that the way to understand the meaning of the cockfight within Balinese culture is as a kind of literary text. Like any art form, the cockfight is "fiction": it has no practical consequences for the people involved; only the roosters are physically harmed and it does not directly alter hierarchical relationships among the human participants.

> What it does is what, for other peoples with other temperaments and other conventions, *Lear* and *Crime and Punishment* do; it catches up these themes—death, masculinity, rage, pride, loss, beneficence, chance—and, ordering them into an encompassing structure, presents them in such a way as to throw into relief a particular view of their essential nature. It puts a construction on them, makes them, to those historically positioned to appreciate the construction, meaningful—visible, tangible, graspable— "real."[77]

As reflected in the style of the above quotes and the substance of Geertz's point of view, the hermeneutic approach to anthropology values literary, narrative style, with its emphasis on language that is dramatic, emotionally laden, subjective, and symbolically suggestive. Human agency and the search for expressing artistically life's larger meaning are highlighted over more sociobiologically connected, functional goals. The concerns of natural science and the positivist paradigm—quantification, demonstrating the objectivity of the observer, operationally defined measures, writing in explicit, formal, abstract, "propositional" terms—are diametrically opposite to Geertz's whole approach. Certainly one of Geertz's aims in the style and content of the essay is to attack the positivist paradigm.

In addition, the focus of the pragmatic paradigm—in defining a social problem to be solved and mounting and evaluating a resulting remedial program—is missing. Geertz's goal is not to account for Balinese behavior by means of a formal theory that can predict or control this behavior. Nor is his goal to reduce problems in Balinese society. Rather, his goal is to appreciate the meaning of established institutions within this culture: to appreciate what is, not to change it. His focus is upon existentially and humanistically "understanding" social behavior, not upon scientifically "explaining" it or pragmatically improving it.

The difference between the hermeneutic and pragmatic paradigms is also highlighted in Geertz's focus on general truths—or dimensions of human existence and society. He uses the example of the Balinese cockfight to talk about universal themes across cultures, about the need to seek meaning dealing with basic human themes such as sexuality, violence, and social status, and to express this meaning in artistic forms. The pragmatist, on the other hand, focuses upon addressing social problems within particular sociopolitical, cultural, and historical contexts, and is not oriented toward the exploration of these general themes.

Louis Sass's *Madness and Modernism*

The differences among the positivist, pragmatic, and hermeneutic paradigms can be illustrated by considering *Madness and Modernism: Insanity in the Light of Modern Art, Literature, and Thought,* a book by the hermeneutically oriented psychologist Louis Sass.[78] In *Madness and Modernism,* Sass describes and analyzes the experiential world of schizophrenics. In dramatic fashion, he shows striking similarities between this world and the experienced world as represented in such post-World War I "high modernist" writers and artists as Eliot, Pound, Virginia Woolf, Valéry, Rilke, Kafka, Picasso, and Matisse, and by such "postmodernist" writers, artists, and composers as Jorge Luis Borges, Thomas Pynchon, Donald Barthelme, Robert Rauschenberg, Jasper Johns, Andy Warhol, and John Cage.[79] The worlds of the schizophrenics and the works of art, music, and literature both reflect such themes as self-referentiality, profound relativism and uncertainty, extreme irony, and tendencies toward fragmentation.

In line with the ontological version of the hermeneutic paradigm, Sass focuses on describing and understanding the similarities between the forms of experience and expression that are characteristic of schizophrenics and of certain modern artistic and cultural movements. He uses these affinities to dispute traditional views of schizophrenia as a form of dementia or regression to infantile forms of consciousness, and to argue instead that schizophrenia is characterized by various forms of exaggerated self-consciousness and by alienation from the body, emotions, and the social world. Sass's interest in these topics differs from what one would expect from a critical hermeneuticist, a positivist, or a pragmatist.

For a writer in the critical-theory camp of the hermeneutic paradigm, the focus would likely be upon the cultural implications of the similarities between schizophrenic experience and art that reflects postmodernist sensibilities. These implications might well suggest that contemporary cultural trends—such as the constant media bombardment of culturally dissonant images and ideas, media commentary upon commentary upon commentary, the emphasis upon diversity and multiculturalism, and the breakdown of physical social communities into "virtual," electronic communities[80]—are literally "driving us crazy." In other words, these trends are pushing us to experience the world in a schizophrenic-like manner, in which a commitment to consistent values and a predictable everyday world of concrete experience is lacking. Critical theory might also relate these trends to the "commodification" of culture due to pervasive capitalism. Consider, for example, the constant punctuation of the hodgepodge of media images of make-believe, real-life tragedy, "docudrama," and so forth by "commercials." Or, remember the earlier quote from Cushman's work, which views the present "self" in contemporary, postmodern culture to be "empty," with a need to be "soothed and made cohesive by becoming 'filled up' with food, consumer products, and celebrities."[81] Thus, a critical theorist might well take Sass's thesis—that there are striking descriptive similarities between the phenomenology of schizophrenia and postmodern literature, music, and art—and use it as a rallying cry for attacking the exploitive, manipulative, alienating, and dehumanizing forces within contemporary industrialized, capitalistic countries.

In contrast, the positivist paradigm has traditionally focused on the kinds of schizophrenic experiences that Sass describes as reflecting "symptoms" of a breakdown of normal, "natural," "healthy" mental functioning. This paradigm has then proceeded to find out what nonphenomenological, "disease-like" factors "cause" these phenomenological symptoms, in the sense that gravity "causes" ocean tides. A variety of such factors have been proposed and investigated, such as problems in genetics, biochemistry, neurology, learning, information processing, affect regulation, or socialization.

Finally, the pragmatic paradigm starts out with the question of whether society views schizophrenic experience as a problem. In present-day industrialized societies, schizophrenia *is* seen as a problem. It is viewed as causing distress and unhappiness in schizophrenics themselves and in their families, and as causing economic losses because schizophrenics are not able to care for themselves or to be productive workers in the economy. Within society (or at least in significant stakeholder groups in society) there is a political consensus about the benefit of achieving certain goals vis-à-vis schizophrenics, namely, increasing their "functional" behavioral patterns. Such functional patterns include self-care and the ability to carry out other "activities of daily living" (such as personal money budgeting and taking public transportation); engagement in nonconflict-causing and nonharmful social relationships (rather than hostility and paranoia); decreased "crazy talk" about bizarre beliefs and experiences; and decreased agitation and anxiety. This consensus having been reached, practitioners of the pragmatic paradigm then try to develop and document the effectiveness of particular intervention programs for reaching these goals.

While positivists share many of these goals, they assume that the goals will be achieved by first finding the "causes" of the dysfunctional behaviors, and then designing intervention programs based upon these "causes."

Pragmatists, on the other hand, begin by focusing on individual cases and developing individually tailored intervention programs based upon holistic, systems-oriented theories of change. These can include components such as psychopharmacology, cognitive therapy, training in social skills and activities of daily living, job training, and family therapy).[82] The results of each case are then evaluated and described in the organizational context in which it took place. This documentation is next entered into a cumulative database of more and less successful cases. Subsequent program developers can then go to this database for ideas about how to adapt previously successful programs to their particular contexts. Also, scholars and researchers can systematically compare and contrast better and worse cases to try and derive general pragmatic principles (not "causal," "scientific" principles) to aid in policy formation and the design of individual, new programs. The pragmatist is not directly interested in the "schizophrenic-like" nature of postmodern literature, art, and music, as is a hermeneutic theorist like Sass. If society approves of these art forms and does not view them as reflecting dysfunctional behavior, the pragmatist does not join into cultural dialogue about them, as does Sass in his role as an ontological hermeneuticist, or as might Cushman in his role as a critical hermeneuticist.

On to the Case Study Method

The contrast between modern positivism and postmodern pragmatism has radical implications for psychological method, that is, for how we seek and evaluate knowledge for addressing human problems and goals. As a bridge to the next four chapters, which explore these methodological implications in detail, it is important to tie together the arguments of the pragmatic thinkers just reviewed and to link them directly to the case study method.

Philosophical pragmatism is founded upon a social constructionist theory of knowledge. The world that exists independently of our minds is an unlimited complex of change and novelty, order and disorder. To understand and cope with the world, we take on different conceptual perspectives, as we might put on different pairs of glasses, with each providing us a different perspective on the world. The pragmatic "truth" of a particular perspective does not lie in its correspondence to "objective reality," since that reality is continuously in flux. Rather, the pragmatic truth of a particular perspective lies in the usefulness of the perspective in helping us to cope and solve particular problems and achieve particular goals in today's world.

How are these problems and goals to be selected, defined, articulated, and addressed? The social constructionist epistemology of postmodernism tells us that human problems and goals are not "given" by the natural world. Instead, these problems and goals represent the purposes, intentions, desires, interests, and values of individuals and groups, who, Pitkin and Shumer remind us, will almost always manifest differences and conflicts. While in many societies, both present and past, these conflicts have been dealt with in dictatorial and militaristic ways, in most industrialized Western countries there is a political and moral consensus that these problems and goals should be articulated and chosen through dialogue and democratically negotiated agreement among the local individuals, groups, and communities who are stakeholders in the particular problems and goals involved. While the positivist search to discover general "laws of nature" is thus doomed, the process of natural science inquiry—which encourages disciplined openness to new experiences and empirical data—is one of the best techniques for deriving pragmatically useful knowledge.

Like other postmodern views, pragmatism is open to the accusation of "anything goes" relativism, that is, to the undermining of any standards for deciding what is true or false, good or bad. This accusation is challenged by Rorty's concept of "pragmatic relativism," which, while denying transhistorical and cross-cultural "foundational" standards, points to the already established and agreed-upon procedures and standards our society now has for determining truth and morality in particular contexts. Examples are the procedures and standards used to elect government officials democratically, to settle civil and criminal disputes in our court system, to conduct academic scholarship in our universities, to carry out investigative journalism, and to describe social behavior "objectively" in quantitative surveys like the U.S. Census, using the statistical methods derived from natural science.

Following Toulmin, we can see that pragmatism focuses on case studies that address particular practical problems in local and time-specific contexts rather than on the abstract, universal, quantitative knowledge of timeless principles and laws. Thus, pragmatic knowledge is more resonant with ethnography, geography, ecology, and history than with the models for positivism: mathematics, physics, and chemistry.

Another crucial theme pervasively underlying the work of pragmatic philosophers is a concern with morality and the striving toward humanistic goals. Throughout his life, John Dewey was a passionate advocate of participatory democracy and the right of each individual to have the opportunity, through proper education, of full self-development. Cornel West sees the appeal of American pragmatism in its "unashamedly moral emphasis" and its unequivocal desire to improve society "in this world-weary period of pervasive cynicisms, nihilisms, terrorisms, and possible extermination." Richard Bernstein argues that we need to go "beyond" objectivism and relativism to productive dialogue so that we can build communities with shared understandings and experiences, shared social practices, and an emotional sense of affinity and cooperation. Richard Rorty focuses on the question, "Why is it in one's interest to be just?" He maintains that socialization, and thus historical circumstance, go "all the way down." In this light, he argues that selfishness is no more a "given" than solidarity, and that there are good reasons to assume that creating the right conditions of socialization and culture can nurture solidarity.

The pragmatic case study method, described and illustrated in the next four chapters, is grounded in pragmatism's primacy of moral concerns. The primary goal of research is not knowledge for its own sake, but to improve the lives of particular individuals, groups, communities, and societies within specific historical and cultural contexts. It is for this reason that, while a positivist psychological project starts with a general theory to be confirmed, a pragmatic psychological project starts with a specific practical problem to be solved. In Stephen Toulmin's framing, the pragmatist identifies with the model of Renaissance humanism and its intellectual virtues of contextuality, modesty, skepticism, toleration, and local, case-based efforts at practical problem solving. In this spirit, Toulmin calls for the redirection of Enlightenment-inspired, modernistic science away from "pure" theory and "pure" technology and toward application to humanistically relevant goals.

PART III

Method

I begin this section, in chapter 6, by translating the philosophical arguments for the pragmatic case study into a methodological framework for this type of research. The pragmatic case study always takes place in the context of a particular human service program intended to address psychological and social pathologies—be it an individual psychotherapy case, a Head Start school, or a large-scale "workfare" program. Written case studies are designed to help program developers, managers, and direct-service personnel apply the lessons of these studies to other, similar cases for enhancing effectiveness. I also spell out the links between the pragmatic case study method and two other, closely interrelated, applied research traditions in psychology: program evaluation and community psychology. Both of these provide important ideas and methods for fleshing out the pragmatic case study paradigm.

Chapter 7 next delves into the nuts and bolts of conducting a rigorous, pragmatic case study. To reveal the structure of such a case study, I begin with the bread-and-butter of the positivist paradigm, the experimental group study, which is conventionally documented in four sections: introduction, method, results, and discussion. I then systematically compare the pragmatist case study method with the positivist and the hermeneutic research study models in terms of these four categories. This demonstrates the variety of ways in which the pragmatic paradigm incorporates and builds upon elements from each of the other two, thus functioning as an integrating force in the discipline. I conclude the chapter by discussing a crucial component of the pragmatic case study method: the grouping of single cases of successful programs into databases. These databases provide a vehicle for matching the contexts of particular past cases to the contexts of cases for which planning is needed—either new cases, or ongoing cases with unsuccessful results. In this way, guidelines from relevant, successful cases can empirically generalize to promote better outcomes in new settings.

6

The Pragmatic Case Study
Psychology's Tool for Enhancing Human Services

Addressing Psychosocial Problems

Today's psychological and social problems press upon us: stress-related anxiety, alcoholism, and antisocial behavior in individuals; child abuse and father absence in families; poor communication, lack of cooperation, and racial tension within business teams; low student achievement test scores, administrative inefficiency, and poor teacher morale in schools; and unemployment, drug abuse, crime, and violence in inner-city communities. Human service programs have been created to address these and a whole spectrum of other troubles. The programs are planned intervention responses designed to reverse the human dysfunctions, environmental deficits, and environmental disincentives that are viewed as underlying the problems.[1]

Rather than the problem-focused, "deficit" language just used, these same ideas can be reframed in positive, "goal-attainment" terms, by saying something like this:

> There are needs in society to help individuals to become upbeat in their affect and good citizens in their conduct; two-parent families to stay together; business teams to achieve effective communication and multicultural collaboration; schools to create high academic performance, administrative efficiency, and high teacher morale; and communities to generate high employment, low drug use, and security and calm. Human service programs have been created to achieve these and many other types of societal goals. The programs are planned intervention responses designed to help create the human skills, environmental supports, and environmental incentives viewed as essential in attaining these goals.

The logical parallel between problem deficit and goal-attainment language results because a problem can be defined as a discrepancy between a present state and a desired state of affairs. The deficit language points to the discrepancy, while the goal-attainment language points to the desired state.[2] (Throughout this book, both the deficit and the goal-attainment frameworks are used.)

Programs to address the above illustrative problems might include psychotherapy for alcoholic individuals; the creation of positive contact for "bonding" between unmarried fathers and their infants right after birth; communication training, sensitivity training, and team building for working groups in organizations; decentralization of decision making in schools; and the creation of anti-drug interventions in inner-city communities.

A psychological inquiry in the pragmatic paradigm is designed to provide practical support for these programs. More specifically, the major purpose of psychological inquiry in the pragmatic paradigm is to aid in the planning, development, implementation, evaluation, and documentation of the individual human service case settings, frequently called "projects," which comprise programs.[3] Typically, pragmatic psychological research involves creating or identifying outstanding "model" projects, investigating and documenting them, and comparing them with "less effective" projects.

Figures I.1 and I.2[4] demonstrated the dramatic differences in how positivist ("applied science") and pragmatic ("disciplined inquiry") approaches develop and run human service projects—be they psychotherapy cases or large social service programs.[5] The positivist approach begins by searching for general, objectively discovered laws of human behavior ("basic science"). These are then studied in natural problem settings ("applied research") to develop technologies that can be packaged into human service programs to help individual clients. There are no feedback loops from the individual case back to the basic science because in the positivist model, individual cases are viewed as idiosyncratic and too contextually specific—only results across groups of individual cases are taken seriously.

Rather than ending with the concerns of the individual client, the pragmatic paradigm *begins* with a particular client presenting with specific problems and goals. Previous theory and research, together with the individual practitioner or practitioner team's professional case experience and conceptual framework (what Peterson calls their "guiding conception") are then mobilized to understand the client's difficulties and aims, and in light of this, to develop an action plan for directly helping the client. Results of implementing the plan are then fed back into the ongoing service process and have an impact on all aspects of the program's functioning. Following from the importance of contextual specificity in constructionist philosophy, a crucial aspect of the pragmatically oriented case study is its emphasis upon holistically assessing and analyzing all the individual components identified in figure 1.2 and the interrelations among these components.

The written case studies emerging from pragmatic projects are intended to provide program developers and managers with templates and guidelines to inform their own guiding conceptions, knowledge bases, and methods for addressing the problems of their clients. In addition, such written case studies provide researchers a database from which to ascertain inductively empirical and theoretical generalizations for enhancing program technology and in turn for guiding policymakers.

Thus, the pragmatic case study in psychology focuses on the design, operation, and impact of projects upon the individuals who provide and receive services within them. Following from the pragmatic emphasis on undertaking programs in order to help particular persons and systems rather than developing theories per se, and in line with the case study literature, the unit of analysis in a pragmatic case study consists of the specific, concrete persons who are impacted by a project within their naturalistic, holistic context. It does not consist of some abstract entity, like a process, a principle, a theory, or an idea.[6] In Peterson's words, the pragmatic case study

> begins and ends in the condition of the client. Whether the client is an individual, a group, or an organization, the responsibility of the practitioner is to help improve the client's functional effectiveness. The practitioner does not choose the issue to examine: the client does. . . . Each problem must be addressed as it occurs in nature, as an open, living process in all its complexity, often in a political context that requires certain forms of actions and prohibits others. All functionally important influences on the process under study must be considered.[7]

Measuring the Bottom Line: Program Evaluation

The principles and methods of the pragmatic case study build upon those from other research traditions. These traditions thus link to and provide concepts and procedures for conducting a pragmatic case study. One of these traditions, discussed in the Introduction and outlined in figure 1.2, is Schön, Polkinghorne, and Peterson's "reflective" model of practice within the context of "disciplined inquiry." In a case study in this tradition, the psychological practitioner or practitioner team describes, analyzes, and interprets the various steps they employ in developing, providing, and evaluating a service program. For example, a clinical psychologist can describe the conduct of therapy with a depressed individual or a dysfunctional family; or a team of organizational psychologists can describe their provision of consultation on changing a corporate culture to place a higher value on product quality.

Two other research traditions—program evaluation and community psychology—are closely connected with the pragmatic case study, and it is to these connections that we now turn.

Program evaluation is an interdisciplinary, applied social science field in which psychologists have played a major role in development and leadership.[8] The typical program evaluation project is a case study, focusing on a particular human services program. In a typical program evaluation study, the researcher stands outside the services, assessing the program but not participating in its intervention activities.[9]

Program evaluation emerged as a coherent field during the 1950s and 1960s from a mixture of positivist social science research, data-based management, and policy formation developed within real-world political contexts.[10] Program evaluation was thus born of a marriage between the positivist and pragmatic paradigms. With such a combination of parents, many observers expected program evaluation research to be embraced eagerly by an information-consuming, science-valuing, and technologically oriented society seeking to make better, more rational decisions and to improve human service programs and organizations emerging from the Great Society of the 1960s. The initial optimism helped stimulate the government to sponsor social program evaluation, whose support went from $17 million in 1969 to about $180 million in 1980.[11]

In line with the initial high expectations for the field, in 1969 Donald Campbell wrote a very influential paper, "Reforms as Experiments." He argued that policy and program decisions should be rooted in positivist experimentation rather than political advocacy. The community and nation, if not the world, should be seen as a laboratory for social experimentation. Statistical comparisons would be made between groups of individuals assigned to social programs that differed systematically. The groups would be composed of randomly assigned individuals in a true experimental design, or groups matched on a variety of background variables in a "quasi-experimental" design. The results of such studies would determine which programs survived, and in this way Campbell envisioned the nation becoming an "experimenting society".

However, by the early and mid-1970s, experts began to agree that the results of the "great evaluation experiment" were very disappointing.[12] During the middle and late 1970s, the positivist paradigm dominating program evaluation up to that time began to be identified as a major cause of the disappointing impact of program evaluation studies. Neigher and Fishman[13] argued that the initial utilization failure in program evaluation was due to an overdependence on theory-testing as compared with a more contextually, pragmatically, and technologically based paradigm. Cronbach and his associates set forth similar arguments, pointing out that until that time, "highly controlled summative studies" (like those proposed by Campbell) had been regarded as the ideal type of evaluation. They concluded that there was then emerging "full recognition that politics and science are both integral aspects of evaluation."[14]

In response to the utilization failures in program evaluation projects, investigators and conceptualizers in the field were stimulated to import into program evaluation more concepts and methods from the pragmatic and hermeneutic paradigms.[15] From the former came a priority on (a) studying the nature of the conceptual, managerial and political contexts of program planning and decision making; (b) linking a program evaluation plan to these contexts; and (c) developing new models of program evaluation that attempt to link data with decision making more explicitly and pragmatically.[16] From the hermeneutic paradigm came the importance of qualitative, ethnographic, and case study research methods.[17]

Over time, the program evaluation field has come to encompass all the components of a human service program as outlined in figure 1.2. This is reflected in Rossi and Freeman's comprehensive definition of the field in their well-known textbook: "Evaluation research involves the use of social research methodologies to judge and to improve the planning, monitoring, effectiveness, and efficiency of health, education, welfare, and other human service programs."[18]

Greene[19] provides a helpful typology of contrasting themes by different groups of program evaluation practitioners. *Postpositivist evaluation* is typified by the quantitative, experimental, "theory-driven" model of Campbell,[20] Chen and Rossi,[21] and large-scale studies of such Great Society programs as Head Start, with a focus not only on accountability but also on developing a causal theory of program action. *Pragmatic evalu-*

ation is typified by Patton's "utilization-focused evaluation."[22] In this model, evaluators pragmatically select their methods—quantitative and qualitative—to match the practical problem in a particular situation, rather than as dictated by some abstract set of principles. The focus is upon describing which parts of a program work well and which need improvement, in the context of the organization's goals.

Greene describes two types of hermeneutic evaluation. *Interpretivist evaluation* is represented in Guba and Lincoln's[23] "fourth generation evaluation." The focus is to enhance qualitative, phenomenologically oriented, contextualized program understanding for stakeholders closest to actual program operations. Second, *critical science [critical theory] evaluation* is exemplified by feminist and neo-Marxist theorists who promote openly ideological forms of inquiry that seek "to illuminate the historical, structural, and value bases of social phenomena and, in doing so, to catalyze political and social change toward greater justice, equity, and democracy."[24]

The "Inside" versus the "Outside" Evaluator

An important issue in the program evaluation field involves trade-offs between an "inside" evaluator, who is an ongoing member of a program, and an "outside" evaluator, who becomes involved with the program for a limited period of time for the sole purpose of a single evaluation of it.[25] For example, as a participant-observer, the inside evaluator generally has the advantage of being more knowledgeable about the detailed context of the program and is more likely to have a sympathetic, richly developed understanding of it. On the other hand, the outside evaluator is likely to have a more varied knowledge base because he or she has involvement with many different programs, not just one. Also, the outside evaluator generally has the advantage of more objectivity. Still again, the outside evaluator's "neutrality" toward the program being evaluated can be replaced with a negative bias based on identification with external interests prejudiced against the program (such as government pressure to save money by defunding the program).

The pragmatic case study researcher recognizes the trade-offs between the insider and outsider roles in a pragmatic case study, and views the importance of integrating both of these perspectives in the design of a project. Thus, the goals of the pragmatic case study are to address all aspects of the evaluation process in a manner that documents (a) the evaluator's role and interests vis-à-vis the case study, (b) the evaluator's capacity to "get inside" the program and show an engaged, proactive understanding of it, (c) the evaluator's capacity and methods for reducing positive or negative bias in the conduct and documentation of the case study, and (d) the evaluator's experience and knowledge from other cases that can be available for comparisons between the present case and those other cases.

Based in the epistemology of constructionism, then, the pragmatic case study recognizes that researchers and practitioners always have preferences, interests, commitments, and ideologies that they bring to any project. The goal is not their elimination but rather their full disclosure, together with the development of information and interpretive methods for either reducing or justifying them. Moreover, from a pragmatic point of view, all knowledge that is created is to be importantly judged by its consequences—for example: Who wins and who loses? How does the new information impact on our psychological, political, and social institutions? and, How does the new information generate new ways for people to understand and relate to one another and better achieve their mutual goals? The answers to these questions are an important component of the pragmatic case study.

Types of Evaluation

The "disciplined inquiry" model outlined in figure 1.2 highlights the importance of the interrelationships among the various components of an applied psychology intervention. Thus, the type of program evaluation that best fits the pragmatic case study is the conception described by Rossi and Freeman's comprehensive definition, mentioned above.

Consistent with the comprehensive approach, Scriven's[26] model lays out the multiple dimensions that program evaluators must consider in conducting a study, and it advocates that they should use multiple approaches to assessing each dimension. Scriven summarizes these in a "Key Evaluation Checklist," emphasizing that an evaluation must be described from a diversity of perspectives, including who is paying for the evaluation, what are the characteristics of the program and the program recipients, by what standards is the program's performance to be assessed, what effects are in fact produced by the program, and what is the cost of the program. The larger the number of different vantage points taken, Scriven believes, the more likely that a "realistic," "truthful," and useful picture will emerge.[27]

Besides comprehensive program evaluation, the field has developed a wide variety of other approaches. Patton has compiled a list of thirty of these.[28] They can be divided into five categories. The first category addresses *input* into planning a program, such as the needs of the clients, the resources required to mount the program, and the extent to which the program deals with the total problem. The second focuses on the *process* of conducting a program, such as the activities involved, whether they meet minimum standards for accreditation and quality, and how the program can be improved ("formative" evaluation). The third concerns the *output* of the program, such as its effect on specific clients, its capacity to meet its original goals, and its unit cost per unit of outcome. The desired outcome can be defined in a variety of ways, from meeting specific, predefined changes in client behavior and behavioral capacity to meeting individually tailored client goals. The fourth category addresses the broader *impact* of the program over time, for example, as reflected in changes in social and economic indicators, and in such issues as whether the program as a whole should be continued ("summative" evaluation). Finally, the fifth category reflects on the process of *program evaluation itself*, addressing such questions as: Is program evaluation feasible in the program as presently structured? Was the program evaluation properly done? and, Was the information emerging from the program evaluation demonstrably helpful to program stakeholders?

Along with Scriven's Key Evaluation Checklist, Patton's list can aid the pragmatic case study designer in reviewing the various facets of a program evaluation and developing a comprehensive plan to interweave many or most of them into any case study project. These efforts help to achieve the holistic picture desired in a pragmatic case study.

Ethical Issues

When program evaluation began, it relied on the positivist epistemology reflected in Peterson's "professional activity as applied science" model (see fig. I.1). Following Campbell's "experimenting society" concept, program evaluators saw themselves as "value neutral" technical experts, setting up social experiments to generate scientific information for use by government and other funders in determining which programs to fund and maintain.

As program evaluators gained field experience in the difference between the "inside" and "outside" evaluator roles, and as postmodern, constructionist ideas challenged the notion of value neutrality, program evaluators became more and more aware of ethical dilemmas raised by their activities.[29]

A crucial theme underlying the work of pragmatic practitioners and pragmatic philosophers is a concern with values, ethics, and morality. For when the possibility of "objectively," "scientifically" arriving at a single, "true" view of reality is rejected on epistemological grounds, the value of any knowledge-seeking project is to be judged on its capacity to achieve independently developed human goals. There is no "knowledge for knowledge's sake." It follows that the pragmatic paradigm of practice does not begin with basic research, but rather starts with the purpose of applied activity, namely to aid a "client" (an individual, group, organization, community, or even a society) and related "stakeholders" (who hold an interest in the client's welfare). The focus is on (a) the client's particular values, interests, purposes, and desires, and (b) the resulting goals for change. Ultimately, it is only relative to these goals that the validity and usefulness of the practitioner's efforts can be evaluated.

Yet two difficulties emerge when trying to define a client's goals. First, *who is the client*? In a narrow sense, one might identify the person or group who directly receives services as the client. But in a broad sense the client includes other stakeholders in a program. For example, who are the stakeholders when a psychotherapist is providing services to an individual client in a "per capita," managed-care plan? A per capita plan is funded by a fixed fee from each person who is covered by the plan. Like other types of health insurance, the fee is based upon the assumption that only a fraction of the plan members will seek therapy. Thus, the plan has to be managed so as to keep funds available for all potential users. While the individual who receives services from the therapist can be viewed as the direct client, there are other important stakeholders in the therapy, including other potential users of the service and the owners of the services (e.g., stockholders for a corporate managed care company, and taxpayers for a government-funded managed care program). It would seem that the interests and goals of these types of stakeholders have to be taken into account when the therapist's performance is evaluated. Yet as more and more stakeholders are included, this accounting becomes increasingly unwieldy.

As another example, consider studying a program involving the implementation of a social problem-solving curriculum for middle-school children.[30] How many of the hundreds or perhaps even thousands of potential stakeholders does the practitioner or program evaluator define as the stakeholders to be formally included in the study? These potential stakeholders can be viewed as including not only the children and their teachers, but also their parents and siblings, school administrators and support staff, school district board members, and even all tax-paying members of the community who don't have children in the school.

Second, once direct clients and other stakeholders are identified, *how are stakeholder goals to be determined?* How does the practitioner or program evaluator deal with conflicts among the interests, purposes, desires, and goals of the different stakeholders? While in many societies, both present and past, such conflicts have been dealt with in dictatorial and militaristic ways, in most industrialized Western countries there is a political and moral consensus that these problems and goals should be articulated and chosen through dialogue and democratically negotiated agreement.[31]

For the pragmatists reviewed in chapter 5, like Bernstein and Rorty, democratic dialogue is the ideal way to decide questions such as who is the client and how can the clients' goals be determined. Moreover, for this dialogue to be most productive, it must be embedded in a community that is built upon shared understandings and experiences, shared social practices, and an emotional sense of affinity and solidarity. Encouraging the development and maintenance of such communities, therefore, is a goal unto itself for the pragmatist.[32] In a broad sense, then, pragmatic practitioners seek, in their programmatic activities, to deal with the issues of identifying clients and their goals in such a way as to promote communities with solidarity and associated democratic dialogue.[33]

To clarify ethical dilemmas, Windle and Neigher[34] have proposed three value-based models of program evaluation for publicly funded social programs. Each has a different overall goal as defined by a particular "key audience." In an "accountability model," the purpose of evaluation is to help high-level policy and decision makers (e.g., the U.S. Congress) and the general public decide on the "bottom line" costs, outcome, and value of a program. In an "amelioration model," the purpose is to aid midlevel program managers and administrators to improve the internal operation of their programs.[35] Finally, in an "advocacy model," the purpose is to help program directors, staff, beneficiaries, their communities, and other "powerless" groups advocate with outside funders for additional resources.

Windle and Neigher discuss the ethical problems inherent in each model. Each approach involves a series of trade-offs, maximizing the values of certain groups in opposition to others. The amelioration model orients to the needs of administrators who want to improve the cost efficiency of a program, but not to the needs of citizens who support a particular program or the high-level decision makers who must decide if a program should be continued, and at what level. The accountability model is the reverse. And the advocacy model blurs the distinction between the goal of evaluating a program in a more "objective" manner and promoting a program in a more "political" manner.

Greene's above-described typology of program evaluation sets forth a commonly held view that each paradigm of program evaluation is primarily associated with one of Windle and Neigher's three models of evaluation. Greene presents "postpositivist" evaluation as focusing on program accountability to *high-level policy and program decision makers* by the use of experiments and quasi-experiments; "pragmatic" evaluation as focusing on program amelioration by the use of descriptive assessments to provide feedback to *midlevel administrators*; and "interpretive" and "critical science" evaluation as focusing on program advocacy by making *program beneficiaries* active participants in the evaluation process through the use of more qualitative, dialogical, and narrative assessment approaches.[36]

In contrast to Greene's narrow view of pragmatism in program evaluation, the scope of the pragmatic case study I am presenting is very broad. The pragmatic case study is driven by its core need to be of practical relevance, and relevance can be defined in different ways depending on the key stakeholders whose interests and values are represented. Thus, the logic and structure of the pragmatic case study must be answerable to all stakeholders—high-level policy and program decision makers, midlevel program managers, and program beneficiaries. Of course, in line with Windle and Neigher's thesis of ethical conflicts between the different models, I am not claiming that a pragmatic case study can address all models and all target audiences simultaneously. In fact, part of the contemporary ethics of program evaluation is to clarify at the beginning who the target audience is and what type of model is being employed.[37] Thus, it is of vital importance in a pragmatic case study to clarify whose values are guiding the study, how those values potentially conflict with the values of other stakeholders, and how the determination of all the relevant values was accomplished.

Collaborating with Clients: Community Psychology

The task of addressing the potentially different and competing values of various stakeholders in a social program has been explored by community psychologists and related community-oriented social scientists.

In the positivist tradition, applied social science researchers have studied disadvantaged communities in a "value neutral" manner, with the goal of developing and testing general sociological, political, and economic theories of the causes of disadvantage—purportedly, to discover general social laws that would provide a scientific basis for rational reform. But in practice, this "scientific inquiry" model has resulted in conflict between the researchers and community activists, who are typically disappointed to find that hypothesis-testing research is of no help to them.[38]

> In the varied topography of professional practice, there is a high hard ground where practitioners can make effective use of research-based theory and technique, and there is a swampy lowland where situations are confusing "messes" incapable of technical solution. The difficulty is that the problems of the high ground, however great their technical interest, are often relatively unimportant to clients and the larger society, while in the swamp are the problems of greatest human concern.[39]

The emergence of the postmodern alternative to positivism contradicted the belief that mainstream social science was value free. Critical theorists like Foucault and Derrida argued the neo-Marxist view that all knowledge-generation is driven by economic, political, and cultural forces, either pitting those in authority against the disadvantaged and disenfranchised, or empowering the latter in their striving toward social dignity, equity, and justice. For example, critical theorists see mainstream, modernistic psychology as a vehicle for maintaining the inequities of the status quo. They contend that it does this by advancing intrapsychic theories to explain away the social inequities to which the poor and disadvantaged are subjected.[40]

Starting in the mid-1960s, this critical theory theme resonated with a growing group of "community psychologists"—disenchanted clinical psychologists who began to realize the role of community dynamics in the support versus the undermining of individuals.[41] Instead of focusing on the psychopathology of the victims of dysfunctional families and communities, they identify their main mission as the study and nurturance of communities, to work toward the *prevention* of mental disorder. This leads them to align their work with the lives, interests, and values of community members and activists. They see their research as flowing from community needs and as designed to have a positive impact on the lives of community members, not just to create theory-building publications. The goal is "citizen participation" in program planning and administration, leading to community "ownership" of a program. In pursuit of this, the community psychologist often becomes a "participant observer," a term taken from anthropology and meaning that the researcher combines systematic observation with participation in the day-to-day life of the communities, organizations, and groups they study.[42]

Illustrating the combination of critical theory and community psychology perspectives, Stringer[43] appeals to human service practitioners—teachers, youth workers, psychotherapists, health workers, social workers, correction officers, school psychologists—who feel burned out by the restrictions and failures of the "scientific" model of modernistic professionalism. Stringer argues that this model has led to the development of centralized policies and programs—generated by research "experts"—who prescribe technical, value-deficient, mechanistic, context-insensitive methods for human service practitioners to apply. To combat burnout and the deleterious effects on needy individuals and communities brought on by the scientific model, Stringer offers the critical postmodern paradigm, which emphasizes the practitioner's creativity in developing collaborative working relationships with clients and a commitment to a variety of progressive values: empowerment, liberation, inclusion, cooperation, equality, human dignity, self-actualization, and the promotion of community. In Stringer's view, then, human service practitioners are burned out because their intrinsic moral passion for helping others has been submerged by modernistic scientific rationality, with its misguided constraints of "rigor" and "objectivity."[44]

In recent years, new, alternative relationships between community researchers and community activists have been developed. These have been embedded within innovative investigatory models, which throughout the research design process recognize the needs, interests, and goals of community members. Sociologist Philip Nyden[45] identifies three of these alternative models:

> [In *advocacy research*], the agenda is set by the [community] client. The role of the research is to help identify and develop this agenda, and to apply

professional expertise to pursue it. However, in case of conflict between the professional judgement of the researcher and the demands of the client, the client must prevail. Advocacy research abandons all claims of neutrality in favor of serving disadvantaged groups. . . .

Action research involves researchers in community projects in order to break through the separation between theory and practice. Change-oriented action is not just the goal of research, but part of its process. Presumably, the action itself uncovers new information about the conditions being studied. . . .

Collaborative research may involve advocacy, and it may involve action. But neither of these are necessary components, and the ultimate subservience of the researcher to the client or community is replaced by an assumption of equality. The researcher needs to be willing to let the community help determine part of the character of the research project, even though the typical "scientific" [positivist] mode of research says that the discipline . . . should determine the shape of research. Research knowledge is not to be used to lord over non-experts; a parallel agenda in collaborative research is the transfer of knowledge, including knowledge of how to complete research, to community organizations.[46]

The pragmatic case study is most closely allied with the collaborative research model. The pragmatic case project designer or researcher does not automatically identify with any particular set of stakeholder goals, as in advocacy research. Moreover, the pragmatic researcher might simply document how a well-functioning program operates, without necessarily taking action, as in action research.

Ideally, the pragmatic researcher establishes values through a three-step collaborative process. First, the values and interests of the various stakeholders in a particular project are set forth. Next, those particular values and goals initially selected for focus by the researcher are outlined, along with a rationale for their selection. To the extent possible, all or most of the stakeholder perspectives are included in the initial selection. Third, these values and goals and their rationale are shared with the various stakeholders, and the final values and goals around which the case study is organized are negotiated with these stakeholders and articulated for all to see. The initial selection and negotiation processes flow from the constructionistic and dialogical notions of postmodernism that see "human beings as cocreating their reality through participation."[47] The specific goal of the whole process results in a mixture of values and goals from the different stakeholder groups, emphasizing the perspectival nature of the project and the validity of each stakeholder group's point of view. A broader goal of the process is to create mutual understanding, networking, collaboration, and partnership among the different stakeholder groups.

For example, in a particular public elementary school, main stakeholders include the state legislators who help to fund the school, the local school board, the teachers, the other school staff, and the students and their families. In documenting this school as a case study in elementary education, the pragmatic researcher can emphasize the values and goals of any of those groups—as long as this is clear and acceptable to all the groups. Moreover, in the case study, the researcher aims to include values from different groups, such as the legislature and school board's typical interest in standardized test scores, and teachers' and the students' typical interest in a stimulating, enthusiasm-generating, "fun" learning environment. While such a learning environment can lead to high test performance, this will not happen if the standardized tests cover material that is impractical or out of context and is based on tedious rote learning. Such a conflict might be resolved through negotiation, in which teachers and students agree to be accountable by standardized tests, and legislators and school board members agree to use tests that tap learning that is practical in content and that engages such competencies as imagination, judgment, and critical thinking in addition to memorization.

"What Works and Why We Have So Little of It"[48]

In *Common Purpose: Strengthening Families and Neighborhoods to Rebuild America*, social analyst Lisbeth Schorr employs pragmatically based concepts to explain the disappointing results of social-science-based programs to address problems like high-risk infants, teen pregnancy, school dropouts, school-to-work transitions, juvenile offenders, drug abuse, and depressed communities. The problem, argues Schorr, is not that we don't have the technical concepts and methods to create such programs. In fact, there are numerous examples of successful programs in almost every type of social problem area. Yet almost all these programs are small, and attempts to "scale up"—that is, to increase their size and scope—fail. When they are expanded, their effectiveness plummets.

Schorr concludes that there are crucial contextual factors in the successful pilot programs—factors that get lost when the programs are scaled up, even though the technical concepts and procedures are maintained. For example, she describes a South Carolina Resource Mothers Program that provided supportive prenatal care to high-risk, pregnant mothers. As a university-based, three-county pilot program, it achieved a significant reduction in babies born at low birth weight. However, when it was scaled up to sixteen counties by the state health department, the reductions in low-birth-weight babies disappeared. While the same procedures were used for identifying pregnant mothers, for counseling, and for education, contextual factors changed and these appeared to undermine the program: "larger caseloads, fewer visits, shorter client contact, less linkage with the community, less training, and less intensity."[49]

Schorr identifies a number of the contextual factors that appeared crucial across a large number of the case examples of "scale-up failure" she studied. These factors reflect a number of the pragmatic themes in our analysis of social programs.

First, successful programs are *comprehensive*, with children seen in the context of their families, and families in the context of their neighborhoods and communities. This emphasizes the systemic interrelationships among social problems. For example, while pressing medical and transportation problems might appear as context in a program that emphasizes job seeking for welfare recipients, that context can undermine the best types of procedures for vocationally educating, training, and motivating welfare recipients.

Second, successful programs have a *clear mission and clear outcome goals*. In the logic of the pragmatic case study, there is no way to assess outcome unless clear goals are established in advance. No matter what the process for reaching them, the bottom line is still the achievement of goals, both the initial goals and other goals that can be conceptually justified for having emerged during the project. Programs without clear initial goals can have "mission creep" and "mission drift." Initial goals—which can be revised as long as at every point there are clear-cut, rationalized goals and the technology in place for measuring change over the course of the program—also aid in ongoing monitoring of program operations, to obtain feedback as to whether they are on target and effective.

Third, successful programs are *flexible in process*. In other words, while successful programs are "tight" about their mission, they are simultaneously "loose" in how the mission is implemented.[50] This is the pragmatic idea that the effective human services practitioner needs flexibility in responding to the unique conditions of the case situation, because knowledge is produced by interaction between an expert's repertoire of cognitive understanding and the environmental cues and response in the case situation at hand. It is Polkinghorne's concept that while novice practitioners follow the rules and procedures they were taught in training in a cookbook type of manner, expert practitioners rework these procedures to meet the unique nature of a particular applied situation.[51] In Schön's words, "When someone reflects-in-action, . . . he is not dependent on the categories of established theory and technique, but constructs a new theory of the unique case."[52]

Fourth, if successful programs are dependent on expert practitioners who require greater front-line discretion, "the greater the importance of *excellent training, monitoring, and supervision*—to ensure that the discretion is exercised in keeping with mission goals and high standards of quality."[53]

Fifth, in the settings in which successful programs operate, practitioners are encouraged to build strong relationships that are imbued with mutual trust and respect. "It is the quality of these relationships that most profoundly differentiates effective from ineffective programs and institutions. But life-transforming relationships do not exist in a vacuum—they must be sustained by supportive institutions."[54] Program relationships—between staff and clients, between staff and other stakeholders, and among staff themselves—are another set of contextual factors that are typically not focused on in positivist studies of human service programs. Instead, in these studies, the focus is on specific technical procedures for achieving a result, be it "motivational counseling" for alcoholics, "systematic exposure" for individuals with phobic disorder, "management skill training" in a corporation, or tax incentives for economic investment in a poverty-stricken neighborhood.

Finally, Schorr discusses how leaders in outstanding programs have the skills to *combine the various factors*:

> These include the willingness to experiment and take risks; . . . to tolerate ambiguity; to win trust simultaneously of line workers, politicians, and the public; to respond to demands for prompt, tangible evidence of results; to be collaborative in working with staff; and to allow staff discretion at the front lines.[55]

Striking another pragmatic theme, Schorr argues that traditional approaches to program evaluation have been positivistically dominated and have worked against finding and documenting successful programs. Valuing conditions that parallel those in the laboratory, traditional program evaluators have looked to evaluate programs that are controlled and circumscribed, with standardized and uniform procedures:

> When it comes to broad, complex, and interactive interventions (early childhood supports, school reform, and better links to employment, for example) aimed at changing multiple outcomes (such as school success, employment rates, and a reduction in the formation of single-parent families), traditional evaluation has been of scant help.[56]

In other words, traditional, positivistically oriented program evaluators have been drawn to study the very programs that seem, based on pragmatic principles and Schorr's analysis of the empirical literature, to be designed for failure! Schorr concludes that we need distinctively different evaluation approaches that are adapted to assess the types of programs that are in fact successful. The pragmatic case study paradigm offers one such new approach.

7

Nuts and Bolts
The Pragmatic Case Study Method

In everyday discourse, stories—who did what to whom, how, and why?—predominate. In personal relationships, in business relationships, in the media, in entertainment, the focus is on particular people in concrete situations.

When we turn to mainstream psychological discourse, the "narrative" mode disappears and is replaced by "propositional" ways of communicating.[1] Here we find an emphasis on statements that are abstract, formal, quantitative, precise, and unemotional. This reflects the positivist psychologist's value on knowledge which can be stated in the form of decontextualized, general laws, like the ideal scientific format for knowledge found in physics and chemistry.

Pragmatism returns psychology to a major focus on contextualized knowledge, about particular individuals in specific concrete situations—in short, to a focus on the specific case—and to reconnecting with the relatively small body of case study literature that does exist in the field. Generally, this literature can be divided into three main categories: models that conceptualize the case study within the positivist paradigm, exemplified by the work of Yin;[2] those that conceptualize the case study within the hermeneutic paradigm, exemplified by the work of Lincoln and Guba;[3] and those that focus on the pragmatic uses of the case study, exemplified by the work of Bromley.[4] These three widely different frameworks demonstrate that the case study method is less a simple data collection technique than a research strategy that can be embedded within different sets of epistemological assumptions. The positivist and hermeneutic approaches offer many ideas that can be adapted to the design and logic of the pragmatic case study, and they are discussed immediately below. The work of Bromley addresses issues reviewed later in the chapter in the section on "case-based reasoning."

We can reveal the structure and process of the pragmatic case study method by analyzing the typical organization and content of a research report emerging from this method. The discussion is enhanced by comparing this organization to that of typical research reports of work conducted in the positivist and hermeneutic paradigms. This analysis is presented below. As a guide to the reader, tables 7.1 and 7.2 (starting on p. 156) provide a summary of the narrative in outline form. It should be noted that because of substantive heterogeneity within the hermeneutic paradigm, it was necessary to choose one representative model of this approach. I choose the work of psychologist Yvonne Lincoln and sociologist Egon Guba,[5] which is notable both for the scholarliness and breadth of its vision and for the specificity of its method—a combination frequently missing or underplayed in hermeneutic writings.

Let the Games Begin

The basic unit of analysis in the positivist paradigm is the quantitative group study. In contrast, the unit of analysis in the pragmatic paradigm and in Lincoln and Guba's hermeneutic paradigm is the case study, in which qualitative and contextual information, in addition to quantitative data, play a very important role.[6] As illustrated by its center location in the tables and as reflected in the discussion below, the pragmatic paradigm is a kind of middle ground between positivism and hermeneutics, borrowing and adapting many concepts and methods from each.[7]

Table 7.1 is organized in terms of the major sections of a positivist research article: introduction, method, results, and discussion. One aspect of the method section that is particularly detailed—the procedures for establishing quality of knowledge—is separately developed in table 7.2.

Introduction

In the positivist paradigm, a research article begins by setting forth a general theory, such as a theory of behavioral causal factors in clinical depression or a theory of the curricular determinants of reading deficiencies in third graders. The article then shows how the study investigates the validity of the theory by testing a series of operationalized hypotheses that are logically derived from it.

In contrast, in the hermeneutic paradigm an article begins by setting forth a topic—a conceptual problem, a program to be evaluated, or a policy option—but no initial theory or hypotheses. These emerge from the study itself rather than being imposed by the researcher.

An article in the pragmatic paradigm is different still. It begins with a particular problem as presented by a specific client (an individual, group, organization, or community). Unlike in the hermeneutic paradigm, the researcher does begin with an explicit guiding conception of the problem. But unlike in the positivist paradigm, this guiding conception is a pragmatic road map for designing a particular program rather than a general theory to be tested.[8] Also, the nature of the guiding conception (e.g., systems-oriented and inclusive of a large number of variables) is more like the hermeneutic than the positivist paradigm. Finally, unlike the hermeneutic paradigm, the pragmatic model does not necessarily involve a guiding conception that is negotiated with the research participants. While the guiding conception is responsive to data that emerge over the course of the research process (cf. the feedback loops in fig. I.2), unlike the hermeneutic approach, the pragmatic paradigm acknowledges expertise that can be brought to the research that is not necessarily up for negotiation with all research stakeholders.

More specifically, in a pragmatic article, the Introduction section includes a description of (a) the particular client who is to be served; (b) the client's particular psychological or social problem that is the focus of the study; (c) a "guiding conception" of the problem, as informed by previous research and relevant experiences of the program practitioners (see fig. 1.2); and (d) a summary of the program for improvement that flows from this conception.

The theory in a positivist study is typically molecular in focus, mechanistic in concept, and limited to a few key variables. This allows for the testing of specific relationships among a few, discrete variables, with all other variables effectively held constant. In contrast, the pragmatic study employs a guiding conception that is not only molecular, to incorporate helpful positivist concepts, but also employs holistic, systems-oriented, and highly multivariate concepts. This type of thinking is required to capture a real-world situation in all its diverse facets: "[The pragmatic case study] begins in the problems and opportunities of natural events. Nature is taken as it comes, in all its complexity. . . . All influences that affect the natural course of events to a significant degree must be taken into account."[9]

Moreover, while a case study can be differentiated by the primary system level of its presenting problem—that is, a case of an individual with

TABLE 7.1

Typical Organization and Content of a Research Report in the Three Paradigms

Section of Article	Positivist Group Study Paradigm	Pragmatic Case Study Paradigm	Hermeneutic Case Study Paradigm[a]
Introduction	Theory to Be Tested	Problem to Be Solved	Topic of the Study
	This section sets forth a general theory of behavior that the study is empirically "testing" by setting up a scientific experiment.	This section sets forth (a) the particular client who is to be served; (b) the client's particular psychological or social problem, which is the focus of the study; (c) a "guiding conception" of the problem, as informed by previous research and relevant experiences of the program practitioners (see figure 1.2); and (d) a summary of the program for improvement that flows from this conception.	This section sets forth the focus of the study, which can be (a) a conceptual problem; (b) a program to be evaluated; or (c) a policy option.
	The theory is typically (a) *molecular* in focus; (b) *mechanistic* in concept; and (c) limited to *a few key variables*.	The guiding conception is typically (a) *both molecular and holistic* in focus; (b) *systems-oriented and organic* in concept; and (c) inclusive of *a large number of variables*.	*At the beginning* of the project, there is *no theory*. Theory emerges during the project. The theory *at the end* is (a) *holistic* in focus; (b) *systems-oriented and organic* in concept; (c) inclusive of *a large number of variables*; and (d) *negotiated* with the research participants.
Method	Settings, Measures, and Procedures for Theory-Testing	Case Context, Program Description, Stakeholders, and Outcome Measures	Case Context, Stakeholders, and Participant Observer Role
setting	This section describes the setting (typically a *"controlled," laboratory-like setting*) in which the study took place.	This section describes the particular *naturalistic case situation* in which the program was implemented, including (a) the cases's context (historical, psychological, social, organization, community, cultural, and	This section provides a detailed, "thick" description of the context of the *naturalistic case situation*.

TABLE 7.1 *(continued)*
Typical Organization and Content of a Research Report in the Three Paradigms

Section of Article	Positivist Group Study Paradigm	Pragmatic Case Study Paradigm	Hermeneutic Case Study Paradigm[a]
Method *(continued)*		physical); (b) the program itself, in terms of different, applicable systems levels: individual staff, teams of staff, and the organization as a whole; and (c) the program itself in terms of direct service versus administrative activities.	
rationale for choosing the study situation	This section describes how the study situation is logically reflective of the theoretical hypotheses to be tested.	This section describes a rationale for choosing the study case. Two general types of rationales are (a) the case is an instance of an exemplary, average, or poor program; or (b) the case is an instance of a rare or unique program.	Explanation of why the conceptual problem, program to be evaluated, or policy option was chosen for study.
case boundaries and relation to other cases	Not applicable.	This section describes (a) the boundaries of the case (e.g., teacher, classroom, school, or school district); and (b) the type of case design in relation to other cases on two dimensions. These dimensions are (1) the "holistic" (single unit of analysis) vs. the "embedded" (multiple levels of analysis) case design; and (2) the "single-case" vs. the "multiple-case" design.	This section describes the boundaries of the case.

TABLE 7.1 *(continued)*
Typical Organization and Content of a Research Report in the Three Paradigms

Section of Article	Positivist Group Study Paradigm	Pragmatic Case Study Paradigm	Hermeneutic Case Study Paradigm[a]
Method *(continued)*			
stakeholder values and goals	Not applicable.	This section outlines (a) the stakeholders in the situation; (b) the stakeholders' values and goals vis-à-vis the client's presenting problem; (c) how and why the researcher derives the final values and goals in the study; and (d) how these final values and goals are shared with the stakesholders.	This section outlines the stakeholders in the situation. The content of the values and goals of the stakeholders are emergent during the study. The Method section describes the process by which the values and goals will be elicited, while the Results section (see below) describes the contents of the values and goals that do in fact emerge.
measures and data collection procedures	This section describes the discrete, operationalized, quantitative measures and procedures used for testing hypotheses associated with the study's theory.	This section describes the measures and procedures employed to assess program impact, typically including participant observation. These measures vary across two dimensions (a) quantitative vs. qualitative measures; and (b) standardized (normative) vs. individualized measures.	This section reviews the procedures and their logic, which consists of an inductive approach that assumes the researcher needs to discover what questions to ask. The procedures emphasize the researcher as a "human instrument." The researcher assumes a participant observer role, building on "tacit" (intuitive, subjective, experiential, empathetic) knowledge, and focusing on narrative and qualitative interactions with the research participants.
quality-of-knowledge procedures	See Table 7.2	See Table 7.2	See Table 7.2

TABLE 7.1 *(continued)*
Typical Organization and Content of a Research Report in the Three Paradigms

Section of Article	Positivist Group Study Paradigm	Pragmatic Case Study Paradigm	Hermeneutic Case Study Paradigm[a]
Results	Theory-Relevant Results	Program Impact	"Grounded Theory"
	This section presents the quantitative results of the study that shed light on testing of the study's theory.	This section summarizes (a) narrative and quantitative evaluation data that shed light on the process and effectiveness of the program, using such data-analytic techniques as "performance indicators," "pattern matching," "cost-effectiveness analysis," and "goal attainment scaling"; and (b) analysis of the guiding conception in terms of what seems to make the program more or less successful, including such emergent analytic techniques as "grounded theory."	This section summarizes the "grounded theory" that emerges from the researcher's participant observation role. The theory emerges as the researcher elicits the constructions of the various stakeholders about the subject of the study; facilitates a mutual dialogue and critique of these constructions; and works toward a negotiated consensual construction among stakeholders. An important goal in writing up the results is to help the reader vicariously grasp the constructions and motives of the stakeholders.
Discussion	Implications for General, Nomothetic Theory	Application to Other Cases	Idiographic Lessons to Be Learned, Empowering Stakeholders
	This section reviews the study results and discusses their implications for the viability of the originally introduced general theory.	This section reviews the study results and discusses them in terms of (a) their applications to other similar case situations; and (b) their relevance for confirming the general usefulness of the original guiding conception and/or for suggesting revisions of the guiding conception to make it more useful.	The emphasis is on an idiographic discussion of the individual case. Application to other cases is always tentative. In an evaluation, the emphasis is on politically empowering the case's stakeholders rather than on the substance of the "findings" of the study per se.

[a] Derived from Lincoln and Guba 1985 and Guba and Lincoln 1989.

TABLE 7.2
Quality-of-Knowledge Procedures in the Three Paradigms

Section of Article	Positivist Group Study Paradigm	Pragmatic Case Study Paradigm	Hermeneutic Case Study Paradigm[a]
Quality-of-Knowledge Procedures	Positivist Group Study Design	Pragmatic Case Design	Hermeneutic Case Design
study design	The design is the plan ensuring that criteria of logical adequacy for theory testing have been met, including the criteria below.	The design is the plan for ensuring that criteria of logical adequacy have been met for documenting the effectiveness of a particular program and for relating program outcomes to the case's guiding conception. The criteria include the items below.	The design is the plan for ensuring that criteria of logical adequacy have been met for meeting the knowledge goals of the study—namely, genuine documentation and articulation of the constructs of the study's participants. Two types of criteria are employed: trustworthiness and authenticity. Trustworthiness consists of hermeneutic criteria that parallel those of positivism, while the authenticity criteria are unique to the hermeneutic approach.
construct validity	*Theoretical construct validity*: showing the correctness of the operational measures in reflecting the theoretical concepts being studied. Since a theoretical construct cannot be fully and directly assessed by any particular operational measure, the technique of *triangulation* is frequently used, that is, multiple and converging operational measures are employed to add validity to the assessment of a theoretical construct.	*Program process and goal construct validity*: showing the reasonableness, logical coherence, and sociopolitical fairness of the operational performance indicators that are used to reflect a program's process and the goals of its stakeholders. Since a program process or program goal is typically not fully and directly assessable by any particular performance indicator, the technique of *triangulation* is frequently used, that is, multiple and converging performance indicators are employed to add validity to the	Not applicable.

TABLE 7.2 *(continued)*
Quality-of-Knowledge Procedures in the Three Paradigms

Section of Article	Positivist Group Study Paradigm	Pragmatic Case Study Paradigm	Hermeneutic Case Study Paradigm[a]
		measurement of program process and goals.	
validity within the study	*Internal-causality validity*: establishing the presence of genuine causal relationships within the study. *Time-Series analysis*, a technique for establishing internal-causality validity in group studies, can be applied to the individual case through *single-subject research*.	(a) *Internal-functionality validity*: establishing the presence of discreet functional relationships between program intervention variables and client outcome variables. The logic of *single-subject research* can be adapted to the pragmatic case study case study as a technique for developing internal-functionality validity. (b) *Internal-connectedness validity*: presenting convincing logic and reasonableness concerning the relations among the various components of a case study—guiding conception, assessment, formulation, action, evaluation, and feedback (see figure 1.2.). The heremeneut's techniques for establishing *credibility*— prolonged engagement, persistent observation, and triangulation in the information gathering process—are also applicable to enhancing internal-connectedness validity.	*Credibility*: establishing isomorphism between the constructed realities of case respondents and reconstructions attributed to them. Credibility can be enhanced by such techniques as prolonged engagement, persistent observation, and triangulation in the information gathering process by using multiple methods, multiple data sources, and multiple investigators.
applicability to other sites	*External validity*: identifying the domain to which the study can be properly generalized.	*Transferability*: providing a "thick" description from which generalizability can be derived.	*Transferability*: providing a "thick" description from which generalizability can be derived.

TABLE 7.2 *(continued)*
Quality-of-Knowledge Procedures in the Three Paradigms

Section of Article	Positivist Group Study Paradigm	Pragmatic Case Study Paradigm	Hermeneutic Case Study Paradigm[a]
reproducibility of the research process	*Reliability*: demonstrating the repeatability of the measurement process.	(a) *Reliability*: employing the positivist paradigm for studying variables that are reflected in standardized, quantitative measures. (b) *Dependability*: employing the hermeneutic paradigm for tracking the process by which the case study was conducted.	*Dependability*: establishing that the process of how the study was conducted is documented in such a way that this process can be tracked and reconstructed by a research auditor.
addressing the researcher's interests and values	*Researcher objectivity*: showing (a) the "value neutrality" of the researcher; and (b) the lack of "experimenter bias," e.g. by use of "double-blind" designs.	(a) *Researcher bias reduction*: showing how the researcher's own personal interests and values that appear to interact and interfere unduly with the design and conduct of the study are reduced, e.g. by use of "double-blind" designs. (b) *Researcher values clarification*: clarifying the values and interests of the researcher that remain. (c) *Confirmability*: assuring that data, interpretations, and outcomes in the research are rooted in contexts and persons of the case apart from the researcher, e.g., by the use of a research auditor's assessment of the content of the research.	*Confirmability*: assuring that data, interpretations, and outcomes in the research are rooted in contexts and persons of the case apart from the researcher, e.g., by the use of a research auditor's assessment of the content of the research.
authenticity	Not applicable.	Not applicable.	Authenticity consists of quality criteria that are intrinsic to hermeneutic study, including (a) the dialectical, dialogical hermeneutic process itself; (b) "fairness"

TABLE 7.2 *(continued)*
Quality-of-Knowledge Procedures in the Three Paradigms

Section of Article	Positivist Group Study Paradigm	Pragmatic Case Study Paradigm	Hermeneutic Case Study Paradigm[a]
			(honoring the whole variety of stakeholder constructions); (c) "ontological authenticity" (improvement in stakeholder constructions); (d) "educative authenticity" (stakeholders' appreciation of others' constructions); (e) "catalytic authenticity" (stimulation to action); and (f) "tactical authenticity" (empowerment for action).

[a] Derived from Lincoln and Guba 1985 and Guba and Lincoln 1989.

depression, a family with poor communication, an organization with low productivity, or a community with a high level of violence—in the real world the different system levels are always interconnected. Every individual is a member of a family, other small groups, organizations, and communities; every small group, organization, and community is ultimately composed of individuals; organizations are composed of small groups, which in turn are impacted by the organization in which they reside; and so forth. Thus, if a pragmatic technology for change involving any one system level is to be effective in the natural environment, its concepts and procedures must include perspectives from other system levels.[10]

In short, the guiding conception of a pragmatic case study employs many of the concepts from living systems theory, such as reciprocally causal interactions among elements, systems within systems, a system as a whole "seeking" equilibrium, and the idea of emergent phenomena. Moreover, living systems theory is designed to apply common concepts, such as boundary and subsystem, across all types of human phenomena, and to be theoretically integrative.[11] Thus the use of living systems theory helps to make lessons learned in one type of social program case (e.g., individual improvement through psychotherapy) applicable to other types of social program cases (e.g., classroom learning through educational programs).[12]

The Case of "Multicom": The Advantages of "Creative Chaos"

In his widely used book, *Images of Organization*,[13] sociologist Gareth Morgan argues for the advantages of a pragmatically focused approach to theoretical formulation that emphasizes complementarity among multiple conceptual models, in contrast to the positivist approach that focuses on demonstrating the competitive superiority of a single theory. While Morgan focuses on organizations, his view is also applicable to individual, small group, and community phenomena.[14]

Morgan illustrates his arguments with the case of "Multicom," a small firm employing 150 people in the public relations field. It was started in 1979 by Jim Walsh, a marketing specialist, and Wendy Bridges, a publications relations expert, who had earlier worked together at a larger communications firm. When they left, they persuaded two colleagues, Marie Beaumont, a film and video professional, and Frank Rossi, a writer and editor, to join them as minority shareholders. Their golden rule: all four would be involved in major policy decisions.

The first two years were challenging, but exciting. Each partner had certain clients for whom he or she felt a special responsibility, while all four and additionally hired staff developed all-around skills so that they could substitute for each other. While this free-wheeling design made intensive time demands on everyone, with frequent early morning and late night hours, it created great flexibility, made the work satisfying, and enhanced the sense of teamwork.

> They also played hard, throwing regular parties to celebrate the completion of major projects or the acquisition of new clients. These helped to keep morale high and to project Multicom's image as an excellent and exciting place to work. The firm's clients often attended these parties, and were usually impressed by the vitality and quality of interpersonal relations.[15]

During the company's third year, however, the long hours and intensive pace got to Walsh and Bridges. Each had demanding family commitments and wanted more leisure time. They talked about "getting more organized" with more formal control mechanisms. Beaumont and Rossi, on the other hand, who were about ten years younger and single, relished their work lifestyle of "creative chaos" and wanted to maintain the status quo. They would have been quite interested in taking on more of the workload in return for greater equity in the company.

In the fourth year, tensions reached such a point that Walsh and Bridges broke the golden rule of joint decision making and exerted their authority as the primary shareholders to reorganize the office, including, for example, a clearer definition of job responsibilities, a more formalized procedure for assigning specific staff to specific projects, and a closer control and closer monitoring of time spent by staff in and out of the office. While they did not actively protest the changes, within a year Beaumont and Rossi had left and set up a new company of their own, Media 2000, taking a number of key staff and clients with them. In the short run, Multicom continued to produce sound financial results, but lost its reputation as an inspiring, leading-edge agency. Media 2000, on the other hand, quickly established a reputation for itself as a talented and innovative agency.

The end result was that Multicom lost two of its top creative professionals and some of its best staff, it had a new competitor, it lost clients, and it lost its distinctive reputation. If organizational consultants had been brought in before the breakup to help develop alternative ways for conflict resolution, how might they have helped? Within the framework of the disciplined inquiry model, Morgan argues that using multiple theoretical models would have enhanced the problem formulation and resultant action plan in comparison to using only one of the models.

For example, while a mechanistic, "scientific management" theoretical model would have been helpful in showing how Multicom could "get organized" and could reduce the stress on Walsh and Bridges, other theoretical models could have highlighted the negative consequences of such an action. Political theory would have shown that Walsh and Bridges's breaking the golden rule of joint decision making among the four partners caused them to move from a democratic to a quasi-autocratic structure, exacerbating differences and tensions between two politically differentiated groups: the two primary shareholders and the two minority shareholders. Moreover, corporate culture theory would have highlighted that the formalizing actions taken by Walsh and Bridges undermined Multicom's early and effective cohesion-building atmosphere based on the originally shared values of the four principals, including role flexibility, joint responsibility for all projects, and working hard and playing hard as a team. In addition, a holographic brain model would have identified vital system characteristics that were being lost by giving up the team-based, client-oriented approach: the ability to create redundant functions and to build the requisite abilities into Multicom's various parts, with each team as a microcosm of the whole. Finally, organismic theory, viewing an organization as a living organism, would have helped to clarify that the bureaucratization brought on by the additional organizational formalizing made Multicom less adapted to its external business environment, which valued creativity, flexibility, and vitality rather than conventionality, predictability, and stability.

Morgan argues that a pragmatic action plan for helping Multicom deal with its organizational tensions would have gained effectiveness by incorporating the various theoretical models. By realizing the trade-offs among interventions generated by different theories, a consultant could have developed a plan that effectively balanced these trade-offs. For example, the consultants might have helped the four principals to agree upon a compromise in which certain elements of Multicom would have become more formalized and differentiated, while other elements would have remained true to the original culture of shared responsibility and being an "all-arounder." Moreover, perhaps the four could also have agreed to have Beaumont and Rossi take on more of the work load in return for being offered a more equal share of ownership in Multicom. By Walsh and Bridges adhering to the golden rule of joint decision making and being willing to compromise on the degree of "getting organized," Beaumont and Rossi would most likely have been much more positively disposed to compromise also, because the continuity of the golden rule was reinforcing the democratic political culture that was of great importance to these financially junior partners. Thus, by making certain adjustments to the original Multicom culture and structure in a manner that preserved its democratic process values, the principals could have retained many of the strengths of the original culture so as to ensure the chances of long-term survival and organizational health for the company.

In sum, Morgan's approach is an example of the pragmatic paradigm, which views different theories as alternative conceptual tools. Just like woodworking implements—a hammer, a saw, a screwdriver—different tools are appropriate to different situations, and frequently multiple tools serve complementary functions when judged against the goal of paradigm: to solve practical problems.

Method

Case Setting and Study Rationale. The positivist study ideally takes places in a laboratory-like setting that allows the "control" of all but a few "independent" (causal) and "dependent" (reactive) variables, which are selected in order to test specific theoretical hypotheses. The focus is upon the theory-relevant variables and procedures for reducing the effect of context upon these variables.

In contrast, the setting of the hermeneutic case study is "wide open." While a rationale is needed for the topic studied, and while the topic can be of practical significance (a program evaluation or a policy-relevant study), the investigation can be driven by "pure" intellectual or philosophical curiosity, without any necessary practical consequences. In describing the setting, emphasis is upon a detailed, "thick" description of the context of the case being explored. No initial theory delimits the way the case situation is studied, since hermeneuts view theory as biasing researchers and closing their eyes to the constructed views of the respondents and experiences of the research participants.

The pragmatic study combines the focus and structure of the positivist model with an emphasis on the hermeneutic thick description of case context. Specifically, the setting of a pragmatic case is described in terms of: (a) the broad, multidimensional nature of the context (historical, psychological, social, organizational, etc.) in which the target program is being applied; (b) the nature of the program itself, both in terms of different, applicable systems levels (e.g., individual staff member, teams of staff members, and the organization as whole), and in terms of direct services versus administrative and support activities. Moreover, the pragmatic researcher is expected to provide a specific rationale for why this case is being studied. Typically, two types of rationales are given: the case is an instance of an exemplary, average, or poor program, to aid in establishing examples of these three categories; or the case is an instance of a rare or unique program that is of interest because of its combination of distinctiveness and relevance.

Case Boundaries. Yin points out that one of the defining characteristics of the case study is that unlike the positivist group study, in the case study "the boundaries between phenomenon and context are not clearly evident."[16] This "boundary problem" means that the limits of any case study are somewhat arbitrary. For example, a therapist might see a client periodically over many years. Should the "case" be limited to a particular episode in that time span or to the total number of contacts? Or should a high school case involve an individual English class teacher working with one specific class or with all the five classes or so she sees over the course of a day? Or should the case involve a broader unit, such as the whole English department, or the whole school, or the whole school district? And what should be the time span of the case—a semester? a year? or multiple years, such as the four years a particular class might spend in the high school before graduation?[17]

Pragmatic researchers address the boundary problem by specifying in detail the boundaries of their cases and why they were chosen. Relevant criteria in this choice include such characteristics as feasibility and what seems to be a "natural unit" in the case situation (such as studying a classroom over the course of a semester or a year). The delineation of the case chosen must be justified in terms of its potential for practical application, since the ultimate rationale for devoting resources to the pragmatic study is its potential for yielding information aiding human service programs dedicated to practical problem solving.

To aid in clarifying the issue of boundaries in case studies, pragmatic researchers utilize Yin's[18] typology of study designs, derived from a grid formed by two dimensions. One dimension distinguishes "single-case" designs from "multiple-case" designs, and the other dimension distinguishes "holistic" (single unit of analysis) from "embedded" (multiple units of analysis) designs.

A single-case design looks at one unit, while a multiple-case design looks at two or more of the same types of units—for example, two or more studies of therapy with individuals with panic disorder, or two or more studies of inner-city high schools in New York City. While as mentioned above, there are times when a single case is studied as such because it is an instance of a rare or unique program, more typical is the study of multiple cases that form a continuum of exemplary, average, or poor programs vis-à-vis achieving a particular set of goals. Even though an individual researcher might study only a single case, that study is frequently part of a multiple-case design in that the single case is intended to be compared and contrasted with other cases dealing with similar initial conditions, problems, and goals.

A holistic study only systematically examines a case as a whole. In contrast, an embedded-design study systematically examines three aspects of a case: subunits of the case, the case as a whole, and how the subunits relate to one another and to the larger case. Thus, the analysis of an elementary school can be viewed holistically, or separate analyses can be conducted of individual classrooms in the school and how they relate to one another and to the school as a whole. Likewise, in studying a therapy case, one can either evaluate the course of therapy as a whole entity only or study both the whole case and individual sessions as separate subunits within themselves and in terms of how they relate to the total case.

Where feasible, there are two potential advantages of embedded-design studies. First, they allow the researcher to recognize variability among subunits, identifying, for example, subunits that are exemplary and deserve recognition and further in-depth study. Also, embedded-design studies provide an opportunity to obtain a more sophisticated and concrete understanding about the case as a whole, as the researcher documents subunit variability and reflects upon how that variability is related to the guiding conception being employed. For example, in studying third-grade achievement in an elementary school, it is useful to study as subunits the classrooms of the individual third-grade teachers. Reviewing the variability among teacher classrooms in light of the fact that all the classrooms are in the same school is then helpful in learning more precisely about the combination of ingredients that leads to high achievement.

Stakeholder Values and Goals. Earlier, I described a three-step collaborative process of value setting between pragmatic researchers and community members involved in their research.[19] The case study write-up includes a description of this process.

Stakeholder values and goals are generally not a part of a positivist study. However, they are vitally important in a hermeneutic study, where the emphasis is on values and goals emerging during the research process.

Measures and Data Collection Procedures. Positivist and hermeneutic researchers collect dramatically different types of data. Positivists focus on discrete, quantitative measures and the operationalized procedures employed to "rigorously" administer them. It is these very qualities to which hermeneutic researchers object. Since hermeneuts are studying phenomenologically based patterns of meaning, they see these positivist qualities as undermining the only valid method they have for assessing these patterns, namely, the "human instrument."[20] This instrument is the empathetic, knowledgeable, and experienced researcher functioning in the role of participant observer. As a partial participant, the researcher has "real" social relationships with the case's clients and other stakeholders. As a partial observer, the researcher is building on his or her "tacit" (intuitive and subjective) knowledge and focusing on qualitative, narrative interactions with the research participants.

Pragmatists select assessment approaches from each of the other two paradigms. In terms of participant observation, it should be remembered that the professional practitioner—therapist, teacher, organizational consultant, physician, lawyer, and so forth—is also a participant observer. This is what is meant by Schön's model of "the reflective practitioner."[21] Schön views the highly functioning practitioner not only as an active participant in the social situation of practice, but also as an observer of and reflector upon that practice. Moreover, by its very nature, the case study draws the researcher into intensive contact with the client and other stakeholders associated with the case. It is not possible—even if it were desirable—to maintain the neutral, detached stance of positivist group researchers who can interact with their "subjects" in a "thin" way because typically they only need a small amount of discrete, quantitative data from any one of the large number of individuals they are studying.

Pragmatists place high value on standardized, quantitative measures, which can descriptively document relevant base rates in the larger context in which case studies take place. For example, a thirty-five-year-old female client's depression score on the Minnesota Multiphasic Personality Inventory[22] helps to place the extent of her depression in the context of the general population of females in the thirty-five-year-old range. And the percentage of students in poverty—as measured by the percentage meeting federal income guidelines for free school lunches—in a New York City elementary school can help to place the problems and academic performance in that school in proper context.[23] More will be said later about quantitative measures in describing the "Results" section of table 7.1. The important point here is that the psychometric criteria for quantitative measurement of social science phenomena that positivist psychologists and other social scientists have developed over the years are very helpful in ensuring fairness and rationality in the quantitative measurement process.[24]

While, as reflected in tables 7.1 and 7.2, Lincoln and Guba in their writings focus almost exclusively on qualitative data, they put forth a position about quantitative data that is highly congruent with the pragmatic approach. They state that there are times when quantitative methods

> will be, and should be, used. The single limitation that a constructivist [hermeneutic] . . . evaluator would put on the use of quantitative methods is that no *causally inferential* statistics would be employed [that is, no use of statistics for positivist theory testing], since the causal linkages implied by such statistics are contrary to the position on causality that phenomenologically oriented and constructivist inquiry takes.[25]

They conclude that in addition to skill in qualitative methods, the hermeneutic researcher must have technical, quantitative skills equal to those of a positivist researcher in areas such as tests, measurements, and descriptive statistics.

Quality-of-Knowledge Procedures. A crucial characteristic that distinguishes a formal psychological investigation from other, less rigorous studies of human behavior (such as journalistic articles, popular biography, or personal memoirs) is the rigor and quality control in the knowledge involved. Psychology can be defined as distinctive from other approaches to human behavior not so much by what it knows than by *how* it knows —that is, by its concern with questions of method and episte- mology. Because of the importance of this aspect of method, it has many dimensions, which are outlined in table 7.2 and described below. In order to maintain the flow of logic as it plays out in research reports within the three paradigms, I will first review the Results and Discussion sections of table 7.1. Then I will turn to the epistemological details of table 7.2.

Results

The Results section of a research study flows directly from the goals of the Introduction and Method sections. In the positivist study, the Re- sults section focuses on presenting statistical analyses of the quantitative data collected in order to see if these results are consistent or inconsistent with the theory-testing hypotheses of the study.

In contrast, in the hermeneutic study, the results consist of the "grounded theory" that emerges from the researcher's participant obser- vation role. This process takes place as the researcher elicits the con- structions of the various stakeholders about the subject of the study; fa- cilitates a mutual dialogue and critique of these constructions; and works toward a negotiated consensual construction among stakeholders. An important goal in writing the Results section is to help the reader vicari- ously grasp the constructions and motives of the stakeholders.

Likewise, the Results section in the pragmatic study flows from the study's "roots" laid out in the Introduction and Method sections. Specif- ically, the setting of the study is a particular human service program de- signed to address the problems of a specific client, within the context of (a) the goals of various stakeholders associated with the problem, and (b) a particular guiding conception of how the program works to achieve positive outcomes. Therefore, the Results section focuses on the degree to which the program is successful and how the program works vis-à-vis its degree of success—all in light of the goals that have been set for the program.

More specifically, the Results section in a pragmatic study summarizes the effectiveness of the program and analyzes the program in terms of whether the guiding conception made the program more or less success- ful, including such analytic techniques as grounded theory. A number of important concepts in the process of evaluating a program's outcome are reviewed below.

Performance Indicators. Performance indicators are quantitative measures that are designed to provide a shorthand, efficient sample picture of how a system is functioning. An example is the information on the dashboard of a car. Fuel level, engine speed, engine temperature, oil pressure, car speed, and so forth are a minute fraction of the possible variables that could be monitored to learn about a very complex engine powering a car at a certain speed in a certain direction. No one would claim that the dashboard indicators provide a full picture of what is happening. Rather, these indicators are chosen because they provide important, practical feedback for the driver to assess whether there is a problem in the moving car's functioning that needs to be addressed.

There are two types of performance indicators. *Process* indicators, such as fuel level and engine speed, provide a measure of how well a system is working internally. *Outcome* indicators, on the other hand, provide a measure of how well the system is accomplishing its goals in the outside world. In the case of the car, this might involve a measure such as the time it takes to drive from New York City to Boston in the summer, late at night, when there is no traffic and without driving over the speed limit. If a car can drive this distance of just over two hundred miles in less than four and a half hours, the car will be successful in its outcome —independent of what the process performance indicators might say.

The same logic applies to human service programs. Examples are therapy, in which process indicators might reflect how many outpatient sessions a client has attended, for what percentage of them the client came on time, and what the credentials of the therapist are; and a high school program, in which process indicators might reflect the attendance and dropout rates of the students or the teachers' credentials. On the other hand, outcome indicators would reflect such therapeutic accomplishments as improvement in life coping and decreased distress, and such educational accomplishments as improvement in academic performance.

The pragmatic case study employs process indicators as a method for understanding how the guiding conception is working, and it employs outcome indicators to assess a program's main impact.

An important caveat is that performance indicators are not direct measures of program processes or program goal attainment, but simply shorthand, operationalized indicators of these. In other words, performance indicators are "proxies," in that they provide only *approximate* measures of what a case's client and stakeholders want to know. Of course it is important to take into account that some indicators arguably come closer to the actual outcomes of interest than others. For example, most would agree that healthy family functioning is relatively more directly measured by a standardized in-home observation instrument than by the lack of reports of child abuse and domestic violence.[26]

Since performance indicators are not direct measures of program processes or program goal attainment, but simply shorthand, operationalized indicators of these, questions arise as to the validity of any particular indicator in representing the more complex construct of program process or outcome. I have labeled these questions the issues of "process construct validity" and "goal construct validity," respectively. They are listed in table 7.2 and reviewed in the "quality-of-knowledge" section below in which the table is discussed.

A good argument for the advantages of outcome over process indicators is represented in the "reinventing government" movement, which is taking hold among the 83,000 governmental units in the United States—one federal, fifty state, and thousands of cities, counties, school districts, water districts, and transportation districts—all encompassing some fifteen million employees.[27] Catalyzed by the work of Osborne and Gaebler,[28] this movement has as one of its themes the idea of "results-oriented government," in which funding is attached to the outcomes of government programs, not to the inner workings—the "rules and red tape"—of government agencies. The traditional focus on inner process has helped to create public cynicism about the value of "government" itself.

The details of developing an outcome-driven performance indicator system in state government is presented in a monograph by Brizius and Campbell for the Council of U.S. Governors' Policy Advisors.[29] Their model, labeled "performance accountability," follows the logic of table 7.1 in detail, emphasizing, for example, both (a) the need to examine the logic of the "program model" (what I have been calling the "guiding conception") behind the design of the program, and (b) the need for careful design and measurement of outcome indicators, because these "drive the accountability system."[30] They describe outcome indicators as reflecting changes in people's lives that should occur if a program is successful, including changes in behavior, life circumstances, knowledge, and skills. In a good performance accountability system, "a few selected indicators will tell us a great deal about whether desired outcomes are being achieved. The object is to have a sufficient number of reasonably valid indicators to guide policy and program decision making, but not so many that the system becomes unmanageable for the users."[31]

According to Brizius and Campbell, a government program— like any organizational program—can be viewed as a system, consisting of input, process, and outcome variables. Input variables include client variables such as the demographic and economic characteristics of the target population; program variables such as the number of staff members hired in an agency and the intensity of service offered; and external variables, such as state economic reversals, population shifts, drug epidemics, or technological advances. Process variables reflect the implementation of a program, such as caseload size, unit cost of service, sources of referrals, number of available program slots, speed of response to reports of abuse, quality of prenatal services, or availability of child care for mothers in a jobs program. In contrast, output variables focus outside of programs per se and reflect the impact of programs upon the lives and functioning of individual citizens and groups of citizens. Examples are a reduction in the rate of unwanted teenage pregnancies, an increase in student performance on achievement tests, an increase in the percentage of functionally literate adults in the general population, a reduction in the percentage of individuals with heart attacks dying before an ambulance service can arrive, a decrease in the number of crack addicts, and an increase in the number of single mothers who are able to leave welfare by gaining decent employment.[32]

Besides stimulating new learning, improved functioning, and improved life circumstances per se, an important dimension of a program's outcomes are the costs (dollarized input) required to achieve them. This is frequently calculated in terms of "cost- effectiveness," that is, in terms of input cost per unit of outcome. This concept is discussed below.

In a related vein, the reinventing government movement argues that the ultimate purpose of government agencies is to impact positively and cost-effectively upon the citizens they serve, and that it is by this criterion that they should be judged. Since the focus is upon the value of services as experienced and viewed by the citizens who receive them, government programs should be "customer driven."

Building on the theme of a results orientation, Osborne and Gaebler view the basic goal of government as facilitating the development of effective services rather than providing them per se—in Peter Drucker's words, "governing" rather than "doing." In this approach, government policies and funds stimulate and empower nonprofit corporations, public-private partnerships, neighborhood associations, volunteer groups, and other nongovernment organizations to become engaged in service provision at the local, community-based level. Through competition, excellence is encouraged.

All of these interrelated themes are reflected in such chapter titles in Osborne and Gaebler's book as "Community-Owned Government: Empowering Rather than Serving"; "Mission-Driven Government: Transforming Rule-Driven Organizations"; "Results-Oriented Government: Funding Outcomes, Not Inputs"; "Customer-Driven Government: Meeting the Needs of the Customer, Not the Bureaucracy"; and "Decentralized Government: From Hierarchy to Participation and Teamwork."

Vice President Al Gore has led a major "reinventing government" initiative at the federal level called the National Performance Review (NPR). Gore documents recent progress in this effort in his book, *Common Sense Government: Works Better and Costs Less.*[33] Here is a sample of some of the achievements of NPR that Gore lists:

- More than 200 agencies have published customer service standards [and distributed them to their customers]. . . .
- $58 billion of NPR's $108 billion in savings proposed in 1993 are already locked in. . . .
- Agencies are sending 16,000 pages of obsolete regulations to the scrap heap, of 86,000 pages of regulations reviewed [thus making the monitoring activities of government less intrusive and time-consuming]. . . .
- Social Security's "800" number is rated better than L. L. Bean's for customer service. . . .
- [EPA has established a philosophy of] tough standards to protect our air, our water, and the health of our people, but common sense, flexibility, innovation, and creativity in how . . . those standards [are met].[34]

Pattern Matching. In developing performance criteria for a program, there is frequently a need for a multidimensional approach, integrating across a variety of different outcome indicators. Campbell and Yin[35] present a relevant approach called "pattern matching," in which several pieces of qualitatively different information that are measured in a case are compared to a predicted pattern. While Campbell and Yin employ pattern matching within the positivist paradigm to compare an observed pattern of results to a theoretically predicted pattern, it is possible to reframe this notion in a pragmatic context. Here, the pattern of interest is an arrangement of a program's outcome indicators that reflect a desirable pattern of program achievement. In other words, the "predicted" pattern in the positivist study is based on theory, while in the pragmatic study, on ideals.

The Malcolm Baldrige Quality Award, created by Congress in 1987 to recognize and encourage the achievement of the highest standards of quality in U.S. businesses, is an excellent example of pragmatic pattern matching. The award was created to recognize excellence and to increase information sharing and the utilization of "best practices." (The award has now been extended to the areas of education and government, and forty-two states and many companies have adapted the idea within their organizations as a technique for recognizing and encouraging achievement.) Many of the principles of the "reinventing government" movement described above were originally derived from the earlier "quality movement" in the corporate world, and it is these concepts that are reflected in the Baldrige Award. Included are principles such as service-oriented, customer-driven goals; leadership through organizational vision and the empowerment of employees; information systems for monitoring product quality, customer satisfaction, key competitors, and employee morale in relation to other comparable organizations (sometimes called "benchmarking"); collaborative rather than hierarchical relationships in working with internal and external constituencies; communications among all constituencies which are clear, explicit, detailed, relevant, and documented; and a commitment by all organization members to continuous improvement.[36]

The quality of an organization is judged by evaluating it multidimensionally across the various quality principles. A high-quality organization is one that demonstrates a *pattern* of effectiveness in *matching* the ideals of organizational quality. The Baldrige Award does this by setting forth a series of seven criteria, with each one weighted by a certain number of points.[37] Organizations then submit detailed, written applications documenting their achievements for each of the criteria. These are reviewed and scored on each of the criteria, and then a total score is attained, using the item weightings. Those organizational candidates rated at or near the top are site visited, during which the criteria are examined in more depth. Organizations that attain high ratings across the seven criteria are granted the award.[38]

Cost-Effectiveness Analysis. As mentioned above, cost-effectiveness is a patterned performance indicator that links units of cost input to units of effectiveness output. The "buyer's guide" approach to cost-effectiveness analysis employed by such product evaluation services as *Consumer Reports* can be usefully adapted to human service programs. In the model, various brands of a product like compact cars or a service like life insurance are compared for relative cost and effectiveness. The brand recommended is that which is less costly and/or more effective. In contrast to cost, which is a unidimensional variable, effectiveness—whether for consumer products or human services—is a multidimensional pattern, as was illustrated above in the example of the Baldrige Award, in which seven different weighted criteria were employed to assess the quality of an organization.

In my own work,[39] I have illustrated the applicability of the buyer's guide model to human services by comparing the logic of a *Consumer Reports* evaluation of (a) different brands of self- buffing floor polishes,[40] and (b) different "brands" of service within Community Mental Health Centers (CMHCs) (e.g., the delivery of outpatient therapy services by different geographic teams within a single CMHC, or the delivery of emergency psychiatric services by different CMHCs). Effectiveness for the self-buffing floor polishes is judged both in terms of "major" criteria, such as wear and scuff resistance, and minor criteria, such as freedom from haze and resistance to yellowing. With parallel logic, the effectiveness criteria for the CMHC services are relative reductions in such psychological impairments as work dysfunction, thought disorder, depression, alcohol abuse, marital conflict, and inability to establish social relationships—with CMHC stakeholders deciding what weights to assign to each of the impairment-reduction criteria.

Each "brand" of floor polish or treatment service is then tested on each of the criteria in conditions that are similar for each of the brands—that is, similar floors for the polishes, similar mixes of psychotherapy patients for the CMHC services. The weighted scores are next combined into a single summary-effectiveness score. These summary scores are then combined, respectively, with the unit cost of the floor polishes (cost per application to a typical floor) and the unit cost of the CMHC treatment service for an average patient. Relative cost-effectiveness between brand *a* and brand *b* (of floor polishes or CMHC treatment services) can then be determined by using a matrix formed by two dimensions: whether brand *A* is less, as, or more effective than brand *B*; and whether brand *A* is less, as, or more costly than brand *B*. In six of the nine possible cells of the matrix, the judgment of cost-effectiveness superiority is clear: one brand is superior on one dimension (more effective or less costly) and also superior or not different on the other dimension. In the other three cells (no difference between the two brands, one brand is more effective and more costly, or one brand is less effective and less costly), there is no clear judgment of superiority to be made.

A recent example of the buyer's guide model is a quality review of the country's largest HMOs by *Newsweek*.[41] The magazine surveyed 150 health plans on forty-three key activities, "from the vaccination of children to the treatment of mental-health problems." The eighty-eight plans that provided adequate data were rated on three measures: "keeping members healthy, treating acute illnesses and managing chronic conditions," with adult care and children's care assessed separately on each of these. The various indicators were then combined into three summary indicators: quality of adult care, quality of children's care, and overall quality. Comparative cost analysis, while not included, would have comprised a very natural extension of this analysis.

Goal-Attainment Scaling. Developed by Kiresuk,[42] this is a pattern-matching assessment approach that allows for individual tailoring of goals to the individual client, rather than applying the same, standardized measures to all who receive services. Rossi and Freeman offer the following illustration of the method:

> An alcohol treatment program may have as its objective the reduction in the number of days workers are absent from work because of excessive drinking. In the case of worker A, who is primarily a "weekend drinker," the goal may be to reduce the number of Sundays of drunkenness over a three-month period so that the worker gets to work on Mondays. For worker B, a "binge drinker," the goal may be to reduce the duration of drinking bouts so that the "drying out" period is also reduced.[43]

Goal attainment expectations can be based on the views of practitioners, of clients, of independent judges, or of some combination of the three. The method can be applied across systems levels, for example, to the goals of work teams or human service organizations as a whole.[44] In each instance, at the beginning of a program intervention, a variety of qualitatively different and qualitatively anchored goals (usually in the feasible range of three to seven) are placed on a numerical scale, where

"-2" describes outcomes that are "the most unfavorable thought likely"; "0," those that are at the "expected level of success"; and "+2," those that are at "the best anticipated success."[45] The client's performance vis-à-vis each of the goal scales is assessed at the end of program intervention. The quantitative scaling of the goals allows for the calculation of summary goal attainment scores per client and for comparison of those scores across clients.

Discussion

At the end of a research article, each of the paradigms reviews the study in terms of its original focus. The positivist discusses the implications of the results for general, "nomothetic" theory, while the hermeneut explores case-study-specific, "idiographic" lessons to be learned, especially regarding the empowering of the study's stakeholders.

The pragmatist takes a middle ground with regard to generality, discussing potential application to other, similar case situations. In addition, the pragmatist discusses the relevance of the findings for confirming the general utility of the study's original guiding conception, and/or for suggesting revisions of the guiding conception to make it more useful.

Quality Control

Study Design

Psychology's distinctiveness is based not so much on what it knows than on how it knows. Table 7.2 outlines quality-of-knowledge issues in a psychological study as viewed by the three different paradigms. These issues emerge from the logical connections between the design of a study and the study's goals. In the positivist model, the design's purpose is to ensure the logical adequacy of the study for testing hypotheses flowing from a general, causal theory of psychological functioning. In the pragmatic model, the design's purpose is to ensure the logical adequacy of the study for drawing conclusions about the effectiveness of a particular program and for relating program outcomes to the guiding conception underlying the program. And in the hermeneutic model, the design's purpose is to ensure that the study genuinely documents and articulates the constructs of the study participants.

Construct Validity

The validity of a measure is the extent to which it assesses what it is intended to measure. Since positivists believe in the objective reality of the abstract constructs about which they theorize, they are interested in demonstrating "theoretical construct validity"—that is, that the operationalized, quantitative measures employed in their studies are valid in accurately reflecting these theoretical constructs. Frequently this is accomplished by showing how the correlations of a particular measure with other relevant variables create a pattern that is consistent with the psychological construct that underlies them all.

While pragmatists are not interested in validating theoretical constructs, they are interested in developing valid performance indicators in measuring stakeholder constructs of program process and program goals, that is, in establishing "process construct validity" and "goal construct validity." This involves demonstrating the conceptual links between process or goal constructs, on the one hand, and measures that purport to be reasonable, logically coherent, and sociopolitically fair indicators of them, on the other.

Rossi and Freeman suggest three criteria that are relevant to the pragmatic validity of a proposed process or outcome performance indicator.[46] First, the proposed indicator typically should be consistent with previous usage of the associated construct: for example, "a measure of 'adoption of innovation' must not contradict the usual ways the term 'adoption' has been used in previous studies of innovation." Second, the proposed indicator should be consistent with alternative indicators that have been used persuasively by researchers. Thus the proposed indicator must either produce similar results as other measures or, if different, "have sound conceptual reasons for being different." Finally, the proposed indicator should be internally consistent, such that if several similar indicators are used to measure a concept, the several indicators "should be related to each other as if they were alternative measures of the same thing."

The federal government's Consumer Price Index (CPI) exemplifies issues in developing a pragmatically valid indicator. The CPI has substantial practical import, since it determines, for example, the cost-of-living increases of individuals receiving Social Security. Recently there has been a rethinking of the conceptual model that underlies how the CPI is measured, because today's marketplace has changed since the CPI was originally conceived—for example, there has been a major growth of consumers shopping in large discount stores.[47] From a pragmatic point of view, the important issue is not the positivist's concern with the "true," "objective" nature of inflation, but how to develop a reasonable, clear, coherent, and sociopolitically fair concept of inflation, and then to operationalize this concept into the CPI in a logical manner.

As indicated in table 7.2, because typically no single operationalized indicator can fully and directly measure either a theoretical construct or a program process or goal, both the positivist and pragmatic paradigms use the technique of "triangulation," that is, they use multiple and converging operational measures to add more validity to the assessment of a construct than is possible with any single construct.[48]

Validity within a Study

In a positivist study, the interest is in "internal-causality validity" (or what positivists simply call "internal validity" to differentiate it from "external validity," described in the next section). The goal of internal-causality validity is in establishing genuine, theory-based causal relationships.[49]

In a pragmatist study, while theories of causality per se are not a concern, there is interest in accomplishing two goals that are logically parallel to internal-causality validity. The first, "internal-functionality validity," involves the establishment of pragmatically useful, functional relationships between program intervention variables and client outcome variables. The second, "internal-connectedness validity," involves the presentation of convincing logic and reasonableness concerning the relations among the various components of a case study (see fig. I.2).

In contrast, the hermeneut is not interested in theoretically causal or pragmatically functional relationships within a study. Rather, the hermeneut is interested in "credibility," which Guba and Lincoln define as establishing "isomorphism between [the] constructed realities of [case] respondents and the reconstructions attributed to them."[50] Lincoln and Guba argue that studies will be more credible if the researcher is able

> to demonstrate a prolonged period of engagement (to learn the context, to minimize distortions, and to build trust), to provide evidence of persistent observation (for the sake of identifying and assessing salient factors and crucial atypical happenings), and to triangulate, by using different sources, different methods, and sometimes multiple investigators, the data that are collected.[51]

As indicated by the placement of text in table 7.2, the pragmatist draws on the ideas of the other two models. Specifically, the hermeneut's techniques for establishing credibility—prolonged engagement, persistent observation, and triangulation—are particularly applicable to the pragmatist's development of internal-connectedness validity; while the positivist's approach to internal-causality validity is particularly applicable to the pragmatist's development of internal-functionality validity.

Single-Subject Research Design. A specific example of an applicable validity technique from positivist group research is "single-subject research."[52] In this research design, which has been most employed by behavioral psychologists studying individual subjects, repeated "dependent variable" measures are collected about the individual over time. At certain points during this period, systematic changes are made in the subject's environment, and these comprise the "independent" variable. Through this design, potential changes in the dependent variable in response to changes in the independent variable can be documented and interpreted.

For example, Lawson[53] worked with a divorced thirty-five-year-old male with a history of problem drinking that began at age sixteen. During a "baseline" period of two weeks, the patient self-monitored the number of his drinks per week, which averaged sixty-five. During the next eleven weeks, the patient received comprehensive behavior therapy treatment, consisting of such techniques as targeted reduction in drinking behavior, learning to avoid drink-inducing situations, development of new social relationships and recreational activities, and learning to be assertive about his wishes. During the treatment there was a dramatic decrease to about ten drinks per week that appeared to be maintained at three-month and eighteen-month follow-ups. In other words, the reduction in drinking appeared functionally related to the therapy.

It is possible that some factor(s) other than the behavior therapy accounted for the change in this client's behavior. For example, he might have started with a new girlfriend at the beginning of treatment, motivating him to cut his drinking, independent of the therapy; the association between the therapy and reduced drinking might just be a coincidence.

In order to address such "threats to internal validity," positivist researchers have developed elaborate single-subject research designs.[54] For example, an intervention variable can be absent (baseline), instituted, withdrawn, reinstituted, and then rewithdrawn—to see if a targeted dependent variable varies as predicted in conjunction with each of the phases. Thus, suppose a child's hyperactive behavior is continuously monitored during the following phases: baseline; institution of a "token-economy" program in which the child is given material rewards for calm, attentive behavior; withdrawl of the token-economy program; reinstitution of the program; and then withdrawal of the program. If variation in the child's hyperactive behavior is closely related to the phase changes, such that low hyperactive behavior occurs during the two token-economy periods and not during the other three periods, the positivist researcher is in a stronger position to conclude that the token-economy changes caused the decrease in hyperactive behavior than if only the baseline and initial token-economy periods were employed in the study. The use of multiple intervention and nonintervention phases greatly reduces the chances that changes in the dependent variable were due to a third variable not related to the intervention. It can be seen that while the major work in single-subject research has been conducted with individuals, the same logic can be applied to larger system units—be they groups, organizations, or communities—as long as the unit is studied as a whole.

The pragmatist researcher views single-subject research designs as useful in identifying effective programs and program elements—with two differences from the approach of the positivist researcher. Whereas the positivist researcher is interested in drawing conclusions with regard to *causal theories* of behavior and behavior change, the pragmatic researcher is interested in the pragmatic implications of the *functional relationships* between the program interventions and the client outcome. Also, whereas the positivist researcher tries to control for context and to focus on the quantitative relationships between independent and dependent variables, the pragmatic researcher believes that qualitative context cannot be controlled and that its in-depth study is in fact as important as quantitative analysis. In line with these differences, it should be noted that the positivist is interested in studying the single case because the presence of only one individual reduces the "error variance" created by intersubject differences in a group study. On the other hand, the pragmatist is interested in studying the individual case because of the opportunity to study the qualitative context in which every individual client is embedded.

Applicability to Other Sites

This criterion deals with the capacity to generalize from the results of a particular study to other, similar situations. The positivist calls this capacity "external validity."[55] Ideally, the positivist achieves external validity by randomly sampling from a given population, so that the results of studying a sample can be directly generalized to the population. In this process, the positivist shows that the sample studied is not distinctive in terms of such characteristics as the particular collection of subjects studied, the particular context in which they are studied, and unique historical factors.[56]

In contrast, the hermeneutic and pragmatist models don't try to control contexts, because they contend that contexts are distinctive in many ways and cannot be "controlled." Rather, these models approach generalizability—or what Lincoln and Guba call "transferability"—by an empirical process. The major technique for doing this is to provide a qualitatively rich and detailed description—that is, a "thick" description—of the subjects, setting, and context of the study. Then the reader can decide to what extent the case as described can be generalized to other case situations.

Reproducibility of the Research Process

Positivists assume a world in which psychological and social transactions are caused by underlying, stable, and quantitatively expressible traits and processes. Positivists thus assume that the measurement of "real" traits and processes should be characterized by stability and repeatability. For example, if the one hundred-item, self-descriptive inventory measure of dependency that I administer to fifty people is a true measure of this trait, I would expect an internal consistency among the responses, such that the dependency score derived from the odd items of the inventory will correlate across the fifty individuals with the score derived from the even items. Thus a high correlation indicates high "odd-even reliability of measurement." Moreover, if my measure of dependency is reliable, I should find that the scores on the first administration of the dependency inventory to my fifty subjects correlates highly with the scores from a second administration at a different point in time, i.e., the inventory should show high "test-retest reliability of measurement."

Hermeneuts reject the assumption of "something tangible and unchanging 'out there.'"[57] Rather, they view the "out there" as "ephemeral and changing."[58] It follows that "noted instabilities cannot be simply charged off to the inquiry procedure; they are at least as much a function of what is being studied as of the process of studying."[59] In short, hermeneuts reject the positivist notion that there are stable phenomena to study and that reliability of measurement is a prerequisite to concluding that one's measurements are tapping what is important and "real." Moreover, there are expected inconsistencies in a hermeneutic study because of its emergent design, which means that deliberate methodological changes and shifts in constructions (as opposed to changes due to sloppiness, boredom, burnout, etc.) are expected.

On the other hand, hermeneuts do recognize the importance of "dependability," that is, being able to document dependably these changes and shifts in such a way that they can be reconstructed by a research auditor. In the words of Guba and Lincoln,

> Such changes and shifts need to be both tracked and trackable (publicly inspectable), so that outside reviewers ["auditors"] of such an evaluation can explore the process, judge the decisions that were made, and understand what salient factors in the context led the evaluator to the decisions and interpretations made.[60]

As indicated in table 7.2, pragmatists selectively use concepts about reproducibility of data from the other two paradigms. Where possible and useful, pragmatists employ positivist criteria of reliability when using standardized, quantitative measures. For example, to the extent that SAT tests can reliably sample verbal and math aptitudes—that is, the kinds of reliability figures called for in the positivist model are attained—and to the extent that SAT tests are useful beyond themselves (e.g., by increasing the fairness of the college admissions process), then the reliability of SAT tests is pragmatically important to establish and maintain. The same can be said of political polls or economic indicators.

On the other hand, the pragmatist does not assume that measures that do not meet the criteria of positivist reliability are not of important meaning and value. For example, the seven ratings in the 1993 Baldrige Award (quality of leadership, information, strategic planning, and so forth)[61] are meaningful and valuable if they conceptually reflect the model of organizational quality around which there is consensus among important corporate stakeholders—independent of whether these ratings are highly intercorrelated. Thus the seven ratings are not viewed as items on a scale of the trait of "quality," but as reflecting different facets of a multidimensional construct. In fact, there might be concern if there was high inter-item reliability because this could imply that only one dimension was in fact being rated, such as a single "halo" dimension of the general impressiveness of an organization.

The hermeneut and positivist positions would seem to concur on the importance of inter-*rater* reliability for measures such as the Baldrige ratings. Here the question is, do different raters (including "research auditors") agree on how they interpret and rate the same collected information? The pragmatist also endorses inter-rater reliability. Even though pragmatists do not believe in objective reality, they do believe in socially constructed views of reality rather than views that are idiosyncratic to each particular individual. Socially constructed reality is based on cultural and historical continuities and convergences upon shared constructs. This is true even though it is recognized that these are only constructs rather than pictures of objective reality and that these constructs are subject to ongoing revision through sociocultural negotiation and action. Moreover, the value of a program from the pragmatic perspective can be judged only on the basis of consensually agreed-upon goals, again emphasizing the importance of social concurrence upon meaning. Thus, for pragmatists, the capacity for different raters to agree on interpretations of data—both quantitative and qualitative—is an important component of a valid and useful measure.

Addressing the Researcher's Interests and Values

Positivists believe in the possibility of accessing objective reality when the researcher's "bias" and "values" are neutralized. This leads them to strive for "value neutrality" of the research and lack of "experimenter bias." (This is one of the reasons why positivists stress quantitative data, because its decontextualized nature strips away the emotional, value-laden content of language, which is intrinsic to qualitative data.) One way of reducing bias in quantitative studies is the use of "double-blind" designs, in which both the researcher and the research subject are ignorant of what experimental conditions are being administered to whom. This design is highly publicized in the testing of medical procedures and medications.

Pragmatists do not believe in the knowability of objective reality or the separability of data, facts, theories, and values. However, pragmatists do affirm the importance of the *relative* reduction in the researcher's personal interests and values that appear to interact unduly and interfere with the design and conduct of a study; and they do emphasize the need for researchers to clarify explicitly their values. In addition, pragmatists acknowledge the advantage of reducing emotionality by quantification for dealing with certain situations. In line with this, pragmatists view the strategies for bias reduction developed by positivists, such as the double-blind design, as very helpful.

Hermeneuts like Lincoln and Guba eschew the notions of objective knowledge, value neutrality, and bias reduction, including the use of double-blind designs.[62] However, they do endorse the notion of "confirmability," which involves assuring that data, interpretations, and outcomes in research are rooted in contexts and persons of the case apart from the researcher, e.g., by the use of a research auditor's assessment of the content of the research. Pragmatists find the strategy of confirmability a useful approach in dealing with qualitative data.

Authenticity

Authenticity criteria are unique to the hermeneutic case. Lincoln and Guba set forth six such criteria, and these are listed in table 7.2.[63]

Linking Frameworks

Peterson's model of professional activity as "disciplined inquiry," shown in figure 1.2, provides an overview of the logic associated with the pragmatic alternative to positivist thinking. The discussion above, summarized in table 7.1, offers a detailed development of the disciplined-inquiry model by translating its logic into a research report framework that parallels that of the positivist and hermeneutic research paradigms.

The categories of activities presented in figure 1.2 and table 7.1 follow the same sequence, outlined in table 7.3. As shown, the Introduction section of a pragmatic case study article describes the *client* and the client's presenting problems, together with three perspectives that the practitioner (or practitioner team) independently brings to the case: the practitioner's *guiding conception* (the theoretical and philosophical approach he or she typically brings to this type of case), the practitioner's previous professional *experience* with this type of case, and previous published *research* that bears on the case.

TABLE 7.3
Major Points of Correspondence between Figure 1.2 and Table 7.1

Professional Activity As Disciplined Inquiry (FIGURE 1.2)	Outline of a Research Article in the Pragmatic Paradigm (TABLE 7.1)
A. Client	Introduction
B. Guilding Conception	
C. Experience, Research	
D. Assessment	Method
E. Formulation	
F. Action	Results
G. Monitoring Evaluation	
H-K. Feedback Loops	
L. Concluding Evaluation	Discussion

The Method section focuses on the practitioner's individualized *assessment* of the client and the client's situation, yielding a *formulation* of what is happening in this particular case. The formulation is then translated into a plan for program intervention services.

The Results section describes the actual intervention services that are administered—that is, the *action* of the practitioner. The effects of the action are next assessed by a *monitoring evaluation*, the results of which comprise *feedback loops* to stimulate possible recycling through earlier phases of the case. Finally, in the Discussion section, reflections upon the study are contained in a *concluding evaluation*.

Note should be made of a very helpful resource that translates many of the case-study issues outlined in tables 7.1 and 7.2 into a set of practice standards for guiding the activities of the pragmatic researcher. Titled *The Program Evaluation Standards: How to Assess Evaluations of Educational Programs* (2d ed.),[64] this book is the consensus product of a wide variety of psychology and other professional associations whose members are involved in evaluations generally, and educational evaluations specifically. The standards are divided into four sections: *utility standards*, which focus on the information needs of intended users; *feasibility standards*, which focus on ensuring that an evaluation will be "realistic, prudent, diplomatic, and frugal"; *proprietary standards*, which focus on ensuring that an evaluation will be conducted "legally, ethically, and with due regard for the welfare of those involved in the evaluation, as well as those affected by its results"; and *accuracy standards*, which focus on ensuring that an evaluation will "reveal and convey technically adequate information about the features that determine worth or merit of the program being evaluated."[65]

From Single Case to Database

More Cases Lead to More Capacity to Generalize

The pragmatic approach to knowledge generation in psychology does not stop with the production of a single case that meets the methodological requirements outlined in tables 7.1 and 7.2. The real payoff of the pragmatic method does not come until cases are assembled and organized into large, accessible databases. In most types of human service situations—say conducting psychotherapy with a forty-year-old female panic disorder client who is also experiencing severe marital problems, or teaching third grade in a blue-collar, "white ethnic," suburban school district—any single successful case is limited in the number of case situations in the future to which it will particularly apply. This is because large contextual differences can occur between a target case and any other case that is randomly drawn out of a heterogeneous case pool. However, as cases in the database grow, they begin to sample a wide variety of contextually different situations in which the target problem can occur. Thus, as the number of cases in the database rises, the probability increases that there are specific cases in the database that are particularly relevant to an ongoing target case. One of the challenges in designing a case study database is therefore to provide methods to "match" a new, ongoing target case with directly relevant and helpful completed cases in the database.

The need for a large number of cases in a useful pragmatic database can be contrasted with the logic of the positivist study. By experimentally or statistically "controlling" for the impact of contextual factors, a single positivist study can test a general theory—say of mechanisms in phobia or of learning processes in third-graders. Results from this one study then have the logical potential of generalizing to the treatment of all phobics or the teaching of all third-graders—or at least to the population from which the study sample was purportedly representatively drawn. Thus, as discussed earlier,[66] the capacity of a positivist study to generalize to new situations is a function of the study's *logical design* vis-à-vis how it relates general characteristics of the study to general characteristics in the new situation. In contrast, the capacity of a pragmatic (or hermeneutic) study to generalize to a new situation is an *empirical question*, dependent upon how much the context and focus of the completed case do in fact correspond with the context and focus of a new or ongoing case.

Contemporary cognitive psychologists discuss the issue of the uniqueness versus the generality of experience in the following way:

> People live in a world of perpetual novelty, in which no experience is ever exactly repeated. Yet paradoxically, many would agree that "there is nothing new under the sun." The "illusion of familiarity," as it might be called, depends on the power of the human mind to find—and, if necessary, to create—similarities between past experiences and the present situation. Perceived similarities enable one to organize objects and events into familiar categories—cats and dogs, friendships and love affairs. But how do categories get formed? One basic mechanism is *analogy*—the process of understanding a novel situation in terms of one that is already familiar.[67]

Over forty years ago, the personality theorist Henry Murray made this same point: "Every person is in some ways like all other people, in other ways like some other people, and in still other ways like no other person."[68] When it comes to "matching" previous cases for generalization to a new case, it is the middle level of generality—the ways in which some of us are the same—that is of most interest. Those aspects of a case that are universal will apply to all of us (all human beings have limited life spans, develop language and other meaning systems, function as information-processing devices, act in both loving and hostile ways, develop and maintain family units and larger social institutions and cultures, and so forth). And those aspects of a case that are unique are by definition not generalizable per se (e.g., an individual or organization being born/created in a particular place at a particular time with particular parents/founders and subsequently being supported or not by particular parents/administrators, and so forth).

In order to determine most effectively the comparability of cases at the "middle level" of similarity, it is necessary to have a detailed, qualitative, "thick" description of the conditions and context of cases—as indicated in the "applicability to other sites" section of table 7.2. A good model for pragmatic psychology in this regard is judicial law. The basic unit in judicial law's knowledge base is the individual case, including transcripts of everything that was said and presented during the case, the judge's or jury's decision and the rationale for that decision, and all similar documents from any appeals associated with the case. The overall process in a judicial case is to view the unique constellation of the case's facts in the context of a legal conceptual framework (parallel to the psychologist's "guiding conception" [see fig. I.2]). This legal conceptual framework is defined in most U.S. law by both legislated principles and English common-law principles, that is, principles that are induced from across a variety of past cases.

Bromley[69] uses the term "quasi-judicial method" to refer to the parallel between case study use in psychology and in the law. "Quasi" acknowledges that rules of evidence in the courtroom are different in important respects from those in psychology, be they positivist, pragmatic, or hermeneutic rules of evidence. However, both case study use in psychology and in the justice system can develop "case law." These are

> the rules and interpretations that emerge from comparisons and contrasts between successive cases. Provided the similarities and differences between cases have been stated explicitly, and justified by means of cogent argument and empirical evidence, the resulting "patterns of meaning" provide convenient conceptual routines for handing subsequent cases of the same type.[70]

"Case-Based Reasoning": Learning by Analogy

Past cases provide guidance for understanding and action in present cases because of those features of past cases which are similar to features of the present cases. In short, we "learn from experience." This principle is the basis of a branch of computerized, artificial-intelligence systems called "case-based reasoning" (CBR). Developed in the early 1980s, CBR is a methodology that solves new problems by adapting previously successful solutions to similar problems.[71]

> At its most simple, case-based reasoning is based on the observation that when we solve a problem we often base our solution on one that worked

for a similar problem in the past. An example would be driving to work. When you get in the car in the morning you don't explicitly plan your route, you take the route you usually take. If you meet a traffic jam you may remember how you avoided a similar jam in the past. If you take an alternate route to avoid a jam and it's a success, you will remember it and perhaps use it again in similar circumstances in the future.

CBR is thus a deceptively simple problem solving paradigm that involves matching your current problem against problems that you have solved successfully in the past.[72]

Parallel to the earlier discussion in chapter 6 about the nature of human service programs, CBR theorists view a case as generally involving three components: "the *problem* that describes the state of the world when the case occurred, the *solution* which states the derived solution, and the *outcome* which describes the state of the world after the case occurred."[73]

The process of matching relevant past cases to solve a present problem can be enhanced by adapting past solutions so that they more closely match the current problem.[74] In CBR logic, when dealing with a present, target problem, a cyclical process is used. First, the target problem is matched against cases in the case base, and one or more similar cases are *retrieved*. This similarity is based on a mapping process in which systematic correspondences between the target problem and past cases are identified. These similarities can involve (a) identical content elements (e.g., both cases involve depressed, older, white males, or both cases involve inner-city schools with a high percentage of students for whom English is a second language); or (b) identical relations among content elements (e.g., the flow of electrons in an electric circuit is analogically similar to the flow of people in a crowded subway tunnel). Once similar past cases have been identified, a solution suggested by these past cases can then be considered, for example, it can be *reused* and tested for success. However, unless the retrieved case is a close match, the solution will probably have to be *revised*, producing a new case. This new case can then be *retained* and added to the original case base. In this way, knowledge accumulates and the growing case base becomes more and more capable of proposing direct solutions—or, in the case of the complex situations addressed by professionals such as psychologists, physicians, and lawyers—more and more capable of generating relevant guidelines for solutions.

In the computerized artificial intelligence field, CBR is contrasted with "knowledge-based systems" (KBS).[75] KBSs were designed primarily in the 1970s to emulate the human diagnostic and classification process. Initially intended for medical diagnosis, they consist of several parts: a collection of facts and their relationships (a "knowledge base"), a collection of IF . . . THEN rules that encode the expert's problem-solving knowledge (a "rule base"), and an interpreter program (an "inference engine") that translates a present problem into the terms of the knowledge base. It can be seen that KBS parallels the positivist, hypothetico-deductive approach to problem solving, in which the "knowledge base" is a validated theory and application of theory to practice involves deducing rules for applying general principles to particular problems. In short, then, the contrast between KBS and CBR parallel, respectively, two distinctions discussed in the Introduction between how professional practice takes place: (a) Peterson's model of professional activity as "applied science" versus "disciplined inquiry"; and (b) Dreyfus and Dreyfus's model of rule-following, "novice practice" versus contextually accommodating "expert practice."[76] While KBS has a track record of many successes in practical decision making, it also has important limitations for situations involving ill-defined, poorly structured, open-ended, complex problems—the type of problems that subsequently lend themselves to several interpretations or require holistic analysis. It is just these types of problems that are the strength of CBR.[77] And these are the kinds of problems that dominate applied psychology and the other human service fields.

It should be noted that the positivist structure of KBS and the pragmatic structure of CBR have parallels in educational theory and practice. Traditional education developed in a modern framework and follows a KBS type of logic, with formal, clearly defined disciplines—like English, math, history, or science—consisting of a body of facts that deductively flow from certain theoretical principles. The pragmatic and proto-postmodern philosopher John Dewey inspired a reaction against traditional education and proposed instead a "progressive education" model, in which teaching is problem focused, case based, and interdisciplinary. Children in a progressive-education class might have a project such as designing locker organizers:

> Designing locker organizers . . . requires the students to understand the variety of ways lockers are used; concepts of geometry; and concepts about physical structures, supports, and materials. They might engage in taking surveys and learn both math concepts (e.g., sampling, averaging, and

probabilities) and social science concepts (e.g., question asking). They might learn concepts in geometry through drawing and manipulation of shapes. They might learn physics concepts from consideration of the kinds of support structures their locker organizers need, and so on.[78]

Cognitive research has found that case-based learning is a distinct advantage in the classroom. Learning is deeper and more effective when the student sees content as relevant and is engaged in real-world problem solving than when knowledge is gained through memorization, prescriptive activities, or word problems.[79] I maintain that this lesson is true of applied knowledge creation generally: problem-driven, contextualized, pragmatic understanding is "deeper" and "more effective" in developing successful human service programs than understanding that is theory driven and based in artificial, experimentally controlled conditions.

PART IV

Application

In this section I explore concrete applications of how the pragmatic case study logic functions and its advantages over positivistic psychology. I illustrate these ideas for two socially important and timely areas: the controversies associated with the "psychotherapy crisis" in professional psychology precipitated by the growth of managed care (chapter 8), and the controversies associated with different ideological approaches to educational reform (chapter 9). In each instance, I explore the polarizing "culture wars" over general principles that pervade the specific area and the role that the pragmatic paradigm can play in transcending these by focusing on individual programs that work and that can be employed as models for other, similar programs.

8

Psychology and Psychotherapy

From "House of Cards" to
"House of Cases"

To be or not to be grounded in the "applied science" model:[1] that is the question faced by clinical psychology therapists. Yes, this model provides the scientific rationale for the privileged societal status that professionals claim for their expertise (e.g., via state licensing of psychologists). Yet to buy into this model relegates the practitioner to the role of a technician mechanically employing basic scientific principles from the laboratory, principles that are contextually peripheral to the systemic complexities and ambiguities of the natural world to which the practitioner is committed.

At the opposite end of the continuum, some therapists who follow a postmodern, hermeneutic paradigm thoroughly reject positivism, and even proudly flaunt this by explicitly advocating for an "unscientific psychology."[2] They deliberately throw off the mantle of science for the artist's smock. While this frees a professional's literary, subjective, and creative capacities from the shackles of positivism, it also raises major questions about the viability of professional psychology as a discipline separate from some combination of literature, journalism,[3] drama,[4] and/or a secular ministry,[5] and thus it seems to undermine any claim that applied psychologists have for special societal status.

Of course, many therapists position themselves somewhere in the middle of this continuum, but wherever they are, they are caught in the dialectical forces built into the continuum itself.

Enter pragmatism, a third alternative championed in this book. Grounded in the "disciplined inquiry" model, pragmatism has the attraction (for some) of being a hybrid, integrating elements from the other two paradigms. Moreover, authors like Peterson, Schön, and Polkinghorne argue cogently that the pragmatic paradigm represents what therapists actually do when they are functioning most effectively; and this book presents a methodology demonstrating that a case-study database can be created with rigorous empirical grounding. However, this database has yet to be implemented; and thus at the present time, the pragmatic paradigm does not have the empirical grounding needed to compete culturally and politically on scientific grounds with the positivist model.[6]

The debate rhetoric among these alternative models for therapy has been increasing dramatically.[7] Nonpositivistic clinicians claim that psychotherapy has been "raped,"[8] that managed care is "a growing crisis and nightmare,"[9] that the therapy of managed care is not "therapy as commonly understood,"[10] that cooperation with managed care companies is like collaboration with the Nazis, and that their livelihoods have been ruthlessly stolen.[11] Positivistically committed, "scientific" psychologists counter that psychotherapy as presently practiced is based on intuition and subjectivity that are in conflict with the process and content of scientific psychology.[12] In fact, these positivists have been working closely with managed care companies to establish "practice guidelines" that require standardized and mechanized treatment packages whose logic does away with the need for doctoral training in professional clinical psychology.[13]

In effect, then, this is clinical psychology's variant of the "culture wars." After reviewing this battle in some detail, the present chapter explores the unrealized potential of the pragmatic paradigm for helping to resolve the conflict and self-destructive battles that permeate clinical psychology today.

An End to Our "Era of Good Feeling"

Over the past thirty-five years, interest and practice in psychotherapy has exploded in the United States. Between 1967 and 1980, the proportion of the U.S. population using mental health services increased from 1 percent to 10 percent, with most of the increase focused on outpatient therapy services.[14] This movement has substantially accounted for the significant growth and prosperity of clinical psychology over this period.[15] Clinical psychologists, whose entry degree is an academic or professional doctorate (the Ph.D. or Psy.D., respectively), have successfully presented themselves as senior, expert therapists because of their advanced training, their association with psychology's history of scientific research on human behavior and experience, and their established licensing status in all fifty states.

All this has taken place in a pluralistic, diversifying period within the discipline, with postmodern voices challenging the traditional positivist paradigm of research and application.[16] This pluralism has spawned a mind-bending variety of therapy models—four hundred by one estimate.[17] Even within such traditional frameworks as psychoanalysis and behavior therapy, there are a dizzying panoply of options. For example, within psychoanalysis there are now long-term and short-term models. And within the short-term models, while there are therapies that focus on traditional Freudian "drive" and "ego" concepts such as aggressive, sexual, and dependent impulses and defenses against them, there are also "object relations" theories that pay particular attention to social relationships, "self psychology" approaches emphasizing the crucial role of empathy in "healing" psychic pain, and others that focus on pathogenic beliefs and the way they are manifested in relation to the therapist.[18]

As another example, behavior therapy is now divided into a variety of submodels. Some of these include (a) "applied behavior analysis," which focuses on the application of Skinner's "radical behavior" principles of operant conditioning to a wide range of clinical and social problems; (b) a "neobehavioral, S-R" model based primarily on the application of Pavlovian classical conditioning; (c) "social learning theory," an approach developed by Bandura and his colleagues which emphasizes observational learning and the integration of classical and operant conditioning and cognitive mediational processes, such as the well-known concept of "self-efficacy"; (d) Staats's "paradigmatic behaviorism," which emphasizes the integration of conditioning theory with traditional concepts in personality, clinical, and social psychology through the concept of "personality repertoires" of sensory-motor, emotional-motivational, and language-cognitive responses; and (e) "cognitive behavior therapy," which derives its main impetus from the "cognitive revolution" in general psychology, emphasizing cognitive processes and private events as mediators of behavior change.[19]

Cross-cutting these types of theoretical differences are epistemological differences underlying the various therapy models. Roughly, the models can be arrayed along a continuum whose poles are represented by the modern positivism versus postmodern constructionism dialectic summarized in chapter 4. For example, traditional cognitive-behavior therapists identify with the modernist, positivist paradigm of mainstream research psychology, striving to base their approach on laboratory-derived principles of human functioning. In contrast to these "objectivist" models are postmodern "constructivist" models, including some of the recent psychoanalytic therapies, other traditional approaches such as humanistic-experiential therapy and strategic family systems therapy, and some very new models explicitly labeled as "narrative" or "constructivist."[20] Traditional cognitive and behavior therapies tend to focus on the remediation of discrete behavioral and cognitive dysfunctions, repairing misdirected conditioning processes and correcting errors and malfunctions in a patient's information processing system.[21] In contrast, the constructivist therapies look more holistically at the personal story or narrative that patients[22]—like all of us—have constructed to describe and explain their lives. The goal of constructivist therapy is a "narrating and renarrating of one's story in the process of which the story gets elaborated, transformed, and repaired."[23] In sum, the therapist is no longer a repairer of broken conditioning or information systems, but rather a "co-constructionist" who helps patients to be aware that there are "multiple realities" to choose from as the patient's life story is reworked so as to result in more positive consequences for the patient's lived experience and concrete life situation.[24]

During the 1970s and 1980s, health insurance funding for psychotherapy was increasing and was able to accommodate the wide variety of different therapies. This co-existence was empirically bolstered during the 1970s by statistical "meta-analyses" of large numbers of therapy outcome studies, which concluded that no one system of psychotherapy had yet to be found to be most successful in addressing the diversity of presenting problems typically encountered in practice.[25] This led to the now famous "Dodo Bird verdict,"[26] which was lifted from *Alice's Adventures in Wonderland*: "Everybody has won, and all must have prizes."

Toward the end of the 1980s, two forces caused an end to the apparent pluralistic calm within the psychotherapeutic community, and within organized psychology generally. First, by 1987 the proportionally higher growth of professional psychologist members in the American Psychological Association (APA) had motivated some of the more research and academically oriented psychologists to break away and form their own association, the American Psychological Society (APS).[27] This split between the research and practice arms of psychology was reflective of the overall diversifying culture within the discipline that was discussed in chapter 2.

Second, by the late 1980s a public consensus emerged that overall health costs—including the cost of outpatient psychotherapy—had spiraled out of control, crossing the 10 percent of gross national product level in 1985, and reaching 14 percent in 1992.[28] The existent fee-for-service, business-and-government-insurance-based system subsequently became less and less economically viable. This stimulated the growth of managed care as a vehicle for controlling the growth of—and perhaps even reducing—health care costs.[29] A crucial cost-cutting strategy of managed care was to decrease the volume of health and mental health services, leading to a reduction in the need for psychotherapists and other health professionals. The resulting oversupply of psychotherapists, including psychologist therapists, has heated up competition for and intensified conflict over limited resources.

These two forces—increasing divergence between scientists and practitioners and reduced opportunities for therapists in the era of managed care—have come together to create a major battle over the "heart and soul" of psychologist-conducted psychotherapy. On one side are "scientist-practitioners," who subscribe to the applied science model, who ally themselves with the American Psychological Society, and who emphasize a positivistic approach to the conduct and evaluation of therapy. For shorthand, I will refer to these clinical psychologists as "scientists."

On the other side of the battle are "scholar-practitioners," who ally themselves with the American Psychological Association (APA).[30] These are by and large psychologists who practice and function outside academic settings and who are not involved in formal research programs. They consist of two groups. The first, which is by far the largest, consists of professionals who purport to ground their assessment and therapy in both positivistic psychological science *and* clinical experience, and whom I will hereafter call "science-purporting clinicians," or simply "clinicians." The second group consists of professionals who explicitly reject positivism and fully embrace a constructionist point of view, whom I will hereafter call "constructivist clinicians." Both types of professionals emphasize their conceptual and theoretical training—hence the phrase "*scholar*-practitioner"—and do not purport to be positivist scientists per se, as do the scientist-practitioners. And both types of scholar-practitioners subscribe to some version of the disciplined inquiry model, which views the clinician as an integrator of theory, positivist and/or nonpositivist research, clinical experience, and the context-based facts of the cases they serve.

The Battle

The scientist-practitioner/scholar-practitioner battle has escalated rapidly in recent years. A lightning rod for directing attacks by scientists on clinicians has been Robyn Dawes's[31] polemical, provocative, and admittedly angry book, *House of Cards: Psychology and Psychotherapy Built on Myth*. Dawes's arguments are based on an assumption that the only "true" clinical psychology is the applied science model, and that science-purporting clinicians have in fact abandoned science in favor of intuition and subjective clinical experience, leading frequently to practice that is unsupported by or even at times contrary to such evidence. (Dawes does not directly address the theory, practice, and rhetoric of constructivist therapists, except by implication he seems at times to reject any approach to psychology that is not thoroughly positivistic.)

Dawes attributes his anger to the misuse of public funds in supporting science-purporting clinicians, who are perpetuating three types of "fraud" in the areas of assessment and therapy. In addition, a fourth kind of "fraud" has been identified by those who have recently extended Dawes's logic.[32]

Dawes's angry accusations (and the support of them by other scientist-practitioners),[33] together with the precipitous decrease in resources for psychotherapy with the advent of managed mental health care, has created a "crisis of survival" for clinical psychology practitioners.[34] Great distress among practitioners has been documented and widely commented upon.[35] For example, in a series of focus groups with practitioners, the Widmeyer Group found "a palpable sense of a proud and caring profession disturbed by the seeming lack of control over their destiny . . . [with] a strong emotional experience of mourning the loss of the way things used to be."[36] And deep concern is expressed that psychology's internal fighting is self-destructive, that the dialectic has become diatribe, and that individual combatants are "fiddling while psychology burns"[37]—that is, the fighting within psychology is ceding leadership and control in the development of managed care to other mental health professions, such as psychiatry and social work.

Below is a review of each of the accusations of fraud that Dawes and other scientists hurl against clinicians, and some of the responses of mainstream clinicians to these charges. What emerges is that while the clinicians are justified in their argument that in many ways the scientists' accusations are too strong and at times clearly unfair, ultimately the clinicians lack the empirical evidence to combat fully the accusations. The last section of the chapter demonstrates how the case-based, pragmatic paradigm can provide a means for clinicians to develop such a body of empirical evidence.

Accusation 1. Clinicians Pay Only Lip Service to Science

Dawes asserts that individually and collectively through its organizations, professional psychologists give the impression that their highest value is the scientific basis of their work, when in fact they often only pay lip service to it. As reviewed earlier, there are still strong modernistic forces in our culture, and being viewed as having a scientific basis of one's work endows it with a privileged status. In fact, this purported scientific basis appears to underlie the public's strong support of psychology as it has mushroomed in growth over the last thirty-five years.

To illustrate his thesis, Dawes provides a number of vivid examples of psychologists and other clinicians whose behavior flies in the face of scientific reasoning, which should be careful, critical, and evidence based.

For example, Dawes cites a licensed California psychologist, Edith Fiore, who claims—along with fourteen colleagues around the country—to overcome the ill effects of being abducted by extraterrestrials (ETs), who frequently sexually abuse their "victims" and then hypnotize the abductees so that they will forget the experience. Some of the symptoms of such abduction, like sleep disturbances, are purported to be similar to those of individuals who have been sexually abused or raised in satanic cults and subsequently "forgotten" the experience. Fiore and her colleagues claim they can help their patients recall the experience because "the subconscious mind has a memory bank of everything we ever experienced, exactly as we perceived it. Every thought, emotion, sound of music, word, taste and sight. Everything is faithfully recorded, somehow in your mind. Your sub-conscious mind's memory is perfect, infallible."[38]

Dawes is particularly incensed by the fact that Fiore and her colleagues are state licensed, an accreditation process justified in part by the purported scientific foundation underlying professional psychology:

> Here we have a striking example of the "license to ignore" gone haywire—in this case, to ignore virtually every study that has ever been conducted on the nature of human memory, especially those that show that memory under hypnosis is *not* more accurate than in a waking state. . . . [The body of scientific research has shown that] the actual process of recalling is that

of recalling bits and pieces of the past ("memory traces") and filling in the gaps with what "makes sense" to us now.[39]

The implications of these studies make it unsurprising that hypnosis produces "recall" of experiences involving ETs and UFOs, since one of the symptoms Fiore lists is obsession with ETs and UFOs. Bridie Murphy lives again, only this time she is sanctified by a state license.[40]

Clinicians Reply

Dawes has found a few blatant examples that the vast majority of us would agree reflect unscientific and unscholarly thinking—whether one is identified as a positivist or a constructionist. However, we repudiate the implication that these examples are typical of clinical thinking. As stated by some of the leaders associated with the scholar-practitioner model, "The profession has a proud history of commitment to inquiry, skepticism, and self-evaluation. . . . There is nothing in the concept of "professional" that implies undisciplined applications of techniques to problems."[41]

It is important in this context to distinguish two meanings of "science." One meaning is identified with modernistic positivism and refers to belief in the discovery, through the experimental method, of objective, universal, and decontextualized laws about the natural, biological, psychological, and social worlds.

The other meaning of "science" refers to disciplined, critical, reflective thought that compares and contrasts evidence arguing for alternative interpretations or explanations of a particular phenomenon. This meaning of science is embedded in Peterson's disciplined inquiry model, and in the use by hermeneutic scholars of the term "human science."[42] Also, this is the meaning of science that James, Dewey, and the other pragmatists had in mind when they championed the "scientific attitude." Because the pragmatists viewed the world as an unlimited complex of variety, change, and novelty, with knowledge consisting of contextually limited guidelines and not general laws, they emphasized openness and a critical perspective on any particular established body of knowledge. It is in this context that Dewey said, "The future of our civilization depends upon the widening spread and deepening hold of the scientific habit of mind."[43]

In sum, many different scholars, theorists, and professionals—pragmatists, psychologist practitioners, physicians, academics in the humanities, hermeneutic writers—are "scientific" in the sense of bringing intellectual discipline and rigor to their work, even though they function out-side the experimental, positivist paradigm modeled by traditional physics and chemistry.

Accusation 2. More Training Does Not Mean More Therapeutic Effectiveness

The whole system of therapist training and credentialing is based on the assumption that the amount of training and experience a clinician has—which are the basis of the credentialing process—are related to that professional's therapeutic effectiveness.[44] This distinguishes "novice" from "expert" therapists, "doctorally trained" from "master's trained" therapists, and so forth. To qualify for state psychological licensing, typ-ically the clinician must have received a doctoral degree and completed a full year of supervised clinical practice. In some states, a professional must keep up with continuing-education courses to retain licensing. There is no criterion in the whole credentialing process which requires that a therapist's patients meet certain standards of outcome for those types of patients, for it is assumed the training and experience are suffi-cient ingredients for clinical effectiveness.

It's a shock to learn from Dawes, then, that psychotherapy outcome studies as a group have not found a consistent and clinically significant advantage of experience as related to therapy outcome. Dawes discusses perhaps the most famous study supporting this conclusion, one in 1979 in which well-credentialed, highly experienced psychoanalytically ori-ented therapists were no more effective in counseling than university pro-fessors who had no training in psychology.[45] To broaden his conclusion, Dawes cites Smith, Glass, and Miller's[46] classic meta-analysis of 375 psy-chotherapy outcome studies which yielded no correlation between expe-rience and outcome; Berman and Norton's later meta-analytic study which concluded that professionals and minimally trained "paraprofes-sionals" do not differ in treatment effectiveness;[47] and Stein and Lam-bert's[48] study review which concluded that level of experience of profes-sional psychotherapists was unrelated to their efficacy.

Clinicians Reply

Yes, it is true that there has not been consistent and dramatic evidence of the advantages of clinical training and experience in the research studies that have been conducted. However, a careful reading of the literature—which is much larger than the study reviews Dawes cites—reveal methodological problems and limitations in these studies.[49] For example, frequently the range of experience sampled is quite limited. In the Smith, Glass, and Miller meta-analysis, the average therapists had only 2.91 years of training plus experience, and in the Stein and Lambert review, most of the therapists had less than five years of practice. Another methodological problem is the fairly consistent finding of a generally higher dropout rate of patients who are in therapy with less experienced clinicians. The efficacy rates of less experienced therapists could thus be elevated since less motivated patients become in essence screened out of their caseload, and they become judged on an unequivalent group of less challenging patients.[50]

Also, not all the reviews cited by applied science advocates that find no differential effect of experience seem to be employing appropriate studies. For example, Christensen and Jacobson[51] recently concluded that "the existing psychotherapy literature . . . has failed to find a relationship between level of therapist training and outcome" by citing a 1993 literature review that they conducted.[52] However, Seligman critically points out that Christensen and Jacobson

> review studies in which manuals are used, mild and uncomplicated clinical problems are the diagnosis . . ., and duration of therapy is brief and fixed. These are precisely the situations in which clinical judgement, experience, and education matter very little. A seven-year-old may be able to fly a one-engine plane in clear weather, but this does not mean he or she can handle a Boeing-747 in a thunderstorm.[53]

Moreover, not all the studies of training and experience achieve negative results. For example, significant correlations between training and experience and outcome were found in a meta-analysis of a large number of studies of rational-emotive therapy[54] and in a parallel study comparing family physicians and specialist mental health workers who worked with psychiatric patients.[55] Also, in a recent meta-analysis completed after Dawes's book was published, Stein and Lambert[56] looked at thirty-six therapy studies and found significant effect sizes for the relationship between experience and outcome, as measured both by pre-post measures of symptoms and by patient self-ratings.[57] This finding was in spite of problems in the definition of experience. For example, Stein and Lambert found that researchers frequently classify experience using global criteria, such as the type of degree held by a therapist, treating as homogeneous both newly degreed therapists and those who have many years of practice experience.

Accusation 3. Statistics Trump Live Clinicians

A result of clinical psychology training and experience is the ability to make uniquely accurate and valid psychiatric diagnoses and clinically relevant predictions. Right? Wrong, argues Dawes. This is the domain of studies of clinical versus actuarial prediction, which were first summarized by Paul Meehl as far back as 1954.[58] In sample studies, clinical versus statistical approaches are used to predict which parolees will commit further crimes, whether the final diagnosis for an inpatient will be one of "neurosis" or "psychosis," which mentally ill individuals are more likely later to commit violent acts, and which officers will later be involuntarily terminated from a police force. Meehl has pointed out that the distinction between clinical and actuarial methods does not refer to the kinds of information on which predictions are based, but rather to the way the information (such as test scores, interview impressions, behavior observation ratings, and performance records) is combined. In "clinical" prediction, "experts" examine all available information, integrate it in terms of their clinical understanding, and offer their judgmental prediction. In "actuarial" prediction, research is carried out to determine which variables in a predictor set are actually correlated with the outcome and how the various factors should be weighted into a formula that maximizes predictive accuracy.

In Meehl's original study, twenty studies were reviewed, and not one showed clinical prediction to be conclusively superior to actuarial prediction. In 1989 Dawes, Faust, and Meehl[59] summarized what by then was one hundred studies, and reached the same conclusion. Dawes points out that the same types of findings hold in other settings, such as predicting bankruptcy in business or predicting future heart attacks. Thus the problem does not seem due to the incompetency of clinical psychologists, but rather to the inferiority of human judgment compared with statistical formulas in combining large and complex amounts of information to make predictions.

Clinicians Reply

We agree that there are situations in which actuarial prediction is more accurate than clinician prediction. But these situations are limited in that they have discrete, clearly operationalized outcomes for which base-rate data have been collected. In the individual case—be it the possibility of suicide, the determination of which parent is better qualified in a custody hearing, or the assessment of whether a criminal defendant is innocent by reason of insanity—context and complexity dictate against operationalizing a discrete outcome or collecting base rates on similar types of situations. Moreover, typically the purpose of psychological assessment is to gain an understanding of an individual's inner experience, dynamics, and pattern of psychological functioning, not to predict discrete behaviors.

Accusation 4. Prepackaged Therapies Trump the Thinking Clinician

The previous section discussed the lack of evidence that expert clinical judgment in psychological diagnosis and prediction is superior to statistical formulas that make such judgments in a standardized and "mechanical" manner. A parallel question emerges in the field of therapy. Here the outcomes achieved by clinicians developing an individualized treatment formulation and plan for each particular patient and implementing it in a flexible, reflective manner is pitted against that of a standardized package of procedures that are operationalized and documented in a formal procedures manual, similar in some ways to a cookbook. This question packs an enormous political and economic wallop. For if so-called "manualized therapy" is as or more effective than "individualized therapy," managed care companies are likely to set their "practice guidelines" to choose manualized therapy, since the managed care companies, as businesses, prefer that which can be objectified and standardized so as to maximize management and control.[60] These "practice guidelines" determine what types of patients will be financially approved to receive what types of treatment. And so the debate between whether managed care's practice guidelines will require manualized or individualized therapy is much more than a theoretical one—it's also about power and money.

Manualized therapy and the so-called "efficacy" research paradigm in which it is embedded emerges directly from the positivist, applied science model. Thus, theoretical principles are discovered in the laboratory and used to derive discrete procedures that are thought to have specific therapeutic value in addressing particular disorders. This therapeutic value is established by operationalizing and standardizing the procedures into a treatment manual, which typically includes a fixed number of patient contact sessions. Research studies are then conducted following a design similar to the "double-blind" drug study. Specifically, patients are randomly assigned to receive either the manualized therapy or some type of presumably less efficacious "control" procedure—parallel to the "placebo" condition in drug studies. Also, there are clearly defined inclusion and exclusion criteria for patients and an adequate sample size to provide proper statistical power. Finally, the outcome of each patient is systematically assessed by evaluators who are blind regarding to which group the patient has been assigned. If a number of these efficacy studies show that patients in the experimental therapy groups consistently achieve better outcomes than those in the control groups, the therapy is said to be scientifically supported and declared to be an "empirically supported treatment" (an "EST"). Once having achieved this state, technicians can be taught to administer the manual on a routine basis. (This type of "efficacy" research is contrasted with "effectiveness" research, which is reviewed later in this chapter.)

With an eye to having concrete input into managed care practice guidelines, in 1995 a task force of the Division of Clinical Psychology of the APA[61] published a report listing twenty-two therapies that they viewed as successful for twenty-one different psychological disorders, as supported by efficacy research, that is, those approaches that are ESTs. Two sets of criteria were employed: one for a "well-established treatment," and one—somewhat less demanding in amount but not type of evidence—for a "probably efficacious treatment."

The use of manuals has a number of straightforward advantages. Since treatment is operationalized and standardized, it is easier (a) to determine exactly what interventions were offered to a patient, (b) to assess degree of therapist adherence to intended procedures, (c) to facilitate replication of a study, (d) to increase the effectiveness of training, and (e) to increase consistency of treatment in dissemination.

While EST studies do focus on a specific disorder, advocates point out that there is frequently heterogeneity in the patients seen in EST studies. Drawing on research studies of bulimia nervosa, one well-known researcher points out that patients enrolled in these studies often have multiple problems and relatively poor prognoses since controlled clinical research is often their last resort after they have failed to improve in previous attempts at therapy.[62]

The results of the Division of Clinical Psychology Task Force, based on reviews of the psychotherapy outcome literature, established a wide variety of "well-established" treatments, most being short-term and cognitive-behavioral. Since the whole process was based on a rational, scientific model and resulted in a substantial number of empirically supported treatments—with all the above-mentioned advantages of ESTs—applied science advocates argue that manualized treatments should form the basis of practice guidelines in managed care, that is, they should be the core treatments that managed care companies approve for reimbursable mental health services.

Moreover, applied-science advocates point to a number of studies that compared manualized to individual treatment for the same disorder, and claim that the results show that manualized is at least as effective, if not more.[63]

Treatment manuals are specifically designed to take precedence over clinical judgment, because advocates claim that clinical judgment is susceptible to cognitive biases. Such biases are also cited by authors like Dawes to account for why there is a superiority of statistical over clinical prediction and diagnosis. In fact, there is a large literature empirically documenting bias in human information processing generally, including a subgroup of studies on clinicians. For example, Turk and Salovey[64] describe two basic types of cognitive errors clinicians commit when faced with difficult judgments about complex diagnostic information. The first type involves overutilization of generally valid, intuitively reasonable strategies. An example is "confirmatory bias," which occurs when clinicians over-rely on their theories about patient personality and diagnostic types as opposed to observation. Another example is the "availability heuristic," which occurs when clinicians estimate the probability of an outcome or event based on salient characteristics brought to mind (e.g., the most recent or the most emotionally loaded information) rather than by a logical analysis of the situation.

The second type of cognitive error involves the underutilization of formal, logical, and statistical decision-making strategies. An example is the "representativeness heuristic," which occurs when the clinician matches a present case with the essential features of an existing schema, and too early discards important information that doesn't fit into that schema. Another example is the cognitive error of "underutilization," which occurs when clinicians ignore important base rate information in favor of intuitive judgment.

Applied-scientist advocates argue that not only do cognitive errors undermine the professional's ability to make accurate and effective judgments and decisions in assessment and therapy, but also there are scientific reasons why professionals don't learn from experience. Specifically, authors like Dawes point to a literature on concept formation and perceptual motor learning (e.g., learning to drive) that concludes that for experience to create new, effective learning, it must involve feedback from emitted responses that is "immediate, systematic, and subject to a minimum of probabilistic distortion."[65] And yet the typical clinical situation involves a patient presenting problems, therapist formulations, treatment interventions, and patient responses, all of which are complex, not always clearly defined, and not formatted in terms to yield clear, undistorted feedback. The ambiguity, complexity, and lack of clear feedback are a recipe for perceptual distortion, such as focusing only on certain types of dysfunctional behaviors, or self-fulfilling prophecies ("when a person is judged to be irredeemably violent and sentenced to death, for example, this judgment itself may be a factor in facilitating later violence").[66]

Applied-science advocates argue that the above constraints on a practitioner's functioning—the likelihood of cognitive error when making judgments and the inability to obtain the type of feedback needed for proper learning—argue against giving the clinician judgmental discretion to individualize therapy or to make assessment-based judgments. By extension, this line of thinking argues for the abolition of doctoral training of professional psychologists,[67] since the technicians required to conduct manualized training don't need more than master's-level training. This is also desirable from the point of view of managed care companies, since master's-level clinicians are less expensive than doctoral-level.

With regard to ESTs limiting the therapist, EST advocates also counter that good manuals have process components built in. Also, a manual can have the flexibility of providing the option of setting aside the manual for treatment of a specific disorder if other patient problems become more pressing (or simply switching to another manual-based treatment), and then returning to the original manual when these problems subside.

In sum, the bottom line of applied-science advocates is that doctoral-level professional psychologists should be phased out, and they should be replaced with master's-level clinical technicians. These technicians would administer the manualized therapy packages designed by scientist-practitioner clinical psychologists, whose training focuses upon scientific research and scientific theory development. This scenario is politically ideal for scientist-practitioners: it makes their scientific research role the *only* role in doctoral clinical psychology, and it places them in a position to gain access to all of the reduced resources now available for doctoral clinical psychologists.

Clinicians Reply

While acknowledging the advantages of manuals vis-à-vis standardization, specifiability of treatment, trainability, and so forth, we hold that manuals do not represent "therapy as commonly understood"[68] and as practiced outside the laboratory and in the field. The constraints placed on therapists and therapy process by manuals and the other EST criteria of the APA Task Force seem almost politically "rigged" in favor of the cognitive-behavioral model.[69] It's a little like the old joke of the inebriated man who is looking for his keys under the street lamp—not because he thinks he lost them there, but because the light is better there! Just because it is easier to conduct research with cognitive-behavioral therapy than with psychodynamic, experiential, or family systems therapies does not make the greater quantity of research in cognitive-behavioral therapy definitive.

Moreover, EST critics point to the discrepancy between (a) the EST findings of the superiority of specific cognitive-behavioral techniques for specific disorders, and (b) the results of most studies, starting with the classic Smith, Glass, and Miller and "Dodo Bird" meta-analytic studies, in which few differences among therapy outcomes as a function of theoretical approach were found. One explanation of this discrepancy is simply that the therapies that are not cognitive-behavioral have not been tested by manualized, experimental studies—in part, because this paradigm seems inappropriate to these therapies. After a recent review of the EST literature, one group of scholars put it this way:

> We were struck by how little research there is within each disorder which directly compared the authors' favored cognitive or behavioral treatments to other well-specified treatments. Time and again, the comparative treatment studies reviewed ended up as horse races between a thoroughbred racehorse and a nondescript nag: one well-defined cognitive or behavioral treatment against a vague psychodynamic "treatment-as-usual" condition.[70]

In any event, findings of nondifferentiation among therapies continue. Two recent examples of large, multimillion dollar, government-sponsored studies specifically designed to meet the methodological criteria of EST research are the National Institute of Mental Health (NIMH) Treatment of Depression Research Program and "Project MATCH," sponsored by the National Institute on Alcohol Abuse and Alcoholism. In the depression study, patients were randomly assigned to one of four conditions, including cognitive-behavioral therapy or "interpersonal therapy" (an offshoot of psychodynamic therapy), with the result that both treatments were found equally effective.[71]

In Project MATCH, patients were randomly assigned to one of three manual-guided, individually delivered treatments, which were designed to be highly contrasting theoretically:

> CBT [Cognitive-Behavioral Coping Skills Therapy] was based on social learning theory and viewed drinking behavior as functionally related to major problems in an individual's life, with emphasis placed on overcoming skills deficits and increasing the ability to cope with situations that commonly precipitate relapse.
>
> TSF [Twelve-Step Facilitation] was grounded in the concept of alcoholism as a spiritual and medical disease with stated objectives of fostering acceptance of the disease of alcoholism, development of a commitment to participate in AA, and beginning to work through the 12 steps. . . .
>
> MET [Motivational Enhancement Therapy] was based on principles of motivational psychology and focused on producing internally motivated change. This treatment was not designed to guide the patient, step by step, through recovery, but instead employed motivational strategies to mobilize the individual's own resources.[72]

It was hypothesized that the treatments would be differentially effective for different types of alcohol patients. For example, CBT was hypothesized to be especially effective for patients with characteristics like cognitive impairment and psychiatric severity; TSF, for patients with characteristics like greater meaning seeking and sociopathy; and MET, for patients with characteristics like high conceptual levels and low readiness to change.[73] The findings revealed that all three treatments were successful in achieving baseline to one-year posttreatment, but that there was little difference in outcomes by type of treatment.

Another example of this trend of nondifferentiation among specific treatment procedures is a large-scale research survey conducted by *Consumer Reports*, under the scientific directorship of Martin Seligman, the 1997–98 president of the APA. Included were 4,100 individuals who had been in psychotherapy or "emotional counseling" with a variety of mental health professionals or family physicians. Among the study's findings was that while patients as a whole "benefited very substantially from therapy," "no specific modality of psychotherapy did better than any other for any disorder."[74]

To explain the lack of differentiation among specific types of therapy, clinicians point to a large, robust research literature on "nonspecific" or "common factors," that is, generic factors that span the different models of therapy and would seem on their face to be therapeutic. In his classic *Persuasion and Healing*, Jerome Frank[75] posited that all psychotherapeutic methods are elaborations and variations of age-old procedures of psychological healing. In the therapy context, these include factors such as an emotionally charged, confiding relationship between patient and therapist; warmth, support, and attention from the therapist in a healing setting; a positive therapeutic alliance between therapist and patient; a new rationale or conceptual scheme offered with confidence by the therapist for patients to frame their problems and goals; a therapeutic ritual; and the passage of time. For example, a meta-analysis of twenty-four studies revealed that 26 percent of the difference in the rate of therapeutic success was associated with the quality of the therapeutic alliance.[76] In contrast to the belief of EST advocates that therapeutic potency resides in specific techniques of intervention,[77] nonspecific-factor advocates view techniques as secondary: "Techniques are ritualized methods of human relatedness and communication. . . . Techniques and the personal meanings they involve are always embedded in human relationships."[78]

Messer and Wachtel,[79] two therapy researchers generally associated with the psychodynamic model, discuss a number of the constraints and limitations intrinsic in the criteria and associated research used for ESTs (or, using an alternative term, what they call "EVTs," "empirically validated treatments"). One limitation focuses on the narrow view of outcome measures employed in the EST research as compared with the broad purview of psychoanalytic therapy research. Psychoanalytic therapy addresses outcome criteria that are more complex and subjective than cognitive-behavioral outcome criteria, and thus they are harder to study:

> Often left out or unable to fit within the research paradigm currently in favor for "EVT" research are not only such considerations as character change, genuineness, integrity, or depth of feeling, in contrast with a narrow focus on symptoms or readily measurable social behavior, but a concern as well, for some psychodynamic and experiential therapists, with the

process by which change is achieved (Gold, 1995). Within this view, therapy crucially involves such processes as exploration, self-discovery, and learning to be more empathic with oneself and others, all of which contribute significantly to symptom reduction and behavioral change but are not reducible to those dimensions of outcome alone.[80]

Messer and Wachtel also question the relevance of the use in EST research of pure diagnostic types, for example, "pure" depressives or "pure" obsessive-compulsives. Even though EST advocates point to heterogeneity in the patients seen in EST studies, Messer and Wachtel counter that the ideology of EST proponents tends to minimize outcome assessment beyond a focus on the target problem.

Some EST critics[81] point out that manuals can function as "straitjackets," overly limiting the therapist's choices. And there is some empirical research to suggest that overly close adherence to a manual can have negative effects, perhaps because a therapist's primary focus on the technique prescribed by the manual can dull his or her interpersonal sensitivity and timing.[82] Finally, disagreeing with the scientists' critique of clinicians' cognitive abilities, EST critics argue that manuals undermine the clinician's capacity to formulate a case and to tailor treatment in response to the unique complexities of a case—thus undermining the clinician's capacity to function as an "expert" practitioner according to Dreyfus and Dreyfus's typology of cognitive process.[83] Manuals also cut off the therapist's creativity in integrating concepts and procedures from different theoretical models. For example, Stricker calls for the integrative therapist to select and mesh together relevant treatment interventions from multiple systems of therapy. This integration, reflecting Peterson's disciplined inquiry model, is then to be "tested in the crucible of the therapeutic experience, and both the therapist and the patient will provide correctives to initial misconceptions. Thus, directionality among the three tiers of experience, technique, and theory is multiple and circular, as each one can influence the others."[84]

A Pragmatic Proposal

The pragmatist approaches the scientist-clinician battle with a constructionist attitude, viewing the scientists and clinicians as each having a viable perspective, but only that—a perspective. There is no single truth, just alternative perspectives, each with its own set of conceptual and practical strengths and weaknesses.

The goal of the pragmatist is to search for the set of concepts and activities that will best serve the needs of those who are stakeholders in psychotherapy. This includes the patients, their families, their work settings, and their neighborhoods; psychologist therapists, other therapists, and their professional associations; managed care administrators; the ultimate payers, be they insurance companies, businesses, or government; and the larger society, which is concerned about whether therapy is a general cultural good. From the pragmatist's point of view, the ultimate focus is upon what benefits patients derive from therapy, and whether these benefits are sufficient in quality and quantity to merit support from the nontherapist community.

Within this framework, the pragmatist draws three conclusions from the battle between the scientists and clinicians explored above. First, the scientists have impressively rigorous data and are correct that there are no strong and systematic, alternative data offered by clinicians to justify their position. Second, the clinicians are correct that the positivist's data are not in tune with the pragmatic paradigm that guides their work, and thus these data are not directly relevant to the monitoring and validating of psychotherapy as it is usually practiced. Third, both sides have persuasive, offsetting theoretical arguments for the advantages of their point of view, for example, therapy permeated by standardization, operationalization, experimental control, and quantitative measurability for the scientists versus therapy permeated by sensitivity to complexity and context, flexibility, and creativity for clinicians.

The pragmatist is not definitively persuaded by the strengths of either side's theoretical arguments, because ultimately the pragmatist is interested in what works empirically with a particular kind of patient in a given set of conditions—not in what is "objectively true" theoretically. Thus, if the conditions of comparison are the same and viewed as fair to each paradigm, it might well be that certain manualized therapies are superior to parallel nonmanualized, more open-ended therapies. But, as pointed out by the scientists themselves,[85] such a finding does not necessarily validate basic science principles and, implicitly, the applied science (as opposed to the disciplined inquiry) paradigm. Rather, the pragmatist views the manualized therapy in this comparison as a technological package that in fact works. Even though it might have been inspired by or is conceptually linked to certain scientific principles, there are always alternative theoretical explanations for why it works.[86] Moreover, any therapy—manualized or not—takes place in a particular context. There are distinctive particulars with regard to the therapist's guiding conception, the therapist's openness to ongoing feedback and possible revision of the guiding conception, the personal and social style and skills of the therapist, the personal and social style and skills of the patient, whether the therapist and patient interpersonally "bond" to create a positive "therapeutic alliance," the patient's present life situation and history, the nature of the patient's presenting problems and goals, and so forth. All of these factors and others reciprocally interact to create the final set of transactions called "therapy" with this individual. While the therapist's guiding conception—which includes the theoretical model engaged in the therapy—is important and to be taken seriously, it is only one factor that leads to the ultimate outcome of the case.

In light of the above, I propose the following six-point plan for conceptually and politically mediating conflict between the scientists and the clinicians. The two groups can then join forces to turn their attention to the common purpose of finding ways to improve (a) the relevance of therapy goals in light of societal and clinical priorities, and (b) the cost-effectiveness of therapy approaches and technologies in meeting these goals. As improvements develop, the groups can work together to take a leadership role in incorporating these improvements into the national system of mental health services.[87]

The Plan

1. There will be a political truce between the scientists and clinicians.
2. The scientists will continue to conduct manualized-treatment-based "efficacy" studies and accrue a body of information about the relationship between packages of therapeutic procedures and therapy outcomes for different types of presenting problems and orders.
3. The scientists will also seek to expand the relevance of their research method to therapy as actually practiced through the development of "effectiveness" studies, which are scientifically complementary to efficacy research (and which are described below).
4. The clinicians will collaborate with the scientists in designing and conducting effectiveness studies, since this type of research integrates scientific and clinical perspectives.

5. In conjunction with pragmatically oriented scientists, the clinicians—both science-purporting and constructivist—will develop a database of pragmatic case studies. In line with the guidelines outlined in tables 7.1 and 7.2, these will comprise systematic, rigorous evidence of the outcome of therapy, thus meeting the calls of scientists for this type of evidence, and yet the form of the research will be in tune with the "disciplined inquiry" epistemological paradigm clinicians use in their practice.

   Moreover, the quantitative and qualitative documentation of the case studies will provide clinicians with the type of explicit, systematic, and rigorous feedback that Dawes has pointed out is necessary for maximal learning from experience and is missing in usual clinical practice.[88]

6. All the resulting efficacy, effectiveness, and case-study data will be pragmatically integrated and interpreted within an adaptation of Kenneth Howard's "patient-focused research" paradigm.[89] This model focuses on (a) the development of a database of expected outcomes of various types of patients—the outcomes and types to be decided on a combination of political, conceptual, and empirical grounds;[90] (b) use of the database to monitor an individual patient's progress over the course of treatment and follow-up; and (c) use of the monitoring data to aid in rational decision making by various stakeholders about the progress of that patient's therapy.

Each of the steps in the plan will be reviewed below.

The Truce

The present battle between scientists and practitioners in clinical psychology is detrimental for both. Scientists use the present accountability pressure of managed care to push for limiting accountability to the efficacy model, over which they exert control. This opens them up to counterattacks from clinicians and could limit the parameters available to behavioral managed-care treatment in the future—not based on evidence, but upon acceptance of a paradigm that excludes all but efficacy evidence. On the other hand, by not generating alternative outcome and accountability data, clinicians undermine their credibility as major players in the evolution of managed-care policy and practice guidelines. Peter Nathan, a clinical psychologist associated with both the worlds of scientific and practitioner training, has framed the situation dramatically, calling for a methodological broadening of the empirical database upon which therapy practice guidelines are grounded:

> Psychologists fiddle while the profession burns. While we've been arguing, the psychiatrists have produced a series of comprehensive practice guidelines [on major depressive, bipolar, substance abuse, nicotine dependence, and schizophrenic disorders]. . . .
>
> It seems time—actually, well past time—to ask whether organized psychology is going to permit psychiatry and the American Psychiatric Association, by *fiat*, to establish the standards of practice by which psychologists are bound. . . . [There is a need] to bring practitioners into more active collaboration with clinical researchers.
>
> . . . The ultimate product [is] ESTs which many more professional psychologists can endorse [that is, ESTs which are open to *both* "applied science" and case-based, "disciplined inquiry" data]. [This] will permit us to move on to creation of our own empirically-derived psychological treatment guidelines: our own standards of practice.[91]

Therapy in the Laboratory versus in the Field

While efficacy studies have many methodological virtues, Seligman—a leading clinical psychologist with excellent experimental and applied credentials—argues that "the efficacy study is the wrong method for empirically validating psychotherapy as it is actually done because it omits too many crucial elements [that is, the appropriate context] of what is done in the field."[92]

For example, some of the contextual properties included in psychotherapy conducted in the field but excluded from efficacy studies include the following:

1. Therapy in the field is *not of fixed duration*. Rather, the time of treatment is tailored to the needs of the individual. In contrast, in an efficacy study the number of sessions are fixed, in order to help "control" and "standardize" the package of therapy administered.
2. Therapy in the field is *self-correcting*. If one technique or approach is not working, the therapist is not constrained to follow particular techniques in a fixed sequence in a manual, as in an efficacy study, but can switch to other techniques or approaches.
3. Patients in therapy in the field often arrive there by *active* shopping, taking an active role in seeking out and selecting the particular therapist and type of therapy they want. In contrast, patients

enter efficacy studies by a *passive* process of random assignment and acquiescence with whom and what are offered in the study.

4. Patients in therapy in the field usually have *multiple problems,* and therapist formulations include the multiple problems as a system as they reciprocally interact. Patients in efficacy studies are typically selected to have one diagnosis by a detailed set of inclusive and exclusive criteria.

5. Therapy in the field is concerned with *broad-based improvement* across a variety of domains, while efficacy studies usually focus only on symptom reduction within the specific disorder targeted.[93]

As an alternative to an efficacy methodology, Seligman identifies a methodology he calls "effectiveness" research. Effectiveness research assesses the outcome of therapy as it is actually delivered, in an "uncontrolled" manner, in the field—without a manual, with duration linked to patient progress or insurance limits, with patients with multiple problems who actively choose their therapist, and so forth.

Seligman emphasizes that efficacy and effectiveness research have different strengths and weaknesses. Generally, efficacy research has high internal validity but low external validity. Since the conditions under which it is conducted are highly controlled, the researcher can have a strong degree of confidence in her ability to infer that any difference found is due to the particular set of therapy procedures varied within the study, since all other possible confounding variables are controlled "in one fell swoop" by random assignment of patients. On the other hand, efficacy research has low external validity, that is, the research has a low degree of confidence in generalizing the results of the particular study to field conditions because of the differences between how efficacy studies are designed and how therapy is conducted in the field—as detailed above.

In contrast, effectiveness studies have the opposite profile of strengths and weaknesses. They have high external validity because they directly sample therapy as practiced in the field, and thus there is little "inferential distance" when generalizing to other therapy populations. Effectiveness studies have low internal validity because there are a number of potential "confounds" in explaining why the results within the study came out the way they did.

Seligman explains that while in his earlier work he favored efficacy designs, it bothered me that I always paid a price when I designed an experiment, and to operationalize the independent variable and choose the population, I had to strip them of much of the reality to which I wanted to generalize. For example, in . . . [my] helplessness experiments, inescapable shock [for a mouse] is quite far removed from the death of a husband, and animals lying down and not moving during shock is quite far removed from passivity and depression in nature. It then took an elaborate chain of argument and further experiment to convince myself and others that I could generalize to uncontrollable life events and depression in humans.[94]

In effectiveness research, then, the independent and dependent variables, although operationalized, are very close to the real target of eventual generalization, and the group investigated is usually a sample of exactly the target population. Alternative causes (both those internal to the participants or external in the situation) are explicitly stated, measured, and controlled for by statistically separating them out—although there is a cost.

The cost here . . . [is that it is] necessary to specify, operationalize, and test explicitly for the influence of [each of the possible] alternative internal and external causes; for unspecified third variables cannot be eliminated in one fell swoop as they can in the experimental method using the right control groups for external third variables and random assignment for participant third variables.[95]

An example can be seen in Seligman's direction of the *Consumer Reports (CR)* study mentioned above. In the study, Seligman found that the longer therapy went on, the more overall improvement occurred. One interpretation of this finding is that therapy is a potent service, and that the more of it there is, the more helpful it is—somewhat like physical therapy for the individual rehabilitating from an accident. However, since the *CR* study did not involve random assignment to the short-term and long-term groups, one could hypothesize, for example, as an alternative explanation that those in long-term therapy were initially more disturbed and that they improved more because they had a longer way to go on the improvement scale (the "ceiling effect"). Another explanatory possibility is that those in long-term therapy were therapy "junkies" and "true believers," individuals so committed to therapy as a way of life that they bias the results in this direction by their combination of commitment to long-term therapy and a highly positive view of its results. To test out both of these alternative hypotheses, analyses were run by statistically separating out from the outcome ratings the effects of initial severity and consumer satisfaction. The correlation between length of therapy and overall improvement remained highly significant, providing empirical evidence that the relationship was not an artifact of severity or therapy "junkies."

In a related analysis, CR looked into the possibility that the benefits of long-term treatment could be an artifact of sampling bias. Specifically, there is a possibility that people who are doing well in treatment selectively remain in treatment, and people who are doing poorly drop out earlier; that is, it might be that "the early dropouts are mostly people who fail to improve, but later dropouts are mostly people whose problem resolves." To test this hypothesis, CR looked at the termination rates of subgroups as a function of how long they were in treatment, from less than one month, to 2 months, to 3–6 months, to 7–11 months, to 1–2 years, to over 2 years. The termination rate across all these subgroups was quite similar, providing evidence to disconfirm the hypothesis of sampling bias as the cause of the correlation between length of treatment and amount of improvement.

While the relationship between long-term therapy and outcome held up when initial severity was statistically separated out, CR did find that the people who received long-term treatment were different. They were more severely troubled, more emotionally disturbed, and more likely to receive psychodynamic treatment. Because of the just-discussed analyses ruling out other interpretations, Seligman concludes that this group of patients chose long-term therapy because they believed it would help, and their therapists made the clinical judgment that this was appropriate. Thus the results can only be generalized to this subgroup. "We cannot infer that long-term therapy would work with patients randomly assigned to long-term therapy who did not believe in long-term therapy and whose therapists did not believe that long-term treatment was the appropriate modality."[96]

Seligman provides many other examples of the use in the CR study of statistical control in place of random assignment and other experimental controls. One of these deals with possible sampling bias. The main sample in the CR study was recruited by a questionnaire which was sent to all of CR's readers, and only 13 percent of the questionnaires sent were returned. One can raise the possibility that those who responded had high motivation because they had unusually positive experiences with therapy, and thus they were unrepresentative of the total population of therapy patients. To test this hypothesis, *CR* conducted a "validation survey," in which postage was paid and the respondent was compensated. While the return rate went up to 38 percent, there were no differences between data from the two samples.

It is important to note that Seligman's model of addressing alternative interpretations to initial findings one by one—instead of in an experimental "one fell swoop"—is similar to the process of analyzing a pragmatic case study. Specifically, in the previous chapter on the case study method, I refer to analysis of the guiding conception in terms of what seems to make the program more or less successful, including such emergent analytic techniques as "grounded theory."[97] In this type of analysis, a first pass is made of the qualitative and quantitative data and a causal interpretation is offered. Then alternative explanations of the initial data discussed are generated, and additional data are mobilized to see if it conforms to the original explanation or seems to point to an alternative explanation.[98]

Let Each Case Speak for Itself: Kenneth Howard's Method

Both efficacy and effectiveness studies focus on the average impact of particular therapy interventions across a group of individual patients, with the former studying therapy under special, experimental conditions, and the latter studying therapy in actual practice. While, as reviewed above, these two models differ in the extent to which they trade off contextual relevance for experimental control, both seek to derive general causal principles about specific factors that are therapeutically potent. With regards to managed care, the goal of this knowledge is to provide input for practice guidelines. These practice guidelines, based on general principles, would then be applied to assign resources to each individual case, without being responsive to the context and complexities directly associated with that individual case.

A decision-making methodology for managed-care psychotherapy that would be more in keeping with the pragmatic paradigm would be to collect systematically relevant process and outcome data from each case, and to employ the cumulating database in the decision-making process. By employing standardized input and outcome measures for each case, norms could be inductively established for superior, average, and inferior outcomes relative to a particular type of case. Then, for example, ongoing decisions over time about how to treat a problem of violent outbursts that interfere with a particular patient's work functioning and close relationships could be based on what is happening in the actual case over time. It would not be based on what a limited number of research studies revealed about the treatment of this *type* of case, independent of the case's *particulars* vis-à-vis the particular therapist, therapy process, and unique life circumstances of the patient. The whole cumulating case database would be used to develop expectations for how this type of patient should progress over the course of therapy, and based upon those expectations, it would be possible to monitor the case over time in terms of its comparative outcome.

If the case deviated from the average expected outcome, the process information about the case would become especially important. In cases with superior outcomes, the process information would help to differentiate whether the deviation from average goal attainment was due to exceptional therapy or to special opportunities and patient strengths in the individual case. In a parallel way, in instances of inferior outcomes, the process information would help to differentiate whether the deviation from average goal attainment was due to problematic therapy, or to special constraints, obstacles, and complexities in the case. In both instances, as the case database developed, there would be more and more cases of a particular type with "superior" or "inferior" outcomes, allowing for cross-case analyses of factors and themes to provide guidelines for improving the overall practice of therapy with that type of patient.[99] As more and more "superior" outcome cases emerge, newly differentiated categories of type of patient might emerge as these cases are shown to have distinct patterns of patient characteristics; and likewise for the emergence of more and more "inferior" outcome cases.

The question might be raised as to why the pragmatic case-study advocate would commit to standardized measures for patient characteristics and patient progress. Isn't this a "nomothetic" (group-focused) approach being imposed upon the "idiographic" process of the individual case study? The answer to this question involves distinguishing between the systematic account of what happens in the case study, which is a "scientific," *descriptive* question, and the goals of the case study project, which is a *value* question. The practical purpose of a national system of therapy funded by various governmental and private groups is to help individuals achieve goals that are valued by various stakeholders, including the larger society; and it is through standardized measures of outcome that these values are operationalized.[100]

In line with this view, the categories of the American Psychiatric Association's *Diagnostic Statistical Manual* (DSM)[101] are viewed by the pragmatist not as psychiatric entities discovered in the natural world. Rather, the DSM categories are viewed as a practical list of constructed types of behavioral, cognitive, and emotional patterns that the mental health profession argues should be labeled as "dysfunctional," with the implied value that societal resources should be devoted to changing these psychological patterns. To the pragmatist, the DSM is more about identifying values than identifying naturally occurring "disease entities."

Standardized therapy outcome measures can thus be viewed as quantitative performance indicators of goal-attainment in areas such as reduced anxiety, depression, and panic attacks; improved assertiveness skills; and increased productivity and job satisfaction at work. In a different society—for example one which is more communally and less individualistically oriented than the United States—there might well be different goals that the society sets for the types of psychological patterns labeled as "dysfunctional" and/or "sick" and for which change is desirable.

The reason why standardized measures of patient typing and therapy outcome are needed, then, is because the capacity to compare individuals is required by the ultimate objective of our national system of therapy, which is to decide how best to allocate resources to achieve our nationally agreed-upon mental health goals.[102]

A methodology to achieve the pragmatic goals just reviewed has been developed and pilot-tested by Kenneth Howard and his research group. In contrast to the "treatment-focused research" paradigms of efficacy and effectiveness studies that focus on specific intervention variables, Howard calls his approach "patient-focused research," because it is focused on the individual patient's course of progress. Howard points out that this type of research is of particular practical interest to "clients" of a particular therapy: the patient, who wants to know how he is doing relative to other patients; the clinician, who wants feedback on her work; the managed-care decision maker, who needs data to help choose how much therapy the patient should continue to receive; and the sponsor, who pays for treatment and wants to know the value of what the money is buying.

Howard's general model for developing patient-focused research is as follows:

1. Establish empirical norms for how patients of a particular type progress at regular time points over the course of therapy. When this is done, there will be data to know the expected, average course of therapy for a particular type of patient over time.
   A. This task involves establishing a series of performance indicators for monitoring outcome over time.
   B. This task also involves establishing a methodology for placing patients into discrete categories by type. For example, in Howard's "COMPASS Treatment System" implementation of the general model approach to be described below, he employed statistical patterns among eighteen intake variables to create patient types.
2. Monitor how each patient progresses over the course of therapy, relative to how the average patient of this patient's type progresses. Then one can conclude whether this patient is doing well, average, or poorly relative to "average" treatment progress.

Following the logic of their general model, Howard and his colleagues have created the COMPASS Treatment System.[103] In designing and developing their system, Howard et al. did not attempt to gain widespread political consensus among the various stakeholders about patient types and outcomes.[104] Thus, Howard et al. do not set forth COMPASS as necessarily the correct implementation of their general model, but use it only as an illustration of an alternative way for implementing the model.

Based on their own program of empirical research, Howard et al. concluded that there are three general, sequential phases of a patient's progress in therapy. The first is "remoralization," which is combating the typical patients' attitude of feeling frantic, hopeless, and desperate upon entering therapy.

The second phase is "remediation" of a patient's symptoms, "the symptoms that led that person to feel so upset and demoralized that he or she had to seek treatment."[105]

The third phase is "rehabilitation," which is focused on "unlearning troublesome, maladaptive, habitual behaviors and establishing new ways of dealing with various aspects of life (e.g., problems of relationship patterns, faulty work habits, and trouble-causing personal attitudes)."[106]

In order to create a comprehensive set of therapy outcome indicators, Howard et al. use outcome criteria associated with each of the three phases, which include subjective well-being, symptom reduction, and life functioning, respectively. They constructed an overall treatment criterion, the "Mental Health Index" (MHI), which consists of the sum of these three scores for any patient at any point in time. Howard validated the MHI by comparing scores of 6,591 patients at the start of therapy with those of 493 nonpatients. This analysis revealed that only about 15 percent of the patient sample had scores higher than 60, while 50 percent of the nonpatient population did.

Howard created patient types by statistically examining how each of eighteen clinical variables impacted upon a patient's profile of outcome scores over time across a large number of therapy outpatients. Those variables and patterns of variables which did statistically differentiate groups of patients were employed as the basis for "grouping" a patient into type. These clinical characteristics included diagnosis, severity of disturbance, chronicity of problems, pattern of presenting problems, and attitudes toward treatment (e.g., confidence that treatment will help).

The utility of Howard's method has been explored in a large group of about 6,500 patients in diverse settings across the country. Two cases from these data illustrate a particularly successful and a particularly unsuccessful course of therapy.

Patient A started at an initial MHI percentile score of 38. His clinical characteristics indicated a profile that would reach a percentile score of 65 percent in fifty-two sessions. Instead, A reached a score of 90 percent in twenty sessions. A is described as follows:

> [He was] a 36-year-old African American, remarried man. His clinical diagnosis was dysthymia. He presented with various family problems, including feeling overwhelmed at home, having financial problems, having a wife with failing health, and experiencing the recent death of a friend. During treatment, he worked on grief issues and on having more realistic expectations regarding his marriage. His wife was brought in for a few sessions, which seemed to help the therapeutic process.[107]

Patient B started at an initial MHI percentile score of 56. His clinical characteristics indicated a profile that would reach a percentile score of about 65 percent in fifty-two sessions. Instead, B only reached a score of 30 percent in fifty-two sessions. B is described as follows:

> This patient was a 36-year-old, employed married man diagnosed with an adjustment disorder. He sought treatment for a "marital relationship problem," with attendant job problems. His clinical characteristics predicted that therapy would be moderately effective at best. However, even the

modest estimated progress and outcome were not achieved, and Patient B spent almost a year in an unproductive treatment.[108]

Howard's Method: Adding More Calories

As presently designed, Howard's case study database only contains quantitative information about patient type and progress over the course of therapy. To expand this model in conjunction with the type of pragmatic case study database described in chapter 7 involves adding to the quantitative information about each case (or at least representative cases) the qualitatively detailed pragmatic case study information outlined in tables 7.1 and 7.2. The Howard group's model thus provides a quantitative framework into which the qualitative information outlined in the tables can be embedded. The qualitative analysis tends to focus on the distinctive processes of the individual case, while the standardized quantitative information provides a basis for comparing the nature and results of the case to other cases and groups of cases.

For example, from the perspective of the pragmatic, disciplined inquiry model, Howard's cases A and B described above are excellent candidates for more detailed, qualitative analyses. Why did patient A do so well and B so poorly? What therapist, patient, patient/therapist match, therapy technique, therapy process, and/or contextually situational factors were associated with these normatively deviant outcomes? And what systemic processes among the factors contribute to the observed outcomes? As multiple, qualitatively analyzed cases like these begin to accumulate, a knowledge base is created for deriving responses to these types of questions that cut across cases—not as general laws, but as conceptual themes and related practical guidelines for future action.

Extending Howard's pragmatic case model provides a vehicle for pragmatically integrating data from efficacy and effectiveness studies with data from individual pragmatic case studies. Integration is possible because any efficacy or effectiveness study investigates groups, and those groups consist of collections of individuals. Each individual in the study can be administered standardized typing and outcome monitoring measures in the COMPASS or in some other agreed-upon system, in addition to whatever other quantitative indicators are distinctive to the study. Moreover, by conducting pragmatic case studies, as described above in chapter 7, on representative patients in these group studies, the processes and outcomes associated with the group studies can be added to a case study database. Thus the fact that an individual patient is in an efficacy or effectiveness study simply provides a distinctive context to the conditions under which the therapy takes place.

Many of the questions about which scientists and clinicians battle can be informed by the expanded Howard model. For example, comparing full case reports of representative cases in which the main difference is a manualized versus an individualized case formulation approach would provide in-depth, qualitative, and process details as to the ways in which these factors seem to contribute or not to contribute to making a clinically significant positive difference in outcome. Thus the present polarized, theoretically focused, and emotionally charged disagreement between scientists, who tout the advantages of operationalized manuals which replace the therapist's clinical judgment, and clinicians, who tout individualized case formulation and treatment process, can be empirically informed with systematic, rigorous case study data.[109]

As another example, comparing two groups of comparable cases (achieved by random assignment or matching on initial characteristics) in which the major difference is therapist experience would provide in-depth, qualitative, and process details as to the ways in which experience seems to or seems not to make a significant positive difference in outcome.

Another therapist factor, besides experience, that is particularly suited to study via the individual case is the identity of the individual therapist. For example, in one study[110] the outcomes of twenty-three therapists offering verbal psychotherapy to 143 patients were assessed. Six therapists achieved success rates of 70 percent or more. At the other extreme, five had a success rate of less than 50 percent, and more than 10 percent of their cases were rated as worse.[111] The expanded Howard model allows for the comparison of the results of an individual therapist in comparison to other therapists with similar types of patients. In fact, an individual therapist can be viewed as offering a particular therapy package, which can be evaluated for its effectiveness by comparing the results of that therapist with the results of other therapists for similar types of patients. Much could be learned by studying the detailed case reports of a therapist with dramatically superior outcome scores relative to the expected outcomes generated by a model like COMPASS.

Also lending itself to the case study method are process and outcome in such therapeutic orientations as psychodynamic, experiential, and family systems therapy, which are not as amenable to efficacy research as is cognitive-behavior therapy. Case studies of these noncognitive-behavioral therapies could supply the empirical information presently missing about these therapies, in a framework—that is, the qualitatively detailed, pragmatic case study—which, unlike efficacy research, is in tune epistemologically with clinicians working in these types of therapies.

In sum, no matter what the factor—manualized versus individualized therapy, therapist experience, therapist identity, therapeutic alliance, theoretical orientation, patient diagnosis, specific therapy procedures, and so forth—the pragmatic case study allows for the study of that factor in the context of the total therapy, that is, for the study of that factor as embedded within the reality of the total therapy process, including the myriad of other variables of potential interest and relevance.

Finally, it should be noted that an expanded Howard model should include an addition to Howard's present system, the extension of Howard's quantitative monitoring of outcome on his Mental Health Index to follow-up assessments after therapy terminates. These assessments are very important as input into resource allocation decisions. For proper resource decision making, it is necessary to know that while Treatment X speeds up the reduction of depression in comparison to a lower-cost Treatment Y, the two treatments are equivalent at six-month follow-up. Then the decision maker has to weigh the limited period of time in which the patient is less depressed against the alternative of a lower-cost treatment achieving the same results by six-month follow-up.

Liberating Therapy Research from Its Positivist Straitjacket: 2,354 Separate Findings *Can* Be Wrong

There is a long tradition of empirical research in psychotherapy. As far back as 1966 Donald Kiesler was describing the dominant paradigm in this research as the positivistic search for "'the one' psychotherapy that would maximally benefit all patients."[112] Implicit in this paradigm was the presence of "uniformity myths"[113] in therapy research, the assumptions that one can select homogeneous groups of therapists who homogeneously administer identical treatments to homogeneous groups of patients with outcome represented by a uniform and homogeneous patient-change dimension (such as "personality reintegration" or "constructive personality change"). The main difference between 1966 and today's era of managed care seems to be that the single search for one psychotherapy system that best works for all patients has been differentiated into multiple searches for the one package of psychotherapy procedures that best works for each DSM-defined type of patient. By one recent estimate, "over 80 percent of the literature on psychotherapy theory is devoted to specific technologies and procedures."[114] This in spite of the fact that analyses of the research data suggest that only about 10–15 percent of the variation in outcome can be attributed to specific approaches, while 30 percent to "common factors" that cut across different therapy techniques and theories.[115] For example, one of these common factors is the quality of the therapeutic alliance between therapist and patient. In a recent meta-analysis of more than twenty-four research reports, the quality of the therapeutic alliance between therapist and patient was found to account for 26 percent of the variation in outcome.[116] These figures suggest the paradoxical power of paradigms over data in scientific research psychology, even though the positivist paradigm purportedly is "data-driven"!

At different points, traditional therapy researchers have attempted to break out of the positivist paradigm as they have bumped up against the presence of complexity and contextuality in those clusters of human transactions labeled "therapy." For example, in 1974 researchers John Gottman and Sandra Leiblum constructed a flowchart to capture the ongoing tasks and decision points a therapist faces in conducting therapy through fifteen sequential action phases, including the following: decide whom to see; learn about initial patient expectations; collect information about presenting problems; negotiate therapeutic contract; implement treatment plan; assess whether there is patient resistance to the specifics of the treatment plan; if there is patient resistance, assess factors underlying it and develop and implement interventions to reduce resistance; and monitor change: (a) if initial goals have been achieved and no new treatment goals have been attained, continue through consolidating learning transfer to posttherapy sessions, termination, and follow-up, or (b) if initial or subsequent goals have not been met, cycle through earlier phases to "self-correct" the therapy process.[117] In a review and expansion of this model, I later added a sixteenth phase: developing and maintaining a positive, working therapeutic alliance throughout therapy contact.[118] The logic of therapy, as reflected in the flowchart, makes it clear that in the individual case, there are a wide variety of ways for manifold variations to evolve as different patterns of choices and decisions occur. In effect, the flowchart can serve as a generic "guiding conception" of therapy process in terms of the disciplined inquiry model (see fig. 1.2).[119]

More recently in 1996, two well-known therapy researchers sounded this same theme as follows:

> Psychotherapy is a highly complex interchange in which a large number of factors interact, any one of which could be significant to outcome. Patients differ along many dimensions, in terms of the socioeconomic circumstances, the stage of their disorder at the time of presentation, and in their premorbid psychological functioning. Similarly, therapists vary in their personality, their skills, their motivation, their ability to comprehend their patients' problems, and their adherence to treatment modalities. Service provision also varies in important ways, including the length of treatment offered, the quality of liaison with other services, the support and supervision offered to practitioners, and the physical resources available.[120]

In spite of this recognition of the severe—if not fatal—limitations of the positivist paradigm, therapy researchers have felt compelled by the paradigm to try and function within this framework. One of the most dramatic examples of this is the work of Orlinsky, Grawe, and Parks,[121] who recently attempted to perform a molecular analysis of 2,354 separate findings in the vast body of positivist psychotherapy research between 1950 and 1992.

Orlinksky et al. begin by presenting an elaborate systems theory analysis of therapy process, viewing an episode of therapy contact between therapist and patient as a system. The *inputs* come from the subsystems of the therapist and the patient, whose impact on the system come both from their roles within the system and from their nontherapy lives outside the boundary of the system. The *outputs* of the therapy system are the influences the system has on both its "internal milieu" (what happens within the therapy itself) and its "external milieu" (the impact of the therapy on the nontherapy lives of the participants). "Treatment outcome" refers to those internal and external milieu changes which create favorable or adverse effects on the patient's well-being.

In an attempt to validate predicted functional relationships in their model, Orlinsky et al. first differentiated sixty-eight input and process variables on the basis of their systems analysis of therapy. Then they classified the 2,354 findings they had found in the literature involving a correlation between an independent process variable and an outcome variable into sixty-eight categories of results. The findings were further differentiated by the role of the outcome rater and the type of outcome assessment method employed. Finally, a "box score" analysis was conducted to determine what specific input and process variables correlated with what specific kinds of outcome measures.

While this was a heroic effort, the ultimate results suggest the deadly limitations of the positivist model from a constructionistic point of view. This follows because the positivist paradigm requires the search for general relationships between a small number of discrete variables across wide varieties of context, and yet it is these contexts, from a constructionist point of view, that have a large impact upon these relationships.

Orlinsky et al.'s systems model reflects the manifold patterns and interactions among large numbers of variables that typically take place in therapy, as in any complex series of personally, socially, and culturally significant human transactions. It is not surprising to find, then, that the yield of the individual, decontextualized impacts of sixty-eight variables across 2,354 findings—what Orlinsky et al. call "facts"—is very meager at best. Those that do emerge generally seem obvious because they appear implicit in the very concept of therapy as requiring a helping transaction between a caring, supportive, respectful professional expert and a patient who, if he or she is to benefit, has to become engaged with the therapist, take responsibility for presenting problems, and be open and cooperative in the change process. Here is a sample of the final summary of Orlinsky et al.'s findings:

> Process variables that have been found consistently related to outcome . . . [include] the overall quality of the therapeutic relationship, therapist skill, patient cooperation versus resistance, patient openness versus defensiveness, and treatment duration.[122]

It's hard to imagine anyone—scientist or clinician—disagreeing with these findings (except for the last one concerning treatment duration, which some researchers argue is not empirically supported). How could a patient be helped if she was completely resistant and defensive and/or didn't "bond" with the therapist? And how could a therapist's lack of skill or inability to engage a patient in a positive relationship not work against any therapeutic gains?[123]

The pragmatically important questions have to do with how, *within the context of a particular patient*, a particular therapist (or a particular treatment manual) can weave together the technical, relationship, and process ingredients in a way to effect change. The argument in this book is that this can only be done by systematically assessing and analyzing—

both quantitatively and qualitatively—individual cases. Thus, from a pragmatic perspective, Orlinsky et al.'s contribution is in providing a conceptual framework of the therapy process that can be used as part of a therapist's (or evaluator's) "guiding conception"[124] in therapy case studies.

The pragmatist views the vast effort associated with designing and carrying out the myriad of studies between 1950 and 1992 resulting in 2,354 findings—perhaps over one-half of them since 1985[125]—as dramatically misdirected. This effort involved vast amounts of time and energy from talented psychologist researchers who conducted many of these studies. The pragmatist argues that this effort—or at least an important portion of it—should have gone into documenting systematic case studies, providing us today with a much more productive empirical base upon which to derive guidelines for the successful conduct of present and future cases.

Moreover, the same conclusion about contextual variations in treatment can be drawn from efficacy outcome studies. While the APA method for establishing "empirically supported treatments" (ESTs) makes it sound as if the results are clear, frequently the actual details of the research results reveal substantial and clinically relevant variation of findings as a function of a variety of nontherapeutic-procedure factors, such as the time point at which the measures are administered (e.g., during therapy, at the end of therapy, or at different follow-up points); the type of statistical analysis employed; and whether full completers or partial completers of the therapy are studied.[126]

Along this same line, the implied consistency in the EST findings appears overstated. For example, Beck's cognitive-behavior therapy for depression is frequently cited as a dramatic example of an approach that has impressive empirical support across a variety of efficacy studies. Yet, in one of the largest and perhaps the most methodologically rigorous, random assignment efficacy studies to date, the above-mentioned NIMH Treatment of Depression Research Program, there were no clear outcome differences between Beck's cognitive-behavior therapy and a placebo with "clinical management" (a weekly meeting of 20–30 minutes to discuss medication, side effects, and the patient's clinical status, that is, in which the only therapeutic factors were "nonspecific"). In addition, the overall impact of this study was disappointing. While 250 depressive patients were selected for the study, only 239 actually entered it, only 155 completed at least twelve of the sixteen planned sessions, and only forty-eight (20 percent of the original 239) met the criteria for recovery with no relapse.[127] Clearly, there seems much room for pragmatic case studies and effectiveness studies to identify further ways to enhance outpatient psychotherapy for individuals with depression!

A Case in Point

Karen Calhoun and Patricia Resick[128] have published the case of "Cindy," a patient presenting with post-traumatic stress disorder (PTSD), which excellently illustrates the components and flow of the pragmatically focused case report. As will be seen below, while the case is conceptually and operationally linked to the cognitive-behavior therapy efficacy research literature on PTSD, the case is also importantly individualized in its implementation. I describe sample portions of the case below to illustrate this integration of individualized, contextualized process with grounding in general theoretical concepts from cognitive-behavioral therapy. The portions are organized in terms of the components of Peterson's disciplined inquiry model (see fig. 1.2). It must be recognized that my summary does not fully provide the rich and relevant details and elaboration of concepts and methods in the Calhoun and Resick report. Rather, my examples are intended to give a sense of how a pragmatic therapy case report might look.

The Patient

At the time of intake, "Cindy" was a twenty-six-year-old married mother of two young children, with a high school education.

> Cindy had become distressed during the fall of the year (3 months before the intake interview) following an affair she had for 5 weeks. During the affair she began to have flashbacks of events that had occurred a decade earlier. When she realized that this affair coincided with the exact time of year she had been raped [10 years earlier], she broke it off and became increasingly depressed and agitated as more memories surfaced. . . .
>
> At the initial interview, Cindy reported that she had been raped repeatedly over a 5-week period by a close friend ["Mark"]. . . . She was subjected to a range of sex acts, including oral, vaginal, and anal intercourse. During the assaults, her most prominent reactions were feeling detached

and numb, guilty, and embarrassed. The incidents were never reported to the police and she received no medical care.[129]

Guiding Conception

The treatment model employed is "Cognitive Processing Therapy" (CPT), a model specifically developed to treat the symptoms of PTSD victims of sexual assault. The model is embedded in the broader theoretical viewpoints of a behavior therapy exposure model and a cognitive information processing model of PTSD. Thus, the symptoms of PTSD—e.g., distressing reexperiencing of the traumatic event through "flashbacks" and intense distress in reaction to cues associated with the trauma, persistent avoidance of stimuli associated with the trauma (such as inability to recall important parts of it), persistent symptoms of increased arousal (like irritability and hypervigilance)—are viewed as inability to have "worked through" emotionally (by exposure) and cognitively (via full information processing) the original, psychologically overwhelming trauma.

The exposure component of CPT is designed to reactivate the original fear memory of the trauma and to provide new information that is incompatible with the current fear structure in order for a new memory to be formed. While the exposure component might alter the perception of fear, a more explicit information-processing component is needed to directly confront conflicts, misattributions, and maladaptive beliefs by providing corrective information.

In addition to their therapy content model, Calhoun and Resick describe the therapy process model they employ. This includes the relevance of such *therapist factors* as the advantages of having a female therapist for female rape victims; the need for the therapist to be knowledgeable about rape and PTSD, including being aware of common misperceptions about rape (e.g., rape is primarily about sex or most rapists are strangers); and heightened awareness of the tendency for non-victims to attribute blame to victims. The process model also includes *patient factors*, such as resistance and ambivalence about therapy, the enacting of avoidance by missing therapy sessions, hypersensitivity to implications of blame, and the special conditions presented by multiple-trauma victims. Finally, the process model addresses *setting factors*, such as the pros and cons for individual versus group therapy.

Experience and Research

In their report, Calhoun and Resick review the research literature from which CPT emerges and is grounded. As part of this review, they describe two promising outcome studies that they have conducted, including clinical experience with sixty-four different cases.

Assessment

Three types of assessment procedures are employed with Cindy. First is an intake interview, which includes an emphasis on supportive, nonevaluative questioning of sexual assault history. Second is the "Structured Clinical Interview," in which a clinician employs questions specifically designed to assess for the symptoms of PTSD and other diagnostic syndromes. Third are a series of psychometrically standardized, self-report questionnaires, which are designed to assess both specific PTSD symptoms and other types of psychopathology, such as depression, somatization, interpersonal sensitivity, and phobic anxiety. All three assessments documented a clear diagnosis of PTSD for Cindy and the presence of major symptoms of depression.

Formulation

In *session 1*, the therapist reviewed the results of the assessment and provided to the patient an information-processing formulation of her PTSD symptoms, which in part included the following:

> The therapist described how rape, for most people, is a schema-discrepant event: It does not fit prior beliefs about oneself, others, or the world. In order to incorporate this event into memory, the information becomes altered (assimilated) or beliefs are changed to accommodate the event. Examples of assimilation are distorting the event so that it is not labelled a rape or blaming oneself for its occurrence. Overaccommodation was described as changing beliefs too much as a result of the rape (e.g., no one can be trusted). Areas of beliefs often affected by rape are safety, trust, power, esteem, and intimacy. . . .
>
> The therapist explained that there would be three major goals for the therapy: to remember and accept the rape, to allow Cindy to feel her emotions and let them run their course (extinguish) so the memory could be put away without such strong feelings still attached, and to get beliefs that had been disrupted and distorted back into balance.[130]

Action

A core structure of the therapy consisted of having Cindy write about the rape experience from different perspectives between sessions and then having her read out loud and process the particular memories that she had written down. The written assignment after the first session was as follows: "Write at least one page on what it means to you that your were raped."

In *session 2*,

> Cindy arrived . . . with obvious emotion and cried periodically through-out the session. She stated that she had been feeling quite angry all week . . . [and was] disgusted with society and particularly politicians and people with money and power. . . . She expressed a great deal of anger over the William Kennedy Smith trial, which occurred just before she started therapy.[131]

After Cindy read aloud her dramatic and articulate statement of what her rape meant to her, Calhoun and Resick commented: "Cindy . . . had difficulty labeling the events as rape and that she believed she had let them happen. She had overaccommodated in her distrust of society and had a great deal of generalized anger."[132] At the end of the session, Cindy was given a three-column form to list rape-related events, her emotionally charged beliefs about them, and the positive or negative emotional consequences of those beliefs.

At the end of *session 3*, in which Cindy's response to the three-column form was processed, she was praised for her ability to recognize and label thoughts and feelings. Then the next homework assignment was introduced: to write a detailed account of the rape, including as many concrete, sensory details as Cindy could provide.

> She was instructed to start as soon as possible and to pick a time and place where she would have privacy and could express her emotions. If she was unable to complete the account in one sitting, she was asked to draw a line where she stopped. (The place where the patient stops is often a place in the event where there is a stuck point, where the patient gave up fighting, where something particularly heinous occurred, and so on.) . . . She was also instructed to read the account to herself every day until the next session.[133]

In *session 4*, Cindy read what she had written, crying most of the time. When she ended, the therapist asked her what she was feeling:

C: (*Long pause, shakes head.*) Bitter.

T: You have a right to that feeling. He blackmailed you.

C: I know.

T: And made you feel guilty.

C: That's why I've blamed myself for all these years and never considered it rape. After a while I just started believing it, seeing him go on to . . . (*drifts off*).

T: But it was rape.

C: I know.

T: And part of the rape was making you feel guilty—that somehow you should have responded differently.

C: And I didn't respond because I didn't want to hurt people, even him!

T: You know how most women respond? (*Cindy looks up.*) They freeze. They go into emotional shock.

C: Yeah, you can't believe it. You're trying to take in what is happening. . . . And then other people all say, "You should have . . ."

    At this point, a discussion ensued regarding how hurtful it is to hear other people's general comments about rape. . . . From there she went on to describe how difficult the week had been with her husband; . . . she was angry that her husband had stopped being supportive. . . . Cindy also expressed disappointment in a friend's reaction.[134]

Toward the end of the session, the therapist helped Cindy to begin to reframe her sense of blame, to realize that she had done "the best she could in an impossible situation."[135]

C: I'll always blame myself.

T: But there's no need for that.

C: And reading back to this [her description of the rape], my god!

T: The ironic part to me is that you chose not to tell, not because you liked it, or because you were a coward, or anything else. You chose not to tell because you didn't want to hurt people.

C: (*Cries.*)

T: You were doing what you considered the right and noble thing to do and then he twisted it around.

C: He used it against me.

T: And he used it against you.

At the end of the fourth session, Cindy's homework was to write the entire account of the details of the rape again, "adding any details she might have left out of the first account and to record any thoughts and feelings she was having now in parentheses along with her thoughts and feelings at the time."[136]

Similar kinds of processes occurred through the final sessions 5–12. For example, in *session 5*, the therapist pointed out that

> perhaps the fact that Mark was popular and went on to the Academy [college] was not relevant to the rape or to whether she could trust people. The more relevant context was that Mark was from a troubled, abusive home and that he was lashing out. Cindy began to accept that she had made a faulty connection between the person who raped her and went on to be successful and everyone else who is successful.[137]

In addition, the therapy dealt with other past and present complexities in Cindy's life: Mark's having come to Cindy's wedding in his handsome Academy uniform and getting her to dance with him; Cindy's starting a new, full-time job during the therapy with some sixty-hour work weeks preventing her from doing her therapy homework; the continuing close friendship between Mark and Cindy's brother, who did not know about the rapes until Cindy finally told him two weeks after completing treatment; Cindy's feeling how unfair life was and like a personal failure because Mark had gone to college with a full four-year scholarship while she had only gone on to business school.

Concluding Evaluation

Cindy came in for follow-up at three months and six months post-treatment. Her questionnaire scores at the last session and at the two follow-up times showed highly dramatic reductions from levels of intense distress to scores in the normal, healthy range. In addition, Calhoun and Resick present assessment information from a follow-up interview two weeks after the three-month follow-up. The qualitative material which emerged in the interview is consistent with the very positive outcome indicated in the psychometric questionnaires. For example,

> Overall, Cindy reported that she was doing very well and that she had a new outlook on life. She feels sad or hurt occasionally when she thinks of Mark and said that it will probably take more time to let go of the feelings completely.

She reported that her relationship with her brother had become some-what strained because he was pushing her to confront Mark, in the hope they [he?] could resolve it. Cindy had not buckled under his pressure and was still debating whether to talk to Mark, but said it is not preoccupying her. She wanted to wait until she felt strong and confident enough to han-dle whatever reactions Mark had. Her job was still going well and Cindy and her husband and children were getting along very well. [In addition, Cindy reported an improving relationship with her father and having made several close friends at work.] . . .

Finally, the therapist asked about Cindy's reactions to successful or powerful people she encounters or sees on the news. She responded that when she sees others who are greedy, she doesn't take it so much to heart and just shrugs them off. "Boy, they're a real case."[138]

The brief summary of this case, while not sufficient in detail to demon-strate any conclusions, does suggest a successful therapy. Some of the crucial elements appear to be the combination of a sensitive, supportive, creative, and skilled therapist (Patricia Resick) flexibly adapting a clearly articulated and research-literature-grounded conceptual framework and set of procedures to the complexities and contextualities of the individ-ual case. As also suggested in the above summary, narratively describing the case within the framework of Peterson's disciplined inquiry model of practice helps to make these elements clear. Moreover, the use of stan-dardized psychometric questionnaires and a standardized, structured di-agnostic interview allows the presenting problems and the outcome of this case to be compared systematically with other cases of similar types of patients.

Certainly, in reading Calhoun and Resick's review of this case, the pragmatist is struck by the exaggeration on both sides of the scientist-versus-clinician battle. Rather, the case suggests that the best therapy in-volves a creative integration of elements from both traditions.

Finally, as another point of integration, it is important to note that Calhoun and Resick place their Cognitive Processing Therapy model pri-marily within the positivist, "scientific" tradition of cognitive-behavior therapy, with its information-processing metaphor. However, in reading the actual conduct of their case, one is struck by the similarity with the postmodern "constructivist" and "narrative" therapy tradition. Thera-pist Resick is not simply correcting Cindy's specific false beliefs and rea-soning errors, as is stressed in the cognitive-behavior therapy tradition. Rather, Resick is helping Cindy to rework the meaning of the rape, which impacts upon Cindy's whole life story and life outlook. In other words, Resick appears in part to be helping Cindy in the "narrating and re-narrating of one's story in the process of which the story gets elaborated, transformed, and repaired"[139]—the quote from above defining constructivist therapy.

9

Educational Reform

From "Culture Wars" and "Silver Bullets"
to the Real Classroom

Today's critiques of American education and calls for reform frequently harken back to a golden age—before drugs, guns, lax discipline, political correctness, entrenched teachers' unions, and widespread cheating "dumbed down" the nation's schools. But when, Peter Schrag[1] asks, was that golden age? In the early years of this century, when Jews, Italians, Chinese, and blacks were portrayed in American textbooks as "mean, criminal, immoral, drunken, sly, lazy, and stupid in varying degrees"? In the 1920s, when most students never went beyond the eighth grade, and large numbers of students in farming areas never went to school between April and November? In the 1930s and 1940s, when a respected survey found that "a large majority of [college] students showed that they had virtually no knowledge of . . . Abraham Lincoln, Thomas Jefferson, Andrew Jackson, or Theodore Roosevelt"? In the 1950s, when *Why Johnny Can't Read* became a best-seller, and when the Soviet success with *Sputnik* in beating us into space was viewed as confirming the failure of America's science education? Or in 1963, when Admiral Hyman Rickover published *American Education, a National Failure?*

Here are today's facts. There are currently 14,000 public school districts, with a total of more than 80,000 schools, 2.5 million teachers, and 44 million public school students.[2] Each school is a case study in how to inculcate certain values and teach certain skills and knowledge, such as the learning of math, English, science, and history; responsible citizenship; cultural values like fairness, honesty, integrity, and compassion; appreciation of the arts; respect for others; a capacity to deal with interpersonal conflict without resorting to physical violence or weapons; a capacity for teamwork; and a capacity to deal with life's stresses without resorting to illegal drugs. In "schools that work" which are committed to all these goals, children thus gain specific knowledge about the world, and they learn to think critically, to cooperate, to be fair, and to develop into insightful, creative, compassionate, and wise citizens able to participate in a democratic society.[3]

While this sounds rather straightforward, the twin forces of postmodern deconstruction and the postmodern "culture wars" have created a volatile mix for the contemporary frontal attacks on U.S. education. This mix fuses (a) pervasive questioning and politicization of the nation's present public education system, in terms of its goals, its methods, its funding, and its method of measuring results; (b) a mind-numbing diversity of approaches to reform; and (c) an attempt at domination by each reform approach. What results is cynicism by the public over the continual coming and going of various, highly politicized educational "fads" and "fashions" and the continual disagreement among educational "experts."

The case-based pragmatic paradigm provides a constructive, depoliticized alternative. It focuses not on trying to prove the superiority of particular educational theories and models, but on the actual empirical outcomes of each classroom, school, and school district, as captured in systematic case studies. As the resultant case studies accumulate in an organized way, they form a knowledge and resource base both for educational practitioners and for the developers of educational policy and planning.

The present chapter will explore how we have arrived at the present uproar over educational quality and performance, and how the case study model offers one alternative for transcending it to focus on the ultimate bottom line: achieving genuine, relevant, continuing, and measurable improvement in our nation's schools.

The Factory Model

From the late nineteenth century to the 1950s, public schools developed and were organized around a modernistic, industrial, "factory" model that prevailed at the turn of the century. In line with Frederick Winslow Taylor's "scientific management" theory, the process of mass production sought to reduce as many aspects of the manufacturing process as possible to simple, repetitive, standardized tasks that could be performed by workers who were easily trained and interchanged. A relatively small number of people—perhaps 20 percent—did the thinking and planning for the entire enterprise. This managerial leadership related to the "line workers" and their "production line" in a centralized, hierarchical manner, preaching the values of standardization, a rigid sense of time, and bureaucratic accountability by documenting conformance to strict rules of procedure.[4] For example, as of 1991, Texas still had a law on its books spelling out precisely how many minutes each teacher had to spend teaching each subject to each student every day.[5]

In the factory school, teachers exercise the same authority over students that school boards, superintendents, and principals exercise over teachers. The assumption is that students will not learn something unless a teacher teaches it. Research in classrooms has documented the continuing prevalence of the factory model. "In most American classrooms, students sit in rows of seats, hour after hour, year after year, listening to adults talk—just like cars lining up at the gasoline pump to have their tanks filled. . . . [Students are passive learners, like] 'sponges'—soaking up lessons with little opportunity to discuss or analyze them."[6]

Another aspect of the factory model is "tracking," the grouping of students by academic ability within age group. In line with Taylor's scientific management, it is assumed that efficiency is increased by providing teachers with classes of homogeneous learners, so they can all receive and absorb information at the same rate.

The factory model was in part a reaction to the need to educate the children of 23 million new immigrants who came to America between 1880 and 1920, more than the entire population in 1850.[7] With the decline of the agrarian society, these immigrants were drawn to the cities, creating many potential social problems. The order, predictability, and control of the factory model school was seen as a "first line of defense against anarchy."[8] In *Middletown*, their classic 1925 study of Muncie, Indiana, sociologists Robert and Helen Lynd vividly captured the culture of the factory school:

> The school, like the factory, is a thoroughly regimented world. Immovable seats in orderly rows fix the sphere of activity of each child. For all, from the timid six-year-old entering for the first time to the most assured high school senior, the general routine is much the same. Bells divide the day into periods. . . . For nearly an hour a teacher asks questions and pupils answer, then a bell rings, on the instant books bang, powder and mirrors come out, there is a buzz of talk and laughter as all the urgent business of living resumes momentarily for the children, minutes pass, another bell,

gradual sliding into seats, a final giggle, a last vanity case snapped shut. "In our last lesson we had just finished"—another class is begun.[9]

Within its time, the factory school achieved certain goals. It facilitated the "melting pot" process by integrating the millions of immigrants into a democratic society, while encouraging a sense of order and discipline. And it trained the kind of "assembly line" worker needed by the industry of the day. On the other hand, there were millions of casualties. In the early years of the century, fewer than 10 percent of American young people graduated from high school,[10] and the number of school dropouts exceeded the number of graduates until the early 1950s.[11] (Today more than 85 percent of American students obtain either a high school diploma or a GED.)[12] Moreover, children who were handicapped, poor, ethnic minorities, and/or non-English-speaking were very ill served; and females as a group were also underserved.

Around the turn of the century, the factory school was dramatically challenged by the pragmatic philosopher, psychologist, and educator John Dewey, who is associated with the Progressive Education movement.[13] His "child-centered" model emphasized such pedagogical innovations as open-ended group projects, involving children in decisions about their own learning, creating a cooperative learning community, and "authentic" assessment that searched for individualized, qualitative alternatives to standardized quantitative testing. Dewey saw the highest purpose of his model to be the education of citizens who become active and effective participants in a democratic society.[14] These ideas and values were embodied in a school he helped to found, the Laboratory School of the University of Chicago, which was active from 1896 to 1904.[15] However, while he was a major public intellectual with an enthusiastic following, Dewey's lifetime—1859–1952—spanned the period in which positivist philosophy, behavioristic psychology, and the factory school model predominated. In light of this, it is not surprising that when Dewey died at the height of modernism, the early 1950s, his influence as a philosopher and educator had reached its lowest point.[16]

Thus, deriving its support from the dominance of modernism and industrial development, and the related conservatism about change associated with the unifying period of the late nineteenth century to the early 1960s, the factory school predominated until the early 1960s. Then, emerging from the countercultural revolt of this time, "radical," "humanistic," "romantic," nontraditional educators such as James Hern-

don, John Holt, Herbert Kohl, and Jonathan Kozol entered the schools—
particularly minority, inner- city schools—as teachers and observers and
wrote up their experiences and reactions in a series of dramatically engaging books.[17] These writers expressed their shock at how children were
being educated, and they reported their attempts to "liberate" classrooms and bring them into the previously disfavored "progressive"
model of education. These efforts raised the public's consciousness about
the need for change, and progressive reforms slowly started to be implemented during the 1970s.

The Combatants Square Off

During the 1980s there was a strong conservative reaction against the
liberal trends of the 1960s and 1970s. It was highlighted in Ronald Reagan's Department of Education by a series of nine reports issued by high-
profile national educational organizations.[18] The best known was the
1983 report, *A Nation at Risk*, by the National Commission on Excellence in Education,[19] which dramatically declared: "If an unfriendly foreign power attempted to impose on America the mediocre educational
performance that exists today, we might well have viewed it as an act of
war. As it stands, we have allowed this to happen to ourselves. . . . We
have, in effect, been committing an act of unthinking unilateral educational disarmament."[20]

This declaration was in a sense the first salvo in the education version
of the postmodern "culture wars," discussed earlier in chapter 2. These
involve the conflict between skeptical and critical postmodernists, on
the left, and modernist conservatives, on the right. As these ideological
wars play out, "tenured radicals" from the 1960s deconstruct the superiority of traditional white, European, male-oriented values and writings, and in their stead these liberals celebrate ethnic and racial diversity, multiculturalism, and feminism. The conservatives counteract by
denigrating these perspectives as simply attempts at "political correctness," originating from the neurotic guilt of misdirected "bleeding
hearts."

While a substantial part of these culture wars have been enacted in the
arena of higher education, the wars also have been intense in the arena
of public education policy. A recent fusillade has come from the journalist and talk show host, Charles Sykes, a veteran of the higher-education

battlefield via his book *Profscam*.[21] Sykes's attack on public education is contained in the title of his recent book, *Dumbing Down Our Kids: Why American Children Feel Good about Themselves But Can't Read, Write, or Add*.[22] A sample of Sykes's rhetoric:

> America's schools are in deep trouble, . . . because they are dominated by an ideology that does not care much about learning. . . . Whether it is called Outcome Based Education or "holistic learning," much of what passes for "reform" among educationists today represents a continued flight from academic standards and expectations.[23]
>
> [There is a] spreading stain of illiteracy among the nation's elaborately and expensively educated students . . . because . . . [educationists teach what they call "higher-order thinking skills" rather than] what it is that students should *think about*. . . . [and because reading and writing are not] taught in American schools. American children are not learning many of the basic facts of history, geography, and science because their schools often are uninterested in teaching them. . . .
>
> The campaign to dumb down the teaching of mathematics will result in an epidemic of mathematical and scientific illiteracy with disastrous consequences for higher education and the national work force. . . .
>
> [Instead of academics,] schools are increasingly emphasizing so-called "affective" learning that deals with the feelings, attitudes, and beliefs of students, rather than addressing what they know or can do. The emphasis on "feelings" means that schools frequently usurp the prerogatives and invade the privacy of families. . . .
>
> The ongoing dumbing down of the nation's schools is reflected in . . . the reliance on vague, impenetrable, and unmeasurable "goals" such as: the "Integration of physical, emotional, and spiritual wellness." . . .
>
> As both standards and achievement have fallen, American schools have inflated grades, adjusted or fudged tests scores, or dumbed down the tests altogether to provide the illusion of success. . . .
>
> American education continues to be dominated by an educational oligarchy [a coalition of "educrats"] that has been aptly called The Blob—a self-interested, self-perpetuating, interlocking directorate of special interest groups that dominates the politics, bureaucracy, hiring, and policy making of American schooling.[24] . . . [They use multiculturalism as] a heavy club wielded against traditional curricula, reading lists, ability tracking, grades, standardized tests, discipline policies, and attempts to raise academic standards.[25]

In short, Sykes condemns the American education system as financially wasteful and an academic failure. He claims students are not achieving in the traditional "3 R's" because teachers, academics, and administrators in the educational establishment—whom he derogatively labels as "educationists" and "educrats"—emphasize the culturally liberal values of multiculturalism, creativity, self-esteem, and "feel-good" psychologizing over the tried-and-true conservative values of self-discipline and the mastery of basic academic content. In addition, the school is undermining the family's role as a value teacher in such private areas as sexuality and through such questionable practices as "values clarification" (versus the clear adult communication of proper values).

In a related conservative salvo, House Speaker Newt Gingrich and University of California regent Ward Connerly, who spearheaded California's drive against race-based affirmative action, charge that, paradoxically, not only have liberally motivated educational policies been outrageously expensive, they have actually hurt the performance of African American students:

> The education bureaucracy won't concede that, despite spending trillions of dollars on education over the past 30 years, American children are further behind today. It doesn't want to admit that the S.A.T. scores of African-American children, which average 100 points less than the scores of white children, are the direct result of the current [Great Society] policies.[26]

In reaction to such highly politicized and provocative conservative rhetoric, two educationally knowledgeable psychologists, David Berliner and Bruce Biddle, have recently written a detailed set of responses and countercharges from a politically liberal position that is supportive of the present educational system. Again, their thesis is in their book title, *The Manufactured Crisis: Myths, Fraud, and the Attack on America's Public Schools.*[27] They charge that there has been a deliberate disinformation campaign on the part of the "far right." This "organized malevolence"[28] can be dated back to the report, *A Nation at Risk*, cited above. Berliner and Biddle investigated in depth the high-profile conservative views of education, particularly those similar to ones espoused by Sykes.

> The more we poked into our story, the more nasty lies about education we unearthed; the more we learned about how government officials and their allies were ignoring, suppressing, and distorting evidence; and the more we discovered how Americans were being misled about schools and their accomplishments.... Many of the myths seem . . . to have been told by powerful people who—despite their protestations—were pursuing a political

agenda designed to weaken the nation's public schools, redistribute support for those schools so that privileged students are favored over needy students, or even abolish those schools altogether.[29]

Berliner and Biddle review the evidence associated with charges of educational decline and decay. For example, one myth is that student achievement has recently fallen across the nation, as exemplified by the following 1992 quote from William Bennett: "[From 1950 to 1989] we probably experienced the worst educational decline in our history. Between 1963 and 1980, for example, combined average Scholastic Aptitude Test (SAT) scores—scores which tests students' verbal and math abilities—fell 90 points, from 980 to 890."[30]

Berliner and Biddle acknowledge that the SAT scores did decline between 1963 and 1975. However, they point out a number of problems with reasoning from that average test score decline to a decline in the educational system. For example, the SAT is a voluntary test associated with college admissions, and thus it is not taken by a representative sample of all high school students. Moreover, the composition of students who take the SAT has varied over time. Specifically, as college opportunities have expanded for groups who traditionally did not aspire to college, proportionately more high school students with characteristics associated with lower scores have been taking the test: specifically, more students with lower grades, more ethnic minority students, and poorer students.[31] Moreover, in response to critics like Gingrich and Connerly, Berliner and Biddle examine SAT scores within ethnic groups for the period 1976 to 1993 to reveal that white students have almost identical scores, and the scores for every minority group have increased during this period, the largest being for African Americans (an increase of 55 points).[32]

A better "report card" for the country's schools is the National Assessment of Educational Progress (NAEP), which includes reading and math tests given to representative national samples of students aged 9, 13, and 17. These show very little change over the past two decades, with the exception of significant gains by Hispanics and blacks in math. In addition, Berliner and Biddle review tests of specific subject areas, such as history and social studies. While these tests show clear limits to the information high school students have acquired, the evidence reveals no decline over time in this area relative to student knowledge attainment in the past.

Berliner and Biddle also point to data that contradict the conservatives' accusation that students today are dumber than they used to be. Retest data from the most widely used intelligence tests show that "since 1932 the mean IQ for white Americans aged two to 75 has risen about .3 points per year, . . . [so that] today's youth average about 15 IQ points higher than did their grandparents and 7.5 points higher than did their parents."[33]

While there are various explanations for this increase—from the effect of students today having more access to schooling to more specific exposure of youth today to the types of items used in these tests—there is certainly no evidence suggesting that youth are not as smart as their parents or grandparents.

Another myth critically reviewed by Berliner and Biddle is that American schools fail in comparative studies of student achievement: "International comparisons of student achievement, completed a decade ago, reveal that on 19 academic tests American students were never first or second and, in comparison with other industrialized nations, were last seven times.—*A Nation at Risk*"[34]

Berliner and Biddle acknowledge that on the tests of the International Association for the Evaluation of Educational Achievement (IEA) American students have frequently done poorly. However, they point out that there are problems in concluding from this that American students as a group lag behind educationally. For example, in many countries there are separate schools for large ethnic minorities who do not speak the dominant language of the country and who are thus excluded from comparative research. Many other countries also operate educational systems in which only selected students are allowed to enter high status high schools, and comparative data from those countries may be collected only from those high-status schools. For example, a quality control observer reported the following conditions for testing in South Korea, a country known for its high scores:

> The math teacher . . . calls the names of the 13-year-olds in the room who have been selected as part of the IEAP sample. As each name is called, the student stands at attention at his or her desk until the list is complete. Then, to the supportive and encouraging applause of their colleagues, the chosen ones leave [to take the test].[35]

In contrast, American public schools serve *all* students and all are typically included in the IEA testing. Moreover, "our over- tested students . .

. are likely to view the tests used in comparative studies as an inconvenience offering no obvious personal advantage."[36]

In addition, disaggregation analyses frequently result in American deficits disappearing. For example, in the 1980–1982 math tests,

> the study found that the aggregate achievement of eighth-grade American students lagged behind that of students in many other countries, notably Japan. This fact was immediately pounced on by critics and by a dutiful press, which enthusiastically vilified American schools for fecklessness.
>
> Nobody at the time seemed to notice that Japanese schools were then *requiring* eighth-grade students to take mathematics courses that stressed algebra, whereas such courses were typically offered to American students a year or two later. . . . [When the American data were disaggregated into those eighth-grade students who had and had not taken algebra, the scores of the former] matched or exceeded those students in the Japanese schools.[37]

As one other example, Berliner and Biddle address those educational experts who tout the advantages of Japanese and Chinese education, such as psychologists Harold Stevenson and James Stigler in their book, *The Learning Gap: Why Our Schools Are Failing and What We Can Learn from Japanese and Chinese Education.*[38] Berliner and Biddle point out the need to look at the total system in these countries and their own internal evaluations, such as the following assessment by a select committee of Japanese educators in a report to their Prime Minister:

> Bullying, suicides among school children, dropping out from school, increasing delinquency, violence both at home and at school, heated entrance exam races, over-emphasis on scholastic ratings, and torture of children by some teachers are the result of the pathological mechanisms that have become established in Japan's educational system.[39]

As a final example, Berliner and Biddle take on the accusations that American education is expensive and wasteful, and that recent increases in expenditures have not been translated into academic gains in the regular classroom. These authors counter by showing that both in per pupil expenditures and in education expenditures as a percentage of per capita income, the United States is in the average range for developed countries,[40] that elementary and secondary schools have a lower number of workers (teachers, assistants, etc.) per executive than business and industry,[41] and that an important portion (perhaps 30 percent) of the new money recently allocated for education went for special-education programs, which now serve 12 percent of all public school children, but which cannot be expected to have any impact on the academic performance of nonhandicapped children.[42]

Many Promising Reform Ideas

The present wave of critique of the status quo in public education begun by *A Nation at Risk* in 1983 has functioned not only as ammunition in the culture wars, but as a general stimulus and rationale for new ideas for change, both progressive and traditional.[43] One set of new ideas that seems particularly promising and far-ranging has been assembled by the education journalist Edward Fiske in his book: *Smart Schools, Smart Kids: Why Do Some Schools Work?*[44] Fiske criticizes the factory school, designed for our pre-1960s industrial economy, as tragically out of date with the demands of today's society, which is postindustrial, computerized, information-and-service focused, and embedded in a world of global economic competition. The factory school is also tragically out of date for the new social and psychological issues that children bring into the classroom today: single-parent families, dual-employed parents, teenage mothers with deficits in parenting and general life skills, divorce, the availability of illicit drugs and their abuse, increasing percentages of ethnic and cultural diversity among students, and an all-pervasive, sex-and-violence-saturated media.

Business and industry have adapted to the changing times by abandoning the industrial and "factory" values of centralization, standardization, and bureaucratic accountability in exchange for "total quality management," which emphasizes decentralization; an emphasis on teams, cooperation, and "line worker" involvement in decision making; more flexible work schedules; and new standards and methods for quality control.

Fiske argues that schools should adapt in a parallel way to the times. Fiske's integrating concept for school reform is the "smart machine," which, instead of simply repeating the same operation over and over in rote fashion, is capable of receiving new information and altering its actions accordingly.

The emerging global economy requires workers who are "smart" in the same sense: workers who can analyze new situations, come up with cre-

ative solutions, and take responsibility for decisions relating to the performance of their jobs. The functioning of a modern democracy requires citizens with similar skills, and to produce "smart" workers and "smart" citizens, we need "smart" schools and "smart" kids.[45]

Fiske proposes that while full-fledged smart schools don't yet exist,
every one of the ingredients for operating them does:

> New ways of managing school systems, running schools, organizing class-
> rooms, using time, measuring results, and so forth exists somewhere in the
> United States.
> . . . [Moreover,] put together, these bold experiments can bring about
> the smart schools that American students need if they are to be prepared
> for the twenty-first century.[46]

Fiske's book is an exposition and series of case examples of these new
"smart school" ideas. Included is "school-based management," in which
authority to make decisions on everything from budgets to hiring to curriculum and textbooks is transferred from a central board of education
to a team associated with the individual school, primarily including the
principal, teachers, and parents, but also sometimes including students
and clerical and custodial workers. As of 1991, ten states were actively
involved in encouraging or requiring school-based management. For example, in Dade County, Florida, a school could decide to participate if
two-thirds of the faculty members in a local school voted to do so.

Another innovation is the "smart classroom," in which the teacher is
more an organizer and coach of activities that provide a setting for students to learn according to their own styles and in ways that they determine to be meaningful, motivating, and relevant to their lives. Smart
classrooms are "learning-oriented, not teaching-oriented."[47] Fiske cites
Theodore Sizer's work[48] in promoting the concept of "essential schools."
The basic idea is to teach "habits of mind" rather than to impart a discrete body of information. This means that schools should do a few
things well rather than try to cover the intellectual waterfront.

> High school schedules should be arranged so that no teacher must know
> and work with more than eighty students. Doing this might require Eng-
> lish teachers to help out with social studies, math teachers with science,
> and so forth. Teachers and administrators should think of themselves as
> generalists first, specialists second.
> . . . Learning is primarily the responsibility of the student. Diplomas
> should be awarded not on the basis of accumulated credits—that is, seat

time—but of "exhibitions" [and "portfolios"], in which students demonstrate and defend what they heave learned.[49]

Sizer has created a "Coalition of Essential Schools." All the schools in the Coalition must agree to commit to the principles associated with the essential school concept, and in return they receive consultation and support. From just a dozen schools in 1985, the Sizer coalition had blossomed into 178 schools across the country by the fall of 1994—87 in cities, 67 in suburbs, 23 in rural areas.[50] Fiske provides a case example of a Sizer-inspired setting: Jim Streible's eleventh-grade history classroom at Fairdale High School in Louisville, Kentucky (see pp. 264–265 below).

In the chapter "Resetting the Clock," Fiske discusses innovations around the country that are restructuring and extending the time the school is open—beyond the 9:00 A.M. to 3:00 P.M., nine months a year of the traditional factory school. For example, year-round schooling makes efficient use of the $250 billion America has tied up in school buildings, rather than leaving the buildings empty for one-quarter of the year during the summer and then frequently going on double-sessions during the nine-month school year. Also, shorter vacations reduce the very significant loss of academic momentum that frequently occurs with the long summer layoff. In addition, in response to the many children whose parents work outside the home, schools are now starting to open their doors from 6:00 A.M. to 6:00 P.M. In San Francisco, there is a Saturday School, which provides a literature program to students scoring below the fortieth percentile nationally on standardized tests. Fiske also discusses the idea of starting students in school when they are developmentally ready, not in terms of arbitrary dates. In this regard, Head Start programs have been receiving a good deal of support on both social equity and cost-benefit grounds.[51]

Fiske's chapter "Beyond Testing" introduces the ideas of alternatives to standardized, quantitative testing to assess how much a child has learned:

Josh Roof [is] a sixth grader at the Key School in Indianapolis, Indiana. He's about to be tested on what he knows about solar energy, and he's been preparing for weeks. But instead of nervously chewing on his number-2 lead pencil while he fills in blanks on a piece of paper, Josh is standing, even smiling, in front of a video camera and talking to a live audience—his teacher, his fellow students—about his topic. He shows them his final product, a model of a solar-powered skyscraper that he decided to use to illustrate what he had learned during the Key School's nine-week school-wide study of the theme, "Harmony."[52]

The Key School is the nation's first to be modeled on Howard Gardner's theory of multiple intelligences,[53] taking into account the different kinds of capacities that students bring to the learning process.

> We are all able to know the world through language, logical-mathematical analysis, spatial representation, musical thinking, the use of the body to solve problems or to make things, an understanding of other individuals, and an understanding of ourselves. Where individuals differ is in the strength of these intelligences—the so-called *profile of intelligences.*[54]

At the Key School, kids get to choose a "special interest pod" that matches their intelligence profile. They spend one class period a day working in the pod with kids from all grades. Sample pods are math pentathlon games, problem solving, communications, art, choir, Spanish, physical sciences, mind and movement, acting, or becoming young astronauts or young naturalists.[55] In addition, all students spend time each day in classes that emphasize different intelligences, such as art, physical education, Spanish, computers, and music. Finally, kids get to demonstrate their learning in a modality, such as an exhibition or a portfolio, that emphasizes their area of intellectual strength, such as Josh Roof's special ability in spatial thinking, which was detected early on by the teachers. Since the video builds on strengths, it typically records a moment of peak learning.

Another innovation in particular schools that Fiske describes is the intensive use of computers, CD-ROMS, and video disks for instruction to create new and more effective ways for students to do research, learn to write, create class newsletters, learn through interactive programs, enhance cooperative learning, and gain a new capability to network with students in other schools around common interests.

In the chapter "The Last Monopoly," Fiske describes the issue of parental and student choice in school selection. While there is contention about the concept of educational vouchers that can take money out of the public school system and place it in religious and other private schools, there is agreement in many school systems that choice *within* public schools—including the concept of "charter schools"—is a positive innovation and way of reducing the disfavored notion of standardization from the factory school model.

One dramatic example is a program for developing "alternative" schools, also called "public academies," in New York City that was started in the early 1970s.[56] The goal was to try out new ideas, and attendance at the schools was voluntary on the part of parents and students who shared the particular school's vision. With these elements in place, the schools had waivers from many of the bureaucratic requirements of the New York City Board of Education (that is, they were virtual "charter schools"), and thus they became a model of decentralized, "school-based management." An early participant was Deborah Meir, a former kindergarten teacher, who opened up the Central Park East Elementary School in a 100 percent minority school in the inner-city area of Harlem in New York City. Using Sizer's principles of "essential schools" and her own unique talents as visionary, creator, and administrator, Meir created a school that became a model of what could be done to transform a factory school mentality into an academically exciting and successful "smart" elementary school. Two spinoff elementary schools were then started, and by the mid-1980s, there were twenty-three separate elementary schools operating on an option basis.[57] In 1985 the Central Park East Secondary School opened, and it also has been a highly documented, stellar success.[58] Building on this success, in late 1993 and 1994, New York City opened eleven more schools, modeled on the philosophy and educational approach at Central Park East; and today there are some fifty alternative schools functioning.[59] Deborah Meir later left Central Park East to help direct the momentum of alternative school developments.

Finally, in the chapter "Learning Communities," Fiske highlights the work of James Comer, a Yale psychiatrist, who has emphasized the linkage between school and community—parents, neighborhood, and social service agencies. Starting in 1968, at two inner-city schools in New Haven, Connecticut, Comer worked at getting parents engaged with the schools through various activities, such as a joint parent-teacher "governing council" for each school, the use of parents as part-time teacher helpers in class, and parent participation in social events. Also, a "mental health" team was established in each school to assist the governing council. The team consists of guidance counselors, school psychologists, special education teachers, nurses, and classroom teachers, and it meets regularly to discuss the developmental needs of individual children and how to combat problems.[60] As of 1994, the Comer method—with its emphasis on child development, parental involvement, and a team approach to problem solving—was being used in more than fifty schools in major American cities.

Fiske also cites the work of the child psychologist and one of the founders of Head Start, Edward Zigler, who advances the idea of the school-community link even further. He views schools not just for teaching, but also as centers for preschool education, day care, parent education, family support counseling, and other social services which support family life. His goal is to make the school, *qua* institution, an integrating force in the community, especially for its own students and teachers.[61] Optimistically, he calls his model "Schools of the Twenty-first Century." As of 1991, New Jersey had set up twenty-nine such one-stop-shopping schools, each of which offers a full package of health, mental health, employment, recreational, substance abuse, and family counseling services in or near the school.

A persuasive reform coming from a traditional educational philosophy is E. D. Hirsch's argument for "cultural literacy." Hirsch summarizes contemporary "schema theory" research on the reading process which concludes that

> the reader . . . is now discovered to be not only a decoder of what is written down but also a supplier of much essential information that is not written down. . . . The reader's mind is constantly inferring meanings that are not directly stated by the words of a text but are nonetheless part of its essential content. The explicit meanings of a piece of writing are the tip of an iceberg of meaning; the larger part lies below the surface of the text and is composed of the reader's own relevant knowledge.[62]

Because reading requires the reader to bring knowledge of context to the reading process, Hirsch argues for the importance of systematically teaching a body of knowledge that helps to define our culture. This knowledge is required for an individual to become an active participant in the culture and to be able to read meaningfully writings which emerge from it. It is not enough to teach only "reading skills" and "critical thinking skills," for these skills alone without the background knowledge are not sufficient for reading for meaning. "You can't learn only *how* to learn about, say, the civil war. . . . [Without the 'intellectual capital' of cultural literacy], just reading a newspaper, with its references like 'supply and demand,' 'Machiavellian tactics,' 'black holes,' or 'The Picture of Dorian Gray,' can be overwhelming."[63]

Hirsch calls the knowledge that forms the context for reading and learning "cultural literacy." In his initial book he listed five thousand "essential names, phrases, dates, and concepts," such as "1066,"

"1861–1865," "Hank Aaron," "eardrum," "generation gap," "lesbian," "rapprochement," "tundra," and "Zeus (Jupiter)."[64] While liberals argue that such a list is "culturally imperialistic," Hirsch counters that there has to be some list, and this list should reflect our actual culture. The goal, he asserts, is not to memorize a list of words or phrases, but to have a working knowledge of enough subject areas to be able to understand new information from a variety of disciplines as it comes along.

Because a core of distinct, culturally relevant knowledge is required for the educational process, Hirsch argues for a national standardized curriculum, which is taught in a standardized cumulative sequence. This has the advantage of efficiently communicating background knowledge, whether students switch teachers, schools, or part of the country. It also provides clear-cut criteria upon which to test students' learning. Following this line of reasoning, Hirsch and his colleagues have developed a "core knowledge" curriculum sequence through the sixth grade, and it has been adopted by some 350 schools. One of them is Mohegan, a K-8, inner-city public school in the South Bronx section of New York City. Journalists' reports from the school suggest impressive qualitative success with the use of Hirsch's program, together with a 13.5 percent increase in reading scores after the first year of the program.[65]

Ideas Are Cheap, Successful Cases Are Not

Refocusing on Results in Practice

In the pragmatist's view, it is important to move beyond the educational culture war, with its battles to decide on one "true" ideological and theoretical approach to education reform. Part of the problem is the pressure from these battles to oversimplify a huge and complex reality such as the national system of schools in order to make it "fit" into a particular ideological or theoretical perspective. In the words of a commentator on the Sykes and the Berliner and Biddle books, "There is so much public education going on in this country that it would be possible for everybody to be correct in the narrow sense: the system probably does contain in its vastness some example of every conceivable kind of success and failure."[66]

The pragmatist views ideas such as those summarized by authors like

Fiske and Hirsch as very promising—but also with many vulnerabilities. For example:

- *School-Based Management.* Decentralizing school governance won't work unless there are talented and committed administrators, teachers, and parents who can work together cooperatively at the individual school level.
- *Smart Classrooms.* The smart classroom requires a teacher who can overcome many obstacles in order to create intrinsic motivation in students. The teacher has to compete with glamorous media for students' attention and to motivate students who are in a local youth culture that frequently denigrates academic achievement.[67] Other problems include the challenge of developing curricula whose content is acceptable to parents of widely differing political, social, religious, and moral views; and the challenge of creating assessment situations in which students' "exhibitions" and "portfolios" can be graded fairly and efficiently.
- *Resetting the Clock.* Keeping schools open longer during the day, on Saturdays, and/or in the summer requires extra money for additional teachers to staff student activities, for additional maintenance staff to handle more wear and tear, and for additional electric, heating, and air conditioning expenses. Changing school hours can also require changing established and comfortable parent and community schedules concerning activities like vacations and summer camp programs.
- *Beyond Testing.* Attempting to individualize assessment by each child's intelligence profile is very labor-intensive, and the non-standardized, qualitative process of assessment is open to charges of subjectivity and lack of fairness. Also, designing a curriculum to be responsive to multiple intelligences requires a trade-off between the traditional "3 R's" and those activities that emphasize other intellectual modalities, such as musical or social skills.
- *New Technologies.* Investing intensively in computers and other technologies draws money away from other needs, such as more teachers for keeping class sizes small.
- *Choice.* Introducing choice into a school system can model cutthroat competition to the students. In addition, it can favor those parents with the resources and initiative to get their children into the limited school slots that are most desirable. Moreover, a situa-

tion with limited slots is highly subject to becoming politicized and compromising the principle of equity.

- *Learning Communities.* Running a school as a self-contained educational institution is hard enough. Can it absorb the extra demands of being an integrated community human service agency and of dealing with family and neighborhood problems?
- *Cultural Literacy.* On one hand, a specific national curriculum would structure and focus the educational process and make accountability more feasible by clarifying learning goals. On the other hand, such a specific curriculum can handcuff the teacher and is not sensitive to the needs, preferences, and cultural contexts of local school districts and schools.

A related problem to the limits of any particular education reform is the extreme way in which many of the reforms are framed in order to make them distinctive. For example, the contrast between Sizer's notion of student-directed projects that capitalize on intrinsic motivation to develop "critical skills" and Hirsch's idea of an externally "imposed" set of cultural concepts to be learned seems overdrawn. In any project, there is curricular content. Why can't a teacher try to coordinate the interests of students with the need to cover certain kinds of material? Perhaps ultimately effective teaching depends on the teacher's capacity to integrate both the development of intrinsic motivation for learning in students and the need to have students learn certain kinds of content.

An apparent example of such integration is described by Evelyn Hernandez, a fifth-grade teacher from the Mohegan School mentioned above, which employs Hirsch's "core knowledge" curriculum.

> The ["core curriculum"] . . . provided the topic, but I could teach it however I wanted. I have a lot [of] . . . freedom and flexibility. . . . In the fifth grade, we learn about the Aztecs and the Incas and the Mayans, but every year I teach it differently, so I don't get bored. Some years, it might be a drama; others, we might make headdresses—whatever the kids are geared to—but they learn the same information.[68]

Another example of the either/or framing of decisions about teaching methods is the "reading wars" debate between the progressive technique of "whole language" and the traditional technique of "phonics" in teaching reading.[69] Proponents of the whole-language approach believe that reading is learned best when the child is immersed in "real" books and "real" writing. The expectation is that children will figure out what words mean by seeing them in personally meaningful contexts. Children are encouraged to skip unfamiliar words if they disrupt the ongoing reading process. The goal is overall understanding, not word-by- word accuracy. While the originators of the whole-language method did not reject all phonics instruction, they emphasized that in the relative emphasis upon "meaning" and "phonics," meaning comes before phonics: "Children learn phonics best *after* they can already read."[70] For the whole-language teacher, phonics are introduced as a follow-up to class time spent in meaningful reading. In contrast, for the phonics advocate, phonic skills are learned as tools *before* meaningful reading can really begin. Proponents of phonics stress specific skills for analyzing words into their parts, for learning about the phonemes and morphemes that are the building blocks of full words. The emphasis is upon such tasks as learning vowels and consonants, letter combinations, correct spelling, and tools for figuring out unfamiliar words.

Instead of being a battle, the advantages of each can be viewed as compensating for the disadvantages of the other. The enthusiasm, fun, and personal relevance of reading stimulated by whole language can provide the intrinsic motivation for students to learn the needed word-decoding techniques of phonics. And there are examples that suggest that the best results are achieved by blending the two.[71]

As implied above in discussing the vulnerabilities of different reform ideas, a crucial factor is how the educational reform is implemented: Does it fit the teaching style, interests, and ideology of the teacher? How does it relate to the learning styles of the students? Is the principal a champion of the idea or a reluctant participant? Importantly, in accounts of successful implementation of different reforms, there appears to be a common enthusiasm and commitment to the idea by the principal and teacher. Consider these common factors in the following two descriptions of seemingly successful implementation of opposite educational models by two very senior male high school teachers, each of whom is passionately and personally in tune with his particular model. The first is Jim Streible, who is the above-described disciple of Theodore Sizer; and the other is Jack Reynoldson, who is singled out as a model by the conservative Charles Sykes for his traditional, "drill sergeant" approach:

> [Jim Streible says that he used to be] a traditional teacher. . . . "I eventually got bored with the whole thing. I decided I just wasn't the person to pump facts into kids' heads." . . . One day Phillip Schlechty, [a colleague of Sizer's, came and] "talked about taking chances and asked us to imagine

what our classes could be like if no holds were barred. . . . He said teachers ought to think in terms of 'what if,' not 'we can't.'" . . . Streible began to change from his lecture approach to coaching students, and while he was doing this Ted Sizer visited [his school]. . . . He liked what Sizer and Schlechty were saying and decided to give it a try. "I got involved in the planning strategy for the second year with other teachers and a lot of good ideas came up. Educationally speaking, Ted Sizer raised me from the dead."[72] . . .

[As evidence of his success, students lavish praise on Steible's classroom. Some sample comments:] "If you don't understand something, . . . here you can ask somebody in a group. They help you, and you all learn together. . . . I wish all my classes were like this." . . . "You really can learn if everybody works together. . . . You learn not only the book skills and facts but the social skills. The student-as-worker approach teaches you responsibility."[73]

[Jack Reynoldson has been teaching since 1955.] "On your feet!" barks the Korean War veteran to his classroom of eighth-graders. With military attention the teenagers jump to attention. "What's wrong with this sentence?" asks [Reynoldson]. . . . He uses his pointer to draw attention to the Blooper of the Day written on the chalkboard: "Of the two girls, Suzy is the most agreeable." Students quietly raise their hands. He calls on one. "It should be, Of the two girls, Suzy is the *more* agreeable." "Correct," says Reynoldson, then addressing the class: "Be seated." A pause, then he barks, "Face west!" The students shift their desks in unison, and then, sitting starched straight, they prepare for what has become a morning ritual: diagramming sentences.[74] . . .

For the last 40 years Reynoldson has resisted every fad and fashion. . . . "I think in education today we have lost a sense of mission and we have substituted politically correct clap trap.". . . [The payoff is that] as a teacher, Reynoldson's record is impressive, both for high-achieving and low-achieving students, including minority students in his classes. . . . Reynoldson is known for working with students closely, especially those who need extra attention. He corrects papers one-on-one. . . . Students say that although he is tough, he is fair in administering discipline and they admire his insistence on academic results.[75]

A related point is the importance of looking at any reform concept in the context of viewing the classroom, school, and school district as one interrelated system. How any particular reform will actually play out is dependent on what else happens in the total system. Fiske draws a related conclusion after his investigation, reviewed above, of specific "smart school" reform ideas. He argues that the real payoff of the reform ideas he's championing will come only when they are put together into one system:

> No one has yet taken a Ted Sizer classroom, put it in a decentralized school system, loaded it up with new technologies, made teachers responsible for student progress, measured this progress with authentic tests, brought social-service agencies into the school, and then given parents the choice of whether this is what they want in the first place.[76]

The pragmatic model helps to refocus professionals on results in practice rather than the staking out of pure and highly differentiated ideological and theoretical positions. In the end, it is not the innovative ideas and models per se that can positively reform education, it is the implementation of the ideas and models in specific settings. As suggested in the Jim Streible and Jack Reynoldson examples presented above, this can very well mean that unrelated or even opposing ideas can both work if implemented in settings in which teachers and administrators communicate to parents an educational vision that is clear, persuasively framed, and enthusiastically believed in.[77]

The pragmatist thus emphasizes the need to study actual embodiments of educational concepts, not just the concepts themselves. This is in contrast to the dominant positivist model in psychology, which is explicitly designed to study the impact of single variables—such as school-based management, cooperative learning through group projects, extending the school year, using "exhibits" and "portfolios" for student assessment, adding computers to the classroom, or introducing a cultural literacy curriculum—while *holding all other variables constant*.[78] Although the pragmatist does not want imperialistically to exclude positivist studies, which do help to develop the individual educational ideas, the pragmatist wants "equal time" and equal access to research resources for performing systematic, holistic case studies.

In sum, the pragmatist emphasizes that the bottom line for evaluating a particular social program, such as a particular school or classroom, is to assess how it actually functions as a whole system, not by its purported ideological or theoretical model per se. All relevant cases must be monitored in an ongoing manner, rather than deciding from a limited number of cases what ideological or theoretical model is best. For ultimately, there is no way—besides actual empirical assessment—of knowing the relationship between a particular organization's purported model and its actual functioning as an organizational system.

The New York City Experience

Who Makes the Honor Roll? It is instructive, then, to consider the results of a recent assessment project in New York City. As part of the first comprehensive "academic accounting" of every school in New York State, third-graders were tested in the spring of 1996 on a standardized test of reading and writing proficiency. New York City grouped its schools into types based on similarities in the income and language backgrounds of their students;[79] and then those schools which scored significantly better on the proficiency scores than their peers within a type were placed on an "honor roll."

The city has not yet completed and released a systematic analysis of the honor roll schools. However, one can gain a sense of the types of diversity associated with honor roll schools from a *New York Times* profile of four of these schools in an article entitled "Best of the City's Schools Share Vision, Not Methods."[80] The first is P.S. 31 in Brooklyn, which is run in a traditional, discipline-and-structure-focused way.

> Sixth graders who misbehave are routinely punished by being demoted, for a week, to the first grade. Kindergartners are seated, not on the cozy rugs that are in vogue across the country, but in long rows of wooden desks, from 9 A.M. to 3 P.M., with no breaks for recess. . . . Once a month, the entire school assembles in the auditorium for a class competition in which students duel using their knowledge of old-fashioned math facts, like multiplication tables.

Rejecting bilingual education, the principal espouses a "sink or swim" philosophy in which every student is put in a mainstream classroom, with extra help available—but only in English. While the school's 772 students speak at least eight languages, this method works: virtually all students have learned to speak English, and 94 percent of the third-graders have achieved minimum competency in reading, with 34 percent reading at a sixth-grade level.

The next school is P.S. 234 in the TriBeCa section of Manhattan. This school has a radically different atmosphere, adhering to the tenets of progressive education. The learning atmosphere is relaxed, informal, fun—even whimsical—with an emphasis on cooperative learning: "Every day, for example, in Maggie Siena's combined fourth-and-fifth-grade class, the 31 students break into groups to research a topic and then reassemble to brief the rest of the class." And with good results: more than half of the third-grade students read at a sixth-grade level, which ranks the school fourth in the city on that scale.

P.S. 29 in the South Bronx, which has a high population of students living in poverty, has the fifth highest third-grade reading scores in the state, adjusting for poverty and foreign languages. Four of its program emphases are particularly distinctive. First is its reward program. Students with the best grades are rewarded with employment at "Kid Card, Inc.," the school's student-run greeting card business, in which students have experience in interviewing prospective colleagues, writing and illustrating their cards, and advertising and selling them from classroom storefronts. Another emphasis is small classes (no more than twenty-two, or ten fewer than allowed by the teachers' contract), achieved by hiring more teachers and fewer teaching assistants. A third emphasis is high teacher training and low turnover, reflecting teacher cohesion and continuity. Finally, the school has an explicit test coaching program, or what it calls its "test sophistication program . . . like Kaplan for the SAT." Every third-grader takes three sample standardized reading tests, beginning in October. Those who do poorly receive remedial help.

In contrast, the principal of P.S. 6, one of the best-performing schools in the state, does not believe in "teaching the test." She does not let her teachers begin test preparation until the end of February. The school is located on the Upper East Side of Manhattan, one of the city's most affluent neighborhoods. However, the school's ranking—it vaulted from seventy-eighth in the city in 1988 to first in the city, and second in the state, in 1996—cannot be attributed only to demographics, since other schools in the area with similar advantages don't score as high. Some of the distinctive characteristics of the program are a curriculum in which all students read a long list of the same books in each grade. For example, fourth-graders read "Sign of the Beaver," written on the fifth-grade level, so that their teachers the next year can build on that knowledge. Also, students identified as falling behind, as early as the first grade, "receive support services, including the part-time attention of an additional teacher, who works with students in class, rather than pulling them out to a separate room, and consultations with a social worker."[81]

Assuming that a more systematic analysis of the honor roll schools were to reveal the amount of diversity we see among these four, what are we to conclude? Is traditional or progressive educational philosophy superior? Should teachers "teach the test" for a school to achieve high standardized scores? How about extrinsic rewards, such as the greeting card company in the South Bronx, for good grades? Should kids learn individually or cooperatively in groups? And what about bilingual education, as opposed to a "sink or swim" policy? It would seem that a reasonable conclusion is to refocus from these types of typical, single-factor questions to concentrate on how multiple factors work together in particular contexts to create successful educational programs in actual practice—that is, to concentrate our efforts on conducting systematic case studies of successful educational settings.

Rudy Crew's "Hands Off" Philosophy. The use of the proficiency report cards in New York City and the celebration of the top-scoring "honor roll" schools reflect the philosophy of the city's schools chancellor, Rudy Crew:

> Unlike previous chancellors, Crew has not got hung up on advocating particular ways of teaching. So long as schools can prove that their students are learning, he doesn't care if their approach is back-to-basics or touchy feely. Crew has set clear guidelines [such as the proficiency scores and related "budget report cards" to start looking at a school's cost-effectiveness], in a kind of franchise approach, about what he expects children to know and when he expects them to know it. Beyond that, he believes that the board's role is solely to assist schools in achieving their performance goals and to intervene swiftly and decisively if they fail.[82]

To put teeth into this philosophy, Crew announced that he was going to write performance standards directly into superintendents' contracts, committing them to raise achievement by a specified percentage over a particular period of time, or to risk losing their jobs.[83]

This philosophy is identical to the pragmatic approach: develop a standardized method for evaluating every program in comparison to its equivalent peers, and then celebrate the high-achieving programs and intervene to change the low-achieving programs. What the pragmatic view adds to Crew's philosophy is the need for rigorously documented representative case studies. The goal of these case studies is not to prove the validity of a particular theory, as positivism dictates, but to develop a database of actual concrete instances of success as a resource for program development and change among less than optimally functioning programs.

Crew points out that the problem in American education (and, I would argue, in all other kinds of human services) is not the creation of isolated individual schools which are successful, but finding a way to replicate, or "scale up" these individual reforms "in a cost-effective way and . . . [in the context of an] organizational culture that gives rise to it on a scale that impacts the life of every child in the system."[84] To provide relevant knowledge for the scaling-up process is one of the goals of the case-study database. In addition, Crew's distinction between the conditions for creating a successful individual school and a successful school system is a most important one. To address these different needs directly, the pragmatist views it as essential to conduct case studies not only of individual schools, but of groups of schools and of whole school systems, like New York City's.

Rudy Crew's "Hands On" Philosophy. Very recently, Rudy Crew partly reversed himself. Instead of permitting school performance data to speak for itself—what Lisbeth Schorr calls being "tight" about outcome standards but "loose" about process[85]—Crew has taken a major move to limit local flexibility and in essence kill the innovative, alternative public academies that have been at the heart of New York City's school-reform efforts in the last decade.[86] As a reflection of the developments that led to this move, the visible champion and director of the effort to consolidate and expand the public academies, Deborah Meir, left the New York City schools in October 1996; and Crew has recently replaced the most active advocate for school reform at the Board of Education, the head of alternative high schools.

Crew has criticized the alternative schools for the very flexibility and freedom from the central administration's rules and regulations that Schorr would argue is part of their strength. For example, taking a bureaucratic path, Crew has proposed that all schools be required to have principals. Presently, about 150 of the small, alternative schools are now run by teacher-directors, who are viewed by these schools as an advantage because they are chosen from a much larger pool of candidates, because they tend to work in collaborative rather than hierarchical ways with their schools' teachers, and because their lower salaries are easier to justify with the smaller number of students.[87]

Crew says: "The issue here is not can you create five schools or 10 schools. . . . The larger question is scalability. And the only things we want to bring to scale are those things which can work and can be replicated, both because they can be done in a cost-effective way and because they measure up and have results."[88] Interpreting these words in terms of his actions, Crew is reverting to a positivist model, claiming that the only programs he wants to scale up are those that can be standardized in process ("replicated"). And yet according to Schorr, this standardization will remove the very qualities—local flexibility and a sense of local staff empowerment—that create successful programs.

On the other hand, if Crew is true to his stated pragmatic commitment to continuous monitoring of cost-effectiveness, all will be able to see the results of his actions. Thus, if Schorr is right, the cost-effectiveness data will indicate a decline in performance of individual schools as they move from local flexibility to centralized control. On the other hand, if Crew is able to achieve the continuous improvement to which he has publicly committed himself, he will have justified his decision to undo the public academies. As the pragmatist sees it, the most important message here is a commitment to ongoing measurement of program results and an openness to abide by the results to resolve theoretical, ideological, and political debates.

Developing a Database of Education Reform Cases: Mike Rose's Cross-Country Journey

The present wave of school reform in its varied and diverse patterns has been blossoming since the 1960s, partly as an outgrowth of postmodern times that question given assumptions and methods. The pragmatic psychologist's approach to improving schools is to search out from among the 14,000 school districts, over 80,000 schools, and 2.5 million teachers in particular classrooms those cases in which exemplary educational outcomes are taking place in context. Once found, and wherever feasible, these successful cases—or a representative sample of them—are documented and assessed two-dimensionally: through the use of standardized, quantitative academic performance measures with different base rates for different types of student populations; and by detailed and systematic, qualitative case studies conducted within a common, disciplined inquiry framework.

The resultant case studies then form an organized and ever cumulative, computerized database of cases. Each case is characterized in an assortment of ways so that types of cases can be defined by a variety of possible criteria, involving single variables and/or patterns of variables. This allows a user to sort through the database and select out those types of cases that address his or her interest, be it a principal or teacher planning an educational program for a school or classroom; a policy planner developing new opportunities, guidelines, or regulations; or a researcher performing comparative studies to find ways to cluster similar cases and to identify common factors of success and failure within particular types of schools.[89]

A number of educational writers have in effect pilot-tested the pragmatic paradigm by searching out particular school districts, schools, and classrooms that are exemplary, and then site-visiting them and documenting in books their functioning and performance as concrete, holistic systems.[90] An excellent representative of these books is *Possible Lives: The Promise of Public Education in America* by Mike Rose,[91] a former public school teacher now training other teachers in a graduate school of education. Rose began by networking with his education colleagues to find model classrooms that would exemplify "the particulars of the potential of public education," sites that showed the potential "for inspired teaching, for courage, for achievement against the odds, for successful struggle, for the insight and connection that occur continually in public school classrooms."[92]

Rose visited nine educational settings scattered around the country. As part of his holistic focus, in each setting Rose paid attention to both the target case at hand and to the larger context in which the case was embedded.

> Schools are nested in complex, often volatile social and political environments, and my trip often coincided with a felicitous shift in policy or a crisis of finances or institutional identity. So another dimension of public education presented itself, and I would change the scope of my inquiry to try to understand the larger forces that encourage or limit good work in our schools.[93]

With his focus on results rather than on a particular ideology or theory, it is not surprising that Rose found heterogeneity in the teachers that he studied:

> There is no single profile of the Good Teacher . . . [and] I recommend no final list of good practices, no particular framework or set of instructional guidelines. Such profiles and lists have value: they can suggest direction and generate discussion. But they also have a tendency to be stripped of context, to become rigid prescriptions, at times reduced to slogan or commodity.[94]

In the final chapter of his book, Rose captures some of the crucial qualitative characteristics that seem to define positive outcomes in particular classrooms:

> Nurturance, social cohesion, the fostering of competence, a sense of growth, a feeling of opportunity, futurity. . . . [These] characteristics combined to create vital public space. The rooms I visited felt alive. People were

learning things, both cognitive and social, and doing things, individually and collectively, making contributions, connecting ideas, generating knowledge. . . . Overall these classrooms were exciting places to be, places of reflection and challenge, of deliberation and expression, of quiet work and public presentation, People were encouraged to be smart.[95]

This is a good start, but the case-based pragmatic paradigm—and the role that psychologists could play in its implementation—add much to work like Rose's: the placing of the case in the formal conceptual framework of disciplined inquiry (see fig. I.2); the conduct of the case according to rigorous methodological principles (see chapter 7) rather than the more informal and journalistic approach of researchers like Rose; the integration of qualitative analysis within a framework of comparative quantitative indicators; and the accumulation of a large number and wide variety of cases into an accessible, computerized, case study database.

"Contingency Theory"—A Rose by Another Name

Beginning in the late 1960s, psychologists have researched the process of planned organizational change in the schools. Following positivist principles, this work has searched for specific variables that could account for the successful adoption of educational reforms, be they the nature of the specific innovation itself (e.g., discovery-oriented teaching techniques to raise student interest) or the process of innovation (e.g., whether the innovations were being implemented as planned). The results of all this work have in effect reached the same pragmatic conclusions Rose did in his journalistic search—namely, that it is the interaction between the content of the innovation and the systemic and contextually based processes within the individual site that account for whether the innovation will be successfully adopted.[96] The educational researchers have formalized this conclusion under the rubric of "contingency theory":

> Given the millions of dollars and countless energy devoted to studying and carrying out the change process, what has really been learned? Essentially this: Some efforts succeed in some settings and not in others; and the setting is the critical factor. . . .
>
> A contingency approach makes several assumptions about change strategies. First, they are bounded by time and place. . . . Second, there is limited generalizability of event relationships . . . [involving] a middle ground between the existence of universal principles of [successful innovation adoption] . . . and the principle that each organization is unique. . . .

Third, interaction between a change strategy and a contextual condition tints subsequent events . . . [that is], a school affects and is affected by the initiation of a change strategy, and the ensuing change process is partially the consequence of this interaction.[97]

The educational literature is filled with lists of organizational factors purported to be associated with successful schools. While the pragmatist, like the contingency theorist, does not assume that they are valid across all settings, they are useful in suggesting promising areas to examine in a systematic case study. For example, one set of factors, emerging from the New York City "honor roll" school analysis, shows striking parallels to certain "nonspecific factors" that are posited to be important in mediating whether specific techniques will work in psychotherapy.[98] The New York City variables, and their therapeutic parallels, include (1) "a strong, [enthusiastic] principal who articulates a clear vision" (a confidant therapist with a clearly articulated vision of the therapeutic process); (2) "a cohesive curriculum, where lessons learned in one grade are built on in the next" (a cohesive model of how therapy proceeds systematically over time to psychological and behavioral improvement); (3) "extensive teacher training" (extensive therapist training in the particular model being employed); and (4) "[capacity of the school to elicit] active support from parents" (capacity of the therapist to form a positive working alliance with the patient).[99] There is also a significant parallel between these characteristics and the following summary of "common factors" that have been found in one summary of the educational research to be associated with the kind of school climate that promotes learning:

High academic expectations and a core academic curriculum for all students. . . .

Schools characterized by clear goals and priorities, teachers who share similar beliefs about the school's mission, and collaboration among faculty.

Positive relationships between students and staff, parental support for learning, high teacher morale, positive student attitudes towards achievement, and low absenteeism.[100]

The Next Step after Lists

The pragmatic study has a formal logic that requires a holistic, systems-oriented qualitative description and analysis of the case. Following the flowchart of a case outlined in figure 1.2,[101] this logic helps to organize the diverse lists of relevant factors that are found in the literature on successful educational innovation. Many of these factors have been discussed above. For example, in the Introduction, the characteristics of educational *clients* and their environments were outlined, including such factors as student and teacher demographics, abilities, learning/teaching styles, and cultures; pertinent characteristics of the central administration, the school board, parents, and other members of the community; and contextual factors such as physical facilities, financial support, and the presence of teaching technologies like computers.

Different *guiding conceptions* underlying educational programs include many of the ideas discussed above on educational models, such as Sizer's principles of essential education, Hirsch's cultural literacy, and the other "smart school" ideas summarized by Fiske.

In the program *formulation*, these general models are operationalized for a particular situation, resulting in specific cases like the Fratney School in Milwaukee, discussed in the Introduction, or the Key School and the four New York City elementary schools described in this chapter. The next part of the case looks at how the program is carried out (*"action"*) through the use of quantitative process statistics and qualitative "thick" description, for example, by reviewing "a day in the life" of representative teachers and students via participant observations of the actual school day and by phenomenologically oriented interviews.[102]

Finally, in addition to a *concluding evaluation* of the educational program, the qualitative evaluation examines in what ways the different components work together, and in what ways they are inconsistent or in conflict.

National Testing: Pragmatic Tool or New Battleground of the Culture Wars

The issue of standardized quantitative testing deserves special comment vis-à-vis the development of an educational, pragmatic case-study database. The logic of the database, which parallels Kenneth Howard's model for developing a database of individual psychotherapy cases described in chapter 8, can be summarized as follows:

1. Collect standardized outcome scores for each individual case, e.g., a single psychotherapy patient, a single teacher's classroom, or a single school.

2. Collect standardized background information about each individual case, so that the case can be "typed," that is, placed in a grouping with other "similar" types of cases. In line with the Howard model, "similar" cases are those which can be expected, *on average*, to have similar outcome scores.

3. On the basis of 1 and 2, a case can be categorized as above average, average, or below average in performance *in comparison to* other cases of the same type. Thus, in the New York City research described above, the "honor roll" schools were those whose reading and writing proficiency scores were significantly higher than schools with students of similar backgrounds, as defined by level of poverty among students in the school and the percentage of students whose primary language was not English.

Today a major controversy has flared up about what types of standardized tests to use in comparing schools. In the early 1980s, when *A Nation at Risk* highlighted the mediocre performance of American schools, achievement was measured primarily by standardized multiple-choice tests. Called "norm based," these tests compare students against one another and not against some specific level of performance, as do "criterion based" tests. In fact, these standardized tests typically measured low-level skills and the simple memorization of facts, independent of the specifics of most curricula.[103] Thus, while these tests were sufficient for meeting the logic of computing comparison scores among schools—that is, they were "standardized"—they did not set "standards" for what each child should know at each level of schooling.

There is also a heated debate about the advisability of setting specific curriculum content standards, within individual states and/or across the whole nation. One prototype for such curriculum standards is E. D. Hirsch's "core knowledge" curriculum discussed earlier. In such a system, "teaching to the test" is not a major problem, since the test taps into the types of knowledge that are the goals of education. In a recent impassioned plea for such a curriculum, one author argued:

> There are . . . no officially recognized, agreed-on expectations of what students should know at each level of schools. Curriculums vary widely, not only within cities and states but also within individual schools. Report after report has shown that American children study too many subjects, too superficially, and spend way too much time taking electives that don't given them the basic skills they need to get even a blue-collar job after high

school. . . . Nearly every other industrialized nation has a core curriculum that stipulates what students must learn in subjects like math, science, literature, and history in order to graduate from one level of schooling to the next. The standardized tests used to measure such progress are limited in number and are content-based, designed for the curriculum, and typically require analytical essays as well as multiple-choice answers. Students know exactly what's expected of them; notions of achievement are associated with effort, not inherent ability.[104]

Another argument in favor of national standards derives from the growing diversity in America's educational setting. This diversity is twofold. First, schools differ in the type of educational model employed, from traditional "back to basics" approaches to Sizer's "Essential Schools." Second, schools differ in the organizational arrangements in which they are embedded, with the emphasis being on consumer "choice" via such options as vouchers, specialized magnet schools, charter schools, other "alternative" schools within large public school districts like New York City, and home schooling. Such diversity greatly reduces the ability to monitor the quality of schooling through central managing of the classroom—the length of class periods, the number of class periods per day, teacher-student ratio, what particular approved textbooks must be used, and so forth. In other words, with the demise of the homogenized and rigidly regulated factory school, it is much harder to control the input into schooling; and there is thus an increased need to monitor quality by monitoring educational output in terms of the effectiveness of schooling. This new emphasis, of course, is very much in line with the pragmatic insistence on measuring and monitoring the ultimate results of a social program, rather than the nature of the inputs into the program or the theory behind the program per se.

The move toward national educational standards was supported by President Bush's America 2000 and then by President Clinton's Goals 2000.[105] However, resistance has come from America's traditional fear of strong national government, voiced in terms of support for "states' rights," "local control," and "parental rights" in determining how and what children will learn. Moreover, the present move toward national standards has become caught up in the education culture wars, reviewed at the beginning of this chapter. "Progressive educators worry that a national curriculum would lead to more rote-learning and a greater reliance on standardized tests. Conservatives, who you might think would cozy up to standards, are deeply suspicious of any sort of outside meddling in their neighborhood schools."[106]

In addition, controversy has surrounded the effort by Goals 2000 to date to create standards in basic academic areas like history. For example, produced largely by liberal, postmodern-oriented academics, the history standards deemphasize the "Eurocentric" and nationalistic American cast of traditional history textbooks. Conservatives loudly protest the standards for downplaying the nation's greatness, for overemphasizing multiculturalism, and for failing to mention by name historical figures such as Paul Revere, Thomas Edison, and Albert Einstein.[107]

A similar controversy has recently erupted over the more recent release of national standards for the English language arts.[108] The standards reflect contemporary postmodern literary theory and question the traditional "great books" approach to literature, emphasizing diversity and openness to the wealth of different written materials that exist. A conservative critic attacks: "So books have no meaning, and nobody can say that Shakespeare is more worthy of study than a baseball card or a cola jingle. . . . [The teacher is a] guide to 'critical thinking,' which turns out to mean not the development of sharp and logical critical skills but the easy accumulation of 'divergent' views on all matters."[109]

On the other hand, there is a governmental program, the National Assessment of Educational Progress (NAEP), which is involved indirectly in standard setting and is less controversial.[110] Mandated by Congress and administered by the National Center for Education Statistics, since 1969 the NAEP has periodically monitored student achievement in reading, writing, math, science, history/geography, and other fields in grades 4, 8, and 12. Known as the nation's "report card," it is the only ongoing national survey of students' educational achievement, and its staying power for over twenty-five years is promising. Until 1988, NAEP was limited to measuring student progress on a national basis. In 1990 thirty-seven states participated in the first state assessment for eighth-grade math. Since that time, participation by states in order to obtain comparisons with one another has been increasing for both math and reading.

The NAEP assessments include both multiple-choice questions and performance tasks that require students to demonstrate directly what they can do, such as writing an essay, creating a map, or solving a math problem. The NAEP tests are criterion based and yield absolute scores of achievement in four categories: advanced, proficient, basic, or below basic. These achievement levels are derived from the collective judgments of a variety of individuals, including a broadly representative panel of teachers.

All in all, while the NAEP is not based on a national curriculum per se, its capacity to garner general support suggests that the curriculum content implied by its test items might be a good starting point for thinking about a national curriculum. Overall, the content of the NAEP is more oriented toward practical skills for coping in real-world situations, like banking, obtaining loans, paying taxes, shopping, and understanding national and world events from a newspaper, that is, to the application of academic knowledge. In contrast, the developmental process of the controversial history and English standards by Goals 2000 was much more dominated by academics advocating from the more theoretical and ideological perspective of their disciplinary focus.

In short, the dialogue about national standards is heated and politicized, and the prospects for developing national standards are mixed. Since this is a value-based dialogue about the goals of a social program, not about what programs are working well to achieve these goals, the pragmatic paradigm is limited in how it can contribute.

However, the pragmatic psychologist can offer to the conversation the study of cases in which a set of curriculum standards have been "successfully" adopted by groups of schools—either within a school district, a state, or in selected sites around the country. In such case studies, "success" would be defined in terms of a number of criteria, including (a) approval and support of the curriculum standards by the various stakeholders associated with the schools studied—politicians, administrators, teachers, students, parents, and the larger community; (b) a persuasive rationale for the process whereby the standards were developed (as just discussed, discipline-focused academics are not the only possible source of such standards: other possible sources are the teachers, parents, politicians, employers, students, and so forth—who are in fact the ultimate "consumers" of the standards); and (c) use of the standards to set expectations and to guide teaching so as to achieve above average performance on the standardized tests now being used (such as the NAEP tests) in comparison to similar types of schools.

Overall, the pragmatist's commitment to quantitative and qualitative empiricism can act as a deescalator of politicized polarization by focusing in detail on actual educational outcomes rather than on the more abstract battles between proponents of opposing ideological and theoretical points of view.

PART V

Implications

Chapter 10 concludes the book with a manifesto for a pragmatic psychology. Here I spell out the steps that must be taken to create pragmatic psychology as a vital, strong, and highly competitive epistemological alternative for meeting the challenges of the twenty-first century.

10

Manifesto for a
Pragmatic Psychology

Prologue: A Call for Pluralism

Postmodernism's political, philosophical, and cultural attacks against modernism, and modernism's predictable counterattacks, have created an intellectual age of polarization and cultural warfare. We saw this vividly embodied in the "psychotherapy wars" and "education wars" reviewed in the last two chapters. If psychology continues to enmesh itself in these debates, the discipline will dissipate many of its resources in a self-destructive struggle. We need instead to focus our energy and creativity upon substantive issues, such as addressing the major psychosocial problems of our times. Psychology's capacity to do this is one of the crucial bases upon which the public supports our discipline. If we are to merit the public's full continuing support, we will have to demonstrate that we can concentrate on producing disciplined, scholarly, insightful, and useful results rather than battling with each other about paradigm differences.

Psychologists must acknowledge that there are different paradigms within our field, and that these paradigms constitute alternative visions of the nature of appropriate psychological knowledge and the methods by which it should be pursued. The strengths of the case-based paradigm lie in practical problem solving for addressing psychosocial troubles, and it is in this arena that pragmatists should concentrate their efforts. Pragmatists affirm that there are interests other than practical problem solving for which the public turns to psychology. These include basic scientific research as an intellectual end in itself, and hermeneutic work that doesn't focus on solving specific problems, but deepens our understanding of some aspect of human life, personality, or psychopathology—in the tradition of the humanities. Pragmatists typically leave these arenas to other paradigms.

My call for pluralism resonates with the multiform, dialogical nature of our postmodern era, particularly with the ideas of postpositivist philosophers like Kuhn, Feyerabend, and Wittgenstein, and pragmatic philosophers like Bernstein, Rorty, Toulmin, and West.[1] The call for pluralism also connects with a long-standing ideal of the academic tradition in which psychology is embedded. While it is recognized that the intellectual life of our universities—both within and across disciplines—is rife with diversity, disagreement, and change over time, most agree that the university as an institution continues to flourish to the extent that its members are committed to the collegial, pluralistic tradition of the academy. Similarly, the health of a democratic society is not dependent upon absolute agreement and consensus on policy issues, but upon a continuing commitment to the institutions of democracy—such as majority rule, regular elections, and "checks and balances" on the different branches of government. A psychology that encourages diversity sends a strong positive message that separates us from those mired in the pervasive culture wars.

The American Psychological Association, as the largest, most powerful, and broadest-ranging organization in American psychology, must take leadership in changing the message from "dueling paradigms" to "strength through diversity" as it communicates to the discipline and the public through its various publications, public statements, and public forums.

Our message should be that disciplinary psychology, unlike "pop" psychology and journalism, is distinctively valuable because it takes a rigorous, systematic, and scholarly approach to the study of human action—be the data experimental or experiential, quantitative or qualitative. Our message should also be that there are different ways in which paradigms can be rigorous (as illustrated in tables 7.1 and 7.2, which compare research reports across three different approaches). Each paradigm should develop its own body of research literature, and the quality of a study should be judged by the methodological standards within the paradigm. This will lead to the continuing development of different bodies of research literature, each documenting particular models, methods, and results.

Scholarly discussion of interparadigm comparisons also constitutes an important component of disciplinary psychology. In light of the postmodern perspective, no one paradigm has a privileged access to the truth. Each paradigm should therefore be judged on its results, its own particular contribution, laying these results out before the public for evaluation. In this way, it is the funders and consumers of psychological research and practice—embodied in such groups as the federal government, managed care companies, the public school system, the media, the academic community, and the larger public—who ultimately will make final judgments concerning the meaningfulness, usefulness, and overall value of these bodies of literature to the larger society.

Pragmatists Unite! An Action Plan for Making Case-Based Psychology a Reality

Given a level playing field in the spirit of pluralism, we pragmatists need to "become competitive" in the marketplace by developing our paradigm and its products in the realm of practical problem solving. This process involves three interlocking activities: becoming organized as a group, creating cumulative databases of properly documented cases, and promoting ourselves to the public.

Pragmatists Must Become Organized

Networking. There are many psychologists who are explicitly pragmatic in their theory and practice, following a version of Peterson's "disciplined inquiry" model. And there are many more who are implicitly so. These psychologists must be encouraged to identify themselves as pragmatists and to join together in networks, through mechanisms such as Internet information-and-discussion groups. The goal is to build a community of pragmatic psychologists, fostering dialogue, sharing insights, and advancing scholarship in the area.

The beleaguered practitioners I discussed earlier[2] are excellent candidates for such networks. These individuals are constantly engaged in pragmatic work with cases, and yet they frequently don't have a clear paradigm to support and enhance their work. Also, fine candidates are those academic researchers with interests in program evaluation, community psychology, and qualitative research, areas with a significant degree of overlap with pragmatism.[3] More generally, the pragmatic paradigm will be appealing to those psychologists who view themselves as "subject experts." These individuals are identified less with particular methodological models than with specific, pragmatically relevant subject areas—like violence, psychopathology, day-care programming, affective education, and organizational downsizing. In this regard, graduate students are an excellent source of recruits, since they typically enter graduate school based on an interest in certain subject areas rather than in a particular methodology.[4] Finally, it is important for pragmatic psychologists to connect with scholars and practitioners in other social science fields—like business, communications, urban anthropology, sociology, and political science—who are attracted to pragmatism and the case study method.

Creating Organizations. As networks of pragmatic psychologists and other social scientists form, they can begin to exert influence on the views and policies of professional organizations to which they already belong. In many of these organizations mechanisms exist for creating new suborganizations around a common interest, such as the divisions of the American Psychological Association or the special interest groups of the Association for Advancement of Behavior Therapy. Also, new organizations structured around a commitment to the pragmatic paradigm and case-based psychology must eventually emerge if the paradigm is to come fully into its own.

Pragmatists Must Create a Cumulative Database of Properly Documented Cases

Infrastructure. We must create a physical and operational structure to store case study reports in a way that provides easy, individually tailored access to them. The most straightforward way to do this is to construct computerized databases, whether located on the Internet, an intranet, or CD-ROMS. To maintain quality and comparability, acceptance of cases must be based on peer review by appropriately constituted editorial boards. In other words, the databases will function as a type of electronic journal.

To bring the database into being will require grappling with a number of thorny policy issues. Two are of particular note: preserving confidentiality and the possible proprietary nature of case data. Because case studies deal with the concrete, personal details of real people in particular situations, it is more difficult to preserve confidentiality with them than when the basic data of a study are abstract numbers across groups of individuals. Systematic guidelines should be developed for aiding case authors in this process. There is also a question of databases intended for authorized professionals being broken into by nonauthorized individuals interested in improper exploitation of the case material. This problem is being addressed in a variety of other domains, such as medical, banking, and Social Security records. We should turn to experts in these domains for advice and procedures for effectively dealing with threats to confidentiality.

There are already precedents in areas such as managed care for private, profit-making companies to amass their own proprietary databases for internal decision making. Ways must be found to employ the financial and logistical resources of for-profit companies so that not only these companies themselves profit from proprietary databases, but so that there is also public benefit by some open data sharing, in the best traditions of academic and scientific partnerships. Also, these private resources must not be viewed as replacing the traditional funders of open, psychological research: government and foundations.

Generating and Valuing Case Reports. Once a database structure is developed, we must fill it with appropriate case reports. This will require providing information and incentives to prospective case authors to stimulate the production of case study reports that meet preestablished quality standards for the database. It is true that presently, practitioners are engaged with cases as their basic activity, and case reports abound in the media, in scholarly biography and history, and in psychology for illustrative purposes. However, few of these meet the pragmatic quality standards outlined in tables 7.1 and 7.2. To receive and disseminate rigorous case study reports, we must create publication vehicles—both the peer-reviewed case study databases discussed above, and books and journals dealing with individual case studies and case study issues. Decision makers associated with research grants and academic promotions must then be persuaded to attach high-level recognition to these types of publications—that is, to turn these case reports into "scholarly currency." As we have seen with positivist publications, success will beget more success: the more case study publications are professionally and academically valued, the more psychologists will be stimulated to publish in this way; and the growing numbers of publications will create a growing acceptance, which in turn will stimulate the creation of even larger numbers of case study manuscripts.

The human resources and incentives for conducting and documenting pragmatically rigorous case studies do already exist: applied researchers funded by government and foundation grants to search for solutions to pressing social problems; academics who function in a "publish or perish culture"; undergraduate and graduate students who are required to complete theses and dissertations;[5] and practitioners and managers who want to diversify their activities and share their experiences with others through reflection and writing. These individuals and groups must be networked together and organized if they are to be effective in developing and advocating for the pragmatic paradigm.

We must also explore opportunities for integrating pragmatic case studies into positivist studies that focus on researching human service programs. Such case studies of selected subjects in a group project can provide a complementary, in-depth picture of program processes and outcomes; and the cases can also be useful on their own.[6]

While APA and other empirical journals abound and there is a wide variety in their topics and subject areas, positivist methods still largely dominate. In pursuit of its professed commitment to pluralism, APA must break this monopoly and initiate case study journals, books, and other publications—in addition to other methodological approaches such as more hermeneutically oriented investigations.[7] In a similar vein, the Association should be encouraged to sponsor some of the pragmatic case study databases that need to be created.

Pragmatists Must Promote Their Ideas to the Public

The public must be educated that science—in the sense of systematic, empirically based, methodologically sophisticated research—does not need to be limited to the experimental laboratory and to quantitative data exclusively. The stuff of ordinary life—concrete events as we experience them qualitatively, narratively, and phenomenologically—is also the stuff of pragmatic case studies, and thus pragmatists should be in a strong position to communicate and engage the public in what we do. We already have the precedents of the attention-getting power of cases in journalism and political advocacy, which are highly dependent on the use of case examples because of their dramatic, engaging, and "real" qualities. In reaching the public, the pragmatic paradigm has the great advantage of tapping into these qualities of case studies. At the same time, pragmatic case studies can educate the public that case studies can be serious, scholarly, and "scientific" (in the broad sense of the word)—in short, it can teach the difference between "disciplined inquiry" and "talk show psychology." It can demonstrate that there is a disciplined alternative to the dichotomy that Robyn Dawes[8] posits: practice that is "scientific" (in the narrow sense of the word), based on experimentally derived, positivist principles versus practice based on the professional's "trained intuition"—a "house of cards" in Dawes's view.

Vision: Staying in Touch with Our Roots

Any action plan can only be truly successful when it is founded upon an inspiring guiding vision. It is imperative that our actions flow from the positive ideals of pragmatism, which are directed toward providing solutions to contemporary psychosocial crises and challenges. Our ideals generate five virtues of pragmatism that are particularly suited to the demands of today's world.

Conceptual Synthesis

In a dialectically divided world, the pragmatic paradigm has a capacity for conceptual integration, incorporating the empiricism and quantitative sophistication of the positivist tradition with the holistic, contextual, and qualitative emphases of hermeneutics.

Pragmatism sees an advantage to the profusion of competing theoretical points of view generated by the dialectics of modernist versus postmodernist debates. The pragmatist views this profusion as a rich resource for assessment, formulation, and intervention ideas in addressing practical problems as they present themselves in complex, real-world case contexts. The difference is that the pragmatist views all theoretical concepts and related methods as potential tools to be employed in practical problem solving—not as positivist pictures of the world, or skeptical postmodern critiques of positivism, or critical postmodern moral visions.

Moreover, the case-driven approach frequently reveals the usefulness of integrating perspectives from seemingly competing, theory-driven points of view. In chapter 8, the therapist of Cindy, the rape victim with post-traumatic stress disorder, began with a positivist, cognitive-behavioral theory that focuses on correcting a patient's false beliefs and reasoning errors. However, the clinical needs of these types of cases and the outcomes obtained with past cases led the therapist to broaden her conceptualization to include as her major therapeutic goal the reworking of Cindy's whole life story and life outlook—an approach very consistent with hermeneutically oriented "constructivist" therapy, in which one's psychological autobiography is "narrated and renarrated" to lead to "repair" through "transformation."[9]

Theoretical Mediation

In a related way, the pragmatic paradigm has the capacity to mediate theory clashes. In addressing socially critical areas such as psychotherapy service delivery reform and education reform, pragmatism takes a *case-driven* position and thereby stands between the contradictory views that emerge when advocates of competing *theory-driven* positions clash. This means, for instance, that psychotherapy service planning should not be dictated by a forced choice between individualized versus manualized treatment; and that educational planning should not be dictated by a forced choice between progressive and "child-oriented" educational models versus those that are traditional and "knowledge oriented." In each instance the proponents argue that based on some sample of relevant therapy patients or schools, their vision is the single true one for *all* patients or *all* schools. In contrast, the pragmatic approach is uncommitted to a single theory per se as it develops appropriate guiding conceptions and case formulations. Rather, each case is judged on its own merits by systematically assessing the case—both quantitatively and qualitatively—within all the distinctiveness and complexity of its context.[10]

Democratic Decision Making

The pragmatic paradigm supports our democratic ideals by requiring collaboration with program stakeholders in program goal setting. The pragmatic paradigm does not attempt to preempt value questions, including questions of what goals human service programs should seek to attain. These are conceived as falling outside the realm of the psychologist's or other social scientist's disciplinary expertise as such. Rather, in line with philosophic pragmatism, goal and other value questions are to be resolved by open, democratic dialogue among relevant stakeholders.

The accessible, "natural," and engaging nature of social science case studies can reinspire the public to become more involved in serious democratic debate about human service programs. Citizens will see that pragmatic psychologists, through their case studies, value the "real" experiences of individuals rather than calculations and formulas summarizing abstract relationships across groups of individuals. Thus, this work will directly connect with the public's own lives and enhance the connection between their personal world and human service program outcomes and policies. It will in turn enhance the public's stake in the basic data of serious psychological and other social science research.

A "Middle Way" to Generalization

The positivist attacks the single case study as too context-specific from which to generalize. The hermeneut attacks the positivist for trying to achieve generalization by merging individual case information into group data and, in the process, stripping away individual context and reducing qualitatively complex processes to numbers. The pragmatist agrees with the positivist about the value of generalizing, but also with the hermeneut about the need to retain context.

The pragmatist provides the alternative of the case study database. Yes, a single pragmatic case is quite limited in its generalization to other cases, because of the unique contextual complexities in any particular case. However, as multiple cases accumulate and are organized into computer-accessible databases, they begin to sample a wide variety of contextually different human service situations in which a particular problem can occur and be addressed. A rising number of cases in the database increases the probability that there are specific cases that as a group generalize to any particular target case. While generalizing by logical deduction is not possible, as in the positivist paradigm, the pragmatic paradigm promises a viable way of attaining a reasonable degree of generalization without giving up context.

Accountability

The pragmatic paradigm meets its accountability to clients in the most direct way possible, by putting the client's needs first, before the program provider's theory. Moreover, the scope of such accountability is very wide. The creation of a database of successful cases facilitates pragmatic program improvement. And this process is applicable not only to therapy and education reform, as illustrated in chapters 8 and 9, but to any type of human service program, such as those dealing with violence, drugs, gangs, homelessness, family dysfunction, poverty, welfare dependence, teenage motherhood, and disease.

More specifically, chapter 8 reviewed a logical model developed and pilot-tested by Kenneth Howard and his research group for establishing psychotherapy base rates by type of case, and for then employing these base rates to assess the relative cost-effectiveness of the therapy in any particular case. Chapter 9 showed how expansion of the Howard model logic, through the development and use of state or national curriculum and achievement standards, makes it possible to manage for excellence a statewide or nationwide network of schools. By extension, the logic of the model can be employed to manage for excellence any type of human service program.

The Challenge Ahead

Pragmatism poses an alternative to the possibility of utopia. In one sense, this is a disappointment. It is hard to compete with positivism's commitment to the Enlightenment view of "Cosmopolis": a vision of a society in which the natural and social worlds are both ordered on underlying rational principles that lead us—as we further reveal them—in one continuous upward movement toward some perfect social state.[11]

It is also hard to compete with the view of critical postmodernists who idealistically focus on closing the vast gap between present social reality and a world without political and cultural domination, oppression, and exploitation.

Yet pragmatism has its own inspirational vision for the future of psychology. The goal of an accessible and crucially relevant database of case studies conducted according to rigorous quantitative and qualitative standards provides a forceful alternative to a psychology that seems to be moving inexorably toward a rigid bifurcation into "theory versus practice," "science versus profession," and "the service-delivery effort . . . called psychology" versus "the academic discipline . . . called behavioral science."[12]

Coming down from the lofty perch of ideological purity, pragmatism meets the world as we find it and asks: How can we improve it—not in some ideal way with a predetermined endpoint, but in a practical way in the here and now, within the context of the social, cultural, political, and economic realities we are given? More specifically, pragmatic psychology directs our attention away from the search for decontextualized general principles toward finding individual, model human services and service programs in context. Through documentation and extension of these "good works," pragmatism doesn't promise an ideal state, but it does offer real, concrete improvement in the social condition.

Pragmatic psychology faces a major challenge in its efforts to gain and promote this vision in today's media environment, dominated as it is by dramatic, combative, dialectical debate.[13] The synthesizer has a harder time getting heard than the purist, the extremist, or the provocateur. The case study method does not present itself as a "magic bullet," and this is disappointing in today's "boom or bust" culture.[14] Pragmatists must remind societal leaders, the media, and the general public that the search for such a magic bullet has only led to a revolving door of fads and fashions. We must counteract the exclusive focus on crisis that pervades the news. Ultimately, the pragmatic psychologist's promotion of lively and rigorously documented case studies of "programs that work" should be able to engage and persuade a public hungry for promising news and reason to be optimistic about the future.

The interested reader is urged to contact the author and to join a Pragmatic Psychology Dialogue Group at the following web site: *http://www.pragmatic-psychology.org.*

Notes

1. Seligman (1995).

2. See Seligman (1996a, 1996b) and the whole October 1996 issue of the *American Psychologist*.

3. Use of the terms "modernism" and "postmodernism" is a controversial issue in contemporary studies of literature and art. Sass (1992) summarizes two very different uses. The first, which I employ in this book, is as follows: "The term *modernism* is sometimes used . . . to refer to the whole trend of rationalistic-scientific thought that begins with Galileo, Newton, and the seventeenth-century Enlightenment. *Postmodernism* then comes to be associated with the adversarial, relativistic, antifoundationalist reactions against this trend that occur in twentieth century art, thought, and culture."

In the second usage, "modernism" started at the turn of the century and continues through the present. It refers to a movement led by writers and artists which is "noted for such stylistic features and aesthetic attitudes . . . as self-referentiality, profound relativism and uncertainty, extreme irony, and tendencies towards fragmentation." It consists of two periods. The first had its heyday in a period of "high modernism," occurring before and just after World War I in the work of writers and artists like Eliot, Pound, Virginia Woolf, Valery, Rilke, Kafka, Picasso, and Matisse." The second period is postmodernism, which began perhaps around 1960. Major figures identified with the postmodernist style, sensibility, or mood would be writers, artists, and composers like Jorge Luis Borges, Thomas Pynchon, Donald Barthelme, Robert Rauschenberg, Jasper Johns, Andy Warhol, and John Cage.

For other discussions of the modern versus postmodern distinction, see Gergen (1991, especially pp. 264–265, note 45); Rosenau (1992, especially p. 5, note 5); and Toulmin (1990, pp. 152–160). For example, Toulmin views postmodernism in many different artistic and intellectual areas as beginning around 1960. In contrast to Sass, Toulmin argues that the 1920–1960 period is highly modernistic, focusing on formalism, rigor, certitude, and rationalism-through-mathematics, as evidenced in such areas as 12-tone music, the art of Piet Mondrian, logical positivism in philosophy, and the functional, "universal-style" architecture of Mies van der Rohe.

4. Ryder (1987).

5. Gergen (1991), pp. 89–95.

6. Gergen (1991) presents intriguing arguments that the expansion of communication technologies (such as cable television, the cellular telephone, the FAX, the modem, the computer, satellite information transmission, video conferencing, and desk-top publishing) forces us to relate to a growing number of persons, roles, institutions, lifestyles, and cultures. This "social saturation" leads to a hyperawareness of diversity, undermining traditional views of a homogeneous, stable, "centered" world. In a parallel but more positive manner, the saturation leads to increasing openness to multiculturalism, which, Gergen argues, is a great strength in an increasingly pluralistic world.

7. Information from the Princeton University Internet web site: *www.Princeton.edu.*

8. A recent social innovation at Princeton, inconceivable in the 1950s, is the "Diversity Table." In the alumni magazine, it is described as a small step in building a "workable pluralism" on a campus that has a history of elitism and exclusivity. Specifically, the Diversity Table is described as

> a grassroots experiment in bridging the cultural differences of the community's various members. At the table, for example, a black custodian may today describe how she avoids walking on the campus when she can, because she doesn't quite feel it's hers. Or a white administrator might recount the difficulty he had explaining to his daughter why blacks at her high school would want to draft their own political agenda. Or one of the town's senior citizens may relate how people patronize her, as if she were a child again. (*Princeton Alumni Weekly*, 1992, p. 10)

9. Fishman and Neigher (1982).

10. I had, in fact, been working within the framework of such a model in developing and pilot-testing a cost-effectiveness methodology for evaluating the services of community mental health centers. The work was supported by the National Institute of Mental Health, and it is described in Fishman (1980) and (1981).

11. Peterson and Fishman (1987).

12. Fishman and Neigher (1987).

13. Nessel (1982).

14. Wade (1982).

15. In the service of simplicity, throughout this book, unless otherwise noted, my use of the terms "pragmatic" and "pragmatism" will refer to the recent, postmodern versions of this way of thinking, and thus will be synonymous with the terms "neopragmatic" and "neopragmatism," respectively.

16. For recent publications applying the pragmatic paradigm to two particular areas—behavior therapy and program evaluation—see Fishman (1988) and Fishman (1991a and 1991b), respectively.

NOTES TO THE INTRODUCTION

1. Barber (1992a).

2. It is difficult to assess whether all these problems are actually worse than in the past, whether there is just a heightened awareness of them with their mushrooming increase in the dramatizing media, or whether, on the assumption that our experienced reality is to a large degree culturally constructed, the media have helped to create new social realities. In any event, as a society we feel an imperative for addressing today's experienced social crises.

3. Hill (1981).

4. Hill (1981).

5. Shaffer (1977).

6. Cited in Fishman and Neigher (1982).

7. This amount is taken from the fiscal year 1998 federal budget, finalized on December 2, 1997. It includes research and development funds for the following federal agencies: National Institute of Mental Health ($750 million); National Institute on Drug Abuse ($527 million); National Institute on Alcohol Abuse and Alcoholism ($227 million); the National Science Foundation's Directorate for Social, Behavioral, and Economic Sciences ($129 million); and the Air Force's Office of Science Research, which supports human factors and training research ($207 million). The figures are from Adler (1998).

8. McFall (1995).

9. Of course, such a prospect raises ethical questions about who would control the controllers, that is, about whether such knowledge would be used for political oppression, as illustrated in such novels as *Brave New World, 1984,* and *Clockwork Orange.*

10. See note 3 in the Preface.

11. Polkinghorne (1992) points out that the original philosophy of "pragmatism," created by Peirce, James, and Dewey, was developed in a modernistic era (the late nineteenth and early twentieth centuries), and as such was less differentiated from "objective science"—that is, was less explicitly epistemologically constructivist—than recent versions of pragmatism, articulated by philosophers such as Rorty, Bernstein, and Toulmin. These recent versions, which are embedded in postmodernity, Polkinghorne calls "neopragmatism." In short, "neopragmatism" is postmodern pragmatism. See note 15 in the Preface.

12. Fukuyama (1989); Toulmin (1990), p. 3.

13. Osborne and Gaebler (1992).

14. Benkov (1994).

15. E.g., see Barker (1992) and Hammer and Champy (1993) concerning business; and Fiske (1991) and Gerstner et al. (1994) concerning education.

16. Horgan (1996).

17. Denzin and Lincoln (1994); Gergen (1991); Polkinghorne (1992); Messer, Sass, and Woolfolk (1988); Rosenau (1992); Sass (in press).

18. Prilleltensky (1994).

19. Sass (in press), p. 3. A major aspect of the pervasive process of interpretation is intentionality, interpreting experience in terms of human goals and purposes. In addition, ontological hermeneutics emphasizes the historicity of human existence, meaning that the phenomenological content of our present experience is highly saturated with interpreted experience from our personal, social, and cultural histories.

20. Polkinghorne (1992), p. 151.

21. Polkinghorne (1992), p. 152.

22. Denzin and Lincoln (1994); Polkinghorne (1992); Rosenau (1992).

23. Rosenau (1992).

24. Sass (in press).

25. Polkinghorne (1992). See note 11, above.

26. For example, in the domain of psychotherapy, see the positivists Dawes (1994) and Held (1995) versus the postmodernists Neimeyer (1995) and Newman and Holzman (1996). And in psychology generally, note the recent splitting of the more purely positivist American Psychological Society from the more pluralist American Psychological Association.

27. Gergen (1991).

28. For an eloquent debate on these issues, see the exchange between M. Smith (1994) and Gergen (1994). Smith's position might be characterized as a combination of positivism and pragmatism, and Gergen's, a combination of skeptical and critical postmodernism.

29. Rosenau (1992).

30. Sass (in press) expresses the central role of ambiguity in ontological hermeneutics in the title of his recent paper, "Ambiguity Is of the Essence," and in the paper's first paragraph:

> "All concepts in which an entire process is semiotically concentrated elude definitions; only that which has no history is definable," wrote Friedrich Nietzsche in his *Genealogy of Morals*. . . . This statement, eminently hermeneutic in spirit, applies to nothing so much as to hermeneutics itself, a concept whose antiquity is matched by a striking, at times maddeningly, ambiguity.

31. See, for example, M. Berman's (1981) and Prilleltensky's (1994) arguments that politically conservative capitalism, which remains politically dominant today, is historically and intrinsically intertwined with modernistic science

and its positivist, mechanistic, atomistic worldview. In contrast, the skeptical and critical postmodern movements emerged from the political left (e.g., Jacoby 1994).

32. For an example of a synthetic, pragmatic reaction to skeptical and critical postmodern books in the area of program evaluation, see Fishman (1992, 1995, 1997).

It should be noted that ontological postmodernism has frequently also presented a bridging role in the dialectical debates. Besides toning down the dialectic by emphasizing intellectual humility and the need for scholarly rigor and philosophical sophistication in light of the complexity and intrinsic limitations of human knowledge, the focus of ontological postmodernism on the intentionality and historicity of human experience (and thus knowledge, which is in effect interpreted experience) resonates strongly with themes of pragmatism. For pragmatism emphasizes that knowledge and "truth" are to be judged in terms of the capacity to accomplish historically situated and socially negotiated goals.

33. Jacoby (1994), pp. xii–xiii.

34. Barber (1992b), p. 146.

35. Scheper-Hughes (1995), p. 22.

36. Peterson (1991), p. 425.

37. E.g., Dreyfus and Dreyfus (1986); Peterson (1991); Polkinghorne (1992); Schön (1983, 1987).

38. Peterson (1991), p. 426.

39. Peterson (1991), p. 427.

40. Peterson (1991), p. 427.

41. Peterson (1991), p. 427.

42. Peterson (1991); Polkinghorne (1992); Schön (1983, 1987).

43. Dreyfus and Dreyfus (1986).

44. Schön (1983), p. 68.

45. Polkinghorne (1992), pp. 162–163. It is important to note that some advocates of a pragmatic paradigm demonstrate the important role that elements from the positivist model can play in effective pragmatic practice. Notable among these are Stricker and Trierweiler, who do just this in their article, "The Local Clinical Scientist: A Bridge between Science and Practice" (1995). They argue that while contextually based practice demands "a recognition of the value of local observations and local solutions to problems, . . . these observations and solutions benefit by the scientific attitude of the clinician and are subjected to the same need for verifiability that greets all scientific enterprises" (p. 995).

46. Gutkin and Reynolds (1990).

47. Greisemer and Butler (1985).

48. The one main exception is the in-home school movement, in which parents take responsibility for educating their children at home. The recent growth

of this movement in part reflects the growing disenchantment with public schools.

49. Olson (1997), p. 8.

50. Comer (1988).

51. See also Wagner (1994).

52. This example is taken from my own graduate teaching experience.

53. Ajzen (1985).

54. For methods to involve the young people themselves in conducting the focus groups, see Krueger and King (1997).

55. Now one could learn something about Fratney School by reading George Wood's (1992) *Schools That Work: America's Most Innovative Public Education Programs*. Wood, a professor of education, not only provides a study of Fratney School, he compares Fratney with a variety of other, diverse schools around the country to derive a set of characteristics associated with "schools that work." From Wood's point of view, these are schools that nurture the skills and attitudes students need for becoming adults eager and ready to fill the role of active and responsible citizens in a participatory democracy.

While Wood is to be commended highly for his efforts, they fall more in the category of investigative journalism than psychological research. Wood describes his own personal experiences in visiting schools that he defines as successful, and he attempts to draw broad generalizations from these experiences, using an informal, intuitive, inspirational, graphic style. What is needed to complement Wood's important work is systematic, formal-research-based case studies. These are studies that use many of the quantitative and rigorously structured qualitative assessment techniques of the positivist and postpositivist traditions to describe, evaluate, and analyze methodically and multiperspectively representative sample cases of different types of schools. It is the results of such studies that would constitute the proposed educational case study database (see chapter 7 on case study method and chapter 9 on educational reform).

56. Baumeister (1991).

57. Baumeister (1991), pp. 12–13. Also see Gergen (1982); Rorty (1979); D'Andrade (1986).

58. Toulmin (1990), p. 147.

59. Messer, Sass, and Woolfolk (1988), p. 8. Two educational researchers put it this way: "electrons, unlike children, have neither motives nor aspirations; they do not strategize, they do not think, they are neither devious nor helpful" (Eisner and Peshkin 1990).

60. Note a certain contradiction here between the Enlightenment emphasis on individual freedom and rationality, on the one hand, and the deterministic models that developed from the application of Enlightenment science to explain social behavior and human experience, on the other.

61. Baumeister (1991), p. 13.

62. Kimble (1985), p. 317.

63. Baars (1986), p. 17.

64. Gergen (1991), p. 40.

65. It should be noted that some of these mental concepts have been incorporated into modernistic psychology via its participation in the "cognitive revolution" of the 1960s, a movement that is described in chapter 2.

66. Cushman (1990), p. 599.

67. To aid the reader in keeping track of the logical connections among the different strands of my argument, I begin each of the five sections with an overview.

68. Postmodernism rejects the possibility of objective truth and replaces it with historically and culturally contextualized and delimited social constructions. This introduces themes of pluralism, subjectivity, reflexivity, and relativism into intellectual discourse. Since objective truth is not attainable, there is a movement among so-called skeptical postmodernists away from the serious pursuit of "reality," "rationality," "authenticity," and "correctness," and toward imaginative playfulness, ironic and ambiguous self-reflexivity, and "anything goes" relativism. In line with this, many nonfiction postmodern writers reject traditional, straightforward expositional writing and adopt a literary voice that is provocative, playful, ambiguous, rich in metaphor and connotation, highly self-aware, self-doubting, and at times deliberately difficult to understand in a traditional, "modern" way. Because of its drama and its "in your face" style, it is not surprising that this writing has gained great visibility and prominence in intellectual circles in recent years. (For a representative example, see Gergen 1991.)

While in this book I champion certain aspects of postmodernism, I do not adopt the literary voice of the skeptical postmodernists. Rather, I select certain lessons from "affirmative" postmodernism in support of a very serious endeavor: to help address the major social crises that most agree challenge us in the United States today. I employ those postmodern ideas that attack the sterility of mainstream psychology and which support a substantive, alternative, case-based pragmatic paradigm. In contrast to skeptical postmodernism, the background of this paradigm is quite "serious" and affirmatively substantive. This will become clear in my review of the ideas of pragmatic philosophers like Cornel West, Richard Bernstein, Richard Rorty, and Stephen Toulmin. The writings of these thinkers reveal their passionate moral commitment to humanistic values such as human solidarity, social justice, respect for diversity, the development of cooperative relationships through respectful and engaged dialogue, and political structures built upon truly participatory democracy.

While it lacks the provocative, playful, and iconoclastic style distinctive of writers of skeptical postmodernism, I view this book as very postmodern in one of its major themes: the strong interrelationships and less than clear-cut boundaries among such different disciplinary approaches as psychology, education, history, epistemological philosophy, moral philosophy, political science, and journalism. In contrast to modernism, which privileges knowledge based on the natural science model and intellectually divides the world into objectively distinctive "disciplines," postmodernism emphasizes that all knowledge is perspectival, and that any particular perspective is ultimately arbitrary and limited. Pragmatism adds to this that therefore the value of any particular disciplinary perspective is to be judged not upon its objective truth in reflecting the "real" world, but rather in its usefulness in accomplishing particular human purposes at particular points in time and in particular geographic and cultural places. Thus, what might be pragmatically most persuasive in one context might not be so in another.

69. For example, Roth's (1987) *Meaning and Method in the Social Sciences: A Case for Methodological Pluralism* presents detailed philosophical arguments supporting my position of a move toward more epistemological and methodological diversity in psychological research.

70. Some examples of these books, which will be included in my discussion, are Bernstein's (1976) *The Restructuring of Social and Political Theory*, which focuses on political science and sociology; Denzin and Lincoln's (1994) *Handbook of Qualitative Research*, which focuses on sociology and anthropology; Fiske and Shweder's (1986) *Metatheory in Social Science: Pluralism and Subjectivities*, which covers the whole span of the social sciences; Rosenau's (1992) *Post-Modernism and the Social Sciences*, which emphasizes political science; Ross's (1991) *The Origins of American Social Science*, which emphasizes sociology, economics, and political science; Seidman and Wagner's (1992) *Postmodernism and Social Theory*, which focuses on sociology; Shweder's (1991) *Thinking through Cultures: Expeditions in Cultural Psychology*, which emphasizes anthropology; and Winch's (1958) *The Idea of a Social Science and Its Relation to Philosophy*, which focuses on sociology and political science.

71. Psychology is frequently viewed in the layperson's mind as focusing on the behavior and experiences of individuals alone and in small groups, while the other social sciences focus on larger systems, such as social institutions (sociology), political institutions (political science), economic structures (economics), and culture (anthropology). However, among professional social scientists these lines of demarcation are not at all so clear. For example, in psychology, formal specialties have developed across the systems spectrum, from the biological (e.g. behavioral neuroscience), to the individual (e.g., clinical and personality psychology), to small groups (social psychology), to organizations (e.g., school, military, and industrial-organizational psychology), to communities (community psychology), and to nations (e.g., peace psychology). (These specialties are represented by Divisions 6, 12, 8, 16, 19, 14, 27, and 48, respectively, of the American Psychological Association.)

In a related vein, Donald Peterson, a major conceptualizer of professional psychology, describes the field as follows:

In aggregate, professional psychology is envisioned as the development and application of knowledge in the assessment and improvement of human function at the psychobiological, individual, group, organizational, and community levels; through direct service . . . , consultation . . . , and public education; and in all settings (mental health, medical and health maintenance, educational, corporate, military, and governmental) in which human conditions might be improved through application of psychological principles and procedures. (1987, p. 21)

Taking the idea of unclear lines of demarcation among the social sciences one step further, James G. Miller, in his book *Living Systems* (1978) proposes a totally unified view of the various social and biological sciences. As described in chapter 2, Miller's work arises out of the "general systems" movement. Miller has proposed a single discipline of "behavioral science" that studies living organisms at seven levels of complexity: the cell, the organ, the individual, the group, the organization, the society, and the supranational system. Each type of system can be described in terms of the same structures, relationships, functions, and terms.

From the modernist point of view, the world consists of various "natural kinds," each deserving its own form of study; and this perspective justifies the existence of discrete academic disciplines, such as psychology versus sociology versus economics. However, the postmodern mindset rejects such "natural kinds" and views all disciplinary distinctions as ultimately arbitrary and only one of multiple possible and reasonable ways to segment our experience. Thus, a postmodern perspective encourages the multidisciplinary extension of the types of issues I raise in this book about psychology to all the social sciences. For example, in a recent handbook documenting various qualitative, postmodern approaches to social science research, the editors emphasize the boundary-crossing nature of such research, which they describe as

interdisciplinary, trans disciplinary, and sometimes counterdisciplinary. . . . It crosscuts the humanities and the social and physical sciences. . . . [Postmodern research is simultaneously drawn to] a broad, interpretive, . . . feminist, and critical sensibility. . . . [and to] more narrowly defined positivist, postpositivist, humanistic, and naturalistic conceptions of human experience and its analysis. (Denzin and Lincoln 1994, pp. 3–4)

Moreover, the multidisciplinary, social science perspective is particularly relevant to two of the areas highlighted in this book. First is the field of educational research, which is inherently interdisciplinary because it is not categorized as one of the "basic" academic disciplines and because it is the object of study of all the different social sciences. Second is the field of program evaluation, which, while sometimes viewed as primarily "owned" by psychology and sociology, ranges across all the social sciences.

It seems clear, then, that from a logical point of view and also from a post-modern perspective, psychology can be viewed as spanning across the major "systems" levels, from the individual to the society, and is thus highly overlapping at times with the other social sciences. Of course it is important not to oversimplify the differences among the various social science disciplines; for from a sociopolitical point of view, each consists of a discrete social group, with its own distinctive training, credentialing, subculture, and history. Yet psychology's wide span of content should certainly make it a major resource in addressing such social problems as education, crime, health, mental health, violence, poverty, and homelessness; and it is to problems like these that this book's arguments are ultimately directed.

72. Lewin (1951).

73. Parloff (1980).

NOTES TO CHAPTER 1

1. In a related way, later chapters argue that the best data we can collect for creating effective human service programs are case histories of individual programs that have proven themselves to be successful.

2. Toulmin (1990).

3. Riger (1992).

4. Garraty and Gay (1972).

5. Hazen and Trefil (1991).

6. As quoted in W. T. Jones (1977).

7. Cited in Ross (1991), p. 6.

8. Ross (1991), p. 3. On the origin of the terms "social science" and "the social sciences," Ross writes that these terms

emerged in the late eighteenth century as one designation for the new political and moral sciences. At times during the nineteenth century, it was more closely associated with a specific kind of social science—the theory of Charles Fournier or Comte, the remedial work of the British and American social science associations—than with the disciplinary traditions established in the universities. . . . The collective designation, the terms "social science" or "the social sciences," did not come into common use until the early 20th century. (1991, p. xx)

9. Flew (1984), p. 150.

10. Flew (1984), pp. 29, 54.

11. Sabine (1950), p. 568.

12. Sabine (1950), p. 686.

13. Cahan and White (1992).

14. Thompson (1975).

15. Koch and Leary (1985), p. 1.

16. Sass (1992).

17. R. Miller (1992), p. 14.

18. For example, see Darwin's two great books, *On the Origin of Species by Means of Natural Selection, or the Preservation of the Favoured Races in the Struggle for Life* (1859), and *The Expression of the Emotions in Man and Animals* (1872).

19. Harre and Lamb (1983), pp. 598–600; Wright (1994); E. O. Wilson (1978, 1998).

20. For example, see Freud's two classics, *The Interpretation of Dreams* (1900), and *Civilization and Its Discontents* (1930).

21. Riger (1992, p. 734) notes that Marxism, psychoanalysis, and postmodernism all challenge "the primacy of reason and the autonomy of the individual." See also Gergen (1982), p. vii.

22. Altman (1987). While Altman uses the terms "centripetal" versus "centrifugal" to describe these contrasting forces, I find it clearer to use the synonymous terms "unifying" versus "diversifying" forces, respectively.

23. Toulmin (1990).

24. Toulmin also makes a strong case for striking parallels between these Renaissance values and those of our present, postmodern time.

25. Altman (1987), p. 1059.

26. Heidbreder (1933).

27. Altman (1987), p. 1059.

28. For a detailed historical documentation of this trend, see Danziger (1990).

29. Danziger (1990).

30. Ronald Miller does a nice job in summarizing the position of the logical positivists:

> Only statements that met . . . [the logical positivists'] verification principle criterion of meaning could qualify as true knowledge claims. This principle claimed that all terms in a proposition had to be open to verification by the senses in order to be meaningful. The only exception to this rule was the logical operators from mathematical logic (e.g., all, a, and, or, not, if-then); thus, the phrase "logical positivism" came into being. No terms or concepts could be introduced into the principles of a discipline unless they were either empirical claims amenable to verification or logical operators. (1992, p. 17)

31. Ayer (1936/1946), p. 31.

32. Ayer (1936/1946), p. 108. It should be noted that postmodernists, who see "value-free" inquiry as impossible, argue that modernist logical positivism has historically been used to support conservative, capitalist politics in the Western countries in which it was developed by rationalizing "free enterprise" science

(as sponsored by those presently in power) as the road to progress. In contrast, postmodernism has been associated with liberal, leftist, and socialist politics, which oppose the status quo and champion the disempowered—women, blacks, other minorities, gays and lesbians, the poor, and so forth. For more discussion of this, see Denzin and Lincoln (1994).

33. Ross (1991)."Scientism" is the position that the natural scientific method used in physics, chemistry, and biology—including components such as the experimental method, the search for general laws, quantified variables, and the use of statistics—must be the defining characteristics of how social science is conducted. For a brief discussion of the resurgence of scientism in the writings of E. O. Wilson (1998), see note 47 in chapter 3.

34. Altman (1987).

35. In the latest manifestation of this process, in August of 1988 the American Psychological Society (APS) was formed by psychologist academics and researchers, after the American Psychological Association turned down a plan to restructure their organization to give more clout to academics, who viewed a domination of the Association by psychologists in private practice (Mangan 1988). In the diversifying, pluralistic era of the 1980s and 1990s, the American Psychological Society has continued to flourish. As of January 1998, the Society had grown to more than 15,000 members (information from the APS Central office, January 1998).

36. Raimy (1950).

37. Ross (1991), p. 429.

38. See Seidman and Wagner (1992, p. 4):

In the twentieth century, social science underwent a process of institutionalization and cultural legitimation. This has shaped social science in distinctive ways. The academicization of social science has meant the heightening of its scientistic claims. In their effort to achieve institutional legitimacy and material resources, contemporary social scientists have often felt compelled to suppress the practice-moral or political role of science.

39. Altman (1987), p. 1061.

40. Riesman (1955).

41. Whyte (1956).

42. Mills (1951).

NOTES TO CHAPTER 2

1. Of course, characterizing the period since 1960 as diversifying does not suggest total breakdown of American society. It only emphasizes that the diversifying trends have been more powerful than the unifying forces. Altman has noted some of these unifying trends:

The continuing identity with American values and norms [such as] egali-
tarianism, independence, patriotism, and pride in our history; . . . the pervasive political and social conservatism of the 1980s; the rise of religious
fundamentalism; . . . [and] Ronald Reagan's political success . . . [which]
exemplifies many Americans' hopes for a simpler life and for the return to
tried and true conservative values. (1987, p. 1062)

On the other hand, it should be noted that while as of this writing in 1998
there are certain large segments of our population who have continued to become
more and more culturally and politically conservative (witness the Republican
takeover of Congress in 1994), these segments appear to be moving into more
and more ideological polarization with other large groups who are outspokenly
liberal advocates for social, political, artistic, and cultural diversity and innovation.

2. Altman (1987), p. 1063.

3. Hogan (1979), p. 4.

4. Fishman and Neigher (1982), p. 539.

5. Gergen (1985a), p. 185.

6. The APA membership figures are available from the American Psychological Association in Washington, D.C.

7. American Psychological Association (1985a), pp. xlii–xlvi.

8. Reich (1971).

9. Reich (1971), pp. 4–8.

10. While there is a side of psychoanalysis that is closely aligned with literature and the humanities, the humanistic psychologists were reacting to the scientistic side of psychoanalysis, involving such elements as its identification with
medical science; its focus on animal instincts and their vicissitudes rather than on
uniquely human, self-actualizing activities; and on its mechanistic models, such
as its notion of a fluidlike libido that hydraulically applies pressure to various impulses to cause particular behavioral tendencies.

11. Urban (1983), pp. 158–159.

12. Maslow (1950).

13. Urban (1983), p. 161.

14. Urban (1983), p. 161.

15. M. Smith (1987). An important offshoot of the "alliance" between humanistic psychology and the counterculture was the "encounter group" movement. The movement flowered in the 1960s and 1970s with leadership by Fritz
Perls at the Esalen Institute in California. Perls's "gestalt" approach featured a
very active group leader using a variety of techniques, including intensive,
weekend "marathon" experiences and psychodrama-like role playing to focus
participants on holistic emotional experience, the here and now, and self-in-
sight.

16. Hull's formula was "sEr = sHr x D x V x K." Baars explains the formula in commonsense terms:

> The expression states that the likelihood of an animal doing something ["sEr"] depends on ["="] how habitual the act is ["sHr"]; how hungry or thirsty [or otherwise motivated] the animal is ["D"]; how intense the stimulus signalling the reward [such as food or water] is ["V"]; and how much reward may come as a consequence of the response ["K"]. Hull maintains that if the product sEr is larger than some reaction threshold "sLr", then the response will be made. (1986, p. 60)

17. Baars (1986), p. 60.
18. Koch (1959), p. 731.
19. G. Miller (1956), p. 90.
20. G. Miller (1956), p. 90.
21. Gardner (1987).
22. Gardner (1987), p. 20.
23. Bruner, Goodnow, and Austin (1956).
24. Gardner (1987), p. 94.
25. Bruner (1990), pp. 4–5.
26. Gardner (1987), p. 37; Bruner (1990), p. 3.
27. Pepper (1942).
28. Altman and Rogoff (1987).
29. Lilienfeld (1978), p. 9.
30. James (1955), p. 58.
31. Dewey and Bentley (1949).
32. Altman and Rogoff (1987).
33. Henderson (1917); Whitehead (1925).
34. J. G. Miller (1978), p. xvii.
35. J. G. Miller (1978), p. xvii.
36. J. G. Miller (1978).
37. For example, the "system boundary" ranges across the seven systems—from the cell membrane, to the outer tissues of the liver, to the individual's skin, to the radio crew of an ocean liner, to the hull of an ocean liner, to the borders of the Common Market, respectively.
38. Gurman and Kniskern (1981).
39. According to Dilthey's conceptualization, there exist two "standpoints," that is, two ways of experiencing the world: (a) standing back separately and observing a world conceived of as composed of natural objects, and (b) living in the world, which means in part that we are intricably bound to the people and things with whom and with which we interact.

To these "standpoints," there correspond two ways of being aware of experience, which Dilthey called (a) *Erklaren*, knowledge of the laws of the causal order of natural phenomena, rigorous scientific knowledge; and (b) *Verstehen*, knowledge of the inner mental life of humans, a function of our "worldview," or system of value-laden and meaningful experience, and a consequence of our being-in-the-world (Chessick 1990, pp. 256–257).

40. Gergen (1982), pp. 86–87.

41. Messer and Winokur (1984).

42. Winch (1958).

43. Winch (1958), p. 122.

44. Gergen (1973).

45. Crider et al. (1989).

46. Gergen (1973), pp. 309–310.

47. Packer (1985).

48. Palmer (1969).

49. Packer (1985), p. 1081.

50. Messer, Sass, and Woolfolk (1988).

51. Messer, Sass, and Woolfolk (1988), pp. xiii–xiv.

52. R. Miller (1992), p. 22.

53. Palmer (1969).

54. Messer, Sass, and Woolfolk (1988), p. 7; and Rorty (1979), p. 319. It is interesting to note the similarity between the hermeneutic circle concept, with its emphasis on the impossibility of simultaneously explaining all assumptions underlying textual passages, and Gödel's First Incompleteness Theorem in mathematics. Published in 1931, the theorem proves that there exist formally undecidable propositions in any formal system of arithmetic (see Gregory 1987, pp. 294–295).

55. Messer, Sass, and Woolfolk (1988), pp. 14–15.

56. Gergen (1985b).

57. Krasner and Houts (1984), pp. 840–841.

58. Gergen (1985b), p. 267.

59. Scarr (1985), p. 499.

60. Gergen (1985b).

61. Gergen (1985b).

62. Roiphe (1993a). See also the book upon which this article is based, Roiphe (1993b).

63. Roiphe (1993a), p. 28.

64. Roiphe (1993a), p. 30.

65. Denzin (1989), p. 7.

66. Miles and Huberman (1984), p. 15.

67. Glaser and Strauss (1967).

68. This is sometimes termed the "hypothetico-deductive method."

69. Strauss and Corbin (1990).

70. See the section in the Introduction headed "Two Faces of Psychology: 'Nature' versus 'Culture.'"

71. Denzin (1989), p. 144.

72. Geertz (1973), pp. 6–7. The example is based on one initially developed by the philosopher Gilbert Ryle, who was the originator of the concept of "thick" versus "thin" description.

73. Bruner (1986).

74. Denzin (1989). Note that some logical positivists, such as the philosopher Carl Hempel (1942) and the psychologist Dean Simonton (1990), contend that historical events can be studied from a natural science perspective, what Simonton calls "historiometry." In counterargument, Bruner (1990) contends: "Trying to 'dechronologize' diachronic historical accounts into synchronic 'social science' propositions . . . succeeds only in losing particularity, in confusing interpretation and explanation, and in falsely relegating the narrator's rhetorical voice to the domain of 'objectivity' (p. 44). For additional counterarguments, see Ricoeur (1981).

75. Burke (1945).

76. White and Epston (1990).

77. Vitz (1990).

78. Bruner (1986).

79. Keller and Flax (1988).

80. Belenky, Clinchy, and Goldberger (1986); Gilligan (1982).

81. Gilligan (1982).

82. Harre and Lamb (1983), pp. 234–235; and Tannen (1990).

83. Denzin (1989); Riger (1992).

84. E.g., Hare-Mustin and Marecek (1992); Roiphe (1993b).

85. E.g., Denzin (1989); Guba and Lincoln (1989); Nyden and Wiewel (1992); Reason (1994); Stringer (1996).

86. Rosenau (1992).

87. P. Berman (1992); Moore (1963); Rosenau (1992); Sass (1992).

88. In breaking away from the medieval authority of the Church, the Enlightenment raised the importance of the independent, free-thinking individual. The modernist idea is that the scientific method allows us to study natural phenomena objectively, without personal and ideological bias; and that by applying this method to human affairs, we will more and more clearly discover the laws of psychological and social behavior. The discovery of these laws will in turn allow us to better and better master our human problems, leading to the cumulative development of progress in our social, political, and cultural life. Many, such as Gergen (1991), have termed this the "grand narrative of modernism," which is one of continuous upward movement—"improvement, conquest, achievement"—toward some utopian social state (Gergen 1991, p. 30).

89. This discussion of characteristics of modernism is taken from Woolfolk and Richardson (1984), pp. 779–782.

90. Nisbet (1976), p. 111.

91. Woolfolk and Richardson (1984), p. 774.

92. Woolfolk and Richardson (1984), p. 780.

93. Brinton (1963).

94. P. Berman (1992); Rosenau (1992).

95. P. Berman (1992); Seidman and Wagner (1992).

96. E.g., Gergen (1991). See also note 6 in the Preface.

97. See Reich's (1971) *Greening of America*, discussed above.

98. P. Berman (1992); Rosenau (1992).

99. A variety of permeating structures were identified. Followers of the philosopher Heidegger, such as Jacques Derrida, focused on the entire problematic tradition of Western thought. Followers of the philosopher Nietzche, such as Michel Foucault, focused on the will to power. Followers of Freud, such as Jacques Lacan, focused on the structures of the unconscious. Followers of Marx, such as Pierre Bourdieu, focused on economic structures. And followers of the anthropologist Claude Lévi-Strauss focused on unchanging cultural structures. Underlying these various structures and providing a unifying theme in the writings of these diverse postmodernist thinkers was the all-pervasive force of language as a metastructure which, more than government or economics or politics, determines the nature of society (P. Berman 1992).

100. Rosenau (1992), p. 6.

101. R. Bernstein (1990).

102. Kimball (1990).

103. Two of the first widely read conservative attacks on the "tenured radicals" were Allan Bloom's (1987) *The Closing of the American Mind* and Charles Sykes's (1988) *Profscam: Professors and the Demise of Higher Education*. Three more books with similar attacking themes and titles have since appeared, including Roger Kimball's (1990) *Tenured Radicals: How Politics Has Corrupted Our Higher Education;* Dinesh D'Souza's (1991) *Illiberal Education: The Politics of Race and Sex on Campus;* and Martin Anderson's (1992) *Impostors in the Temple.*

104. P. Berman (1992).

105. Gergen (1991).

106. As described in note 3 in the Preface, Sass discusses how the term "modernism" has two very different uses in describing Western culture. On one hand, it refers to rational-scientific thought since the Enlightenment, and on the other, to the artistic and literary movement that began around 1900 in the work of such individuals as Eliot, Pound, Kafka, Picasso, and Matisse, and which includes characteristics such as profound relativism and uncertainty. My use of the term throughout the book and Gergen's use of the term in this context obviously follow Sass's first meaning.

Gergen (1991, pp. 30–36) describes the modernist search for objective "essence" in the humanities. Rejecting a concern with an author's heart or mind, literary theory focused on systematic, empirical analysis of a novel or poem's language, viewing a literary work as a thing-in-itself, searching for "some quality common and peculiar to all objects that provoke the esthetic emotion" (quoted from Clive Bell, *The Esthetic Hypothesis*). The Bauhaus school of arts and crafts in the 1920s worked to create an environment in which all the arts could investigate "the fundamentals of design," leading to "a general solution," which became the International Style. Architecture abandoned decorative styling, like Victorian gingerbread, seeking the essence of architectural esthetics in a building's reflection of the function it serves. Modern dance abandoned the stylized and decorative vocabulary of the ballet, and sought "the essentials of movement." Modern music turned away the romantic composer's attempt to express emotion to look at the inner structure of the music itself, as illustrated in the development of 12-tone technique. The turn from personal expression to the art form itself also occurred in painting, with an interest in pure color, pure form, and "object-free art." Thus, each art is to be "rendered 'pure', and in its 'purity' find the guarantee of its standards of quality as well as its independence" (quoted from the art critic Clement Greenberg).

NOTES TO CHAPTER 3

1. Fiske and Shweder (1986).
2. Popper (1959).
3. Flew (1984), p. 281.
4. Kuhn (1962).
5. Kuhn (1970), p. 93. Note here the parallel between Kuhn's description of scientific paradigms and the concept of the hermeneutic circle, discussed in chapter 2.
6. Gleick (1987), p. 7; Hawking (1988).
7. Gleick (1987), p. 8.
8. Gleick (1987).
9. Gleick (1987), p. 27. A second example of sensitive dependence on initial conditions given by Gleick is the development of a snowflake:

> As a growing snowflake falls to earth, typically floating in the wind for an hour or more, the choices made by the branching tips at any instant depend sensitively on such things as the temperature, the humidity, and the presence of impurities in the atmosphere. The six tips of a single snowflake, spreading within a millimeter space, feel the same temperatures, and because the laws of growth are purely deterministic, they maintain a near-perfect symmetry. But the nature of turbulent air is such that any pair of snowflakes will experience very different paths. The final flake records the history of all the changing weather conditions it has experienced, and the combinations may as well be infinite. (1987, p. 311)

10. Gleick (1987), pp. 37–39. As chaos theory has developed, in the 1980s it has expanded into what is termed "complexity theory" (e.g., Lewin 1992). This model extends chaos theory into the realm of biological, sociological, and cultural "self-organizing systems," which evolve over time. In terms of Pepper's "worldviews," described in chapter 2, complexity theory embraces organicism, which puts it in direct paradigm clash with the Darwinian concept of natural selection by adaptation, which is grounded in mechanism.

11. Gleick (1987), p. 36. For an example of the dynamics of paradigms in psychology, see Fishman, Rotgers, and Franks (1988).

12. Quine (1951); Quine (1960).

13. In Quine's (1953) words, "Any statement can be held true come what may, if we make enough drastic changes elsewhere. . . . [We can even retain a belief that runs counter to our surroundings] by pleading hallucination or by amending certain statements of the kind called logical laws" (p. 43).

14. Quine (1960).

15. Quine (1975), p. 81.

16. Quine (1981), p. 22.

17. Quine (1975), p. 68.

18. Feyerabend (1975), p. 52.

19. Feyerabend (1975), p. 52.

20. Feyerabend (1975), p. 27.

21. Feyerabend (1975), p. 19.

22. For an excellent, detailed discussion of Quine's and Feyerabend's ideas and their use in a larger argument for methodological pluralism in the social sciences, see Roth (1987).

23. Wittgenstein (1995; originally published in 1921).

24. Wittgenstein (1953).

25. Wittgenstein's point here is illustrated by Geertz's contextual analysis of the meaning of a wink, discussed in "Qualitative Research," of chapter 2.

26. Wittgenstein (1953), remark 11.

27. Wittgenstein (1953), remark 66.

28. Wittgenstein (1953), remark 43.

29. Wittgenstein (1953), remark 246. See also Magill (1990), p. 656.

30. Wittgenstein (1953), remark 693.

31. At one point, Wittgenstein defines a "form of life" as a collection of "language games" bound together by a "family resemblance" (Mehon and Wood 1994, p. 328).

32. Skinner (1957).

33. In the words of Van Fraassen (1980), scientific realism commits us to the view that "science aims to give us, in its theories, a literally true story of what the world is like; and acceptance of a scientific theory involves the belief that it is true" (p. 8).

34. Regarding modernism's support of scientific realism, Gergen frames it this way:

> [In modernism], the search for knowledge proceeds towards an essence—a fundamental *thing-in-itself*. That twentieth-century physics should rediscover the idea of the atom, the irreducible particle, is hardly surprising. However, the promise that reasoned observation will lead to the truth is intoxicating. Any discipline laying claim to scientific methods could also claim to search for its essence: the essence of the political process, the economy, mental illness, social institutions, foreign cultures, education, communication, and so on. (1991, pp. 32–33)

35. Sometimes electromagnetic radiation acts as a wave, and sometimes it acts as a particle.

36. Hazen and Trefil (1991), pp. 124–127.

37. Hazen and Trefil (1991).

38. Flew (1984), pp. 320–321.

39. MacCorquodale and Meehl (1948). Also see Marx and Cronan-Hillix (1987), pp. 309–310.

40. Fine (1986).

41. Horgan (1996).

42. H. Bloom (1973).

43. H. Bloom (1973), p. 21.

44. Horgan (1996), pp. 1–8.

45. Penrose (1989).

46. Horgan (1996), pp. 1–2.

47. For a recent attempt to reassert the privileged truth status of the hard sciences, see E. O. Wilson's (1998) *Consilience: The Unity of Knowledge*. In line with his advocacy of evolutionary psychology (E. O. Wilson 1978), Wilson, a prominent biologist, argues that the "real" world is the physical one of nature, and that culture is a type of epiphenomenon of that physical world. "Nature is organized by simple universal laws of physics to which all other laws and principles can eventually be reduced," including any principles of human behavior. Thus, "all the meaning [the brain] can master, and all the emotions it can bear, and all the shared adventure we might wish to enjoy, can be found by deciphering the hereditary orderliness that has borne our species through geological time." In short, "all tangible phenomena, from the birth of stars to the workings of social institutions, are based on material processes that are ultimately reducible, however long and tortuous the sequences, to the laws of physics." For a very cogent critique of Wilson's thesis, following from many of the arguments in this chapter against the privileged truth status of scientific materialism, see Todorov (1998).

NOTES TO CHAPTER 4

1. Redhead (1997).
2. Manning and Cullum-Swan (1994).
3. Table 4. 1 is taken from Fishman (1988). For related analyses and tables, see Guba and Lincoln (1994) and Greene (1994).
4. Kimble (1984).

NOTES TO CHAPTER 5

1. The interaction of postpositivism and Continental philosophy can be viewed in terms of the three paradigms outlined in table 4.1. Specifically, the "conservative" wing of postpositivism has refined the traditional positivism of A. J. Ayer and the Vienna Circle, and this refined version provides the philosophical rationale for the *positivist paradigm*. The "liberal" wing of postpositivism joined forces with Continental philosophy to create the philosophical rationale for the *hermeneutic paradigm*. Between these conservative and liberal poles, the *pragmatic paradigm* has emerged.

2. See the chapter 2 sections on "Humanistic Psychology" and "Hermeneutics." Also, methodological, ontological, and critical hermeneutics generally correspond, respectively, to skeptical, ontological, and critical postmodernism, described in the Introduction.

3. For a recent example of these critiques, see Gottlieb (1991).

4. See chapter 3.

5. Mary Hesse makes this point in the following manner:

[In the logical positivist view,] natural science [involves] a *one-way* logic and method of interpretation, . . . since theory is dependent on self-subsistent facts, and testable by them. In human science, on the other hand, the "logic" of interpretation is irreducibly *circular*: part cannot be understood without whole, which itself depends on the relation of its parts; data and concepts cannot be understood without theory and context, which themselves depend on relations of data and concepts. (1980, p. 171, italics added)

6. R. J. Bernstein discusses this point:

It would be a mistake to think that postempirical [postpositivist] philosophers of science have been directly influenced by hermeneutics [and its related strands in Continental philosophy]. In the main, . . . they have been virtually ignorant of the hermeneutical tradition. It is primarily because of the internal dialectic of contemporary philosophy of science [postpositivism], by reflection on and argumentation about a correct understanding

of scientific inquiry, that they have stressed those features of science . . .
that are hermeneutical. (1983, p. 33)

7. R. Miller (1992), p. 23.

8. West (1989).

9. West (1989), p. 4.

10. "Contextualism" is one of Stephen Pepper's "worldviews," as described
in the section on "General Systems Theory" in chapter 2.

11. Lilienfeld (1978), p. 9.

12. Lilienfeld (1978).

13. As cited in Thilly and Wood (1957), p. 635.

14. Hartshorne, Weiss, and Burks (1958), p. 400.

15. James (1955), p. 58.

16. Hollinger (1985), p. 30.

17. Dewey (1910).

18. Hollinger (1985), p. 31.

19. E.g., R. J. Bernstein (1983); Rorty (1982); Rorty (1991); and Toulmin
(1990), respectively. Note that while Toulmin was educated in England, I consider him an American philosopher since he has written much of his work in
America. See also the work of Joseph Margolis (e.g., 1986), another important
American pragmatist.

20. R. J. Bernstein (1983), p. 8.

21. R. J. Bernstein (1983), p. 9.

22. Woolfolk (1992, p. 221) summarizes this idea in the tautology: "If there
is no truth without objectivism, then without objectivism there is no truth."

23. Geertz (1989), p. 15.

24. Geertz (1989).

25. Kernan (1992), p. 11.

26. Spiro (1978).

27. R. J. Bernstein (1983), pp. 16–17. In Descartes' own words:

It is now some years that I detected how many were the false beliefs that I
had from my earliest youth admitted as true. . . . [I became convinced that]
I must once for all seriously undertake to rid myself of all the opinions
which I had formally accepted, and commence to build anew from the
foundation, if I wanted to establish any firm and permanent structure in
the sciences. . . . [Like Archimedes] I shall have the right to conceive high
hopes if I am happy enough to discover one thing only which is certain and
indubitable. (From Descartes' *Meditations,* as quoted in R. J. Bernstein
1983, 16)

28. From Descartes' *Meditations,* as quoted in R. J. Bernstein (1983), p. 17.

29. R. J. Bernstein (1983), p. 17–18.

30. R. J. Bernstein (1983), p. 19.

31. Geertz (1989).

32. Geertz (1989), p. 15.

33. Hughes (1992), p. 46. Another assault on relativism has been made by the conservative historian Paul Johnson (1991), who views the relativism of the early twentieth century, as evidenced by the ideas and artistic works of Einstein, Freud, Dada, Stravinsky, and Proust, as undermining "a settled and objectively true moral code, which was at the centre of nineteenth-century European civilization." Jacoby (1994) presents a cogent rebuttal, pointing out, in part, that "if several categories must be selected to capture a twentieth-century experience, racism, nationalism, militarism, absolutism, or intolerance would be more appropriate than relativism" (pp. 124–125).

34. R. J. Bernstein (1983), p. 24.

35. R. J. Bernstein (1983), p. 223.

36. Pitkin and Shumer (1982), pp. 47–48.

37. R. J. Bernstein (1983), p. 226.

38. R. J. Bernstein (1983), p. 230.

39. R. J. Bernstein (1983), p. 231.

40. R. J. Bernstein (1983), p. xv.

41. Rorty as quoted in R. J. Bernstein (1983), p. 203.

42. Rorty (1979).

43. Rorty (1991), p. 89. The hermeneutic slogan, "interpretation all the way down" (Geertz 1973, pp. 28–29), is a cogent way of summarizing Rorty's position here. Sass also is very articulate in elaborating a position very much like Rorty's:

> The domain of human practices is highly articulated and differentiated, of course; it contains inertias and constancies of all kinds; but it is a mistake to view these enduring patterns as but the reflections or instantiations of some purer world of Platonic essences. . . . They are just the practices themselves, being constituted ever anew by the interpretive habits of the beings who live them. (In press, p. 13)

44. Rorty (1982).

45. Rorty (1982), p. 191.

46. See the Introduction and chapter 4.

47. Rorty (1982), p. 198.

48. Rorty (1982), p. 197.

49. Rorty (1982), p. 205.

50. Rorty (1982), pp. 204, 208.

51. See chapter 3.

52. Fishman (1992).

53. Rorty (1979).

54. Rorty (1989a), pp. 37–38.
55. Rorty (1989a), p. 37.
56. Rorty (1989a), p. 37.
57. Rorty (1989a), p. 38.
58. Rorty (1989b).
59. Rorty (1989b), p. xiii.
60. Rorty (1989b), p. xiii.
61. Toulmin (1990).
62. See chapter 1.
63. Toulmin (1990), pp. 169–170.
64. Toulmin (1990), p. 170.
65. Toulmin (1990), p. 170.
66. Toulmin (1990), p. 157.
67. See chapter 1.
68. Toulmin (1990), p. 154.
69. Toulmin (1990), p. 31.
70. Toulmin (1990), p. 32.
71. Toulmin (1990), p. 33.
72. Toulmin (1990), p. 34.
73. Geertz (1973).
74. Geertz (1973), p. 422.
75. Geertz (1973), p. 417.
76. Geertz (1973), p. 420.
77. Geertz (1973), pp. 443–444.
78. Sass (1992).
79. See Preface, note 3.
80. Gergen (1991).
81. Cushman (1990), p. 599. See earlier quote, Introduction.
82. Anthony (1990); Lieberman (1992).

NOTES TO CHAPTER 6

1. Yin (1993), p. 66.
2. Kanfer and Schefft (1988); Bromley (1986).
3. Wholey et al. (1970), Horst et al. (1974), and Shadish, Cook, and Leviton (1991) distinguish between human service "programs" and the "projects" of which they are comprised. A program involves the allocation of funds to accomplish a prescribed set of objectives through the conduct of specified activities, such as the federal funding of the Title 1 program of compensatory education in the public schools. A project is the implementation level of a program, such as a particular Title 1 program in a particular school. Wholey and his colleagues emphasize the extensive heterogeneity that is frequently found at the project level:

"An examination of 20 case settings in the same program will often reveal 20 very different program intervention designs, different in activity and purpose" (Horst et al. 1974, p. 303).

To aid the flow of the text, in the discussion to follow I frequently use the term "program" to refer to the broader sense of the word and/or to a particular project. In these instances, the context indicates which meaning is intended. In instances where the context is not clear, I employ the distinction between "programs" and "projects" outlined above.

4. See the Introduction.

5. See the Introduction and chapter 7 for an elaboration of the logic compared in figures I.1 and I.2.

6. The focus on specific, concrete persons in a social science case is reflected in illustrative quotes from well-known case study theorists:

> Custom has it that not everything is a case. A child may be a case. A doctor may be a case—but *his doctoring* lacks the specificity, boundedness, to be called a case. An agency may be a case. The reasons for child neglect or the policies of dealing with neglectful parents would seldom be considered a case. Those topics are generalities rather than specificities. The case is specific. Even more, the case is a functioning specific, . . . a bounded system. In the social sciences and human services, it [the case] has working parts, it probably is purposive, even having a self. It is an integrated system. The parts do not have to be working well, the purposes may be irrational, but it is a system. (Stake 1994, p. 236)

> In the classic case study, a "case" may be an individual. Thus you can imagine case studies of clinical patients, of exemplary students, or of certain types of leaders. In each situation, an individual person is the case being studied, and the individual is the primary unit of analysis. . . . Of course, the "case" also can be some event or entity that is less well defined than a single individual. Case studies have been done about decisions, about programs, about implementation process, and about organizational change. Beware of these types of topics—none is easily defined in terms of the beginning or end points of the "case." (Yin 1989, p. 31)

> "Case-study" [is] a general term widely used in the social and behavioral sciences, to refer to the description and analysis of a particular entity (object, person, group, event, state, condition, process, or whatever). Such entities are usually natural occurrences with definable boundaries, although they exist and function within a context of surrounding circumstances. (Bromley 1986, pp. 7–8)

7. Peterson (1991), pp. 426–427.

8. For an overview of this field as both a content area and profession, see

Rossi and Freeman (1993); Shadish, Cook, and Leviton (1991); and recent issues of the journal *Evaluation and Program Planning*.

9. See figure 1.2, components G and L, "Monitoring Evaluation" and "Concluding Evaluation."

10. Morell (1979); Rossi and Freeman (1985).

11. Shadish, Cook, and Leviton (1991), p. 27.

12. For example, Wholey and his associates (1970, p. 46) concluded that "the recent literature is unanimous in announcing the general failure of evaluation to affect decision-making in a significant way." Carol Weiss (1972, pp. 10–11) viewed underutilization as one of the foremost problems in evaluation research: "Evaluation research is meant for immediate and direct use in improving the quality of social programming. Yet a review of evaluation experience suggests that evaluation results have not exerted significant influence on program decisions." Cohen and Garet (1975, p. 19) found that "there is little evidence to indicate that government planning offices have succeeded in linking social research and decision-making." Finally, Deitchman (1976, p. 390) concluded that "the impact of the research on the most important affairs of state was, with few exceptions, nil."

13. Neigher and Fishman (1985).

14. Cronbach et al. (1980), p. 35.

15. Shadish, Cook, and Leviton (1991).

16. Examples of the results of this process are Scriven's (1967, 1972) "formative" versus "summative" evaluation; Patton's (1978, 1997) "utilization-focused" evaluation"; Gold's (1983) "stakeholder-based evaluation"; Stake's (1980) "responsive," "case-based," and "qualitative" evaluation; Wholey's (1983) "evaluability assessment"; and Guba and Lincoln's (1989) "responsive, constructivist evaluation."

17. Guba and Lincoln (1989); Lincoln and Guba (1985); Patton (1980).

18. Rossi and Freeman (1985), p. 19. Note that in ordinary language use, to conduct an "evaluation" of a human activity is to study it and come to a judgment about its value. And this is the meaning of the term as it is used in components G and L in figure 1.2. However, as seen in Rossi and Freeman's definition, in the contemporary field of "program evaluation," the term "evaluation" has a much broader meaning, referring not only to judging the results of an activity, but also to studying its conceptualization, plan, and process. To aid in keeping these two meanings separated, I will hereafter use the term "evaluation" to refer to the narrower meaning, and the term "program evaluation" to refer to the broader meaning.

19. Greene (1994).

20. Campbell (1969).

21. Chen and Rossi (1983).

22. Patton (1978, 1997).

23. Guba and Lincoln (1989).

24. Greene (1994), p. 533. Note that Greene's typology parallels my tripartite conception of three contrasting epistemological paradigms in psychology, shown in table 4.1. Greene's "postpositivist evaluation" corresponds to my "positivist paradigm"; her "pragmatic evaluation," to my "pragmatic paradigm"; and her "interpretivist evaluation" combined with her "critical science [critical theory] evaluation," to my "hermeneutic paradigm."

25. Note that the pros and cons of the inside evaluator are magnified in cases where the psychologist is not only an evaluator, but also a participant in service planning and delivery.

26. Scriven (1980, 1983).

27. For an excellent summary of Scriven's ideas, see Shadish, Cook, and Leviton (1991).

28. Patton (1997).

29. In the words of Shadish, Cook, and Leviton (1991, pp. 46–47):

Early evaluators mostly ignored the role of values in evaluation—whether in terms of justice, equality, liberty, human rights, or anything else. Scriven suggests that such evaluators believed their activities could and should be value-free. But it proved to be impossible in the political world of social programming to evaluate without values becoming salient. Social programs are themselves not value-free.

30. Elias (1991).

31. Peterson (1995); Pitkin and Shumer (1982).

32. R. J. Bernstein (1983), p. 226.

33. One theorist of pragmatically focused "action research" puts it this way:

Community-based action research is not just a tool for solving problems; it is a valuable resource for building a sense of community. . . . [Thus,] the heart of community-based action research is not the techniques and procedures that guide action, but the sense of unity that holds people to a collective vision of their world and inspires them to work together for the common good (Stringer 1996, pp. 96, 102).

The role of "community" in the pragmatic paradigm is explored in the next section on community psychology.

34. Windle and Neigher (1978).

35. Note that the differentiation between the accountability and amelioration models respectively parallels the contrast between "summative" and "formative" evaluation mentioned earlier.

36. In hermeneutic studies generally, the differentiation of researcher and subject is replaced by an egalitarian, collaborative relationship between program evaluator and program client. More specifically, in interpretivist evaluation, the focus is upon bestowing dignity and respect to beneficiaries through the use of

phenomenologically oriented assessment of their experiences in the program, and through an emphasis upon two-way dialogue between program evaluator and client. And in critical science evaluation, the focus is on politically empowering beneficiaries by paying special attention to how the program is serving to maintain power, resources, and inequities in society.

37. Shadish, Cook, and Leviton (1991), pp. 455–463.

38. Nyden and Wiewel (1992).

39. Schön (1983), p. 42.

40. Prilleltensky (1994).

41. Heller et al. (1984).

42. Price and Cherniss (1977).

43. Stringer (1996).

44. For further development of this theme, see Schorr (1997).

45. Nyden and Wiewel (1992).

46. Nyden and Wiewel (1992), pp. 43–44. See also Nyden et al. (1997). Schensul and Schensul use the same term, "collaborative research," to describe their approach. Their model, while overlapping with Nyden's, has a more explicit pragmatic focus:

> Collaborative research may be defined as building multisectoral networks that link researchers, program developers, [program funders], and members of the community or group under study [and/or receiving service] with the explicit purpose of utilizing research as a tool for joint problem-solving and positive social change. Collaborative research is based on expressed organizational and/or community needs and is conducted in partnership with those most invested in the problem and its solution. (1992, p. 162).

47. Reason (1994).

48. Schorr (1997), p. 3.

49. Schorr (1997), p. 4.

50. Schorr (1997), p. 8.

51. See the section on the "Postmodern, Pragmatic Model" in the Introduction.

52. Schön (1983), p. 68.

53. Schorr (1997), p. 10.

54. Schorr (1997), p. 10.

55. Schorr (1997), p. 9.

56. Schorr (1997) p. 141.

NOTES TO CHAPTER 7

1. See the section on "Narrative versus Propositional Modes of Thought" in chapter 2.

2. Yin (1989, 1993).

3. Lincoln and Guba (1985); Guba and Lincoln (1989). See also Stake (1994, 1995) and Eisner (1991).

4. Bromley (1986). See also Patton (1980, 1997).

5. Lincoln and Guba (1985); Guba and Lincoln (1989); Guba and Lincoln (1994).

6. While the group study is the basic unit of analysis in the positivist paradigm, Yin (1989, 1993) has shown how the case study can be adapted to the logic of positivist research—that is, to the testing of causal relationships predicted by theory.

7. In this regard, Yin's work is quite helpful since he adapts positivist logic to the contextually rich case study research design; and Lincoln and Guba make a most useful contribution by concretely laying out the purposes and methods of a hermeneutic case study.

8. In line with chapter 6, note 3, in tables 7.1 and 7.2, the term "program" refers to a specific intervention "project," as opposed to a funding vehicle for supporting a wide variety of individual projects. For example, in tables 7.1 and 7.2, a typical "program" could be a single, cognitive-behavioral therapy case or a single Head Start school, as opposed to the cognitive-therapy movement or all the federally funded Head Start projects as a whole.

9. Peterson (1987), p. 31.

10. Fishman and Peterson (1987).

11. See the Preface and chapter 2.

12. Living systems theory was originally proposed by James Miller as a vehicle for placing the results of positivist studies into an integrative, systems framework; and in 1978 his 1,102-page book carrying out this proposal was hailed as a major positivist, scientific contribution. However, Miller's systems concepts—with their multivariate, reciprocally interdependent character—clash with the need for limited, discrete, and causally linear variables in positivist thinking. It is thus no surprise that Miller's massive book has since disappeared from positivist discourse. On the other hand, practitioners have found Miller's system concepts particularly useful for the reasons given above. Thus Miller's systems concepts are very helpful when employed in the guiding conceptions of pragmatic, disciplined inquiry case projects, but not as the theories to be tested in positivist research studies.

For another example of positivist thinking strait-jacketing systems thinking, see the description of Orlinsky et al.'s psychotherapy process research in chapter 8 (in the section headed "Liberating Therapy Research from Its Positivist Strait Jacket"). As in Miller's work, intrinsic logical and epistemological problems underlie Orlinsky et al.'s work, since these authors attempt to incorporate discrete, linear positivist relationships into a systems model in which large numbers of interdependent variables simultaneously interact at different levels of systems complexity.

13. Morgan (1986). Note that a second edition of this book was published in 1997.

14. For an example of the complementary use of multiple conceptual models in the field of behavior therapy, see Fishman and Franks (1997). Also note the variety of conceptual frameworks available in today's pluralistic environment in psychology, such as the cognitive, systemic, humanistic/experiential, hermeneutic, and social constructionistic theoretical models that are reviewed in chapter 2.

15. Morgan (1986), p. 323.

16. Yin (1989), p. 23.

17. Also relevant to the boundary issue is the discussion of the difference between a "program" and a "project," discussed in chapter 6, note 3.

18. Yin (1989), p. 46.

19. See the section in chapter 6, "Collaborating with Clients: Community Psychology."

20. It should be noted, however, that hermeneutic researchers like Lincoln and Guba (1985) do not reject quantification altogether. See text below.

21. Schön (1983). See the discussion of Schön's ideas in the Introduction chapter.

22. Colligan et al. (1983).

23. Steinberg (1997a).

24. For example, see the American Psychological Association's *Standards for Educational and Psychological Testing* (APA, 1985b).

25. Guba and Lincoln (1989), p. 259.

26. Brizius and Campbell (1991), p. A-27.

27. Osborne and Gaebler (1992), p. xxi.

28. Osborne and Gaebler (1992).

29. Brizius and Campbell's 1991 book, *Getting Results*, does an excellent job of spelling out the technology of the pragmatic paradigm in down-to-earth terms for officials involved in the development, administration, and evaluation of government programs.

30. Brizius and Campbell (1991), p. A-10.

31. Brizius and Campbell (1991), p. 19.

32. Brizius and Campbell (1991), pp. A-16 to A-18.

33. Gore (1995).

34. Gore (1995).

35. Campbell (1975) and Yin (1989).

36. Ruben (1995).

37. As of April 1998, the criteria were worded as follows: "1. customer satisfaction/retention; 2. financial and marketplace performance; 3. product and service performance; 4. productivity, operational effectiveness, and responsiveness; 5. human resource performance/development; 6. supplier performance/de-

velopment; and 7. public responsibility/good citizenship" (from the Baldrige Award Web Site 1998).

38. Boyett et al. (1993); Ruben (1995).

39. Fishman (1980, 1981).

40. *Consumer Reports* (1975).

41. Spragins (1997).

42. Kiresuk (1973); Kiresuk and Lund (1978); Kiresuk and Sherman (1968).

43. Rossi and Freeman (1985), p. 71.

44. Kiresuk and Lund (1978).

45. Kiresuk and Lund (1978).

46. Rossi and Freeman (1985), p. 201.

47. Baker (1997).

48. Note that while hermeneutic psychologists do not seek to establish "construct validity," they do employ triangulation for the purpose of establishing "credibility," as described in the text below (see also Lincoln and Guba 1985, pp. 305–307).

49. In their well-known methods monograph, Cook and Campbell (1979, p. 37) describe internal validity as the rational basis with which to infer that either the relationship between two variables is causal or that the absence of a relationship implies the absence of cause.

50. Guba and Lincoln (1989), p. 237.

51. Lincoln and Guba (1985), p. 307. Note that in their later work, these authors are less enthusiastic about triangulation because of its positivist connotations (Guba and Lincoln 1989, p. 240).

52. Kratochwill (1978). This type of research is also called "time-series methodology" (Barlow, Hayes, and Nelson 1984) or "single case experimental designs" (Barlow and Hersen 1984).

53. Lawson (1983).

54. E.g., Barlow and Hersen (1984); Kazdin (1982).

55. Cook and Campbell (1979, p. 37) define external validity as the rational basis with which we infer that a presumed causal relationship can be generalized to and across alternate measures of the cause and effect and across different types of persons, settings, and times.

56. Guba and Lincoln (1989); Yin (1989).

57. Lincoln and Guba (1985), p. 299.

58. Lincoln and Guba (1985), p. 299.

59. Lincoln and Guba (1985), p. 299.

60. Guba and Lincoln (1989), p. 242.

61. Boyett et al. (1993), pp. 341–342.

62. The reader is reminded that there is diversity among advocates of skeptical, ontological, critical, and "mixed" versions of hermeneutics. For example, on the issue of objective knowledge, ontological hermeneuts—as the name "onto-

logical" implies—do believe in a kind of objective knowledge gained through phenomenologically based understanding, that is, gained through our fundamental "being-in-the-world."

63. Guba and Lincoln (1989).

64. Sanders (1994).

65. Sanders (1994), pp. 23, 65, 81, 125.

66. See the "applicability to other sites" section in table 7.2 and the accompanying text.

67. Gentner and Holyoak (1997).

68. Murray and Kluckhohn (1953).

69. Bromley (1986).

70. Bromley (1986), p. 7.

71. Gentner and Holyoak (1997), p. 33; Kolodner (1997); Watson (1994), p. 1.

72. Watson (1994), p. 2.

73. Watson (1994), p. 2 (italics added).

74. Gentner and Holyoak (1997), p. 33; Watson (1994).

75. These are also called "rule-based systems."

76. See figures I.1 and I.2 and the accompanying text in the Introduction.

77. Kolodner (1997), p. 58.

78. Kolodner (1997), p. 61.

79. E.g., Brown (1988).

NOTES TO CHAPTER 8

1. See figure 1.1 in the Introduction.

2. Newman and Holzman (1996).

3. Held (1995).

4. Newman and Holzman (1996).

5. Messer and Wachtel (1997).

6. G. T. Wilson (1996), p. 301; Nathan and Gorman (1998).

7. Nathan (1997); Widmeyer Group (1994).

8. Fox (1995).

9. Karon (1995).

10. Messer and Warren (1995).

11. Macchia (1995).

12. Dawes (1994).

13. G. T. Wilson (1996, 1997).

14. Roth and Fonagy (1996).

15. For example, in 1959, twenty-five hundred members of APA listed specialties in clinical or counseling psychology, compared with 40,000 in 1988. During this time, the percentage in clinical and counseling out of the total APA membership climbed from 14 percent to 59 percent (Dawes 1994, p. 12).

In 1985 an estimated $2.8 billion was spent on the therapy services of "office-based, licensed, clinical psychologists" (Dawes 1994, p. 11, note 3). Based on an average annual rate of increase of 13.9 percent from 1985 to 1988, the 1990 costs have been estimated at $5.4 billion (Dawes 1994, p. 11).

16. See chapter 2.
17. Karasu (1986).
18. Messer and Warren (1995).
19. Fishman and Franks (1997).
20. Neimeyer (1995).
21. Meichenbaum (1995).
22. In this chapter, I will follow the distinction between therapy "patient" and therapy "client" that the psychotherapy researcher Kenneth Howard draws:

> At least six parties can be identified who have a vested interest in the evaluation of mental health treatments: patients, clients, clinicians, managers, sponsors, and researchers. . . . *Patients* are the persons who directly receive the treatment. *Clients* are the persons or institutions whose interests are intended to be served by the treatment. . . . *Clinicians* are the persons who conduct the treatment. *Managers* are the persons who make decisions regarding the allocation of treatment resources. . . . *Sponsors* are the persons or institutions who pay for the treatment. Finally, *researchers* are persons who are concerned with the application of proper scientific [or disciplined inquiry] methodology (measurement technology and standards of evidence) for assessing treatment effects. (Howard et al., 1996, p. 1059)

23. Messer and Wachtel (1997), p. 13.
24. Meichenbaum (1995).
25. Luborsky, Singer, and Luborsky (1975); M. L. Smith and Glass (1977); M. L. Smith, Glass, and Miller (1980); Stiles, Shapiro, and Elliott (1986).
26. Luborsky, Singer, and Luborsky (1975).
27. See chapter 1, note 35.
28. *Consumer Reports* (1992), p. 436.
29. Note that the debate over President Clinton's national health care plan in 1994 was a debate over what kind of managed health plan the country would have—a centrally organized or a decentralized one—not a debate over the concept of managed care per se.
30. There are some scientist-practitioners in APA, and APA makes active efforts to encourage scientists and scientific activities in the Association. On the other hand, a comparison of APA and APS creates a clear differentiation between a more science-driven versus a more practice-driven organization, respectively.
31. Dawes (1994).
32. E.g. G. T. Wilson (1996, 1997).
33. McFall (1995); G. T. Wilson (1996, 1997); Hayes et al. (1995).

34. Seligman (1996a), p. 1077.

35. E.g., Nathan (1997); Widmeyer Group (1994).

36. Widmeyer Group (1994), p. 1.

37. Nathan (1997).

38. Dawes (1994), p. 167.

39. Dawes (1994), pp. 167, 211.

40. Dawes (1994), pp. 167–168.

41. Fox, Kovacs, and Graham (1985), p. 1045.

42. Peterson (1997) responds to positivistic defenders of the applied science paradigm (see figure 1.1). These defenders hold the cardinal principle that *scientific clinical psychology* is the only legitimate and acceptable form of clinical psychology. Peterson replies that "as long as 'science' is defined in a sufficiently comprehensive and flexible way to accommodate the problems with which professional psychologists are concerned, no one I know will disagree" (p. 185). Further, he states: "To me, inclusion of a procedure as 'scientific' need not require rock-hard prior proof of effectiveness, but it does require that the procedure be subject to systematic scientific inquiry and that large bodies of sound research do not indicate persuasively that the procedure fails to do what it is purported to do" (p. 234).

43. Dewey (1910).

44. Fishman and Neigher (1982).

45. Strupp and Hadley (1979).

46. M. L. Smith, Glass, and Miller (1980).

47. Berman and Norton (1985).

48. Stein and Lambert (1984).

49. Roth and Fonagy (1996).

50. Stein and Lambert (1995).

51. Jacobson and Christensen (1996), p. 1032.

52. Christensen and Jacobson (1993).

53. Seligman (1996a), p. 1077.

54. Lyons and Woods (1991).

55. Seligman (1995).

56. Stein and Lambert (1995).

57. These effect sizes were .30 for symptoms and .27 for the patient self-ratings.

58. Meehl (1954).

59. Dawes, Faust, and Meehl (1989).

60. Hayes et al. (1995); G. T. Wilson (1996, 1997).

61. Task Force on Promotion and Dissemination of Psychological Procedures (1995).

62. G. T. Wilson (1996).

63. G. T. Wilson (1997), p. 208.

64. Turk and Salovey (1985).
65. Dawes (1994), p. 120.
66. Dawes (1994), p. 120.
67. Dawes (1994); Hayes et al. (1995); G. T. Wilson (1996).
68. Messer and Warren (1995).
69. Nathan (1997), p. 5.
70. Elliott, Stiles, and Shapiro (1993), p. 459.
71. Roth and Fonagy (1996), pp. 62–67.
72. Project MATCH Research Group (1997), p. 13.
73. Project MATCH Research Group (1997), p. 8.
74. Seligman (1996a), abstract.
75. Frank (1973).
76. Horvarth and Symonds (1991).
77. G. T. Wilson (1996).
78. Michael Mahoney, as quoted in S. Miller et al. (1997), p. 28.
79. Messer and Wachtel (1997).
80. Messer and Wachtel (1997), p. 22.
81. Goldfried and Wolfe (1996).
82. Henry et al. (1993).
83. Dreyfus and Dreyfus (1986; see discussion in Introduction). This point has also been made by such leading thinkers within the cognitive-behavioral therapy model as Gerald Davison (1998), who frames the argument as follows: "Because manuals can constrain clinician behavior and because they are almost always associated with categorically defined diagnostic categories, one can lose sight of the idiographic analysis of single cases. Reliance on manualized treatment can discourage functional analysis of the complexities of individual cases. Achieving some synthesis of this dialectic poses a significant challenge to the continuing development of the science and profession of applied psychology" (p. 163). (See also Goldfried and Davison 1976/1994; and Davison and Lazarus 1994).
84. Stricker (1994, p. 7). See also Hoshmand and Polkinghorne (1992, p. 60). As of this writing, the work of the APA task force on empirically supported treatments over the past few years has just resulted in the publication of an impressive, encyclopedic volume edited by Nathan and Gorman (1998) that documents hundreds of relevant efficacy studies and makes a strong argument for the advantages of the efficacy approach as the "gold standard" of therapy outcome research. However, in the context of the intense debate within APA over the merits of efficacy versus effectiveness research, the book contains a foreword and afterword by APA's incumbent president, Martin Seligman, who argues for the complementarity and integration of efficacy and effectiveness research. For a lively debate over the superiority of efficacy research, see Nathan (1998) for the pro, and Messer (1998) for the con.
85. E.g., Follette (1995).

86. Gergen (1982), pp. 77–78.
87. Nathan (1997).
88. Dawes (1994), p. 120.
89. Howard et al. (1996).

90. To achieve consensus on a typology of patients and patient outcomes will be a challenging process, integrating a variety of considerations. Some of these include: What are the different political interests of various stakeholders, such as patients, payors, and therapists? Is it possible to negotiate a political consensus among them upon a common set of outcome goals? What are alternative conceptual frameworks for typing patients and outcomes? For example, there are striking conceptual differences in how therapists of different theoretical orientations—such as cognitive-behavioral versus psychodynamic approaches—conceptualize relevant patient type and therapy outcome variables. In light of such conceptual differences, can a common framework be rationally derived and agreed upon—especially in light of the political considerations? Also, how do patient typing variables (like diagnosis and severity of disorder) empirically correlate with outcome criteria, and is it possible to statistically control for these correlations?

91. Nathan (1997), pp. 1, 5.
92. Seligman (1995), p. 966.
93. Seligman (1995), pp. 966–967.
94. Seligman (1996a), p. 1075.
95. Seligman (1996a), p. 1075.
96. Seligman (1996a), p. 1076.
97. See chapter 7, the beginning of the section on "Results."

98. For a heated and informative discussion of the relative pros and cons of efficacy versus effectiveness research designs, see the whole October 1996 issue of the *American Psychologist*.

99. Developing a typology of cases is a complex political, conceptual, and empirical process. See note 90.

100. Taube, Mechanic, and Hohmann (1989).
101. American Psychiatric Association (1994).

102. Again, developing a typology of cases is a complex political, conceptual, and empirical process. See note 90.

103. Howard et al. (1996); Lyons et al. (1996); Sperry et al. (1996).
104. See note 90.
105. Howard et al. (1996), p. 1061.
106. Howard et al. (1996), p. 1061.
107. Howard et al. (1996), p. 1062.
108. Howard et al. (1996), p. 1062.

109. One group of therapy researchers recently framed the issue this way: "Research should be focused, not only toward continuing to evaluate in con-

trolled settings the efficacy of our interventions, but toward systematically evaluating the effectiveness of various delivery models in clinical settings" (Bologna et al. 1998, p. 108).

110. Orlinsky and Howard (1986).

111. Also see Lambert and Okiishi (1997); and Luborsky et al. (1997).

112. Kiesler (1971).

113. Kiesler (1966).

114. Beutler (1986), p. 94.

115. Lambert (1992), p. 97.

116. Horvarth and Symonds (1991).

117. Gottman and Leiblum (1974), p. 4.

118. Fishman (1988), pp. 284–285.

119. For another example of an elaborately phased and flowcharted generic model of therapy process, see Fischer's (1986) "PRAISES" model. Fischer comments on the actual complexity of therapy as reflected in the model: "Despite the fact that it looks like a General Motors wiring diagram at first glance, the flowchart on closer examination consists simply of the varied aspects that constitute the flow of eclectic practice" (p. 342).

120. Roth and Fonagy (1996), p. 14.

121. Orlinsky, Grawe, and Parks (1994).

122. Orlinsky, Grawe, and Parks (1994), p. 364.

123. Certainly, scientists who advocate for manualized treatments claim to build these into their manuals and training. As one ardent believer in manualized therapy states:

> The importance of developing rapport and building a positive therapeutic alliance is not less important in manual-based therapy than conventional therapy. The quality of the therapeutic relationship will help determine the extent to which patients comply with treatment interventions. Therapists have a critical role to play in overcoming ambivalence about behavior change, and in nurturing commitment to change despite psychological setbacks. (G. T. Wilson, 1996, p. 305)

124. See figure 1.2.

125. Orlinsky, Grawe, and Parks (1994), p. 352.

126. E.g., Roth and Fonagy (1996).

127. See summaries of this study in Roth and Fonagy (1996), pp. 62–67; and in Persons (1993), pp. 308–309.

128. Calhoun and Resick (1993).

129. Calhoun and Resick (1993), pp. 62–63.

130. Calhoun and Resick (1993), pp. 63–65.

131. Calhoun and Resick (1993), p. 66.

132. Calhoun and Resick (1993), p. 67.

133. Calhoun and Resick (1993), p. 69.
134. Calhoun and Resick (1993), p. 72.
135. Calhoun and Resick (1993), p. 73.
136. Calhoun and Resick (1993), p. 73.
137. Calhoun and Resick (1993), p. 76.
138. Calhoun and Resick (1993), p. 95.
139. Messer and Wachtel (1997).

NOTES TO CHAPTER 9

1. Schrag (1997).
2. Olson (1997), p. 8.
3. Wood (1992).
4. Fiske (1991), pp. 25–26.
5. Fiske (1991), p. 33.
6. Fiske (1991), p. 63.
7. Fiske (1991), p. 31.
8. Fiske (1991), p. 31.
9. As quoted in Fiske (1991), p. 33.
10. Graham (1992), p. 12.
11. Wilson and Daviss (1994), p. 6.
12. Graham (1992), p. 12.
13. Dewey's predecessors in the movement include Horace Mann, Frances Parker, and the psychologist G. Stanley Hall.
14. Westbrook (1991), p. 104.
15. Westbrook (1991), p. 111.
16. Westbrook (1991), p. 537. Starting in the 1960s, there has been a major renewal of interest in Dewey's work, which is so in tune with the pragmatic, moral, and case-study-based themes of postmodernism. Examples are the recent appearance of major intellectual biographies by Robert Westbrook (1991) and Alan Ryan (1995), and the celebration of Dewey as one of the three most important philosophers of the twentieth century by Richard Rorty, a pragmatist who himself is perhaps the most widely read philosopher alive today (Gottlieb 1991).
17. E.g., Herndon (1968); Holt (1970); Kohl (1968); and Kozol (1967). Also an important influence on suburban schools in the 1960s and '70s was the British Infant School model, which led to open classrooms and a radical rethinking of the education process.
18. Greisemer and Butler (1985).
19. Gross and Gross (1985).
20. National Commission on Excellence in Education (1983), p. 1.
21. Sykes (1988).

22. Sykes (1995).

23. Sykes (1995), p. ix.

24. Sykes (1995), pp. 8–11.

25. Sykes (1995), p. 89.

26. From a recent *New York Times* op-ed piece, as quoted in Schrag (1997), pp. 72–73.

27. Berliner and Biddle (1995).

28. Berliner and Biddle (1995), p. xi.

29. Berliner and Biddle (1995), p. xii. Schrag provides the following supportive example. In the spring of 1991 the Sandia National Laboratories, a federal institution with an excellent reputation, compiled a careful, detailed, statistical report showing that the picture in American education was complex and not as gloomy as the federal reports of the 1980s claimed.

> [The report was] buried by the Department of Energy, which had commissioned it. The document, said James Watkins, George Bush's Secretary of Energy, was "dead wrong," and would be regarded as "a call for complacency at a time when just the opposite is required." . . .
>
> Even after the Clinton Administration finally released it in 1993, neither the Sandia data nor similar findings from other sources got much attention. Mixed reports don't make for good headlines. (1997, p. 72)

30. Bennett (1992), p. 15.

31. For example, at present the average SAT score earned by students goes down by *fifteen points* for each decrease of $10,000 in family income (Berliner and Biddle 1995, p. 19).

32. Berliner and Biddle (1995), p. 22. Schrag (1997) frames the point in this way: "Although SAT verbal scores declined over the years 1975 to 1990, . . . if the same population that took the SATs in 1975 had taken them this year, the average score would be significantly higher than it was then—and higher than it was in 1990" (p. 73).

33. Berliner and Biddle (1995), p. 43.

34. National Commission on Excellence in Education (1983), p. 8.

35. As quoted in Berliner and Biddle (1995), p. 54.

36. Berliner and Biddle (1995), p. 54.

37. Berliner and Biddle (1995), pp. 55–56.

38. Stevenson and Stigler (1992).

39. As quoted in Berliner and Biddle (1995, p. 2), from *Japan Times* (November 20, 1985). For a detailed picture of the "dark side" of the Japanese education system, see Schooland (1990).

40. Berliner and Biddle (1995), pp. 67–68.

41. Berliner and Biddle (1995), p. 80.

42. Berliner and Biddle (1995), p. 82. Schrag (1997) points to a related find-

ing: "[The Sandia National Laboratories report (1993)] estimates that from 1960 to 1988 constant-dollar spending for 'regular' students increased by 39 per cent per pupil while spending for all students increased by roughly 150 percent" (p. 76).

43. For example, in the book reviewed below, which stresses progressive reforms, Edward Fiske introduces his proposals for change as follows:

It's no secret that America's public schools are failing. Since the early 1980s Americans have been deluged with reports and studies, backed by abundant anecdotes, documenting the academic deficiencies of our young people. One survey of high school juniors discovered that only one in three could put the Civil War in the correct half century. The National Assessment of Educational Progress [NAEP] found that only one in five young adults between the ages of 21 and 25 could read a bus timetable or draft a simple letter asking for a job in a supermarket. In the nation that first landed a man on the moon, a full quarter of adults cannot say whether the earth goes around the sun or vice versa. In 1987 the New York Telephone Company had to screen 57,000 applicants to find 2,000 with the skills to become entry-level operators and repair technicians. (1991, p. 13)

44. Fiske (1991).

45. Fiske (1991), p. 27. For related and similar analyses of the need for educational reform that flows from and is attuned to the changing nature of American business and industry, see K. Wilson and Daviss (1994) and H. Smith (1995).

46. Fiske (1991), p. 27.

47. Fiske (1991), p. 66.

48. Sizer (1984, 1992, 1996).

49. Fiske (1991), p. 67.

50. H. Smith (1995), 170.

51. Fiske (1991), p. 102.

52. Fiske (1991), p. 115.

53. Gardner (1991).

54. Gardner (1991), p. 12.

55. Fiske (1991), p. 127.

56. Rose (1995), pp. 194–197.

57. Fiske (1991), p. 182.

58. E.g., see Fiske (1991); Meir (1995); H. Smith (1995); Wiseman (1994); Wood (1992).

59. Mosle (1996b), p. 46. But see the text below, pp. 270–271.

60. Comer (1988).

61. Zigler (1989). See also Dryfoos (1994).

62. Hirsch (1988), pp. 33–34.

63. Mosle (1996a), p. 15.

64. Hirsch (1988), Appendix, "What Literate Americans Know," pp. 154–215.

65. Sykes (1995), p. 287; Mosle (1996b), p. 68.

66. Lehmann (1995), p. 14.

67. LeCompte and Preissle (1992).

68. As quoted in Mosle (1996b), p. 68.

69. Adams and Bruck (1995); Hancock and Wingert (1996); Rothman (1990); Sykes (1995), chapter 8.

70. Routman (1988), p. 44.

71. Hancock and Wingert (1996); Collins (1997). Very recently, after two years of study on methods for teaching reading, a prestigious panel of national experts concluded that the whole language and phonics methods are complementary and should be combined. A journalist summarized the findings as follows:

> The panelists wrote that a variety of studies have shown that emergent readers who are given direct instruction in phonics "learn to read more quickly." But it cautioned that phonics has its limits, and that without an understanding of context, the word "spring," for example, can refer to a season or a coiled piece of metal. . . . For that reason, the panel stopped far short of calling for a return to the era of Dick-and-Jane books . . . (and) implored teachers to use rich literature to hook youngsters as lifelong readers. (Steinberg 1998)

72. Fiske (1991), pp. 68–69.

73. Fiske (1991), p. 75.

74. Stone (1994).

75. Sykes (1995), p. 268.

76. Fiske (1991), p. 248.

77. Of course, it is very possible that there are some educational ideas that won't work anywhere, and other ideas that are distinctive in their capacity to work in a great many settings. The pragmatist sees both of circumstances as possibilities to be empirically determined, not to be theoretically accepted or rejected in principle.

78. As described in the previous chapter on psychotherapy, "holding constant" can be done either experimentally or statistically—referred to in psychotherapy investigations as "efficacy" versus "effectivness" research, respectively.

79. Specifically, New York City examined the correlations between their schools' proficiency scores, on the one hand, and the percentage of students who were poor and/or bilingual, on the other. Then, on the basis of these correlations, each school's expected percentage of students who were at or above grade level in reading and writing was calculated on the basis of the school's student poverty

and bilinguality levels. For example, a school with the highest percentages of poor students and of bilingual students was expected to have only 17 percent of their students reading and writing at or above grade level; and a school with the lowest percentages of poor and of bilingual students was expected to have 70 percent of their students reading and writing at or above grade level.

80. Steinberg (1997a).

81. Steinberg (1997a).

82. Mosle (1997), p. 49.

83. Steinberg (1997b); Hartocollis (1997b).

84. Rudy Crew, as quoted in Mosle (1997), p. 32. For more on "scaling up," see the chapter 6 section, "What Works and Why We Have So Little of It," which reviews the contribution of Lisbeth Schorr (1997).

85. See note 84.

86. Hartocollis (1997a). Also, see the text above, pp. 258–259.

87. Hartocollis (1997a).

88. As quoted in Hartocollis (1997a).

89. Note that each case holistically describes actual students and teachers in a particular learning environment. An alternative approach that is often employed is to collate educational "best practices." Here, each educational program or technique—such as a special way of teaching math, Sizer's common principles for "essential schools," or Hirsch's "cultural literacy" approach to curriculum—is presented in generalized form, detached from its embodiment in any particular classroom situation. This is parallel to presenting therapy techniques as techniques, independent of particular case situations. This approach is quite different from examining how a particular therapeutic or educational technique works when it is concretized and contextualized in a particular therapeutic or educational setting, as is being proposed here.

90. E.g., Fiske (1991); Friedman (1990); Kidder (1989); Mosle (1996b); Rose (1995); H. Smith (1995); Wood (1992).

91. Rose (1995).

92. Rose (1995), p. 4.

93. Rose (1995), pp. 5–6.

94. Rose (1995), p. 9.

95. Rose (1995), p. 416.

96. Firestone and Corbett (1988).

97. Firestone and Corbett (1988), p. 333.

98. See chapter 8.

99. Steinberg (1997a), p. 28.

100. Olson (1997), p. 17. In a related way, Nathan Tarcov, an educational specialist at the University of Chicago, points out that debates over teaching technologies or policies typically leave out a fundamental factor: "Whatever the curriculum, ultimately it comes down to the teacher, especially the teacher's energy

and character and sense of humor and ability to relate to young people, and not just the policies the teacher follows" (quoted in Steinberg 1997c, p. 14).

Note that the "common factors" associated with educational success and the "nonspecific factors" associated with psychotherapy success fall under the umbrella of the "contextual factors" Schorr (1997) identifies as essential for the success of any human service program. See the discussion of these factors in the chapter 6 section, "What Works and Why We Have So Little of It."

101. Also see table 7.3.

102. LeCompte and Preissle (1992); Wagner (1994).

103. *Education Week* (1997), p. 32.

104. Mosle (1996b), p. 46.

105. Mosle (1996b); Short and Talley (1997); Toch (1996).

106. Mosle (1996b), p. 47.

107. Sykes (1995); Toch (1996).

108. Leo (1996).

109. Leo (1996), p. 61.

110. *Education Week* (1997), p. 27.

NOTES TO CHAPTER 10

1. See chapters 3 and 5, respectively.

2. See Introduction and chapter 8.

3. See chapter 6.

4. See "A Tale of Two Studies" in the Introduction.

5. See "A Tale of Two Studies" in the Introduction.

6. See Fishman (1990, 1991a, 1991b).

7. See Denzin and Lincoln (1994).

8. Dawes (1994).

9. For a related discussion of the practical intervention advantages of integrating perspectives from different theoretical points of view, see the section in chapter 7, "The Case of 'Multicom': The Advantages Of 'Creative Chaos.'"

10. In the words of Steinberg, progressive versus traditional educational proponents view their arguments as "clashing over education's one truth faith," while teachers pragmatically ask, "Why choose?"

> Listening to the discussion of education reform is like walking into an ice cream parlor that says it serves only vanilla and chocolate—with no hope of swirling them together. Whatever the subject, educators and parents are presented with stark, politicized choices that are often uncomplicated by the realities of the classroom. (1997c, p. 1).

11. Gergen (1991); Toulmin (1990).

12. Rice (1997), p. 1178.

13. For example, in his book *Breaking the News: How the Media Undermine American Democracy*, investigative journalist James Fallows (1996) documents the news media's preference for the drama of conflict over careful, substantive evaluation of the issues. The goal is to make the news entertaining in order to achieve audience share. This is done by viewing public life as a competitive game, where the emphasis is upon who wins rather than whether they should win. "The entire press," he concludes, "has become the sports page." (Also see Schechter's 1997 *The More You Watch, the Less You Know: News Wars/(Sub)merged Hopes/Media Adventures*.)

14. Hall (1997).

References

Adams, M. J., & Bruck, M. (1995). Resolving the "great debate." *American Educator*, 19, 10–20.

Adler, A. (February, 1998). New federal budget holds some funding increases. *APA Monitor*, 1–2.

Ajzen, I. (1985). From intention to actions: A theory of planned behavior. In J. Kuhl & J. Beckman, *Action control: From cognition to behavior*, 11–39. Heidelberg: Springer.

Altman, I. (1987). Centripetal and centrifugal trends in psychology. *American Psychologist*, 42, 1058–1069.

Altman, I., & Rogoff, B. (1987). World views in psychology: Trait, interactional, organismic, and transactional perspectives. In D. Stokols & I. Altman, eds., *Handbook of environmental psychology*, 7–40. New York: John Wiley.

American Psychiatric Association (1994). *Diagnostic and statistical manual of mental disorders*. 4th ed. Washington, D.C.: American Psychiatric Association.

American Psychological Association (APA) (1985a). *Directory of the American Psychological Association*. Washington, DC: American Psychological Association.

———. (1985b). *Standards for educational and psychological testing*. Washington, DC: American Psychological Association.

Anderson, M. (1992). *Impostors in the temple*. New York: Simon & Schuster.

Anthony, W. (1990). *Psychiatric rehabilitation*. Boston: Boston University Center for Psychiatric Rehabilitation.

Ayer, A. J. (1936/1946). *Language, truth, and logic*. New York: Dover.

Baars, B. J. (1986). *The cognitive revolution in psychology*. New York: Guilford Press.

Baker, D., ed. (1997). *Getting prices right : The debate over the accuracy of the consumer price index*. Armonk, NY: M. E. Sharpe.

Baldrige Award Web Site (April 21, 1998). *www.baldrige.com/KEY.HTM.*

Barber, B. R. (1992a). Jihad vs. McWorld. *Atlantic Monthly*, 269, 53–65.

———. (1992b). *An aristocracy of everyone: The politics of education and the future of America*. New York: Oxford University Press.

Barker, J. A. (1992). *Paradigms: The business of discovering the future.* New York: HarperCollins.

Barlow, D. H., Hayes, S. C., & Nelson, R. O. (1984). *The scientist-practitioner: Research and accountability in clinical and educational settings.* Elmsford, NY: Pergamon Press.

Barlow, D. H., & Hersen, M. (1984). *Single case experimental designs: Strategies for studying behavior change.* 2d ed. Elmsford, NY: Pergamon Press.

Baumeister, R. F. (1991). *Meanings of life.* New York: Guilford.

Belenky, M. F., Clinchy, B. M., & Goldberger, N. R. (1986). *Women's ways of knowing: The development of self, voice, and mind.* New York: Basic Books.

Benkov, L. (1994). *Reinventing the family.* New York: Crown.

Bennett, W. (1992). *The declining of America: The fight for our culture and our children.* New York: Summit Books.

Berliner, D. C., & Biddle, B. J. (1995). *The manufactured crisis: Myths, fraud, and the attack on America's public schools.* Reading, MA: Addison-Wesley.

Berman, J. S., & Norton, N. C. (1985). Does professional training make a therapist more effective? *Psychological Bulletin, 98,* 401–407.

Berman, M. (1981). *The reenchantment of the world.* Ithaca, NY: Cornell University Press.

Berman, P., ed. (1992). *Debating P.C.: The controversy over political correctness on college campuses.* New York: Bantam Doubleday Dell.

Bernstein, R. (April 8, 1990). Academic left finds the far reaches of postmoderism. *New York Times,* 5E.

Bernstein, R. J. (1976). *The restructuring of social and political theory.* New York: Harcourt Brace Jovanovich.

———. (1983). *Beyond objectivism and relativism.* Philadelphia: University of Pennsylvania Press.

Bertalanffy, L. von (1968). *General system theory: Foundations, development, applications.* New York: Braziller.

Beutler, L. E. (1986). Systematic eclectic psychotherapy. In J. C. Norcross, ed., *Handbook of eclectic psychotherapy,* 94–131. New York: Brunner/Mazel.

Bloom, A. (1987). *The closing of the American mind.* New York: Simon & Schuster.

Bloom, H. (1973). *The anxiety of influence.* New York: Oxford University Press.

Bologna, N. C., Barlow, D. H., Hollon, S. D., Mitchell, J. E., & Huppert, J. D. (1998). Behavioral health treatment redesign in managed care settings. *Clinical Psychology: Science and Practice, 5,* 94–114.

Boyett, J. H., Schwartz, S., Osterwise, L., & Bauer, R. (1993). *The quality journey: How winning the Baldrige sparked the remaking of IBM.* New York: Dutton.

Brinton, C. (1963). *The shaping of modern thought.* Englewood Cliffs, NJ: Prentice Hall.

Brizius, J. A., & Campbell, M. D. (1991). *Getting results: A guide for govern-ment accountability*. Washington, DC: Council of Governors' Policy Advi-sors.

Bromley, D. B. (1986). *The case-study method in psychology and related disci-plines*. New York: John Wiley.

Brown, A. L. (1988). Motivation to learn and understand: On taking charge of one's own learning. *Cognition and Instruction, 5,* 311–322.

Bruner, J. (1986). *Actual minds, possible worlds*. Cambridge, MA: Harvard Uni-versity Press.

———. (1990). *Acts of meaning*. Cambridge, MA: Harvard University Press.

Bruner, J., Goodnow, J., & Austin, G. (1956). *A study of thinking*. New York: John Wiley.

Burke, K. (1945). *A grammar of motives*. New York: Prentice Hall.

Cahan, E. D., & White, S. H. (1992). Proposals for a second psychology. *Amer-ican Psychologist, 47,* 224–235.

Calhoun, K. S., & Resick, P. A. (1993). Post-traumatic stress disorder. In D. H. Barlow, ed., *Clinical handbook of psychological disorder: A step-by-step treatment manual,* 48–98. 2d ed. New York: Guilford Press.

Campbell, D. T. (1969). Reforms as experiments. *American Psychologist, 24,* 409–429.

———. (1975). Degrees of freedom and the case study. *Comparative Political Studies, 8,* 178–193.

Chen, H., & Rossi, P. H. (1983). Evaluating with sense: The theory-driven ap-proach. *Evaluation Review, 7,* 283–302.

Chessick, R. D. (1990). Hermeneutics for psychotherapists. *American Journal of Psychotherapy, 44,* 256–273.

Christensen, A., & Jacobson, N. S. (1993). Who or what can do psychotherapy: The status and challenge of nonprofessional therapies. *Psychological Science, 5,* 8–14.

Cohen, D. K., & Garet, M. S. (1975). Reforming educational policy with applied social research. *Harvard Educational Review, 45,* 17–41.

Colligan, R. C., Osborne, D., Swenson, W. M., & Offord, K. P. (1983). *The MMPI: A contemporary normative study*. New York: Praeger.

Collins, J. (October 27, 1997). How Johnny should read. *Time, 150,* 78–81.

Comer, J. P. (1988). Educating poor minority children. *Scientific American, 259,* 42–48.

Consumer Reports (February, 1975). Floor polishes. *Consumer Reports, 40.*

———. (1992). Wasted health care dollars. *Consumer Reports, 57,* 435–448.

Cook, T. D., & Campbell, D. T. (1979). *Quasi-experimentation: Design and analysis issues for field settings*. Chicago: Rand McNally.

Crider, A. B., Goethals, G. R., Cavanaugh, R. F., & Solomon, P. R. (1989). *Psy-chology*. 3d ed. Glenview, IL: Scott, Foresman, & Company.

Cronbach, L. J., Ambron, S. R., Dornbusch, S. M., Hess, R. D., Hornik, R. C., Phillips, D. C., Walker, D. F., & Weiner, S. S. (1980). *Toward reform of program evaluation*. San Francisco: Jossey-Bass.

Cushman, P. (1990). Why the self is empty: Toward a historically situationed psychology. *American Psychologist, 45*, 599–611.

D'Andrade, R. (1986). Three scientific world views and the covering law model. In D. W. Fiske & R. A. Shweder, eds., *Metatheory in social science: Pluralisms and subjectivities,* 19–41. Chicago: University of Chicago Press.

Danziger, K. (1990). *Constructing the subject: Historical origins of psychological research*. New York: Cambridge University Press.

Davison, G. C. (1998). Being bolder with the Boulder model: The challenge of education and training in empirically supported treatments. *Journal of Consulting and Clinical Psychology, 66*, 163-167.

Davison, G. C., & Lazarus, A. A. (1994). Clinical innovation and evaluation: Integrating practice with inquiry. *Clinical Psychology: Science and Practice, 1*, 157–168.

Dawes, R. M. (1994). *House of cards: Psychology and psychotherapy built on myth*. New York: Free Press.

Dawes, R. M., Faust, D., & Meehl, P. E. (1989). Clinical versus actuarial judgment. *Science, 243*, 1668–1674.

Deitchman, S. (1976). *The best-layed schemes: A tale of social research and bureaucracy*. Cambridge, MA: MIT Press.

Denzin, N. K. (1989). *Interpretive interactionism*. Newbury Park, CA: Sage.

Denzin, N. K., & Lincoln, Y. S., eds. (1994). *Handbook of qualitative research*. Thousand Oaks, CA: Sage.

Dewey, J. (January 28, 1910). Science as subject-matter and as method. *Science, 36*, 127.

Dewey, J., & Bentley, A. F. (1949). *Knowing and the known*. Boston: Beacon.

Dreyfus, H. L., & Dreyfus, S. E. (1986). *Mind over machine*. New York: Free Press.

Dryfoos, J. G. (1994). *Full-service schools: A revolution in health and social services for children, youth, and families*. San Francisco: Jossey-Bass.

D'Souza, D. (1991). *Illiberal education: The politics of race and sex on campus*. New York: Free Press.

Education Week (January 22, 1997). Quality counts: A report card on the condition of public education in the fifty states. *Education Week (Supplement), 16*, 1–238.

Eisner, E. W. (1991). *The enlightened eye: Qualitative inquiry and the enhancement of educational practice*. New York: Macmillan.

Eisner, E. W., & Peshkin, A. (1990). *Qualitative inquiry in education: The continuing debate*. New York: Teachers College Press.

Elias, M. J. (1991). An action research approach to evaluating the impact of a social decision-making and problem-solving curriculum for preventing behavior and academic dysfunction in children. *Evaluation and Program Planning*, 14, 397–401.

Elliott, R., Stiles, W. B., & Shapiro, D. A. (1993). Are some therapies more equivalent than others? In T. R. Giles, ed., *Handbook of effective psychotherapy*, 455–479. New York: Plenum.

Fallows, J. (1996). *Breaking the news: How the media undermine American democracy.* New York: Pantheon Books.

Feyerabend, P. (1975). *Against method: Outline of an anarchistic theory of knowledge.* London: New Left Books.

Fine, A. (1986). Is scientific realism compatible with quantum physics? In A. Fine, *The shakey game*, 151–171. Chicago: University of Chicago Press.

Firestone, W. A., & Corbett, H. D. (1988). Planned organizational change. In N. Boyan, ed., *Handbook of research on educational administration*, 321–341. White Plains, NY: Longman.

Fischer, J. (1986). Eclectic casework. In J. C. Norcross, ed., *Handbook of eclectic psychotherapy*, 320–352. New York: Brunner/Mazel.

Fishman, D. B. (1980). A computerized, cost-effectiveness methodology for community mental health centers. In J. B. Sidowski, J. H. Johnson, & T. A. Williams, eds., *Technology in mental health care systems*, 43–63. Norwood, NJ: Ablex.

———. (1981). *A cost-effectiveness methodology for community mental health centers: Development and pilot test.* DHHS Pub. No. (ADM) 81–767 (reprinted 1984). Washington, DC: U.S. Government Printing Office.

———. (1988). Pragmatic behaviorism: Saving and nurturing the baby. In D. B. Fishman, F. Rotgers, & C. M. Franks, eds., *Paradigms in behavior therapy: Present and promise*, 254–293. New York: Springer.

———. (1990). The quantitative, naturalistic case study: A unifying element for psychology. *International Newsletter of Uninomic Psychology*, 9, 1–10.

———. (1991a). An introduction to the experimental versus the pragmatic paradigm in evaluation. *Evaluation and Program Planning*, 14, 353–363.

———. (1991b). The experimental versus the pragmatic paradigm: Summary and conclusions. *Evaluation and Program Planning*, 14, 403–409.

———. (1992). Postmodernism comes to program evaluation: A critical review of Guba and Lincoln's *Fourth Generation Evaluation. Evaluation and Program Planning*, 15, 263–270.

———. (1995). Postmodernism comes to evaluation, II: A review of Denzin and Lincoln's *Handbook of Qualitative Evaluation. Evaluation and Program Planning*, 18, 301–310.

———. (1997). Postmodernism comes to program evaluation, III: A critical review of Stringer's *Action research: A handbook for practitioners. Evaluation and Program Planning*, 20, 231–235.

Fishman, D. B., & Franks, C. M. (1997). The conceptual evolution of behavior therapy. In P. L. Wachtel and S. B. Messer, eds., *Theories of psychotherapy*, 131–180. Washington, DC: American Psychological Association.

Fishman, D. B., & Neigher, W. D. (1982). American psychology in the eighties: Who will buy? *American Psychologist, 37,* 533-546.

———. (1987). Technological assessment: Tapping a "third culture" for decision-focused psychological measurement. In D. R. Peterson & D. B. Fishman, eds., *Assessment for decision,* 44–76. New Brunswick, NJ: Rutgers University Press.

Fishman, D. B., & Peterson, D. R. (1987). On getting the right information and getting the information right. In D. R. Peterson & D. B. Fishman, eds., *Assessment for decision,* 395–451. New Brunswick, NJ: Rutgers University Press.

Fishman, D. B., Rotgers, F., & Franks, C. M., eds. (1988). *Paradigms in behavior therapy: Present and promise.* New York: Springer.

Fiske, D. W., & Shweder, R. A., eds. (1986). *Metatheory in social science: Pluralism and subjectivities.* Chicago: University of Chicago Press.

Fiske, E. B. (1991). *Smart schools, smart kids: Why do some schools work?* New York: Simon & Schuster.

Flew, A., ed. (1984). *A dictionary of philosophy.* 2d ed., rev. New York: St. Martin's Press.

Follette, W. C. (1995). Correcting methodological weaknesses in the knowledge base used to derive practice standards. In S. C. Hayes, V. M. Follette, R. M. Dawes, & K. E. Grady, eds., *Scientific standards of psychological practice: Issues and recommendations,* 229–247. Reno, NV: Context Press.

Fox, R. E. (1995). The rape of psychotherapy. *Professional Psychology: Research and Practice, 26,* 147–155.

Fox, R. E., Kovacs, A. L., & Graham, S. R. (1985). *Proposals for a revolution in the preparation and regulation of professional psychologists, 40,* 1042–1050.

Frank, J. D. (1973). *Persuasion and healing: A comparative study of psychotherapy.* Rev. ed. Baltimore: Johns Hopkins University Press.

Friedman, S. G. (1990). *Small victories: The real world of a teacher, her students, and their high school.* New York: Harper & Row.

Fukuyama, F. (1989). The end of history? *National Interest, 16,* 3–19.

Gardner, H. (1987). *The mind's new science.* New York: Basic Books.

———. (1991). *The unschooled mind: How children think and how schools should teach.* New York: Basic Books.

Garraty, J. A., & Gay, P., eds. (1972). *The Columbia history of the world.* New York: Harper & Row.

Geertz, C. (1973). *The interpretation of cultures.* New York: Basic Books.

———. (1989). Anti anti-relativism. In M. Krausz, ed., *Relativism: Interpreta-*

tion and confrontation, 12–34. Notre Dame, IN: University of Notre Dame Press. Reprinted from the *American Anthropologist*, 86, 2 (June 1984): 263–278.

Gentner, D., & Holyoak, K. J. (1997). Reasoning and learning by analogy: Introduction. *American Psychologist*, 52, 32–34.

Gergen, K. J. (1973). Social psychology as history. *Journal of Personality and Social Psychology*, 26, 309–320.

———. (1982). *Towards transformation in social knowledge*. New York: Springer-Verlag.

———. (1985a). Selves in search of an identity. Review of J. Suls & A. G. Greenwald, eds., *Psychological perspectives on the self*, vol. 2. *Contemporary Psychology*, 30, 184–186.

———. (1985b). The social constructionist movement in modern psychology. *American Psychologist*, 40, 266–275.

———. (1991). *The saturated self: Dilemmas of identity in contemporary life*. New York: Basic Books.

———. (1994). Exploring the postmodern: Perils or potentials? *American Psychologist*, 49, 412–416.

Gerstner, L. V., Semrad, R. D., Doyle, D. P., & Johnson, W. B. (1994). *Reinventing education: Entrepreneurship in America's public schools*. New York: Dutton.

Giles, T. R. (1993). *Managed mental health care: A guide for practitioners, employers, and hospital administrators*. New York: Allyn & Bacon.

Gilligan, C. (1982). *In a different voice: Psychological theory and women's development*. Cambridge, MA: Harvard University Press.

Glaser, B., & Strauss, A. (1967). The discovery of grounded theory. Chicago: Aldine.

Gleick, J. (1987). *Chaos: Making a new science*. New York: Penguin.

Gold, N. (1983). Stakeholder and program evaluation: Characterizations and reflections. In A. S. Bryk, ed., *Stakeholder based evaluation*. San Francisco: Jossey-Bass.

Goldfried, M., & Wolfe, B. (1996). Psychotherapy practice and research: Repairing a strained alliance. *American Psychologist*, 51, 1007–1016.

Goldfried, M. R., & Davison, G. C. (1994). *Clinical behavior therapy*. (Expanded edition). New York: Wiley. (Originally printed in 1976.)

Gore, A. (1995). *Common sense government: Works better and it costs less*. New York: Random House.

Gottlieb, A. (June 2, 1991). The most talked about philosopher. *New York Times Book Review*, 30.

Gottman, J. M., & Leiblum, S. R. (1974). *How to do therapy and how to evaluate it*. New York: Holt, Rinehart, & Winston.

Graham, P. A. (1992). *S.O.S.: Sustain our schools*. New York: Farrar, Straus, & Giroux.

Greene, J. C. (1994). Qualitative program evaluation: Practice and promise. In N. K. Denzin & Y. S. Lincoln, eds., *Handbook of qualitative research*, 530–544. Thousand Oaks, CA: Sage.

Gregory, R. L., ed. (1987). *The Oxford companion to the mind*. New York: Oxford University Press.

Greisemer, J. L., & Butler, C. (1985). The national reports on education: A comparative analysis. In B. Gross & R. Gross, eds., *The great school debate: Which way for American Education?*, 50–71. New York: Simon & Schuster.

Gross, B., & Gross, R. (1985). *The great school debate: Which way for American Education?* New York: Simon & Schuster.

Guba, E. G., & Lincoln, Y. S. (1989). *Fourth generation evaluation*. Newbury Park, CA: Sage.

———. (1994). Competing paradigms in qualitative research. In N. K. Denzin & Y. S. Lincoln, eds., *Handbook of qualitative research*, 105–117. Thousand Oaks, CA: Sage.

Gurman, A. S., & Kniskern, D. P., eds. (1981). *Handbook of family therapy*. New York: Brunner/Mazel.

Gutkin, T. B., & Reynolds, C. R. (1990). *Handbook of school psychology*. 2d ed. New York: John Wiley.

Hall, S. (1997). *Commotion in the blood*. New York: Henry Holt.

Hammer, M., & Champy, J. (1993). *Reengineering the corporation: A manifesto for business revolution*. New York: HarperCollins.

Hancock, L. N., & Wingert, P. (May 13, 1996). If you can read this . . . you learned phonics. Or so its supporters say. *Newsweek*, 75.

Hare-Mustin, R. T., & Marecek, J., eds. (1992). *Psychology and the construction of gender*. New Haven, CT: Yale University Press.

Harré, R., & Lamb, R., eds. (1983). *The encyclopedic dictionary of psychology*. Cambridge, MA: MIT Press.

Hartocollis, A. (October 13, 1997a). Small schools face limits on autonomy. *New York Times*, B–1.

———. (December 23, 1997b). NYC schools chancellor drafts new standards for principals. *New York Times*, 1.

Hartshorne, C., Weiss, P., & Burks, A. W., eds. (1958). *Collected papers of Charles Sanders Peirce*, vol. 7. Cambridge, MA: Harvard University Press.

Hawking, S. (1988). *A brief history of time: From the big bang to black holes*. New York: Bantam.

Hayes, S. C., Follette, V. M., Dawes, R. M., & Grady, K. E., eds. (1995). *Scientific standards of psychological practice: Issues and recommendations*. Reno, NV: Context Press.

Hazen, R. M., & Trefil, J. (1991). *Science matters: Achieving scientific literacy*. New York: Doubleday.

Heidbreder, E. (1933). *Seven psychologies*. New York: Appleton-Century-Crofts.

Held, B. S. (1995). *Back to reality: A critique of postmodern theory in psychotherapy.* New York: W. W. Norton.

Heller, K., Price, R. H., Reinharz, S., Riger, S., & Wandersman, A., & D'Annuo, T. A. (1984). *Psychology and community change: Challenges of the future.* 2d ed. Chicago: Dorsey Press.

Hempel, C. (1942). The function of general laws in history. In C. Hempel, *Aspects of scientific explanation and other essays in the philosophy of science.* New York: Free Press.

Henderson, L. J. (1917). *The order of nature.* Cambridge, MA: Harvard University Press.

Henry, W. P., Strupp, H. H., Butler, S. T., Schacht, T. E., and Binder, J. L. (1993). Effects of training in time-limited dynamic psychotherapy: Changes in therapist behavior. *Journal of Consulting and Clinical Psychology, 61,* 434–440.

Herndon, J. (1968). *The way it spozed to be: A report on the classroom war behind the crisis in our schools.* New York: Simon & Schuster.

Hesse, M. (1980). *Revolutions and reconstructions in the philosophy of science.* Brighton, U.K.: Harvester Press.

Hill, G. (August 30, 1981). Of mice and men and now computers. *New York Times,* E–18.

Hirsch, E. D., Jr. (1988). *Cultural literacy: What every American needs to know.* New York: Vintage Books.

Hogan, R. (April, 1979). An interview with Robert Hogan. *APA Monitor,* 4–5.

Hollinger, D. A. (1985). *In the American province: Studies in the history and historiography of ideas.* Bloomington: Indiana University Press.

Holt, J. (1970). *How children learn.* New York: Dell.

Horgan, J. (1996). *The end of science: Facing the limits of knowledge in the twilight of the scientific age.* Reading, MA: Addison-Wesley.

Horst, P., Nay, J. N., Scanlon, J. W., & Wholey, J. S. (1974). Program management and the federal evaluator. *Public Administration Review, 34,* 300–308.

Horvarth, A. O., & Symonds, B. D. (1991). Relation between working alliance and outcome in psychotherapy: A meta-analysis. *Journal of Consulting and Clinical Psychology, 38,* 139–149.

Hoshmand, L. T., & Polkinghorne, D. E. (1992). Refining the science-practice relationship and professional training. *American Psychologist, 47,* 55–66.

Howard, K. I., Moras, K., Brill, P. L., Martinovich, Z., & Lutz, W. (1996). Evaluation of psychotherapy: Efficacy, effectiveness, and patient progress. *American Psychologist, 51,* 1059–1064.

Hughes, R. (February 3, 1992). The fraying of America. *Time,* 44–49.

Jacobson, N. S., & Christensen, A. (1996). Studying the effectiveness of psychotherapy: How well can clinical trials do the job? *American Psychologist, 51,* 1031–1039.

Jacoby, R. (1994). *Dogmatic wisdom: How the culture wars divert education and distract America*. New York: Anchor/Doubleday.

James, W. (1955). *Pragmatism and four essays from "The Meaning of Truth."* New York: Meriden Books.

Johnson, P. (1991). *Modern times: From the twenties to the nineties*. Rev. ed. New York: HarperCollins.

Jones, W. T. (1977). The age of reason. In *The World Book Encyclopedia*, vol. 1, 130–130a.

Kanfer, F. H., & Schefft, B. K. (1988). *Guiding the process of therapeutic change*. Champaign, IL: Research Press.

Karasu, T. B. (1986). The specificity versus nonspecificity dilemma: Towards identifying therapeutic change agents. *American Journal of Psychiatry, 134*, 687–695.

Karon, B. P. (1995). Provision of psychotherapy under managed care: A growing crisis and national nightmare. *Professional Psychology: Research and Practice, 25*, 5–9.

Kazdin, A. E. (1982). *Single-case research designs: Methods for clinical and applied settings*. New York: Oxford University Press.

Keller, E. F., & Flax, J. (1988). Missing relations in psychoanalysis: A feminist critique of traditional and contemporary accounts of analytic theory and practice. In S. B. Messer, L. A. Sass, & R. L. Woolfolk, eds., *Hermeneutics and psychological theory*, 334–366. New Brunswick, NJ: Rutgers University Press.

Kernan, A. B. (January 22, 1992). The death of literature. *Princeton Alumni Weekly*, 11–15.

Kidder, T. (1989). *Among schoolchildren*. Boston: Houghton Mifflin.

Kiesler, D. J. (1966). Some myths of psychotherapy research and the search for a paradigm. *Psychological Bulletin, 65*, 110–136.

———. (1971). Experimental designs in psychotherapy research. In A. E. Bergin & S. L. Garfield, eds., *Handbook of psychotherapy and behavior change: An empirical analysis*, 36–74. New York: John Wiley.

Kimball, R. (1990). *Tenured radicals: How politics has corrupted our higher education*. New York: Harper & Row.

Kimble, G. A. (1984). Psychology's two cultures. *American Psychology, 39*, 833–839.

———. (1985). Conditioning and learning. In S. Koch & D. E. Leary, eds., *A century of psychological science*, 284–321. New York: McGraw-Hill.

Kiresuk, T. J. (1973). Goal attainment scaling at a county mental health service. *Evaluation, 1*, Special Monograph, 12–18.

Kiresuk, T. J., & Lund, S. H. (1978). Goal attainment scaling. In C. C. Attkisson, W. A. Hargreaves, M. J. Horowitz, & J. E. Sorensen, eds., *Evaluation of human service programs*, 341–370. New York: Academic Press.

Kiresuk, T. J., & Sherman, R. E. (1968). Goal attainment scaling: A general method for evaluating comprehensive community mental health programs. *Community Mental Health Journal, 4,* 443–453.

Koch, S. (1959). Epilogue. In S. Koch, ed., *Psychology: A study of a science,* vol. 3. New York: McGraw-Hill.

Koch, S., & Leary, D. E. (1985). *A century of psychology as a science.* New York: McGraw-Hill.

Kohl, H. (1968). *Thirty-six children.* New York: New American Library.

Kollock, P., & O'Brien, J. (1994). *The production of reality: Essays and readings in social psychology.* Thousand Oaks, CA: Pine Forge/Sage.

Kolodner, J. L. (1997). Educational implications of analogy: A view from case-based reasoning. *American Psychologist, 52,* 57–66.

Kozol, J. (1967). *Death at an early age: The destruction of the hearts and minds of Negro children in the Boston Public Schools.* Boston: Houghton Mifflin.

Krasner, L., & Houts, A. C. (1984). A study of the "value" systems of behavioral scientists. *American Psychologist, 39,* 840–850.

Kratochwill, T. R., ed. (1978). *Single-subject research: Strategies for evaluating change.* New York: Academic Press.

Krueger, R. A., & King, J. A. (1997). *Involving community members in focus groups.* Thousand Oaks, CA: Sage.

Kuhn, T. S. (1962). *The structure of scientific revolutions.* Chicago: University of Chicago Press.

———. (1970). *The structure of scientific revolutions.* 2d ed. Chicago: University of Chicago Press.

Lambert, M. J. (1992). Psychotherapy outcome research: Implications for integration. In J. C. Norcross & M. R. Goldfried, eds., *Handbook of psychological integration,* 94–129. New York: Basic Books.

Lambert, M. J., & Okiishi, J. (1997). The effects of the individual psychotherapist and implications for future research. *Clinical Psychology: Research and Practice, 4,* 66–75.

Lawson, D. M. (1983). Alcoholism. In M. Hersen, ed., *Outpatient behavior therapy: A clinical guide,* 134–172. New York: Grune & Stratton.

LeCompte, M. D., & Preissle, J. (1992). Toward an ethnology of student life in schools and classrooms: Synthesizing the qualitative research tradition. In M. D. LeCompte, W. L. Millroy, & J. Preissle, eds., *The handbook of qualitative research in education,* 815–859. San Diego: Academic Press.

Lehmann, N. (November 12, 1995). Grading the public schools: They're a disaster, they're a triumph, they're beyond evaluation. Choose up to three. *New York Times Book Review,* 14–16.

Leo, J. (April 1, 1996). Shakespeare vs. spiderman. *U.S. News & World Report,* 61.

Lewin, K. (1951). *Field theory in social science.* New York: Harper & Row.

Lewin, R. (1992). *Complexity: Life at the edge of chaos.* New York: Macmillan.

Lieberman, R. P., ed. (1992). *Handbook of psychiatric rehabilitation.* New York: Elsevier.

Lilienfeld, R. (1978). *The rise of systems theory: An ideological analysis.* New York: John Wiley.

Lincoln, Y. S., & Guba, E. G. (1985). *Naturalistic inquiry.* Newbury Park, CA: Sage.

Luborsky, L. L., McLellen, A. T., Diguer, L., Woody, G., & Seligman, D. A. (1997). The psychotherapist matters: Comparisons of outcomes across twenty-two therapists and seven patient samples. *Clinical Psychology: Research and Practice, 4,* 53–65.

Luborsky, L., Singer, B., & Luborsky, L. (1975). Comparative studies of psychotherapies: Is it true that "everyone has won and all must have prizes?" *Archives of General Psychiatry, 32,* 995–1008.

Lyons, J. S., Howard, K. I., O'Mahoney, M. T., & Lish, J. D. (1996). *The measurement and management of clinical outcomes in mental health.* New York: John Wiley.

Lyons, L. C., & Woods, P. J. (1991). The efficacy of rational-emotive therapy: A quantitative review of the outcome research. *Clinical Psychology Review, 11,* 357–369.

Macchia, P. (1995). Quality care: Who's kidding whom. *New Jersey Psychologist, 45,* 10.

MacCorquodale, K., & Meehl, P. E. (1948). On the distinction between hypothetical constructs and intervening variables. *Psychological Review, 55,* 95–107.

Magill, F. N. (1990). *Masterpieces of philosophy.* New York: HarperCollins.

Mangan, K. S. (September 1, 1988). Rift among psychologists prompts academics to form new society: Two thousand are said to join. *Chronicle of Higher Educations, 35,* A1, A10.

Manning, P. K., & Cullum-Swan, B. (1994). Narrative, content, and semiotic analysis. In N. K. Denzin & Y. S. Lincoln, eds., *Handbook of qualitative research,* 463–478. Thousand Oaks, CA: Sage.

Margolis, J. (1986). *Pragmatism without foundations: Reconciling realism and relativism.* New York: Basil Blackwell.

Marx, M. H., & Cronan-Hillix, W. A. (1987). *Systems and theories in psychology.* 4th ed. New York: McGraw-Hill.

Maslow, A. H. (1950). Self-actualizing people: A study of psychological health. In W. Wolff, ed., *Personality symposium,* no. 1. New York: Grune & Stratton.

McFall, R. M. (July 21, 1995). The future of mental-health care. *Chronicle of Higher Education,* B1–B3.

Meehl, P. E. (1954). *Clinical versus statistical prediction: A theoretical analysis and a review of the evidence.* Minneapolis: University of Minnesota Press.

Mehan, H., & Wood, H. (1994). Five features of reality. In P. Kollock & J. O'Brien (Eds.), *The production of reality: Essays and readings in social psychology,* 314–330. Thousand Oaks, CA: Pine Forge Press.

Meichenbaum, D. (1995). Changing conceptions of cognitive behavior modification: Retrospect and prospect. In M. J. Mahoney, ed., *Cognitive and constructive psychotherapies: Theory, research, and practice,* 20–26. New York: Springer.

Meir, D. (1995). *The power of their ideas: Lessons for America from a small school in Harlem.* Boston: Beacon.

Messer, S. B. (1998). Practice guidelines: Too behavioral? [Response to Nathan's "Practice guidelines: Not yet ideal."] Comment submitted to *American Psychologist.*

Messer, S. B., Sass, L. A., & Woolfolk, R. L., eds. (1988). *Hermeneutics and psychological theory.* New Brunswick, NJ: Rutgers University Press.

Messer, S. B., & Wachtel, P. L. (1997). The contemporary psychotherapeutic landscape: Issues and prospects. In P. L. Wachtel & S. B. Messer, eds., *Theories of psychotherapy: Evolution and current status,* 1–38. Washington, DC: APA Books.

Messer, S. B., & Warren, S. (1995). *Shortterm psychodynamic therapy.* New York: Guilford Press.

Messer, S. B., & Winokur, M. (1984). Ways of knowing and visions of reality in psychoanalytic therapy and behavior therapy. In H. Arkowitz & S. B. Messer, eds., *Psychoanalytic therapy and behavior therapy: Is integration impossible?* 63–100. New York: Plenum.

Miles, M. B., & Huberman, A. M. (1984). *Qualitative data analysis: A sourcebook of new methods.* Newbury Park, CA: Sage.

Miller, G. A. (1956). The magical number seven, plus or minus two: Some limits on our capacity for processing information. *Psychological Review, 63,* 81–97.

Miller, J. G. (1978). *Living systems.* New York: McGraw-Hill.

Miller, R. B. (1992). *The restoration of dialogue: Readings in the philosophy of clinical psychology.* Washington, DC: American Psychological Association.

Miller, S. D., Duncan, B. L., & Hubble, M. A. (1997). *Escape from Babel: Toward a unifying language for psychotherapy practice.* New York: W. W. Norton.

Mills, C. W. (1951). *White collar: The American middle classes.* New York: Oxford University Press.

Moore, W. E. (1963). *Social change.* Englewood Cliffs, NJ: Prentice-Hall.

Morell, J. A. (1979). *Program evaluation in social research.* Elmsford, NY: Pergamon Press.

Morgan, G. (1986). *Images of organization.* Newbury Park, CA: Sage.

Mosle, S. (September 29, 1996a). Doing our homework: Two books examine the new debates about achieving better and more equitable education. *New York Times Book Review,* 14–16.

———. (October 27, 1996b). The answer is national standards. *New York Times Magazine*, 44–47, 56, 68.

———. (August 31, 1997). The stealth chancellor. *New York Times Magazine*, 31–33, 36–37, 48–52, 60–61.

Murray, H. A., & Kluckhohn, C. (1953). Outline of a conception of personality. In C. Kluckhohn, H. A. Murray, & D. Schneider, eds., *Personality in nature, society, and culture.* 2d ed. New York: Knopf.

Nathan, P. E. (1997). Fiddling while psychology burns? *Register Report, 23,* 1, 4–5, 10.

———. (1998). Practice guidelines: Not yet ideal. *American Psychologist, 53,* 290–299.

Nathan, P. E., & Gorman, J. M., eds. (1998). *A guide to treatments that work.* New York: Oxford University Press.

National Commission on Excellence in Education (1983). *A nation at risk: The imperatives for educational reform.* Washington, DC: U.S. Government Printing Office.

Neigher, W. D., & Fishman, D. B. (1985). From science to technology: Reducing problems in mental health evaluation by paradigm shift. In P. H. Rossi, H. F. Freeman, & L. Burstein, eds., *Improving data collection reliability in program evaluation,* 263–298. Beverly Hills, CA: Sage.

Neimeyer, R. A. (1995). Constructivist psychotherapies: Features, foundations, and future directions. In R. A. Neimeyer & M. J. Mahoney, eds., *Constructivism in psychotherapy,* 11–38. Washington, DC: American Psychological Association.

Nessel, J. (1982). Understanding psychological man: A state-of-the-science report. *Psychology Today, 16,* 40–59.

Newman, F., & Holzman, L. (1996). *Unscientific psychology: A cultural-performatory approach to understanding human life.* Westport, CT: Praeger.

Nisbet, R. (1976). *Sociology as an art form.* London: Oxford University Press.

Nyden, P., Figert, A., Shibley, M., & Burrows, D., eds. (1997). *Building community: Social science in action.* Thousand Oaks, CA: Pine Forge Press.

Nyden, P., & Wiewel, W. (1992). Collaborative research: Harnessing the tensions between researcher and practitioner. *American Sociologist, 23,* 43–55.

Olson, L. (January 22, 1997). Keeping tabs on quality: America's public school systems are riddled with excellence but rife with mediocrity. *Education Week (Supplement), 16,* 7–17.

Orlinsky, D. E., Grawe, K., Parks, B. K. (1994). Process and outcome in psychotherapy. In A. E. Bergin & S. L. Garfield, eds., *Handbook of psychotherapy and behavior change,* 270–378. 4th ed. New York: John Wiley.

Orlinsky, D. E., & Howard, K. I. (1986). Process and outcome in psychotherapy. In A. E. Bergin & S. L. Garfield, eds., *Handbook of psychotherapy and behavior change.* 3d ed. New York: Wiley.

Osborne, D., & Gaebler, T. (1992). *Reinventing government: How the entrepreneurial spirit is transforming the public sector.* Reading, MA: Addison-Wesley.

Packer, M. J. (1985). Hermeneutic inquiry in the study of human conduct. *American Psychologist, 40,* 1081–1093.

Palmer, R. E. (1969). *Hermeneutics: Interpretation theory in Schleiermacher, Dilthey, Heidegger, and Gadamer.* Evanston, IL: Northwestern University Press.

Parloff, M. B. (1980). Psychotherapy and research: An anaclitic depression. *Psychiatry, 43,* 279–293.

Patton, M. Q. (1978). *Utilization-focused evaluation.* Beverly Hills, CA: Sage.

———. (1980). *Qualitative evaluation methods.* Beverly Hills, CA: Sage.

———. (1997). *Utilization-focused evaluation.* 3d ed. Beverly Hills, CA: Sage.

Penrose, R. (1989). *The emperor's new mind.* New York: Oxford University Press.

Pepper, S. (1942). *World hypotheses: A study in evidence.* Berkeley, CA: University of California Press.

Persons, J. B. (1993). Outcome of psychotherapy for unipolar depression. In T. R. Giles, ed., *Handbook of effective psychotherapy,* 305–323. New York: Plenum.

Peterson, D. R. (1987). The role of assessment in professional psychology. In D. R. Peterson & D. B. Fishman, eds., *Assessment for decision,* 5–43. New Brunswick, NJ: Rutgers University Press.

———. (1991). Connection and disconnection of research and practice in the education of professional psychologists. *American Psychologist, 46,* 422–429.

———. (1995). The gift of diversity. Invited address at the Annual Convention of the American Psychological Association, New York City.

———. (1997). *Educating professional psychologists: History and guiding conception.* Washington, DC: American Psychological Association.

Peterson, D. R., & Fishman, D. B., eds. (1987). *Assessment for decision.* New Brunswick, NJ: Rutgers University Press.

Pitkin, H. F., & Shumer, S. M. (1982). On participation. *Democracy, 2,* 43–54.

Polkinghorne, D. E. (1992). Postmodern epistemology of practice. In S. Kvale, ed., *Psychology and postmodernism,* 146–165. Newbury Park, CA: Sage.

Popper, K. R. (1959). *The logic of scientific discovery.* London: Hutchison.

Price, R. H., & Cherniss, C. (1977). Training for a new profession: Research as social action. *Professional Psychology, 8,* 222–231.

Prilleltensky, I. (1994). *The morals and politics of psychology: Psychological discourse and the status quo.* Albany: SUNY Press.

Princeton Alumni Weekly (January 22, 1992). The diversity table. *Princeton Alumni Weekly, 92,* 10.

Project MATCH Research Group (1997). Matching alcoholism treatments to client heterogeneity: Project MATCH posttreatment drinking outcomes. *Journal of Studies on Alcohol*, *58*, 7–29.

Quine, W. V. O. (1951). The two dogmas of empiricism. *Philosophical Review*, *60*, 20–43. Reprinted in W. V. O. Quine, *From a logical point of view*, 20–46. Cambridge, MA: Harvard University Press, 1953.

———. (1953). *From a logical point of view*. Cambridge, MA: Harvard University Press.

———. (1960). *Word and object*. Cambridge, MA: MIT Press.

———. (1975). The nature of natural knowledge. In S. Gutterplan, ed., *Mind and language*. Oxford: Clarendon Press.

———. (1981). *Theories and things*. Cambridge, MA: Belknap Press of Harvard University Press.

Raimy, V. C., ed. (1950). *Training in clinical psychology*. New York: Prentice Hall.

Reason, P. (1994). Three approaches to participative inquiry. In N. K. Denzin & Y. S. Lincoln, eds., *Handbook of qualitative research*, 324–339. Thousand Oaks, CA: Sage.

Redhead, M. (September 28, 1997). What we don't know: Science has not got as far as the public thinks it has. *New York Times Book Review*, 27.

Reich, C. A. (1971). *The greening of America*. New York: Bantam.

Rice, C. E. (1997). Scenarios: The scientist-practitioner split and the future of psychology. *American Psychologist*, *52*, 1173–1181.

Ricoeur, P. (1981). *Hermeneutics and the human sciences*. Ed. and trans. J. B. Thompson. New York: Cambridge University Press.

Riesman, D. (1955). *The lonely crowd: A study of the changing American character*. New York: Doubleday.

Riger, S. (1992). Epistemological debates, feminist voices: Science, social values, and the study of women. *American Psychologist*, *47*, 730–740.

Roiphe, K. (June 13, 1993a). Date rape's other victim: In their claims of a date-rape epidemic on campus, feminists subvert their own cause. *New York Times Magazine*, 26, 28–30, 40, 68.

———. (1993b). *The morning after: Sex, fear, and feminism on campus*. New York: Little, Brown & Company.

Rorty, R. (1979). *Philosophy and the mirror of nature*. Princeton, NJ: Princeton University Press.

———. (1982). *Consequences of pragmatism*. Minneapolis: University of Minnesota Press.

———. (1989a). Solidarity or objectivity. In M. Krausz, ed., *Relativism: Interpretation and confrontation*, 35–50. Notre Dame, IN: University of Notre Dame Press. Also in R. Rorty, *Objectivity, relativism, and truth*, 21–34. New York: Cambridge University Press, 1991.

———. (1989b). *Contingency, irony, and solidarity*. New York: Cambridge University Press.

———. (1991). *Objectivity, relativism, and truth*. New York: Cambridge University Press.

Rose, M. (1995). *Possible lives: The promise of public education in America*. New York: Penguin Books.

Rosenau, P. M. (1992). *Post-modernism and the social sciences: Insights, inroads, and intrusions*. Princeton, NJ: Princeton University Press.

Ross, D. (1991). *The origins of American social science*. New York: Cambridge University Press.

Rossi, P. H., & Freeman, H. E. (1985). *Evaluation: A systematic approach*. 3d ed. Beverly Hills, CA: Sage.

———. (1993). *Evaluation: A systematic approach*. 5th ed. Thousand Oaks, CA: Sage.

Roth, A., & Fonagy, P. (1996). *What works for whom? A critical review of psychotherapy research*. New York: Guilford Press.

Roth, P. A. (1987). *Meaning and method in the social sciences: A case for methodological pluralism*. Ithaca, NY: Cornell University Press.

Rothman, R. (March 1, 1990). From a "great debate" to a full-scale war: Dispute over teaching reading heats up. *Education Week*, 1.

Routman, R. (1988). *Transitions: From literature to literacy*. Portsmouth, NH: Heinemann

Ruben, B. D., ed. (1995). *Quality in higher education*. New Brunswick, NJ: Transaction.

Ryan, A. (1995). *John Dewey and the high tide of American liberalism*. New York: W. W. Norton.

Ryder, R. G. (1987). *The realistic therapist: Modesty and relativism in therapy and research*. Newbury Park, CA: Sage.

Sabine, G. H. (1950). *A history of political theory*. New York: Henry Holt.

Sanders, J. R., ed. (1994). *The program evaluation standards: How to assess evaluations of educational programs*. 2d ed. Thousand Oaks, CA: Sage.

Sandia National Laboratories (1993). Perspectives on education in America: An annotated briefing. *Journal of Educational Research*, 86, 259–310.

Sass, L. (1992). *Madness and modernism: Insanity in the light of modern art, literature, and thought*. New York: Basic Books.

———. (in press). Ambiguity is of the essence: The relevance of hermeneutics for psychoanalysis. In P. Marcus & A. Rosenberg, eds., *Psychoanalytic versions of the human condition and clinical practice*. New York: New York University Press.

Scarr, S. (1985). Construing psychology: Making facts and fables for our times. *American Psychology*, 40, 499–512.

Schechter, D. (1997). *The more you watch, the less you know: News wars/(sub)merged hopes/media adventures*. New York: Seven Stories Press.

Schensul, J. J., & Schensul, S. L. (1992). Collaborative research: Methods of inquiry for social change. In M. D. LeCompte, W. L. Millroy, & J. Preissle, eds., *The handbook of qualitative research in education*, 161–200. San Diego: Academic Press.

Scheper-Hughes, N. (May 7, 1995). The end of anthropology: Clifford Geertz reflects on a much reduced science. *New York Times Book Review*, 22–23.

Schön, D.A. (1983). *The reflective practitioner: How professionals think in action.* New York: Basic Books.

———. (1987). *Educating the reflective practitioner: Toward a new design for teaching and learning in the professions.* San Francisco: Jossey-Bass.

Schooland, K. (1990). *Shogun's ghost: The dark side of Japanese education.* New York: Begin & Garvey.

Schorr, L. B. (1997). *Common purpose: Strengthening families and neighborhoods to rebuild America.* New York: Anchor/Doubleday.

Schrag, P. (October 1997). The near-myth of our failing schools. *Atlantic Monthly, 280,* 72–74, 76, 78, 80.

Scriven, M. (1967). The methodology of evaluation. In R. W. Tyler, R. M. Gagne, & M. Scriven, eds., *Perspectives in curriculum evaluation*, 39–83. AERA Monograph Series on Curriculum Evaluation, no. 1. Chicago: Rand McNally.

———. (1972). Pros and cons about goal-free evaluation. *Evaluation Comment, 3,* 1–7.

———. (1980). *The logic of evaluation.* Inverness, CA: Edgepress.

———. (1983). Evaluation ideologies. In G. F. Madaus, M. Scriven, & D. L. Stufflebeam, eds., *Evaluation models: Viewpoints on educational and human services evaluation,* 229–260. Boston: Kluwer-Nijhoff.

Seidman, S., & Wagner, D. G., eds. (1992). *Postmodernism and social theory.* Cambridge, MA: Blackwell.

Seligman, M. E. P. (1995). The effectiveness of psychotherapy: The *Consumer Reports* study. *American Psychologist, 50,* 965–974.

———. (1996a). Science as an ally of practice. *American Psychologist, 51,* 1072–1079.

———. (1996b). A creditable beginning. *American Psychologist, 51,* 1086–1088.

Shadish, W. R., Cook, T. D., & Leviton, L. C. (1991). *Foundations of program evaluation: Theories of practice.* Newbury Park, CA: Sage.

Shaffer, L. S. (1977). The golden fleece: Anti-intellectualism and social science. *American Psychologist, 32,* 814–823.

Short, R. J., & Talley, R. C. (1997). Rethinking psychology and the schools: Implications of recent national policy. *American Psychologist, 52,* 234–240.

Shweder, R. A. (1991). *Thinking through cultures: Expeditions in cultural psychology.* Cambridge, MA: Harvard University Press.

Simonton, D. K. (1990). *Psychology, science, & history: An introduction to historiometry.* New Haven, CT: Yale University Press.

Sizer, T. R. (1984). *Horace's compromise: The dilemma of the American high school*. Boston: Houghton Mifflin.

———. (1992). *Horace's school: Redesigning the American high school*. Boston: Houghton Mifflin.

———. (1996). *Horace's hope: What works for the American high school*. Boston: Houghton Mifflin.

Skinner, B. F. (1957). *Verbal behavior*. New York: Appleton-Century-Crofts.

Smith, H. (1995). *Rethinking America: A new game plan from the American innovators—schools, business, people, work*. New York: Random House.

Smith, M. B. (1987). Humanistic psychology. In R. J. Corsini, ed., *Concise encyclopedia of psychology*, 540–543. New York: John Wiley.

———. (1994). Selfhood at risk: Postmodern perils, and the perils of postmodernism. *American Psychologist*, 49, 405–411.

Smith, M. L., & Glass, G. V. (1977). Meta-analysis of psychotherapy outcome studies. *American Psychologist*, 32, 752–760.

Smith, M. L., Glass, G. V., & Miller, T. I. (1980). *The benefits of psychotherapy*. Baltimore: Johns Hopkins University Press.

Sperry, L., Brill, P. L., Howard, K. I., & Grissom, G. R. (1996). *Treatment outcomes in psychotherapy and psychiatric interventions*. New York: Brunner/Mazel.

Spiro, M. (1978). Culture and human nature. In G. Spindler, ed., *The making of psychological anthropology*, 330–360. Berkeley: University of California Press.

Spragins, E. E. (December 15, 1997). How to choose an HMO. *Newsweek*, 72–74, 77, 81.

Stake, R. E. (1980). Program evaluation, particularly responsive evaluation. In W. B. Dockrell & D. Hamilton, eds., *Rethinking educational research*, 72–87. London: Hodder & Stoughton.

———. (1994). Case studies. In N. K. Denzin, & Y. S. Lincoln, eds., *Handbook of qualitative research*, 236–247. Thousand Oaks, CA: Sage Publications.

———. (1995). *The art of case study research*. Thousand Oaks, CA: Sage.

Stein, D. M., & Lambert, M. J. (1984). On the relationship between therapist experience and psychotherapy outcome. *Clinical Psychology Review*, 4, 127–142.

———. (1995). Graduate training in psychotherapy: Are therapy outcomes enhanced? *Journal of Consulting and Clinical Psychology*, 63, 182–186.

Steinberg, J. (January 4, 1997a). Best of the city's schools share vision, not methods. *New York Times*, 1, 28.

———. (January 4, 1997b). Crew to add performance standards to superintendents' contracts. *New York Times*, 28.

———. (December 14, 1997c). Class wars: Clashing over education's one true faith. *New York Times Week in Review*, 1, 14.

———. (March 19, 1998). Report urges hybrid approach to reading education. *New York Times on the Web: www.nytimes.com.*

Stevenson, H. W., & Stigler, J. W. (1992). *The learning gap: Why our schools are failing and what we can learn from Japanese and Chinese education.* New York: Simon & Schuster.

Stiles, W. B., Shapiro, D. A., & Elliott, R. (1986). Are all psychotherapists equivalent? *American Psychologist, 41,* 165–180.

Stone, D. (May 1, 1994). This teacher commands attention. *Wisconsin State Journal.*

Strauss, A., & Corbin, J. (1990). *Basics of qualitative research: Grounded theory procedures and techniques.* Newbury Park, CA: Sage.

Stricker, G. (1994). Reflections on psychotherapy integration. *Clinical Psychology: Research and Practice, 1,* 3–12.

Stricker, G., & Trierweiler, S. J. (1995). The local clinical scientist: A bridge between science and practice. *American Psychologist, 50,* 995–1002.

Stringer, E. T. (1996). *Action research: a handbook for practitioners.* Thousand Oaks, CA: Sage.

Strupp, H. H., & Hadley, S. W. (1979). Specific versus nonspecific factors in psychotherapy. *Archives of General Psychiatry, 36,* 1125–1136.

Sykes, C. J. (1988). *Profscam: Professors and the demise of higher education.* Washington, DC: Regnery Gateway.

———. (1995). *Dumbing down our kids: Why America's children feel good about themselves but can't read, write, or add.* New York: St. Martin's Press.

Tannen, D. (1990). *You just don't understand.* New York: William Morrow.

Task Force on Promotion and Dissemination of Psychological Procedures. (1995). Training in and dissemination of empirically validated psychological treatments. *Clinical Psychologist, 48,* 3–23.

Taube, C. A., Mechanic, D., & Hohmann, A. A. (1989). *The future of mental health services research.* Washington, DC: U.S. Department of Health and Human Services.

Thilly, F., & Wood, L. (1957). *A history of philosophy.* New York: Henry Holt.

Thompson, K. (1975). *Auguste Comte: The foundation of sociology.* New York: Wiley.

Toch, T. (April 1, 1996). The case for tough standards. *U.S. News & World Report,* 52–56.

Todorov, T. (April 27, 1998). The surrender to nature: A review of E. O. Wilson's *Consilience: The unity of knowledge. New Republic,* 29–33.

Toulmin, S. (1990). *Cosmopolis: The hidden agenda of modernity.* Chicago: University of Chicago Press.

Turk, D. C., & Salovey, P. (1985). Cognitive structures, cognitive processes, and cognitive-behavior modification: II. Judgements and inferences of the clinician. *Cognitive Therapy and Research, 9,* 19–33.

Urban, H. B. (1983). Phenomenological-humanistic approaches. In M. Hersen, A. E. Kazdin, & A. S. Bellack, eds., *The clinical psychology handbook*, 155–175. Elmsford, NY: Pergamon Press.

Van Fraassen, B. C. (1980). *The scientific image*. Oxford: Clarendon Press.

Vitz, P. C. (1990). The use of stories in moral development: New psychological reasons for an old educational method. *American Psychologist, 45*, 709–720.

Wade, N. (April 30, 1982). Smart apes, or dumb? *New York Times*, 28.

Wagner, T. (1994). *How schools change: Lessons from three communities*. Boston: Beacon.

Watson, I. (1994). The case for case-based reasoning. Unpublished manuscript, available on the internet and from Ian Watson, University of Salford, Bridgewater Building, Salford, M5 4WT; e-mail: i.d.watson@surveying.salford.ac.uk.

Weiss, C. H., ed. (1972). *Evaluating social action programs*. Boston: Allyn & Bacon.

West, C. (1989). *The American evasion of philosophy: A genealogy of pragmatism*. Madison: University of Wisconsin Press.

Westbrook, R. B. (1991). *John Dewey and American democracy*. Ithaca, NY: Cornell University Press.

White, M., & Epston, D. (1990). *Narrative means to therapeutic ends*. New York: Norton.

Whitehead, A. N. (1925). *Science and the modern world*. New York: Macmillan.

Wholey, J. S. (1983). *Evaluation and effective program management*. Boston: Little, Brown & Company.

Wholey, J. S., Scanlon, J. W., Duffy, H. G., Fukumoto, J. S., & Vogt, L. M. (1970). *Federal evaluation policy: Analyzing the effects of public programs*. Washington, DC: Urban Institute.

Whyte, W. H., Jr. (1956). *The organization man*. New York: Simon & Schuster.

Widmeyer Group (July/August, 1994). American Psychological Association (APA) member focus groups on the health care environment: A summary report. Conducted for the APA Practice Directorate. Washington, DC: American Psychological Association.

Wilson, E. O. (1978). *On human nature*. Cambridge, MA: Harvard University Press.

———. (1998). *Consilience: The unity of knowledge*. New York: Alfred A. Knopf.

Wilson, G. T. (1996). Manual-based treatments: The clinical application of research findings. *Behaviour Research and Therapy, 34*, 295–315.

———. (1997). Treatment manuals in clinical practice. *Behaviour Research and Therapy, 35*, 205–210.

Wilson, K. G., & Daviss, B. (1994). *Redesigning education*. New York: Henry Holt.

Winch, P. (1958). *The idea of a social science and its relationship to philosophy* (originally published in 1946.) London: Routledge & Kegan Paul.

Windle, C., & Neigher, W. D. (1978). Ethical problems in program evaluation: Advice for trapped evaluators. *Evaluation and Program Planning, 1,* 97–108.

Wiseman, F. (1994). *High School II.* Documentary film for the Public Broadcasting System (PBS).

Wittgenstein, L. (1953). *Philosophical investigations.* Trans. G. E. M. Anscombe. New York: Macmillan.

———. (1995). *Tractatus logico-philosophicus* (originally published in 1921). London: Routledge & Kegan Paul.

Wood, G. H. (1992). *Schools That work: American's most innovative public education programs.* New York: Penguin Books.

Woolfolk, R. L. (1992). Hermeneutics, social constructionism, and other items of intellectual fashion: Intimations for clinical science. *Behavior Therapy, 23,* 213–223.

Woolfolk, R. L., & Richardson, F. C. (1984). Behavior therapy and the ideology of modernity. *American Psychologist, 39,* 777–786.

Wright, R. (1994). *The moral animal: Evolutionary psychology and everyday life.* New York: Random House.

Yin, R. K. (1989). *Case study research: Design and methods.* Rev. ed. Newbury Park, CA: Sage.

———. (1993). *Applications of case study research.* Newbury Park, CA: Sage Publications.

Zigler, E. (1989). Addressing the nation's child care crisis: The school of the twenty-first century. *American Journal of Orthopsychiatry, 59,* 485–491.

Index

The references to the figures are rendered in italics.

accountability: managed care exerting pressure for, 220; performance accountability, 174; in pragmatic psychology, 291–92

accountability model of evaluation, 144, 145, 321n.35

accuracy standards, 190

action: culture in rational agency, 22; practical action, 113–15, 131; relativism and moral responsibility for, 112. *See also* human behavior

action component in disciplined-inquiry model: in "Cindy" PTSD case, 240–42; in disciplined-inquiry model, *11, 12;* in educational reform, 275; in pragmatic and disciplined-inquiry models compared, 189, *189;* in pragmatic psychology, 136–37

action research, 27–28, 148, 321n.33

adoption of innovation, 181

advocacy model of evaluation, 144, 145

advocacy research, 147–48

affective learning, 250

alien abduction, 205; and licensing and accreditation, 205–6

alternative schools: in New York City, 258–59, 270; for school choice, 277

Altman, Irwin: on pendulum swings in history, 29, 36–37; on psychology before 1879, 38; on psychology from 1879 to 1960, 39, 42; Toulmin compared with, 121; on unifying trends since 1960, 306n.1; on worldviews in psychology, 55

"Ambiguity Is of the Essence" (Sass), 298n.30

amelioration model of evaluation, 144, 145, 321n.35

America 2000, 277

American Education, A National Failure? (Rickover), 245

American Evasion of Philosophy, The: A Genealogy of Pragmatism (West), 107

American Psychiatric Association, 227

American Psychological Association (APA): APS splits from, 202, 298n.26, 306n.35; centenary of Wundt's laboratory celebrated by, 35; clinical psychology's growth in, 326n.15; encouragement of diversity required of, 284; formation of, 38; growth since 1960s, 46; a pragmatist division for, 286; PsycINFO database, 19; for publishing and sponsoring pragmatic case studies, 288; scholar-practitioners allied with, 203; scientist-practitioners in, 327n.30; splits in, 41; Task Force on Promotion and Dissemination of Psychological Procedures, 211–12, 214, 329n.84

American Psychological Society (APS), 202, 203, 298n.26, 306n.35

American Psychologist (journal), 62, 330n.98

"American Psychology in the 1980s: Who Will Buy?" (Fishman and Neigher), xxii

amorality, as modernist value, 69

analytic/synthetic distinction, 80–81

Anglo-American philosophy: British empiricism, 33, 103; and Continental philosophy, 103–6; logical positivism as dominating, 103. *See also* pragmatism

animal learning research: of Hull, 49–50; as not applicable to war requirements, 41; in psychological research of 1950s, 22–23, 47 anthropology: and the cognitive revolution, 53; cultural relativism in, 110–11; Geertz on Balinese cockfights, 125–27; the local as focus of ethnography, 123

antifoundationalism: counterculture of the 1960s associated with, xxi; foundationlessness as postmodern theme, 5, 6, 295n.3; of Rorty, 119

anti-Vietnam War protests, 44

application, 197–279; as preceding theory in pragmatic paradigm, 2; theory as preceding in positivism, 1; Toulmin's call for science to turn toward, 132. *See also* applied psychology

applied behavior analysis, 201

applied psychology: educational psychology as first, 14; the only meaningful psychology as, 28; open-ended complex problems in, 194; positivist model of, 9–10; pragmatic model of, 10–14; pragmatic paradigm in, 199–244; technological model of, xxii, xxiii, xxiv. *See also* clinical psychology; practitioners

applied science model, 9–10, *10*; for clinical psychology, 199–200; community psychology contrasted with, 146, 147; Peterson on, 9–10, 328n.42; scale-up failure in, 149–50; scientist-practitioners subscribing to, 203

Archimedean point, 109, 111

Arendt, Hannah, 114

argumentation, 123

Aristotle, 120–21

artificial intelligence, 51, 53, 192, 193

assessment: in "Cindy" PTSD case, 239; in disciplined-inquiry model, *11, 12*; in pragmatic and disciplined-inquiry models compared, 189, *189*

Assessment for Decision (Peterson and Fishman), xxiii

association, laws of, 34

Association for Advancement of Behavior Therapy, 286

atomic statements, 84, 94

Austin, George, 52

authenticity, *160, 162*, 188

availability heuristic, 212

Ayer, A. J.: and conservative postpositivism, 315n.1; on meaninglessness of metaphysics and ethics, 103; statement of logical positivism, 40; "yea-boo" theory of ethics, 40

Baars, B. J., 23, 301n.63, 308n.16

Baldrige Quality Award, 177, 178, 186–87, 324n.37

Balinese cockfights, 124–27

Bandura, A., 201

Barber, Benjamin, 9

basic research: in applied science model, 10; technology contrasted with, xxii; as value for pragmatism, 283

Bauhaus, 312n.106

Baumeister, R. F., 21

Beaumont, Marie, 164–65

Beck, Aaron, 236–37

behavior, human. *See* human behavior

behavioral science: defined, 303n.71; University of Chicago Committee on Behavioral Sciences, 56. *See also* social science

behaviorism: Bruner's information-processing model contrasted with, 52; disagreement on significance of, xxiv; dominance from 1930s to 1950s, 39; in Hull's learning theory, 49–50; humanistic psychology as alternative to, 48; human science eclipsed by, 58; as natural science approach to human action, 94; as paradigm, 77; during period of systems and schools, 39; in psychological research of 1950s, 22–23; Wittgenstein as attacking foundations of, 86–87

behavior therapy: Association for Advancement of Behavior Therapy, 286; constructivist therapies contrasted with, 202; diversity within, 201. *See also* cognitive behavioral therapy

being-in-the-world, 61–62

benchmarking, 177

Bennett, William, 252

Bentley, Arthur, 55

Berliner, David, 251–55

Berman, J. S., 207

Berman, M., 298n.31

Berman, P., 71

Bernstein, Richard J., 109–15; *Beyond Objectivism and Relativism: Science, Hermeneutics, and Praxis,* 109; on Cartesian Anxiety, 111, 316n.27; con-

structionism of pragmatism of,
297n.11; humanistic values of,
301n.68; objectivism and relativism
contrasted by, 109–11; postmodern
pragmatism of, 102, 109; on postpositivism and Continental philosophy,
315n.6; on practical action, 113–15,
131; on relativism and objectivism as
either/or, 111–13; *The Restructuring of
Social and Political Theory,* 302n.70
Bertalanffy, Ludwig von, 56
*Beyond Objectivism and Relativism: Sci-
ence, Hermeneutics, and Praxis* (Bernstein), 109
bias: clinical judgment as susceptible to
cognitive, 212–13; experimenter, 162,
187. *See also* value-neutral inquiry
Biddle, Bruce, 251–55
bilingual education, 267, 268–69
Bloom, Allan, 311n.103
Bloom, Harold, 91
Bologna, N. C., 331n.109
Boulder model, 41
boundary problem, 157, 168–70
Bourdieu, Pierre, 311n.99
*Breaking the News: How the Media Un-
dermine American Democracy* (Fallows), 338n.13
Bridges, Wendy, 164–66
British empiricism, 33, 103
British Infant School model, 332n.17
Brizius, J. A., 174–75, 324n.29
Bromley, D. B.: on case studies, 319n.6;
pragmatic case studies of, 153; on
quasi-judicial method, 192
Bruner, Jerome: in cognitive revolution,
50–51, 52; on dechronologizing historical events, 310n.74; on meaning versus
information, 53, 97; on propositional
thought, 65, 66; in *Psychology Today*
survey, xxiv; *A Study of Thinking,* 52
Burke, Kenneth, 66
Bush, George, 277
butterfly effect, 79
"buyer's guide" model, 178–79

Calhoun, Karen, 237–44
Campbell, Donald T., 138–39, 142,
176–77, 325nn. 49, 55
Campbell, M. D., 174–75, 324n.29

Camus, Albert, 49
capitalism: logical positivism associated
with, 305n.32; modernist science associated with, 298n.31; positivism associated with, 7; Smith's free market economics, 34
Carnap, Rudolf, 39
Carter, Hodding, xxi
case-based evaluation, 320n.16
case-based reasoning (CBR), 192–95
case histories, 304n.1
cases: components of, 193; in law, 192; as
learning experiences in disciplined-inquiry model, 12; as particular, 123; of
schizophrenia, 129; as starting and ending points for pragmatic psychology, 2.
See also case studies
case studies: boundary problem, 157,
168–70; in disciplined-inquiry model,
138; for educational effectiveness,
15–16, 266; as holistic, systems approach, 16; the individual as focus of,
319n.6; journals as databases of,
20–21; as method for psychology,
130–32; pragmatism focusing on, 131,
153; proprietary nature of case data,
286–87; as unit of analysis in pragmatic
and hermeneutic paradigms, 154. *See
also* databases of case studies;
hermeneutic case studies; pragmatic
case studies; quantitative (positivist)
group studies; written case studies
catalytic authenticity, 163
ceiling effect, 223
Central Park East Elementary School (New
York City), 259
Central Park East Secondary School (New
York City), 259
certainty: conceptual frameworks as lacking absolute, 113; Heisenberg's Uncertainty Principle, 89; pragmatism as
evading quest for, 107; Toulmin on
modernist quest for, 121–22. *See also*
foundationalism
chaos theory, 79–80, 89, 313n.10
charter schools, 258, 259, 277
Chen, H., 139
child-centered education, 248
choice in school selection, 258, 262–63,
277

Christensen, A., 208
"Cindy" case, 237–44, 289–90
civil rights movement, 44
classical humanism, 69
class size, 268
client: in "Cindy" PTSD case, 237–38; in
    community psychology, 146–49; in dis-
    ciplined-inquiry model, 10, *11*; in edu-
    cational reform, 275; identifying,
    143–44; in pragmatic and disciplined-
    inquiry models compared, 188, *189*;
    pragmatic paradigm meeting its ac-
    countability to, 291; pragmatic psychol-
    ogy as beginning with, 136–37
client-centered psychotherapy, 49
clinical management, 236
clinical psychology: applied science model
    in, 199–200; Boulder model for training
    in, 41; community psychology, 146–49;
    culture wars in, 200; fads and fashion
    in, xxii; growth and prosperity of, 200,
    326n.15. *See also* practitioners; psy-
    chotherapy
clinical technicians, 213–14
clinicians. *See* practitioners
Clinton, Bill, 277, 327n.29
Coalition of Essential Schools, 257
cognitive behavioral therapy: Beck's work
    on depression, 236–37; in "Cindy" case,
    243, 289; in diversification of therapeu-
    tic models, 201; EST criteria as rigged in
    favor of, 214; in Project MATCH, 215;
    research in noncognitive-behavioral
    therapies contrasted with, 232
cognitive dissonance, 59
Cognitive Processing Therapy (CPT), 238,
    243
cognitive revolution, 49–53; cognitive be-
    havior therapy deriving from, 201; con-
    trasting inspirations in, 97; as postmod-
    ern, 96
Cohen, D. K., 320n.12
collaborative research: in hermeneutic
    studies, 321n.36; Nyden on, 148; the
    pragmatic case study as allied with,
    148; Schensul and Schensul on,
    322n.46
Comer, James, 16, 259
Committee on Behavioral Sciences (Uni-
    versity of Chicago), 56

*Common Purpose: Strengthening Families
    and Neighborhoods to Rebuild America*
    (Schorr), 149
community mental health, xxii, 296n.10
Community Mental Health Centers
    (CMHC), 178
community psychology, 146–49
COMPASS Treatment System, 228, 230,
    231
complexity theory, 313n.10
computers: artificial intelligence, 51, 53,
    192, 193; for case study databases, 286;
    in education, 258, 262; the mind com-
    pared with, 52, 97
Comte, Auguste, 34–35, 88
concept formation, 52
concluding evaluation: in "Cindy" PTSD
    case, 242–43; in disciplined-inquiry
    model, *11, 12*; in educational reform,
    275; in pragmatic and disciplined-in-
    quiry models compared, 189, *189*
confidentiality, 286
confirmability, *162*, 188
conflict: in democratic politics, 114,
    130, 144; media preference for,
    338n.13
Connerly, Ward, 251
consciousness: as foundational for Conti-
    nental philosophy, 105; Hume's mental
    mechanics of, 33–34; as not objectively
    observable, 23; Penrose on science and,
    91; in postmodern psychology, 24; in
    psychology grounded in culture, 22. *See
    also* intentionality
constructionism. *See* social constructionism
constructive personality change, 232
constructivist clinicians, 203
constructivist therapies, 202, 243–44,
    290
construct validity, *160, 174*, 181–82,
    325n.48
Consumer Price Index (CPI), 181–82
Consumer Reports (magazine), xx, 178,
    215–16, 223–25
content analysis, 98
contextualism, 53–54, 55–56, 57, 97,
    107
Continental philosophy: and Anglo-Ameri-
    can philosophy, 103–6; attacks on logi-
    cal positivism, 102, 104–6; considered

as soft-headed and muddled, 105; convergence with postpositivism, 106, 315nn. 1, 6; five strands of, 103–4. *See also* critical hermeneutics; existentialism; methodological hermeneutics; ontological hermeneutics; phenomenology
Contingency, Irony, and Solidarity (Rorty), 120
contingency theory, 273–74
Cook, T. D., 321n.29, 325nn. 49, 55
cooperative learning, 266
Copernicus, 32
Corbett, H. D., 273, 336n.96
"core knowledge" curriculum, 261, 263, 276
correspondence theory of truth, 108, 115, 130
Cosmopolis: The Hidden Agenda of Modernity (Toulmin), 120
cost-effectiveness analysis, 159, 178–79
counterculture of the 1960s, xxi, 44, 49, 97, 248
credibility, 161, 182–83
Crew, Rudy, 269–71
criterion based tests, 276, 278
critical hermeneutics, 62; in Continental philosophy, 103, 104; and critical postmodernism, 315n.2
critical postmodernism: and community psychology, 147; as controversial, 70; and critical hermeneutics, 315n.2; defined, 6; as leftist, 9; modernism compared with, 69; and positivism, 7, 8; in psychology, 7; and skeptical postmodernism, 7; utopian vision of, 292
critical science evaluation, 140, 145, 321n.24, 322n.36
critical theory: Anglo-American view of, 105; attack on logical positivism, 104; critical hermeneutics as outgrowth of, 62; on limitation of knowledge, 106; as postmodern theme, 6; on power in knowledge-generation, 146; schizophrenia as analyzed by, 128
critical thinking skills, 260, 263
Cronbach, L. J., 139
cultural criticism, xxi
cultural literacy, 260–61, 263
cultural relativism, 69, 110–11
culture: humanities for study of, 21; mind-

as-culture researchers, 97; modern positivism on subjectivity of, 94; and narrative thinking, 66; and nature as interrelated for postmodern constructionism, 96; versus nature in psychology, 21–24, 57; as operating through narrative, 66; rational agency in, 22; thick description for, 65; E. O. Wilson on reducibility of, 314n.47. *See also* multiculturalism
culture wars: in clinical psychology, 200; cultural relativism as at heart of, 110; in current social climate, 1; as diverting attention from real problems, 9; in education, 246, 249–55, 277–78; political correctness debate, 70–71; pragmatic psychology as response to psychology's, 7–9; the psychology wars, 45
curriculum: "core knowledge" curriculum, 261, 263, 276; "great books" approach, 44, 70, 278; national curriculum, 261
Cushman, Philip, 24, 128
"customer driven" programs, 175
cybernetics, 51–52, 56

Dade County, Florida, 256
Darwin, Charles, 36, 88
databases of case studies, 190–95; educational reform cases, 269, 271–73, 275, 336n.89; empirical grounding for, 200; as facilitating program improvement, 291–92; generating and valuing case reports, 287–88; infrastructure for, 286–87; for managed care decision-making, 225–26; matching new cases to, 190–92; plan for creation of, 286–88; in plan to mediate scientist-clinician conflict, 220; purpose of, 133
"Date Rape's Other Victim" (*New York Times Magazine* article), 63–64
Davison, Gerald, 329n.83
Daviss, B., 334n.45
Dawes, Robyn: on actuarial prediction as more accurate than that of clinicians, 209; as catalyst for this study, xix–xx; on clinicians as paying only lip service to science, 205–7; disciplined alternative to dichotomy of, 289; *House of Cards*, xix–xx, 204; on more training as not meaning more therapeutic effective

Dawes, Robyn *(continued)*
ness, 207–9; as natural-science psychologist, xix; as positivist, 298n.26; in sci-
entist-practitioner/scholar-practitioner
battle, 204–17
deconstruction, xxi, 7, 70, 246
"Deep Play: Notes on the Balinese Cockfight" (Geertz), 125
deficit language, 135–36
deinstitutionalization of the mentally ill,
44
Deitchman, S., 320n.12
democracy: conflict in politics of, 114,
130, 144; Dewey on participatory, 131;
education for, 256; pluralism as essential to, 284; pragmatic paradigm as supporting, 290–91; Western tradition of,
113
Denzin, N. K., 64, 65, 302n.70, 309n.65,
310n.74
dependability, 162, 186
dependency inventory, 185
depression, 171, 215, 236
Derrida, Jacques, 146, 311n.99
Descartes, René: Bernstein on Cartesian
Anxiety, 111, 316n.27; Toulmin on
quest for certainty of, 122
design of studies. *See* study design
Dewey, John: low point of influence of,
248; on participatory democracy and
individual fulfillment, 131; in pragmatism's development, xxiv, 103, 107; on
progressive education, 194, 248; renewal of interest in, 332n.16; on scientific habit of mind, 108–9, 206; on self-
action, interaction, and transaction, 55
Diagnostic and Statistical Manual (DSM),
227
dialectic: between formal rationalism and
humanistic pragmatism, 123; of modernism and postmodernism, 93–101;
philosophy as, 26; positivist/modernist
debate in psychology, 7; understanding
as dialectical, 61
dialogue: for dealing with conflict, 114,
130, 144; in interpretivist evaluation,
322n.36
Dilthey, Wilhelm, 57, 60, 308n.39
disciplinary boundaries, 301n.68, 303n.71
disciplined-inquiry model, 10–14, *11*; case

studies in, 138; in "Cindy" PTSD case,
238–44; contrasted with "talk show"
psychology, 289; educational reform
application, 274–75; as integrative,
217; pragmatic case studies compared
with, 188–90, *189*; pragmatic psychology as grounded in, 199, 285; scholar-
practitioners adhering to, 203; science's
meaning in, 206
discussion section of a research article,
159, 180
diversifying forces, 36–37, 96–97
"Dodo Bird verdict," 202, 214
double-blind designs, *162*, 187, *188*, 211
double hermeneutic, 61
Dreyfus, H. L., 13, 194, 217
Dreyfus, S. E., 13, 194, 217
drives, 201
Drucker, Peter, 175
drug abuse, 44
D'Souza, Dinesh, 311n.103
Du Bois, W. E. B., 107
*Dumbing Down Our Kids: Why American
Children Feel Good about Themselves
But Can't Read, Write, or Add* (Sykes),
250

economics, 34, 41
education: bilingual education, 267,
268–69; case-based learning in, 195;
computers in, 258, 262; as in crisis, 1;
critiques of contemporary, 245; culture
wars in, 246, 249–55, 277–78; diversity
of American, 277; expenditures on,
254–55, 334n.42; factory model of,
246–49, 255; the facts about contemporary, 245–46; international comparisons
of, 253–54, 333n.29; knowledge-based
logic in traditional, 194; multiculturalism in, 250, 251, 278; politicization of,
246; pragmatic case studies in, 149;
progressive education, 194, 248, 249,
290; "reinvention" of, 4; research as interdisciplinary in, 303n.71; school-community link, 259–60; schools as excellent sites for preventing problems, 14;
stakeholders in, 143–44; the 3 R's, 251,
262. *See also* curriculum; educational
reform; higher education; testing (educational)

educational psychology, 14
educational reform, 245–79; America
    2000 plan, 277; avoiding forced
    choices in, 290, 337n.10; charter
    schools, 258, 259, 277; choice in
    school selection, 258, 262–63, 277; co-
    operative learning, 266; critical think-
    ing skills, 260, 263; database of case
    studies of, 269, 271–73, 275, 336n.89;
    disciplined-inquiry model applied in,
    274–75; exhibits and portfolios, 257,
    258, 266; Goals 2000 plan, 277, 278,
    279; in-home school movement,
    299n.48; learning communities, 259,
    263; limits of particular programs,
    261–66; one-stop shopping schools,
    260; pragmatic psychology for address-
    ing, 14–16; promising ideas for,
    255–61; school-based management,
    256, 259, 262, 266; smart classrooms,
    256, 262; smart schools, 255–56,
    265–66; special interest pods, 258;
    vouchers, 15, 258, 277; year-round
    schooling, 257, 262, 266. *See also* al-
    ternative schools
educative authenticity, 163
effective ingredients, 19
effectiveness research: *American Psycholo-
    gist* article on, 330n.98; Bologna on,
    331n.109; as focusing on averages, 225;
    in plan to mediate scientist-clinician
    conflict, 219–20; Seligman on efficacy
    research and, 222–23, 329n.84
efficacy research: *American Psychologist*
    article on, 330n.98; Bologna on,
    331n.109; and contextual variations in
    treatment, 236; as focusing on aver-
    ages, 225; in plan to mediate scientist-
    clinician conflict, 219–20; as positivist,
    210–11; Seligman on effectiveness
    research and, 221–23, 329n.84
ego psychology, 201
Einstein, Albert, 56, 89
Elliott, R., 214
embedded-design study, 157, 169
Emerson, Ralph Waldo, 107
emotions: as socially constructed, 63;
    E. O. Wilson's evolutionary account of,
    314n.47
empathy, 201

empirically supported treatment (EST),
    211–12, 213, 214, 216–17, 236
empirically validated treatments (EVTs),
    216–17
empiricism: British empiricism, 33, 103;
    Enlightenment glorification of, 32, 68;
    in logical positivism, 39
"encounter group" movement, 307n.15
End of Science, The (Horgan), 4, 90
English language arts, 278
Enlightenment: empiricism and reason
    glorified by, 32, 68; freedom and de-
    terminism as conflicting in, 300n.60;
    the independent individual's place in,
    310n.88; modernism associated with,
    3, 32, 37, 68, 311n.106; nineteenth-
    century attacks on, 36; social sciences
    originating in, 32; Toulmin on quest
    for certainty of, 121–22; as unifying
    period, 37–38; utopian Cosmopolis
    of, 292
epistemology: diversity as required in, 26;
    the general as focus of, 124; natural sci-
    ence's privileged status, 38; paradigms
    of, 99; and politics, 71; Rorty's metacri-
    tique of, 115–16; six themes of post-
    modernist, 5–6; underlying therapeutic
    models, 201–2. *See also* empiricism;
    foundationalism; knowledge; objec-
    tivism; perspectivism; positivism; post-
    positivism; relativism
Erklaren, 308n.39
Esalen Institute, 307n.15
essentialism: critical postmodernism ac-
    cused of, 7; in feminist psychology, 68
essential schools, 256–57, 259
EST (empirically supported treatment),
    211–12, 213, 214, 216–17, 236
ethics: logical positivism on, 39–40; mod-
    ernist belief in objectivity of, 71; the
    universal in, 123. *See also* morality
evaluability assessment, 320n.16
evaluation: in disciplined-inquiry model,
    10, 11, 12. *See also* concluding evalua-
    tion; monitoring evaluation; program
    evaluation
evolutionary psychology (sociobiology),
    36, 94, 314n.47
evolution by natural selection, 36, 77, 94,
    313n.10

EVTs (empirically validated treatments), 216–17
exhibits and portfolios, 257, 258, 266
existentialism: Anglo-American view of, 105; attack on logical positivism, 104–5; in Continental philosophy, 103, 104; in humanistic psychology, 49; on the inconsistent act, 59; on limitation of knowledge, 106
experience and research, professional. *See* professional experience and research
experiential therapy, 214, 216, 231–32
experimental group study. *See* quantitative (positivist) group study
experimental method, 33
experimental psychology, 49
experimenter bias, *162*, 187
"experimenting society" concept, 139, 142
experiments, 81
expert practitioners, 13, 194, 207, 217
external validity, *161*, 182, 185, 325n.55
extraterrestrials, 205

factory model of education, 246–49, 255
fact/value distinction, 34, 96, 103
Fairdale High School (Louisville, Ky.), 257
Fallows, James, 338n.13
falsifiability, 75–76
family resemblance, 85, 313n.31
family systems therapy, 57, 202, 214, 231–32
Faust, D., 209
feasibility standards, 190
feedback mechanisms, 51–52, 59, 189, *189*, 213, 220
feminine science, 96
feminism: critical science evaluation of, 140; date rape controversy, 63–64; and postmodern diversity, 97; research methods of, 67–69
Feyerabend, Paul, 82–84; critique of logical positivism, 105–6; on limitation of knowledge, 87–88
field theory, 56
Fiore, Edith, 205–6
Firestone, W. A., 273, 336n.96
Fischer, J., 331n.119
Fishman, Daniel B., xxii–xxiii, 139, 233, 324n.14
Fiske, D. W., 302n.70

Fiske, Edward, 255–60, 265–66, 334n.43
Flew, Antony, 76, 89–90, 312n.3
folk psychology, 66
Fonagy, P., 234, 331n.120
formal rationalism, 121
formative evaluation, 142, 320n.16, 321n.35
formism, 53–54
forms of life, 84, 313n.31
formulation: in "Cindy" PTSD case, 239; in disciplined-inquiry model, *11, 12*; in educational reform, 275; in pragmatic and disciplined-inquiry models compared, 189, *189*
Foucault, Michel, 146, 311n.99
foundationalism: an Archimedean point, 109, 111; and Cartesian Anxiety, 111; critical postmodernism accused of, 7; objectivism as, 109; pragmatism as evading foundation, 107. *See also* antifoundationalism
foundationlessness, 5, 6
fourth generation evaluation, 140
Fox, R. E., 206, 328n.41
fragmentariness, 5, 6
Frank, Jerome, 216
Franks, C. M., 324n.14
Fratney School (Milwaukee), 20–21, 300n.55
Freeman, H. E., 139, 141, 179, 181, 320n.18
Free Speech Movement, 44
Freud, Sigmund: the Enlightenment attacked by, 36; skeptical postmodernism influenced by, 311n.99. *See also* psychoanalysis
functionalism, 39

Gadamer, Hans-Georg, 6, 61, 114
Gaebler, T., *174*, 175–76
Galileo, 32, 116–17, 121
Gardner, Howard, 51, 258
Garet, M. S., 320n.12
Geertz, Clifford: on Balinese cockfights, 124–27; on cultural relativism, 110; on movement beyond objectivism and relativism, 111–12; on thick and thin description, 65; and Wittgenstein's theory of meaning, 313n.25
Geisteswissenschaften. See human science

gender: in feminist psychology, 67, 68; as socially constructed, 63
general, the, 123–24
generalizability, 185, 190–92, 291
general laws: for educational effectiveness, 15; focusing on social goals rather than, 20; Gergen contrasting psychological theories with, 58; and logical positivism, 39; modernism on scientific method as leading to, 310n.88; modern positivism on, 94; natural science paradigm as promising, 3–4; positivism on, 108, 153; search for as doomed, 130
general relativity, 91–92
general systems theory, 53–57, 97, 303n.71
geometrical theorems, 66
Gergen, Kenneth J.: on animal learning research, 23; on cultural effects of communications technology, 296n.6; exchange with Smith, 298n.28; on grand narrative of modernism, 310n.88; on modernism and scientific realism, 314n.34; on modernist belief in knowability of values, 71, 311n.106; on modern/postmodern distinction, 295n.3; on psychological theories as historical, 58–59; "Social Psychology as History," 58; on specialization in psychology, 46; on theoretical categories and observation, 63, 309n.58
gestalt psychology, 56, 307n.15
Gilligan, Carol, 67
Gingrich, Newt, 251
Glaser, Barney, 65
Glass, G. V., 207, 208, 214
Gleick, James, 79–80, 312n.9
goal-attainment language, 135–36
goal-attainment scaling, 159, 179–80
goal construct validity, 160, 174, 181
Goals 2000, 277, 278, 279
Gödel's First Incompleteness Theorem, 309n.54
Gold, N., 320n.16
Goldfried, M., 217, 329n.81
Goodnow, Jacqueline, 52
Gore, Al, 176
Gorman, J. M., 329n.84
Gottman, John, 233

government, movement to "reinvent," 174–76, 177
graduate students, 286, 288
Graham, S. R., 206, 328n.41
Grand Unified Theory, 78
Grawe, K., 234–36
"great books" approach, 44, 70, 278
Greek philosophy, 120–21
Greenberg, Clement, 312n.106
Greene, J. C., 139, 140, 145, 321n.24
Greening of America, The (Reich), 47–48
grounded theory, 65, 96, 158, 172
Guba, Egon G.: on confirmability, 188; on credibility, 182; on dependability, 186; fourth generation evaluation, 140; hermeneutic paradigm in, 153, 154; on quantitative measures, 171; responsive, constructivist evaluation, 320n.16; on transferability, 185
guiding conception: in "Cindy" PTSD case, 238; in disciplined-inquiry model, 11, 12; in discussion section of research article, 159, 180; in educational reform, 275; in introduction to a research article, 155, 156; judicial cases compared with, 192; as only one factor in ultimate outcome, 219; in pragmatic and disciplined-inquiry models compared, 188, 189; in pragmatic psychology, 136; psychotherapy flowchart as generic, 233; in results section of a study, 172, 174

Habermas, Jürgen, 62, 114
Handbook of Qualitative Research (Denzin and Lincoln), 302n.70
Head Start, 139, 257
health care: costs, 203; review of plans, 179. *See also* managed care
Heidegger, Martin, 6, 48, 61–62, 105, 311n.99
Heisenberg's Uncertainty Principle, 89
Held, B. S., 298n.26
heliocentric system, 32
Hempel, Carl, 310n.74
Henderson, L. J., 56
hermeneutic case studies: addressing the researcher's interests and values, 162, 188; applicability to other sites, 161, 185; authenticity, 162; case boundaries,

hermeneutic case studies *(continued)*
157; case setting and study rationale, *156, 157,* 167; construct validity, 325n.48; discussion section of research article, *159,* 180; introduction to research article, 154–55, *156;* measures and data collection procedures, *158,* 170; method section of research article, *156,* 167; quality of knowledge procedures, *160;* reproducibility of research process, *162,* 185–86; results section of research article, *159,* 172; stakeholder values and goals, *158,* 170; study design, *160,* 180; validity within a study, *161,* 182–83

hermeneutic circle, 61; Gödel's Incompleteness Theorem compared with, 309n.54; Kuhn's paradigms compared with, 312n.5; and the limitation of knowledge, 106; in postmodern constructionism, 95; postpositivism compared with, 87–88

hermeneutic paradigm: case study as unit of analysis in, 154; case study literature of, 153; characteristics of, *99;* contrasted with positivist and pragmatic paradigms, 98–101; pragmatic paradigm contrasted with, 127; pragmatic psychology combining positivist paradigm and, 8, 101, 154; in program evaluation, 139, 140; representative for this study, 154; unscientific psychology advocated by, 199. *See also* hermeneutic case studies

hermeneutics, 59–62; collaborative relationship of researcher and subject in, 321n.36; on conceptual frameworks as not arbitrary, 113; counterculture of the 1960s associated with, xxi; the double hermeneutic, 61; examples of hermeneutically oriented research, 124–29; "interpretation all the way down," 317n.43; in postmodern constructionism, 95; in qualitative research, 98; as science and art of interpretation, 6, 60; sense of "science" in, 206; types of, 60. *See also* critical hermeneutics; hermeneutic circle; hermeneutic paradigm; methodological hermeneutics; ontological hermeneutics

Hernandez, Evelyn, 263
Herndon, James, 248–49
Hesse, Mary, 315n.5
higher education: "great books" approach, 44, 70, 278; pluralism as essential to, 284; postwar boom in, 45; "tenured radicals," 70, 71, 249, 311n.103
high modernism, 127, 295n.3
Hirsch, E. D., 260–61, 263, 276
historiometry, 310n.74
history: as the closest we come to objective reality, 31; the local as focus of, 123; pendulum swings in, 36–38; positivism on natural science approach to, 310n.74; postmodernism on, 31; standards for teaching, 278
history of psychology, 29–71; coming of age from 1879 to early 1960s, 38–43; foundation of modern, 29, 31, 35, 38; origins from 1600 to 1879, 32–36; phases of, 31–32, 37; the postmodern invasion since the 1960s, 44–71; postwar boom in higher education, 45–47; from 1600 to the early 1960s, 31–43; systems and schools of early modern psychology, 38–39; unifying development reflecting unifying forces of American society, 42–43; during World War II, 40–41
HMOs, 179
Hobbes, Thomas, 33, 88
holistic study design, *157,* 169
Holt, John, 249
Holzman, L., 199, 298n.26, 326n.2
homelessness, 44
honor roll schools, 267–69, 274, 276
Hook, Sidney, 107
Horgan, John, 4, 90–92
House of Cards: Psychology and Psychotherapy Built on Myth (Dawes), xix–xx, 204
Houts, A. C., 63, 309n.57
Howard, Kenneth: COMPASS Treatment System, 228, 230, 231; educational data base compared with that of, 275; extending model of, 230–32, 292; Mental Health Index, 229, 232; on patient/client distinction, 327n.22; patient-focused research paradigm, 220, 227–30

Huberman, A. M., 64, 309n.66
Hughes, R., 112, 317n.33
Hull, Clark, 49–50, 308n.16
human behavior: consciousness and intentionality in, 22; feedback as altering,
  59; Gergen on animal studies for investigating, 23; hermeneutic approach to,
  60; Hull's model of, 49–50; human science studying from the inside, 58, 96;
  modern positivism on, 94; natural science studying from the outside, 58;
  postmodern constructionism on, 96;
  Rorty on different vocabularies for
  dealing with, 117; as self-reflexive, 59,
  61; theory of planned behavior, 17
human instrument, 170
humanism: classical humanism as modernist value, 69; in humanistic psychology, 48
humanistic experiential therapy, 202
humanistic psychology, 47–49, 96,
  307n.10
humanities: in the cognitive revolution, 53;
  in contemporary psychology, 23–24; in
  humanistic psychology, 48; natural science contrasted with, 21; social science
  as caught between natural science and
  the, 60
human science: boundary with natural science as blurring, 92; human behavior as
  studied from inside in, 58; natural science distinguished from, 57–71,
  315n.5; and natural science for Rorty,
  117; postmodern psychology as, 96;
  sense of "science" in, 206; understanding as goal of, 96. *See also* social science
human service programs: for addressing
  psychosocial problems, 135; "buyer's
  guide" model of cost-effectiveness applied to, 178; contextual differences between cases in, 191; databases of case
  studies facilitating, 292; examples of,
  136; open-ended complex problems in,
  194; positivist approach to, 136; pragmatic approach to, 136–37; pragmatic
  paradigm stimulating democratic debate on, 291; projects distinguished
  from programs, 318n.3; Schorr on factors in success of, 150–51; social welfare programs, 42. *See also* program
  evaluation
Hume, David, 33–34, 88
Husserl, Edmund, 48
hypnosis, 206
hypothetical construct, 90

*Idea of a Social Science and Its Relation to
  Philosophy, The* (Winch), 58, 302n.70
identity politics, 69, 70
idiographic theory, 99, 159, 180, 226
Images of Organization (Morgan), 164
indeterminacy of radical translation, 82
individualized therapy, 210, 290
induction, 75–76
Industrial Revolution, 35–36
Infant School model, 332n.17
inflation, 182
information theory, 51
in-home school movement, 299n.48
innovation: adoption of, 181; as criterion
  for publication, 46
inside evaluators, 140–41
instinct theory, 39
intelligence test scores, 253
intentionality: as cultural reality, 21; in interpretation, 298n.19; in postmodern
  psychology, 24, 96; in psychology
  grounded in culture, 22
interdisciplinary (multidisciplinary) approach, 138, 303n.71
internal-causality validity, 161, 182, 183
internal-connectedness validity, 161, 182,
  183
internal-functionality validity, 161, 182, 183
internal validity, 183, 325n.49
International Association for the Evaluation of Educational Achievement (IEA),
  253–54
interpersonal therapy, 215
interpretation: circularity in logic of,
  315n.5; in ethnographic writing, 125;
  the hermeneutic circle in, 61; hermeneutics as science and art of, 6, 60; intentionality as aspect of, 298n.19; "interpretation all the way down," 317n.43;
  psychology seen as, 60
interpretive theory, xxi
interpretivist evaluation, 140, 145, 321nn.
  24, 36

introduction to a research article, 154–55, 164–67; in hermeneutic paradigm, 154–55, *156;* in positivist paradigm, 154, *156;* in pragmatic paradigm, 155, *156,* 164–67
introspection, 39, 52
ironic science, 91
irony, 59

Jacobson, N. S., 208
Jacoby, Russell, 9, 317n.33
James, William: on pragmatic theory of truth, 108; in pragmatism's development, xxiv, 102, 107; scientific attitude of, 109, 206
Japanese education, 254, 333n.39
Johnson, Paul, 317n.33
Journal of Personality and Social Psychology, The, 59–60
journals: as case study databases, 20–21; case study databases as electronic, 286; for case study publication, 287; methodological rigor in, 46
judicial law, 131, 192

Kernan, A. B., 110, 316n.25
Key Evaluation Checklist, 141
Key School (Indianapolis, Ind.), 257–58
Kierkegaard, Søren, 49
Kiesler, Donald, 232
Kimball, Roger, 311n.103
Kimble, G. A., 23, 100, 301n.62
Kiresuk, T. J., 179
knowledge: "core knowledge" curriculum, 261, 263, 276; critical theory on, 146; for knowledge's sake, 143; logical positivism on, 39; ontological hermeneutics on, 325n.62; in positivist paradigm, 153; postpositivism on limitations of, 87–88, 105–6; pragmatic view of, 108, 131; Rorty on, 116; social and economic forces affecting, 36, 146. *See also* epistemology; truth
knowledge-based systems (KBS), 194
Koch, Sigmund, 50
Kohl, Herbert, 249
Kolodner, J. L., 194–95, 326n.78
Kovacs, A. L., 206, 328n.41
Kozol, Jonathan, 249
Krasner, L., 63, 309n.57

Kuhn, Thomas: critique of logical positivism, 105–6; on limitation of knowledge, 87–88; on paradigms in science, 76–81

laboratory mice, 23
Laboratory School of the University of Chicago, 248
Lacan, Jacques, 311n.99
Lambert, M. J., 207, 208
language: linguistics, 53; oral versus written, 123; postmodern constructionism on, 95–96; private language thesis, 85–86; Quine on scientific, 82; Skinner's behavioral explanation of, 87; Wittgenstein's picture theory of, 84. *See also* meaning
language arts, 278
language games, 84–87, 96
law cases, 192
laws of association, 34
laws of nature. *See* general laws
Lawson, D. M., 183
Lazarus, Richard, xxiv
learning: affective learning, 250; cooperative learning, 266; social learning theory, 201. *See also* animal learning research; education
learning communities, 259, 263
Learning Gap, The: Why Our Schools Are Failing and What We Can Learn From Japanese and Chinese Education (Stevenson and Stigler), 254
Leiblum, Sandra, 233
Leo, J., 278, 337n.109
Lévi-Strauss, Claude, 311n.99
Leviton, L. C., 321n.29
Lewin, Kurt, 27–28
life functioning, 228–29
Lilienfeld, R., 55, 308n.29
Lincoln, Yvonne S.: on confirmability, 188; on credibility, 182; on dependability, 186; fourth generation evaluation, 140; *Handbook of Qualitative Research,* 302n.70; hermeneutic paradigm in, 153, 154; on quantitative measures, 171; responsive, constructivist evaluation, 320n.16; on transferability, 185
linguistics, 53
literary criticism, 60, 91, 92

lived experience: in hermeneutics, 64; in postmodern psychology, 24
living systems theory, 56–57, 164, 323n.12
local, the, 123–24
logical positivism, 39–40; consensus about, 26; as conservative and capitalist, 305n.32; Continental philosophy's attacks on, 102, 104–6; as dominating Anglo-American philosophy, 103; on natural science approach to history, 310n.74; as reducing philosophy to philosophy of science, 40, 103; on scientific realism, 90; Toulmin on, 122–23; verification principle, 305n.30; Vienna Circle, 39, 122, 123, 315n.1; Wittgenstein's *Tractatus* as rationale for, 84. *See also* postpositivism
Lonely Crowd, The (Riesman), 42
long-term therapy, 201, 223–24
Lorenz, Edward, 79
Lynd, Robert and Helen, 247–48

Madness and Modernism: Insanity in the Light of Modern Art, Literature, and Thought (Sass), 127–29
"Magical Number Seven, Plus or Minus Two, The: Some Limits on Our Capacity for Processing Information" (Miller), 51
managed care: accountability pressure from, 220; and alternative models for psychotherapy, 200; in Clinton plan, 327n.29; decision-making methodology for, 225; decreasing volume of mental health services, 203; and manualized therapy, 210; per capita managed care, 143; practice guidelines, 200, 210, 220–21, 225; proprietary databases in, 287
manualized therapy: in applied science model, 10; avoiding forced choice between individualized therapy and, 290; manuals as "straightjackets," 217, 329n.83; as more effective than clinicians, 210, 211, 212; pragmatic approach to, 218–19, 235; as rigged in favor of cognitive behavioral therapy, 214; therapeutic alliance in, 331n.123
Manufactured Crisis, The: Myths, Fraud, and the Attack on America's Public Schools (Berliner and Biddle), 251

Margolis, Joseph, 316n.19
Marx, Karl: the Enlightenment attacked by, 36; skeptical postmodernism influenced by, 311n.99
Marxism: critical hermeneutics in, 62; neo-Marxism, 6, 48, 62, 105, 146
masculine science, 95
Maslow, Abraham, 48
mathematics tests, 252, 254, 278
Maxwell's equations, 89
May, Rollo, 48
meaning: in anthropological research, 126; Bruner on, 53, 97; content analysis of, 98; as cultural reality, 21; the hermeneutic circle in interpreting, 61; as not objectively observable, 23; pragmatic theory of, 107–8; in psychology grounded in culture, 22; in reading instruction, 264; Wittgenstein on, 84, 85
mechanism: contextualism replacing, 56; of modernism, 22; natural selection as mechanistic, 313n.10; in Newtonian science, 33; in Pepper's framework, 53–54; psychology shifting away from, 97
media: conflict preferred by, 338n.13; in the construction of reality, 297n.2; in critical theory analysis of schizophrenia, 128; multiculturalism associated with, 296n.6; postmodernism's growth stimulated by, xxi, 69
Media 2000, 165
Meehl, Paul, 209
Meir, Deborah, 259, 270
"melting pot" concept, 4, 42, 44, 95, 248
memory traces, 205–6
mental health: community mental health, xxii, 296n.10; Community Mental Health Centers, 178; decreasing volume of services for, 203; deinstitutionalization of the mentally ill, 44; prevention of mental disorder, 147; school teams for, 259. *See also* psychosocial problems
Mental Health Index (MHI), 229, 232
mental phenomena: behaviorism rejecting, 22, 39; in the cognitive revolution, 52; psychology of the 1950s as rejecting, 23; Wittgenstein's analysis of mentalistic terms, 87. *See also* consciousness
Messer, S. B., 60, 202, 216–17, 309n.51, 327n.23

Metatheory in Social Science: Pluralism and Subjectivities (Fiske and Shweder), 302n.70

method, 133–95; case studies as method for psychology, 130–32; diversity as required in, 26; experimental method, 33; Feyerabend on anarchism in, 82–84; modernism on scientific method as leading to objective knowledge, 95, 310n.88; of positivism, 8; psychology allying with natural scientific, 39. *See also* methodological pluralism; methodological rigor

methodological hermeneutics, 60–61; in Continental philosophy, 103, 104; and skeptical postmodernism, 315n.2

methodological pluralism: Feyerabend on, 83; pragmatic manifesto as calling for, 283–85; in psychotherapy, 201–2

methodological rigor: as criterion for publication, 45–46; in positivist psychology, 8, 39; in propositional thinking, 66

method section of a research article, *156*, 167–72; case boundaries, *157*, 168–69; case setting and study rationale, *156*, *157*, 167–68; measures and data collection procedures, *158*, 170–71; quality of knowledge procedures, *158*, 171–72; stakeholder values and goals, *158*, 170

"Method, Social Science, and Social Hope" (Rorty), 116

Middle Ages, 121

Middletown (Lynd and Lynd), 247–48

Mikulski, Barbara, 2–3

Miles, M. B., 64, 309n.66

Milgrim, Stanley, xxiii

Miller, George, 50–51, 97

Miller, James G., 56–57, 97, 303n.71, 323n.12

Miller, Ronald, 106, 305n.30

Miller, T. I., 207, 208, 214

Mills, C. Wright, 43, 107

mind, the: computers compared with, 52, 97; the unconscious, 36. *See also* mental health; mental phenomena

mission creep, 150

mission drift, 150

model projects, 136, 168

modern art, 127, 295n.3, 311n.106

modernism: in the arts, 127, 295n.3, 311n.106; as conservative, 71; critical postmodernism compared with, 69; dialectic of postmodernism and, 93–101; on disciplinary boundaries, 302n.68; and the Enlightenment, 3, 32, 37, 68, 311n.106; four interrelated values characterizing, 68–69; grand narrative of, 310n.88; high modernism, 127, 295n.3; mechanistic view of humans in, 22; modernist science associated with capitalism, 298n.31; modern positivism, 94–95; natural science as source of psychology of, 21; the 1950s as high point of, xx; in Pepper's framework, 53–54; in political correctness debate, 71; positivist paradigm as predominating due to misplaced faith in, 3; postmodern critique of, 4; postmodernism contrasted with, xxi; pragmatism as originally modernist, 297n.11; psychological practitioners for, 9–10; on scientific method as leading to progress, 4, 310n.88; and scientific realism, 90, 314n.34; technology as modernist concept, xxiv; Toulmin on quest for certainty of, 121–22; two senses of term, 295n.3, 311n.106; women in, 67

Mohegan School (New York City), 261, 263

monitoring evaluation: in disciplined-inquiry model, *11*, 12; in pragmatic and disciplined-inquiry models compared, 189, *189*

Montesquieu, 33

morality: amorality as modernist value, 69; logical positivism on questions of, 39; moral authority of Western democratic tradition, 113; pragmatism's moral emphasis, 131, 143; relativism and responsibility for action, 112; in Rorty's pragmatic relativism, 120. *See also* ethics; value

Morgan, Gareth, 164–67

Mosle, S., 260, 276–77, 334n.63, 337n.104

Motivational Enhancement Therapy (MET), 215

Multicom, 164–67

multiculturalism: accepted authority challenged by, 44; in education, 250, 251,

278; media saturation leading to openness to, 296n.6; as postmodernist value, 70, 71

multidisciplinary (interdisciplinary) approach, 138, 303n.71

multiple-case study design, 157, 169

multiple intelligences, 258, 262

Murray, Henry, 191

narrative mode of thought, 65–67, 96, 153

narrative therapy models, 202, 203

Nathan, Peter E., 220–21, 329n.84

National Assessment of Educational Progress (NAEP), 252, 278–79, 334n.43

National Commission on Excellence in Education, 249

national educational testing, 275–79

National Institute of Mental Health (NIMH) Treatment of Depression Research Program, 215, 236

National Performance Review (NPR), 176

national standardized curriculum, 261

Nation at Risk, A (National Commission on Excellence in Education), 249, 251, 255, 276

natural kinds, 303n.71

natural science: boundary with human disciplines as blurring, 92; critical hermeneutics on political role of, 62; for deriving pragmatically useful knowledge, 130; empiricism and reason as hallmarks of, 32; evolution by natural selection, 36, 77, 94, 313n.10; evolution of, 32–33; human behavior as studied from outside in, 58; humanities contrasted with, 21; human science distinguished from, 57–71, 315n.5; and human science for Rorty, 117; in logical positivism, 39, 40; objective observation as hallmark of, 23; positivism on natural science approach to history, 310n.74; positivist view of, xx; privileged epistemological status of, 38; psychology allying with method of, 39; Rorty on success of, 116–17; social science as caught between the humanities and, 60; social science evolving from, 32; technology contrasted with, xxii; truth as goal of, xxii. *See also* physics

natural science-based psychology: defined, xix; disappointing substantive results of, xxii, xxiii–xxiv, 3; humanistic reaction to, 48; pragmatic psychology contrasted with, xx. *See also* applied science model

natural unit, 168

nature: causal interaction in, 22; and culture as interrelated for postmodern constructionism, 96; versus culture in psychology, 21–24, 57; mind-as-nature researchers, 97; natural sciences for study of, 21; and propositional thinking, 66; thin description for, 65; E. O. Wilson's materialist view of, 314n.47. *See also* natural science

Naturwissenschaften. See natural science

Neigher, William, xxii, 139, 144–45

Neimeyer, R. A., 298n.26

Neisser, Ulric, xxiii

neobehavioral, S-R model, 201

neo-Marxism, 6, 48, 62, 105, 146

neopragmatism: counterculture of the 1960s associated with, xxi; as postmodern pragmatism, xxiv; as postmodern theme, 6; term as used in this book, 296n.15. *See also* pragmatism

New Haven, Connecticut, 259

New Jersey, 260

New Left movement, 44

Newman, F., 199, 298n.26, 326n.2

Newton, Isaac, 32–33, 34, 56, 88, 121

Newton's laws of motion, 66

New York City: alternative schools in, 258–59, 270; Crew's policies, 269–71; Mohegan School, 261, 263; proficiency testing in, 267–69, 274, 276, 335n.79

Niebuhr, Reinhold, 107

Nietzsche, Friedrich, 49, 311n.99

nihilism, skeptical postmodernism accused of, 7, 27

Nisbet, R., 68, 310n.90

nomothetic theory, 99, 159, 180, 226

nonlinear theories, 89

normal science, 78

norm based tests, 276

Norton, N. C., 207

novice practitioners, 13, 194, 207

Nyden, Philip, 147–48

objectivism: defined, 109; Geertz on movement beyond relativism and, 111–12;
practical action for moving beyond relativism and, 113–15, 131; and relativism as either/or, 111–13; relativism
contrasted with, 109–11; in therapy
models, 202
objectivity: contextualism on, 55; as hallmark of natural science, 23; history as
the closest we come to objective reality, 31; modernism on scientific
method as objective, 95, 310n.88;
modernist belief in objectivity of values, 71; ontological hermeneutics on,
325n.62; postmodernism denying pure
objectivity, 5; postmodernism rejecting
objective truth, 301n.68; pragmatism
rejecting, 108; social constructionism
rejecting, 62
object-relations theories, 201
Olson, L., 274, 336n.100
one-stop shopping schools, 260
ontological authenticity, 163
ontological hermeneutics, 61–62; Anglo-
American view of, 105; attack on logical positivism, 105; in Continental philosophy, 103, 104; on historicity of
human existence, 298n.19; on limitation of knowledge, 106; on objective
knowledge, 325n.62; and ontological
postmodernism, 315n.2; as postmodern
theme, 6; in Sass's work on schizophrenia, 127
ontological postmodernism: ambiguity and
complexity emphasized by, 8, 298n.30;
bridging position of, 229n.32; defined,
6; and ontological hermeneutics,
315n.2; practical problem solving as
deemphasized by, 8; pragmatism compared with, 229n.32
oral language, 123
organicism, 53–54, 56, 97, 313n.10
Organization Man, The (Whyte), 42–43
organizations, quality of, 177
Origins of American Social Science, The
(Ross), 302n.70
Orlinsky, D. E., 234–36, 323n.12
Osborne, D., 174, 175–76
outcome indicators, 173–74
outside evaluators, 140–41

Packer, M. J., 60, 309n.49
paradigmatic behaviorism, 201
paradigms: changes of, 78–80; defined, 77;
the hermeneutic circle compared with,
312n.5; Kuhn on, 76–81; in postmodern constructionism, 95
paradox, 59
paraprofessionals, 207
Parks, B. K., 234–36
Parloff, Morris, 28
participant observation, 140, 147
particle physics, 89
particular, the, 123
patient factors, 238
patient-focused research, 220, 227–30
patients: clients distinguished from,
327n.22. *See also* client
pattern matching, 159, 176–77
Patton, M. Q., 140, 142, 320n.16
peer review, 286
Peirce, Charles Sanders, 107, 108
pendulum swings in history, 36–38
Penrose, Roger, 91–92
Pepper, Stephen, 53–55, 97, 313n.10
per capita managed care, 143
performance accountability, 174
performance indicators, 159, 173–76
Perls, Fritz, 48, 307n.15
personality reintegration, 232
personality repertoires, 201
perspectivism: defined, 118; of postmodernism, xxi, 38; of pragmatic psychology, 217–18; of Rorty, 117–19
Persuasion and Healing (Frank), 216
Peterson, Donald: on applied science
model, 9–10, 328n.42; assessment conference, xxii–xxiii; disciplined-inquiry
model of, 10, 12, 13, 14, 138, 285; on
guiding conceptions, 136; on the pragmatic case study, 137; on the pragmatic
paradigm, 199–200; on professional
psychology, 302n.71
phenomenology: Anglo-American view of,
105; attack on logical positivism, 105;
in Continental philosophy, 103, 104; in
humanistic psychology, 48–49; on limitation of knowledge, 106
Philosophical Investigations (Wittgenstein), 84, 85
philosophy, 73–132; in the cognitive revo-

lution, 53; consensus in, 26; as dialectic, 26; Greek philosophy, 120–21; logical positivism as reducing to philosophy of science, 40, 103; Rorty's metacritique of, 115–16; as therapeutic for Wittgenstein, 86; the timeless as focus of, 124; Toulmin on two worldviews in Greek, 120–21. *See also* Anglo-American philosophy; Continental philosophy; epistemology; ethics; positivism

Philosophy and the Mirror of Nature (Rorty), 115

phonics, 263–64, 335n.71

physics: chaos theory, 79–80, 89, 313n.10; evolution of modern, 32–33; as fundamental for E. O. Wilson, 314n.47; paradigm change in, 78–79; particle physics, 89; quantum mechanics, 91–92; relativity, 89, 91–92; scientific realism and contemporary, 89–90; social physics, 35; unified theory, 78, 91–92; Wundt's laboratory associated with, 35

picture theory of language, 84

Pitkin, H. F., 114, 130

Plato: logical argument against relativism, 110; Toulmin on rational formalism of, 121

pluralism: as postmodern theme, 301n.68. *See also* methodological pluralism

political correctness, 70–71, 249

political science, 33, 41

Polkinghorne, Donald: on disciplined-inquiry model, 12, 14, 138; on expert versus novice practitioners, 13, 151; neopragmatism of, xxiv, 6, original and recent versions of pragmatism contrasted by, 297n.11; on pragmatic epistemology in psychology, 14; on the pragmatic paradigm, 199–200

Popper, Karl, 75–76, 87–88, 105–6

positivism: Comte, 34–35, 88; and critical postmodernism, 7, 8; disagreement regarding, 26; mainstream psychology building on assumptions of, 1; modern positivism, 94–95; political and economic dominance of psychology, 8; versus postmodernism in psychology, 7; as predominating due to misplaced faith in modernism, 3; as rightist, 9; and skeptical postmodernism, 7, 8, 27; as under-

lying modernism, xx; utopian vision of, 292. *See also* logical positivism; positivist paradigm

positivist case studies. *See* quantitative (positivist) group studies

positivist paradigm: case study literature of, 153; characteristics of, 99; contrasted with pragmatic and hermeneutic paradigms, 98–101; correspondence theory of truth in, 108; as dominating contemporary psychology, 3; Geertz's anthropology contrasted with, 126; human service programs in, 136; integrating pragmatic case studies into positivist studies, 288; knowledge-based systems following, 194; knowledge in, 153; and managed care, 200; pattern matching in, 176; pragmatic psychology as combining hermeneutic paradigm and, 8, 101, 154; pragmatic psychology containing elements of, 8, 299n.45; in program evaluation, 138, 139; psychological practitioners for, 9–10; on psychotherapy as currently practiced, 200; quantitative group study as unit of analysis, 154; schizophrenia as analyzed by, 128, 129; in therapy models, 201–2; therapy research of, 232–37; value-neutrality in, 146. *See also* quantitative (positivist) group studies

Possible Lives: The Promise of Public Education in America (Rose), 272

postmodernism, 5–6, 68–71; in the arts, 295n.3; core idea of, 5; counterculture of the 1960s associated with, xxi; deconstruction, xxi, 7, 70, 246; dialectic of modernism and, 93–101; on disciplinary boundaries, 301n.68, 303n.71; emergence of postmodern pragmatism, 102–32; feminist acceptance of, 67; four types of, 6; on history, 31; humanities as source of psychology of, 21; as leftist, 306n.32; literary style of, 301n.68; on logical positivism, 305n.32; the media in the growth of, xxi, 69; modernism as criticized by, 4; modernism contrasted with, xxi; neopragmatism as postmodernist pragmatism, 297n.11; objective truth rejected by, 301n.68; origins in 1960s France,

postmodernism *(continued)*
69; Pepper's framework compared with, 54, 55; versus positivism in psychology, 7; postmodern constructionism, 95–97; postmodernization of science, 90; pragmatic postmodernism, 6; pragmatism as embraced and incorporated into, xxiv; the psychological practitioner for, 9–14; psychology as influenced by, xxi–xxii; science and technology in development of, 69; six epistemological themes of, 5–6; Toulmin on, 295n.3; usage of term, 295n.3. *See also* critical postmodernism; ontological postmodernism; skeptical postmodernism

Postmodernism and Social Theory (Seidman and Wagner), 302n.70

Post-Modernism and the Social Sciences (Rosenau), 302n.70

postpositivism, 75–92; on conceptual frameworks as not arbitrary, 113; conservative and liberal wings of, 315n.1; convergence with Continental philosophy, 106, 315nn. 1, 6; the end of scientific realism, 88–92; Feyerabend's anarchism, 82–84; and the hermeneutic circle, 87–88; Kuhn's paradigms, 75–81; on limitations of knowledge, 87–88, 105–6; Popper's falsifiability, 75–76; Quine's webs of belief, 80–82; Wittgenstein's language games, 84–87

postpositivist evaluation, 139, 145, 321n.24

post-traumatic stress disorder (PTSD), 237–44

practical action, for moving beyond objectivism and relativism, 113–15, 131

practical rationality, in shared community, 114

practice guidelines, 200, 210, 220–21, 225

practitioners: as caught between two unattractive alternatives, 13; as "co-constructionists," 202; from 1879 to early 1960s, 40–41; expert practitioners, 13, 194, 207, 217; increasing divergence between scientists and, 203; modern positivist model of, 9–10; in networks of pragmatic psychologists, 285; novice practitioners, 13, 194, 207; postmodern pragmatic model of, 10–14; supporting,

9–21; two models of, 9. *See also* scholar-practitioners; scientist-practitioners

pragmatic case studies, 135–52; action plan for promoting, 285–89; addressing the researcher's interests and values, *162*, 187–88; as answerable to all stakeholders, 145; applicability to other sites, *161*, 185; case boundaries, *157*, 168–70; case setting and study rationale, *156*, *157*, 167–68; and collaborative research, 148; and community psychology, 146–49; construct validity, *160*, 181–82; disciplined-inquiry model compared with, 188–90, *189*; discussion section of research article, *159*, 180; goals of, 140–41; holistic orientation of, 137; the individual as focus of, 137; integrating into positivist studies, 288; introduction of research article, 154–55, *156*, 164–67; living systems theory compared with, 164, 323n.12; measures and data collection procedures, *158*, 170–71; method section of research article, *156*, 167–72; the nuts and bolts of, 153–95; pattern matching in, 177; performance indicators for, 173–76; and program evaluation, 137–45; public promotion of, 288–89; quality of knowledge procedures, *160*; reproducibility of research process, *162*, 186–87; results section of research article, *159*, 172–80; from single case to database, 190–95; single-subject designs, 184; social constructionism in, 141; stakeholder values and goals, *158*, 170; strengths of case-based paradigm, 283; study design, *160*, 180; as taking place in a context, 133; validity within a study, *161*, 182–84. *See also* databases of case studies

pragmatic evaluation, 139–40, 145, 321n.24

pragmatic paradigm. *See* pragmatic psychology

pragmatic postmodernism, 6

pragmatic psychology: accountability in, 291–92; application as preceding theory in, 2; becoming organized, 285–86; as beginning with the client, 136–37; cases as starting and ending points for, 2; case study as unit of analysis in, 154; case study literature of, 153; as centrist, 8–9; challenge to, 293; characteristics of, 99; clinical application of, 199–244; conceptual synthesis in, 289–90; contextualist worldview as basis of, 55; contrasted with positivist and hermeneutic paradigms, 98–101; democratic decision making in, 290–91; educational reform application, 245–79; Geertz's anthropology contrasted with, 126–27; hermeneutic and positivist paradigms combined in, 8, 101, 154; hermeneutic paradigm contrasted with, 127; human service programs in, 136; implications of, 281–93; as integrative, 8; knowledge as contextual in, 153; a manifesto for, 283–93; for mediating scientist-clinician conflict, 217–44; mediating theory clashes, 290; as middle way to generalization, 291; natural science-based psychology contrasted with, xx; positive elements in, 8, 299n.45; the psychological practitioner for, 9–14; public promotion of, 288–89; research generated by, 16–20; as response to psychology's culture wars, 7–9; schizophrenia as analyzed by, 128–29; technological paradigm evolving into, xxiv; utopia eschewed by, 292–93; vision of, 289–92. *See also* pragmatic case studies

pragmatism: agreement regarding, 26; case studies as focus of, 131, 153; on disciplinary boundaries, 302n.68; emergence of postmodern, 102–32; as evading foundation and certainty, 107; on knowledge, 108, 131; modernist and postmodernist, 297n.11; moral emphasis of, 131, 143; neopragmatism as postmodernist, 297n.11; ontological postmodernism compared with, 229n.32; originators of, 107–9; postmodernism as embracing and incorporating, xxiv; reinvigoration of, 102, 106–9; relativism attributed to, 130–31; Rorty's pragmatic relativism, 119–20, 131; social constructionism of, 130; term as used in this study, 296n.15; on truth, 107–8, 119–20, 130, 299n.32.

See also neopragmatism; pragmatic psychology

PRAISES model, 331n.119

praxis: Bernstein on importance of, 114–15; defined, 109

prevention of mental disorder, 147

Prilleltensky, I., 298n.31

Princeton University, xxi, 296n.8

private language, 85–86

problem-driven research, 18

process construct validity, 160, 174, 181

process indicators, 173–74

process information, 226

"professional activity as applied science" model. *See* applied science model

professional experience and research: in "Cindy" PTSD case, 239; in disciplined-inquiry model, 11, 12; in introduction to a research article, 155, 156; in pragmatic and disciplined-inquiry models compared, 188, 189

"professional practice as disciplined inquiry" model. *See* disciplined-inquiry model

Profscam (Sykes), 250

program: in disciplined-inquiry model, 10, 11; in pragmatic and disciplined-inquiry models compared, 189, 189. *See also* human service programs

program evaluation, 137–45; accountability model, 144, 145, 321n.35; advocacy model, 144, 145; amelioration model, 144, 145, 321n.35; approaches to, 142; critical science evaluation, 140, 145, 321n.24, 322n.36; emergence as coherent field, 138; ethical issues in, 142–45; failure of, 139, 320n.12; formative evaluation, 142, 320n.16, 321n.35; hermeneutical concepts in, 139, 140; inside versus outside evaluator, 140–41; as interdisciplinary, 138, 303n.71; interpretivist evaluation, 140, 145, 321nn. 24, 36; positivist and pragmatic elements in, 138; postpositivist evaluation, 139, 145, 321n.24; pragmatic evaluation, 139–40, 145, 321n.24; Rossi and Freeman's comprehensive definition of, 139; Schorr on traditional, 151–52; Scriven's Key Evaluation Checklist for, 141; summative evaluation, 139, 142,

program evaluation *(continued)*
320n.16, 321n.35; types of, 141–42;
the typical evaluation program, 138; typology of themes in, 139–40; utilization-focused evaluation, 140, 320n.16;
value-based models of, 144–45; value-
neutral approach to, 142–43, 321n.29
*Program Evaluation Standards, The: How
to Assess Evaluations of Educational
Programs* (Sanders), 189–90
progress, social. *See* social progress
progressive education, 194, 248, 249, 290
Project MATCH, 215
projects: defined, 136; model projects,
136, 168; programs distinguished from,
318n.3
proof, 123
propositional mode of thought, 65–67,
153
proprietary databases, 286–87
proprietary standards, 190
provincialism, 112
P.S. 6 (Manhattan), 268
P.S. 29 (South Bronx), 268
P.S. 31 (Brooklyn), 267
P.S. 234 (Manhattan), 267
psychoanalysis: ego psychology, 201; humanistic psychology as alternative to,
48, 307n.10; object-relations theories,
201; outcome criteria of, 216; plurality
of models in, 201; self psychology, 201;
the unconscious in, 36
psychodynamic therapies, 214, 215, 216,
231–32
psychology: allying with logical positivism,
40, 103; being more responsive to
today's social crises, 27–28; as doubly
self-reflexive, 61; educational psychology, 14; evolutionary psychology, 36,
94, 314n.47; experimental psychology,
49; feminist research methods, 67–69;
folk psychology, 66; formal publications since 1887, 19; formal specialties
of, 46, 302n.71; gestalt psychology, 56,
307n.15; humanistic psychology,
47–49, 96, 307n.10; as male dominated, 67; nature versus culture in,
21–24; polarization within the field, 7,
298n.26; postmodernism as influencing,
xxi–xxii; postmodern psychology as

human science, 96; pragmatic psychology as response to culture wars in, 7–9;
Psychology Today magazine survey on
most significant work in, xxiii–xxiv;
reinventing, 1–28; seen as source for
solving social problems, 2; as social science, 27, 302n.71; three paradigms for,
98–101; turning mainstream psychology upside down, 1–5; two cultures in,
100. *See also* applied psychology; applied science model; behaviorism; clinical psychology; cognitive revolution;
disciplined-inquiry model; history of
psychology; pragmatic psychology
Psychology: A Study of a Science (Koch),
50
Psychology Today (magazine), xxiii–xxiv
psychometrics, 39
psychosocial problems: addressing,
135–37; arising from the 1960s, 44; defined, 135–36; depression, 171, 215,
236; education affected by, 255; interrelations among, 150; post-traumatic
stress disorder, 237–44; schizophrenia,
127–29; schools as sites for addressing,
14
psychotherapy: in "Cindy" PTSD case,
237–44; client and patient distinguished
in, 327n.22; client-centered psychotherapy, 49; *Consumer Reports* magazine
article on, xx, 215–16, 223–25;
Dawes's critique of, xix–xx, 204–17;
empirical research tradition in, 232; experiential therapy, 214, 216, 231–32;
family systems therapy, 57, 202, 214,
231–32; flowchart analysis of, 233,
331n.119; growth between 1967 and
1980, 200; individualized therapy, 210,
290; insurance funding for, 202; interpersonal therapy, 215; in the laboratory
versus in the field, 221–25; long-term
therapy, 201, 223–24; and managed
care, 200, 203; meta-analyses of outcomes of, 202, 207, 208, 214, 216;
methodological pluralism in, 201–2;
narrative therapy models, 202, 203;
performance indicators for, 173; polarization within the field, 298n.26; positivist research on, 232–37; positivists
on current practice of, 200; pragmatic

paradigm applied to, 199–244; psychodynamic therapies, 214, 215, 216,
231–32; rational-emotive therapy, 208;
short-term therapy, 201, 223–24; therapeutic alliance, 216, 219, 233,
331n.123; therapist identity in outcomes, 231; therapy junkies, 223–24.
See also behavior therapy; psychoanalysis
PsycINFO, 19
publication vehicles for case studies,
287–88
public education. *See* education
"publish or perish," 45
pure experience, 48

qualitative evaluation, 320n.16
qualitative research, 64–65; complexity in,
97–98; as postmodern, 96
quality control, 160, 180–88; addressing
researcher's interests and values, 162,
187–88; applicability to other sites,
161, 185; Baldrige Quality Award, 177,
178, 186–87, 324n.37; construct validity, 160, 174, 181–82; quality-of-
knowledge procedures in studies, 160,
171–72; reproducibility of research
process, 162, 185–87; study design,
160, 180; total quality management,
255; validity within the study, 161,
182–84
quantification: in positivist methodology,
170, 187; pragmatists valuing, 171;
qualitative research contrasted with, 64;
in scientific methodology, 39; standard
ized quantitative testing, 246, 248, 257,
262, 268, 275–76; as value-neutral, 187
quantitative (positivist) group studies: addressing researcher's interests and values, 161; applicability to other sites,
161, 185; case boundaries, 157, 168;
case setting and study rationale, 156,
157, 167; construct validity, 160, 181,
182; discussion section of research article, 158, 178; documentation for, 133;
generalizing from, 190–91; introduction
to research article in, 154, 156; measures and data collection procedures,
159, 170; method section of research
article in, 156, 167; quality control in,

160, 180–88; quality of knowledge procedures, 160; reproducibility of research process, 161; results section of
research article, 159, 172; single-subject
research design, 183; stakeholder values
and goals, 158, 170; study design, 160,
180; as unit of analysis in positivist paradigm, 154; validity within a study,
161, 182, 183
quantum mechanics, 91–92
quasi-judicial method, 192
Quine, Willard Van Orman: critique of
logical positivism, 105–6; in development of pragmatism, 107; Feyerabend
compared with, 83; on limitations of
knowledge, 87–88; on webs of belief,
80–82, 313n.13

rape: in "Cindy" PTSD case, 237–44; date
rape debate, 63–64
rational-emotive therapy, 208
rational formalism, 121
rationality. *See* reason
reading: cultural literacy, 260; tests, 252,
268; whole-language versus phonics,
10, 263–64, 335n.71; *Why Johnny
Can't Read*, 245
Reagan, Ronald, xxii, 249, 307n.1
realism, scientific. *See* scientific realism
reality: as constructed for postmodernism,
xxi; as divided into nature and culture,
21, 57; history as the closest we come to
objective reality, 31; as interpreted for
postmodernism, 5; logical positivism on
discovering the nature of, 39; the media
in the construction of, 297n.2
reason: Darwin on, 36; Enlightenment glorification of, 32, 68; nineteenth-century
challenges to, 305n.21; Plato's rational
formalism, 121; practical rationality in
shared community, 114; rationality as
modernist value, 68–69, 95
Redhead, M., 93, 315n.1
reflection-in-action, 13, 151
reflexivity: human behavior as self-reflexive, 59, 61; as postmodern theme,
301n.68; psychology as doubly self-reflexive, 61
"Reforms as Experiments" (Campbell),
138

rehabilitation, 228
Reich, Charles, 47–48
"reinventing government" movement, 174–76, 177
relativism: cultural argument against, 110; cultural relativism, 69, 110–11; Geertz on movement beyond objectivism and, 111–12; logical argument against, 110, 112–13; and objectivism as either/or, 111–13; objectivism contrasted with, 109–11; as postmodern theme, 301n.68; practical action for moving beyond objectivism and, 113–15, 131; pragmatism accused of, 130–31; rise in belief in, 38; Rorty's pragmatic relativism, 119–20, 131; skeptical postmodernism accused of, 7; standard arguments against, 110
relativity, 89, 91–92
reliability of measurement, 162, 185
remediation, 228
remoralization, 228
Renaissance: as diversifying period, 37; humanistic pragmatism of, 121; postmodernism compared with, 123, 305n.24; received view of, 121
representativeness heuristic, 212
research articles. *See* written case studies
Resick, Patricia, 237–44
responsive, constructivist evaluation, 320n.16
responsive evaluation, 320n.16
Restructuring of Social and Political Theory, The (Bernstein), 302n.70
"results-oriented" government, 174
results section of a research article, *159*, 172–80; cost-effectiveness analysis, 178–79; goal-attainment scaling, 179–80; pattern matching, 176–77; performance indicators, 173–76
Reynoldson, Jack, 264, 265
Rice, C. E., 292, 337n.12
Richardson, F. C., 310n.89
Rickert, Heinrich, 57
Rickover, Hyman, 245
Riesman, David, 42
Riger, S., 305n.21
rigor, methodological. *See* methodological rigor
Rogers, Carl, 48, 49

Rogoff, Barbara, 55
Roiphe, Katie, 64, 309n.62
Rorty, Richard, 115–20; in Bernstein's synthesis, 114; constructionism of pragmatism of, 297n.11; *Contingency, Irony, and Solidarity*, 120; on Dewey, 332n.16; humanistic values of, 301n.68; implications for social science, 116–19; metacritique of philosophy, 115–16; "Method, Social Science, and Social Hope," 116; *Philosophy and the Mirror of Nature*, 115; postmodern pragmatism of, xxiv, 103, 107, 109; pragmatic relativism of, 119–20, 131; principle themes in work of, 115
Rose, Mike, 272–73
Rosenau, P. M., 295n.3, 302n.70
Ross, Dorothy: *The Origins of American Social Science*, 302n.70; on origins of term "social science," 304n.8; on scientism, 40, 41, 306n.33
Rossi, Frank, 164–65
Rossi, P. H., 139, 141, 179, 181, 320n.18
Roth, A., 234, 331n.120
Roth, P. A., 302n.69, 313n.22
Ryan, Alan, 332n.16
Ryle, Gilbert, 310n.72

"salad bowl" concept, 4, 44
Salovey, P., 212
Sanders, J. R., 189, 326n.64
Sandia National Laboratories, 333n.29, 334n.42
San Francisco, California, 257
Sartre, Jean-Paul, 49
Sass, Louis: "Ambiguity Is of the Essence," 298n.30; *Madness and Modernism*, 127–29; on methodological hermeneutics, 60–61, 309n.51; on ontological hermeneutics, 6, 298n.30; Rorty compared with, 317n.43; on two uses of "modernism," 295n.3, 311n.106
SAT tests, 186, 251, 252, 333nn. 31, 32
Saturday school, 257, 262
scaling-up, 149–50, 269–70
Scarr, S., 63, 309n.59
schema theory, 260
Schensul, J. J., 322n.46
Schensul, S. L., 322n.46
Scheper-Hughes, Nancy, 9

schizophrenia, 127–29
Schleiermacher, Friedrich, 60
Schlick, Moritz, 39
scholar-practitioners: actuarial prediction as
  more accurate than that of, 209–10; battle with scientist-practitioners, 204–17;
  cognitive biases alleged in, 212–13; defined, 203; more training as not meaning
  more therapeutic effectiveness, 207–9; as
  paying only lip service to science, 205–7;
  pragmatic psychology for mediating scientist-clinician conflict, 217–44; prepack-
  aged therapies as superior to, 210–17.
  See also disciplined-inquiry model
Schön, D. A.: on conflict between research
  and the client, 146, 322n.39; on disciplined-inquiry model, 12, 13, 14, 138;
  on the pragmatic paradigm, 199–200;
  on reflection-in-action, 13, 151; on the
  reflective practitioner, 170
school-based management, 256, 259, 262,
  266
school hours, 257, 262
school reform. *See* educational reform
schools. *See* education
"Schools of the Twenty-first Century"
  model, 260
*Schools That Work: America's Most Inno-
  vative Public Education Programs*
  (Wood), 300n.55
Schorr, Lisbeth, 149–52, 270–71,
  337n.100
Schrag, Peter, 245, 333nn. 29, 42
science: Dewey on scientific habit of mind,
  108–9; feminine science, 96; ironic science, 91; Kuhn on revolutions in,
  76–81; masculine science, 95; normal
  science, 78; in postmodernism's development, 69; postmodernization of, 90;
  the timeless as focus of, 124; Toulmin's
  call to turn toward application, 132;
  two meanings of, 206; unified science,
  123. *See also* human science; natural
  science; social science
science-purporting clinicians, 203
scientific inquiry model. *See* applied science model
scientific realism, 88–92; and contemporary physics, 89–90; defined, 88; Horgan's critique of, 90–92; logical posi-

tivism as agnostic regarding, 90; and
  modernism, 90, 314n.34; Van Fraassen
  on, 313n.33
scientism, 40, 41, 58, 94–95, 306n.33
scientist-practitioners: in APA, 327n.30;
  battle with scholar-practitioners,
  204–17; defined, 203; pragmatic psychology for mediating scientist-clinician
  conflict, 217–44. *See also* applied science model
Scriven, M., 141–42, 320n.16, 321n.29
Seidman, S., 302n.70
self, the, in postmodern psychology, 24
self-actualization, 48
self-efficacy, 201
self-esteem, 251
self-organizing systems, 313n.10
self psychology, 201
Seligman, Martin: *Consumer Reports*
  study of psychotherapy, xx, 215–16,
  223–25; on differential effect of therapist training, 208; on effectiveness and
  efficacy research, 221–23, 329n.84
sensitive dependence on initial conditions,
  79, 312n.9
setting factors, 238
Shadish, W. R., 321n.29
Shannon, Claude, 51
Shapiro, D. A., 214
short-term therapy, 201, 223–24
Shumer, S. M., 114, 130
Shweder, R. A., 302n.70
Siena, Maggie, 267
Simonton, Dean, 310n.74
single-case study design, 157, 161, 169,
  183–84
Sizer, Theodore, 256–57, 259, 263, 264,
  266
skeptical postmodernism, 70; "anything
  goes" character of, 301n.68; as controversial, 70; and critical postmodernism,
  7; as deconstructive, 7; defined, 6; as
  leftist, 9; and methodological hermeneutics, 315n.2; origins of, 70; and positivism, 7, 8, 27; in psychology, 7
Skinner, B. F., xxiii–xxiv, 87, 201
smart classrooms, 256, 262
smart schools, 255–56, 265–66
*Smart Schools, Smart Kids: Why Do Some
  Schools Work?* (Fiske), 255

Smith, Adam, 33, 34, 88
Smith, H., 334n.45
Smith, M. Brewster, 49, 298n.28
Smith, M. L., 207, 208, 214
social constructionism, 62–64; feminist acceptance of, 67; in original and postmodernist pragmatism, 297n.11; postmodern constructionism, 95–97; in postmodernist vision, xxi; as postmodern theme, 5, 6, 301n.68; in pragmatic case studies, 141; of pragmatism, 130; rise in belief in, 38; in therapy models, 201–2; Wittgenstein as anticipating, 86
social learning theory, 201
social Newtonianism, 34
social physics, 35
social progress: as modernist promise, 4, 310n.88; postmodern constructionism on, 95; Adam Smith on, 34
"Social Psychology as History" (Gergen), 58
social science: allying with logical positivism, 40, 103; as apolitical, 41; as caught between natural science and the humanities, 60; Comte's three-part, 35; contextual elements in, 56; critical hermeneutics on political role of, 62; economics, 34, 41; Enlightenment origins of, 32; fact/value distinction in, 34; federal budget for, 3, 297n.7; implications of Rorty's work for, 116–19; institutionalization and academicization of, 306n.38; linguistics, 53; natural science in evolution of, 32; origins of term, 304n.8; political criticism of, 2–3; political science, 33, 41; popular books of 1950s, 42–43; in postwar boom in higher education, 45; pragmatic psychologists connecting with other fields of, 286; psychology as, 27, 302n.71; scientism in, 41; seen as source for solving social problems, 2; sociology, 35, 41. *See also* anthropology; psychology
social welfare programs, 42
sociobiology (evolutionary psychology), 36, 94, 314n.47
sociology, 35, 41
special interest pods, 258
Spiro, Melford, 110–11
Staats, Arthur W., 201

Stake, R. E., 319n.6, 320n.16
stakeholder-based evaluation, 320n.16
stakeholders, 143–44; in community psychology, 148–49; pragmatic case studies as answerable to all, 145; pragmatic psychology focusing on, 218; values and goals in case study write-up, *158, 170*
standardized measures, 171
standardized quantitative testing, 246, 248, 257, 262, 268, 275–76
standardized therapy outcome measures, 226–27
Stein, D. M., 207, 208
Steinberg, J., 335n.71, 337n.10
Stevenson, Harold, 254
Stigler, James, 254
Stiles, W. B., 214
storytelling, 65–66, 96
Strauss, Anselm, 65
Streible, Jim, 257, 264–65
Stricker, G., 217, 299n.45
Stringer, E. T., 147, 321n.33
structuralism, 38–39
Students for a Democratic Society (SDS), 44
study design, 169–70; double-blind designs, *162, 187, 188, 211*; embedded-design study, *157, 169*; holistic study design, *157, 169*; multiple-case study design, *157, 169*; quality control for, *160, 180*; single-case study design, *157, 161, 169, 183–84*
Study of Thinking, A (Bruner, Goodnow, and Austin), 52
subjective well-being, 228–29
subjectivity: of culture for modern positivism, 94; as postmodern theme, 301n.68
summative evaluation, 139, 142, 320n.16, 321n.35
Sykes, Charles, 249–51, 264
symptom reduction, 228–29
system boundaries, 57, 308n.37

tactical authenticity, *163*
talk therapy: Dawes's critique of, xix, xx. *See also* psychoanalysis
Tarcov, Nathan, 336n.100
Task Force on Promotion and Dissemina-

tion of Psychological Procedures (APA), 211–12, 214, 329n.84

Taylor, Frederick Winslow, 246

"teaching the test," 268, 276

technicism, 68

technological model of applied psychology, xxii, xxiii, xxiv

technology: in applied science model, 10; guiding practical action as goal of, xxii; as modernist concept, xxiv; natural science contrasted with, xxii; in postmodernism's development, 69; theories as constructs in development of, 90

"tenured radicals," 70, 71, 249, 311n.103

test coaching, 268

testing (educational): international testing, 253–54; mathematics tests, 252, 254, 278; national testing, 275–79; reading tests, 252, 268; SAT tests, 186, 251, 252, 333nn. 31, 32; standardized quantitative testing, 246, 248, 257, 262, 268, 275–76; "teaching the test," 268, 276; test coaching, 268

test-retest reliability of measurement, 185

texts: Geertz on seeing the Balinese cockfight as, 126; hermeneutics approaching action as textual, 60; hermeneutics as means of interpreting, 60

theoretical construct validity, *160*, *181*

theory: application as preceding in pragmatic paradigm, 2; grounded theory, 65, 96, *158*, *172*; as hypothetical construct, 90; Kuhn's paradigms, 76–81; in mechanistic systems, 54; Popper's falsifiability criterion for, 75–76; of positivism, 8; pragmatic psychology for mediating between theories, 290; as preceding application in positivism, 1; psychological theories as historical for Gergen, 58–59; Quine on linguistic embeddedness of, 82; for scientific realism, 313n.33

"Theory of Open Systems in Physics and Biology, The" (Bertalanffy), 56

theory of planned behavior (TPB), 17

therapeutic alliance, 216, 219, 233, 331n.123

therapist factors, 238

therapy, psychological. *See* psychotherapy

therapy junkies, 223–24

thick description: in anthropology, 125; in educational reform research, 275; for generalizing cases, 185, 192; in hermeneutic case studies, 167, 168; in qualitative research, 65, 96; Ryle originating concept of, 310n.72

thin description, 65, 94, 310n.72

Thinking through Cultures: Expeditions in Cultural Psychology (Shweder), 302n.70

3 R's, 251, 262

timeless, the, 124

timely, the, 124

time-series methodology. *See* single-case study design

token-economy program, 184

total quality management, 255

Toulmin, Stephen, 120–24; constructionism of pragmatism of, 297n.11; *Cosmopolis: The Hidden Agenda of Modernity,* 120; on Enlightenment as unifying period, 37; on four themes distinguishing rationalism and pragmatism, 123–24; on Greek worldviews, 120–21; humanistic values of, 301n.68; on logical positivism, 122–23; on modernist quest for certainty, 121–22; on postmodernism, 295n.3; postmodern pragmatism of, 102, 109; on the Renaissance and postmodernism, 305n.24; on science turning toward application, 132

tracking (educational), 247

Tractatus Logico-Philosophicus (Wittgenstein), 84

transferability, *161*, *185*

treatment-focused research, 227

treatment manuals. *See* manualized therapy

triangulation, *161*, *182*, *183*, 325n.48

Trierweiler, S. J., 299n.45

Trilling, Lionel, 107

trustworthiness, *160*

truth: in contextualism, 55; correspondence theory of, 108, 115, 130; as natural science's goal, xxii; postmodernism rejecting objective, 301n.68; pragmatic theory of, 107–8, 119–20, 130, 299n.32

Turk, D. C., 212

Twelve-Step Facilitation (TSF), 215

Uncertainty Principle, 89
unconscious, the, 36
understanding: as dialectical, 61; as goal
  of human science, 96; *Verstehen,*
  309n.39
underutilization, 212
unified science, 123
unified theory, 78, 91–92
uniformity myths in therapy research, 232
unifying forces, 36–37, 95
universal, the, 123
University of California, Berkeley, 44
University of Chicago, 56, 248
utility standards, 189–90
utilization-focused evaluation, 140, 320n.16

value: fact/value distinction, 34, 96, 103;
  modernist belief in knowability of, 71,
  311n.106; pragmatic paradigm as not
  preempting questions of, 290; researcher's interests and values, 162,
  187–88; stakeholder values in research,
  158, 170; value-based evaluation,
  144–45. *See also* morality; value-neutral inquiry
value-neutral inquiry: in applied social science, 146; in natural science, xx; positivist adherence to, 187; postmodernist
  rejection of, 305n.32; program evaluation as, 142–43; in propositional thinking, 66; in social science, 34
"values clarification," 251
Van Fraassen, B. C., 313n.33
Verbal Behavior (Skinner), 87
verifiability, 299n.45
verification principle, 305n.30
Verstehen, 309n.39
Vienna Circle, 39, 122, 123, 315n.1
vouchers, 15, 258, 277

Wachtel, P. L., 202, 216–17, 327n.23
Wagner, D. G., 302n.70
Walsh, Jim, 164–66
Watkins, James, 333n.29
Watson, I., 192–93, 326n.72
webs of belief, 80–82, 95
Weiss, Carol, 320n.12
West, Cornel: *The American Evasion of
  Philosophy: A Genealogy of Pragma-*

tism, 107; on chronological develop-
  ment of pragmatism, 107; humanistic
  values of, 301n.68; on moral emphasis
  of pragmatism, 131
Westbrook, R. B., 332n.16
White Collar: The American Middle Class
  (Mills), 43
Whitehead, Alfred North, 56
whole-language approach, 10, 263–64,
  335n.71
Wholey, J. S., 318n.3, 320nn. 12, 16
Why Johnny Can't Read (Flesch), 245
Whyte, William, 42–43
Widmeyer Group, 204
Wiener, Norbert, 51–52, 56
Wilson, E. O., 314n.47
Wilson, G. T., 327n.32, 331n.123
Wilson, K., 334n.45
Winch, Peter, 58, 302n.70
Windle, C., 144–45
Witmer, Lightner, 14
Wittgenstein, Ludwig: critique of logical
  positivism, 105–6; on forms of life, 84,
  313n.31; on language games, 84–87;
  Philosophical Investigations, 84, 85; on
  philosophy as therapeutic, 86; *Tractatus
  Logico-Philosophicus,* 84
Wolfe, B., 217, 329n.81
Wood, George, 300n.55
Woolfolk, R. L., 60, 309n.51, 310n.89
World Hypotheses: A Study in Evidence
  (Pepper), 53
worldviews: in Greek philosophy, 120–21;
  Pepper's schema of, 53–55
written case studies, 154–80; discussion,
  180; introduction, 154–67; method,
  167–72; from pragmatic projects, 137;
  purpose of, 133; results, 172–80
written language, 123
Wundt, Wilhelm, 1, 29, 31, 35, 38

"yea-boo" theory of ethics, 40
year-round schooling, 257, 262, 266
Yin, R. K.: on case boundary problem,
  168; on case studies, 319n.6; on case
  study in positivist research, 323n.6; on
  pattern matching, 176–77; positivist
  paradigm in, 153; typology of study designs, 169

Zigler, Edward, 260

About the Author

Daniel B. Fishman is professor of clinical and organizational psychology at the Graduate School of Applied and Professional Psychology of Rutgers University. He holds a B.A. degree (1960) in philosophy and psychology from Princeton University, and a Ph.D. (1965) in clinical psychology and social relations from Harvard University. His prior appointments were as associate director of a large community mental health center in metropolitan Denver, principal investigator of a major National Institute of Mental Health contract to develop a cost-effectiveness methodology for community mental health centers, and assistant professor of behavioral medicine at the University of Colorado Medical School. As a practicing clinical and consulting psychologist, Fishman has specialized in work and career problems, employee-management conflict, organizational development, program planning, and program evaluation. He is past president of the Eastern Evaluation Research Society, past president of the Society for Studying Unity Issues in Psychology, a former board member of the Association for Advancement of Behavior Therapy, and a fellow of the Society for Community Research and Action of the American Psychological Association.

Fishman's eighty articles, books, and book chapters and his numerous invited addresses span interests in the case-study method, psychological paradigms, pragmatism and postmodernism, program planning and evaluation, cost-effectiveness analysis, community psychology, cognitive behavior therapy, and professional psychology training. A former consulting editor for *Professional Psychology* and the *Journal of Community Psychology,* he is presently on the editorial boards of *Evaluation and Program Planning* and the *Journal of Applied Behavioral Science.*

Fishman's previous books include *A Cost-Effectiveness Methodology for Community Mental Health Centers* (1981), *Assessment for Decision* (1987, with D. R. Peterson), *Paradigms in Behavior Therapy* (1988, with F. Rotgers and C. M. Franks), and *The Human Side of Corporate Competitiveness* (1990, with C. Cherniss).